THE BEST AMERICAN

NONREQUIRED
READING

2013

THE BEST AMERICAN

NONREQUIRED
READING™
2013

■

EDITED BY

DAVE EGGERS

INTRODUCTION BY

Walter Mosley

MANAGING EDITOR

DANIEL GUMBINER

A MARINER ORIGINAL
HOUGHTON MIFFLIN HARCOURT
BOSTON · NEW YORK
2013

www.hmhbooks.com

ISSN: 1539-316X
ISBN: 978-0-544-10550-8

Printed in the United States of America
DOC 10 9 8 7 6 5 4 3 2 1

CONTENTS

EDITOR'S NOTE

It feels very strange to tell you that this is the last *Best American Non-required Reading* I'll be editing. On the other hand, if you'd told me back at the turn of the century that the series would go this long—this is the twelfth edition, good lord—I would have been highly skeptical. This series has lasted nearly as long as the Second Polish Republic.

The original idea was Houghton Mifflin Harcourt's. They'd been putting out, and expanding, the Best American series for 120 years or so, always looking for new permutations of the brand. It all started back in the 1860s, I think, with *The Best American Buffalo-Curing Manifestoes,* and the success of that series begat *The Best American Women's Suffrage Thwarting Pamphlets,* and eventually *The Best American Short Stories* and *The Best American Essays,* the two series that eventually became flagships of the fleet.

They offered us at 826 Valencia—a nonprofit writing and tutoring center in San Francisco—the chance to edit a book with the help of local high school students, and we thought it was a great chance to see the landscape of contemporary literature through the eyes of very smart teenagers. So starting in 2002, I gathered a wide-ranging dream team of high schoolers from all over the Bay Area, and we started meeting every week to read and talk about new writing.

We had no particular methodology. We asked every journal we could find for free subscriptions, they sent us their issues, and the students and I would page through them, looking for extraordinary things. Our process has always been unscientific, even haphazard, but very simple. We try to find things we love.

For over a decade, it's been a highlight of my week. This past year, like every year before it, the class met once a week, from 6 to 8 p.m. The students, after full days of school and whatever extracurricular activities they're attached to, make their way, by bus and subway and foot, to our office on Valencia Street. We take attendance, we pass out photocopies of whatever stories we've chosen to read that week, and for the first hour, the room is quiet as a tomb.

We read in a very amateur way. We read each story knowing absolutely nothing about the origin of the piece, the author, or the author's intentions or astrological sign or anything else. As you can imagine, this is more difficult than ever before—to read something new, completely relying on its merits, without extraneous noise, theories, conjectures, or presuppositions. But it's the best, and perhaps the only honest way, to read.

When we're done reading, we all look up from the page and talk about whether or not the piece struck us. We talk about whether or not it worked. Whether or not we learned something new, whether or not the voice was fresh. Whether or not we were moved. The students are asked to explain why they like something, why they don't, what works and what doesn't. Every year, in the white-hot crucible of our discussions—I think I just exaggerated, but anyway—I've seen shy and taciturn students become eloquent and incredibly well-read young adults, ready for whatever they pursue in college or after.

Many of these students have gone to and finished college. Some of them now work in publishing; most do not. Yesterday I saw one student from the very first year; he'd just gotten back from Chile, where he was involved in an Internet start-up. One former *BANR* member, wanting badly to work with her hands and with delicate things, is now studying to become a florist. Another is getting a second degree at Oxford. And one is now the managing editor of this book.

His name is Daniel Gumbiner, and after being a part of the *BANR* committee, he went to college, graduating from UC Berkeley in 2012. When we needed a managing editor for the book, Daniel came to mind. I asked him, and he took the job. How's that for continuity? He's done an exceedingly good job this year, and he'll be continuing next year. He'll be joined by next year's editor, the novelist and essayist Daniel Handler, who has somehow convinced Lemony Snicket, a writer of entertainments for younger readers, to write the introduction. The collection will be in good hands.

And I've said this just about every year, but the future of the written word is in good hands, too. The students with whom I've had the honor to share editorial duties over these many years have proven, beyond any doubt, that young people read as much or more than their predecessors—certainly more than I did at their age—and that both their analytical skills and their willingness to judge what they read with pure hearts bode well for books and those who write them.

We hope the contents of this anthology, as varied as they are, confirm this. From the start, *The Best American Nonrequired Reading* was a hybrid of many of the other Best Americans. We were allowed to include just about anything: fiction, nonfiction, and journalism; essays, comics, humor, poetry, oral history, and primary source documents. And over the years we've published all of this and more. We've included commencement speeches, web rantings, tweets, even voicemail messages. We hope that this year and every year *BANR* presents a look at how humans were thinking and writing during the twelve months we gathered material.

I'd like to thank the people of Houghton Mifflin Harcourt for their faith and indulgence over these many years. From the start, they've given us the longest of leashes, and, because all proceeds from this book go to 826 National, Houghton Mifflin Harcourt has done a great deal for our network of writing and tutoring centers.

While I have some paper left, I'd like to thank the honorable Mr. Walter Mosley for writing the beautiful introduction to this year's edition, and for understanding so intuitively the spirit behind this collection and the spirit inside these young people who make it happen. Mr. Mosley was the first big-time author to speak at our center in Los Angeles, 826LA, when it was a tiny room on the second floor of a former police station in Venice. He demonstrated his great generosity and genius then, and his humanity is undiminished ten years later.

Indulge me, too, while I thank all the past managing editors of the series. It was many years before I realized I needed some help getting the collection together, and their help made the last five years possible. So thank you Scott Cohen, Elissa Bassist, Jesse Nathan, Maxwell Klinger, Kevin Collier, and Em-J Staples. And thank you to our colleagues in Michigan, who do all we do in San Francisco and do it as Michiganders do: well, and while wearing many layers.

Finally, thank you, readers, for picking up this collection, this year and any year. It's been a distinct pleasure to put this anthology together, and I know I'll miss it. After a decade or so, it's time for me to free up some time to do other things, including but not limited to amateur dentistry. But hearing from so many of you readers, and knowing that the collection has meant something to people, means the world to me. Thank you kindly.

DAVE EGGERS
San Francisco, 2013

INTRODUCTION

When asked to write the introduction for the *Best American Nonre-quired Reading* 2012 I was at first stumped and a little mystified. The potential palette for such a collection seemed so large, unwieldy, and subjective that I wondered how any specific presentation could do it justice; I mean, what is meant by the best, after all? When I talked to the managing editor, he told me that my relationship to reading was what the editorial staff, and readers in general, would find most in-teresting. This added request, requirement, or desire only served to increase my consternation. Reading is such a personal and private activity that, in some ways, it seemed impossible to talk about with any shared sense of truth, verity.

And so, before addressing the task at hand, I had to make sure that I had a workable definition of what reading, for me, actually is.

This is what I came up with:

> In the modern world reading is an essential activity like eating or lov-ing, going to war or even surrendering to a truth that, because it is undeniable, is also inescapable. Reading, I believe, is one of the few activities that increases, deepens, and expands the capacity of the hu-man mind; it is a process that is at once conscious and unconscious, personal and solitary but also interpersonal and even social. We read works by women and men long dead, by living writers that we can see

and touch, and words that we ourselves have written just yesterday or maybe years ago in a forgotten journal or some letter that was never mailed. Shopping lists and love letters, angry declarations of separation and long explanations of acts we wished we had never taken are often the subjects of our writing. These words are meant to express very specific feelings and ideas but when they are read by others they go through miraculous transmogrifications. People interpret intentions and glean meanings that the writer may not have intended or might not have realized that he or she was saying. Even the original writer can find new meaning in words she wrote years ago.

The written word grows in meaning with every reading and rereading. No two people ever understand language in exactly the same way. Even simple one-word assertions like yes or no might have dozens of possible meanings.

Having come this far in my fractured, and necessarily incomplete, interpretation of the process of reading, it occurred to me what was most interesting about the *BANR* project: that is, the two processes of the young editors who gathered together the contents of this aspect of the Best American series.

First, it intrigued and impressed me that these readers could come together and agree on fragments, stories, and essays that they all saw somewhat differently. Maybe one editor thought that an idea presented was fascinating or important where another reader saw something exhilarating in the style of writing. A third contributor didn't understand what was being said and a fourth had issues with the author's implied opinions about gender. They all came together in a room in San Francisco and danced around and around the language and ideas celebrating, classifying, considering, and finally agreeing upon what would make the final cut and what would not.

This process alone I would find extremely daunting. A long time ago, in 1965, the Lovin' Spoonful released a pop song called "Did You Ever Have to Make Up Your Mind?" It was a tune about a young man who, again and again, found that he was in love with two women but had to decide on one. I always felt that this was a central challenge in life and that I have never, or at least rarely, been up to the task. That is why I shy away from editing jobs: there's just too much to love.

Never just the question of better or the best, the outcome of editing is, rather, the ecstasy of being in tune with something and the heartbreak of turning away from other beauty.

But as much as I am impressed with the job of deciding, it is the other fundamental step in this process that arrests me. Reading is good enough but rereading is sublime. In the mad rush of our modern "scientistic" world people often tell me that they read some iconic piece of literature like *Man's Fate, Dead Souls,* or *One Hundred Years of Solitude.* I have taken to asking the person making this claim to literacy how many times they read the document. Usually, I get a quizzical stare and then the claim, "One very close reading."

But "Once is never enough," to quote another pop song: "Do That to Me One More Time" by The Captain and Tennille, this time from 1979.

You don't propose marriage after one date. You don't decide on a career after one article or class session. You don't cast your vote based on one opinion of the candidate in question. Stories, essays, novels, and memoirs all deserve to be, indeed have to be read multiple times. Every writer worth his or her salt knows that writing is rewriting. Every reader should know the same thing about understanding text: that is, real reading is rereading.

The editors of this book by example and for the love of writing have shown us in the words represented here that they have read and reread and reread again the ocean of words that we are about to embark upon. They, the editors, will have gotten more from this process than most readers in the modern world. It is the work of editing, of going over every word and then discussing those words and then diving back in again that makes real readers.

So what is the best? A group of young scholars that has taken to heart the task of deepening their own minds in order to present to us a world that is at once known and hidden. They have examined and reexamined linguistic interpretations of the world we live in and so have become curators of our culture by the lovely example of making impossible choices.

WALTER MOSLEY

BEST AMERICAN FRONT SECTION

EVERY YEAR, the *BANR* committee comes across extraordinary work that does not fit in the main section of the book. The committee collects this work and publishes it here, in the Best American Front Section. You will love it so much.

Best American American Poem

SHERMAN ALEXIE

FROM *Tin House*

Sherman Alexie is the author of over twenty-two books, including The Absolutely True Diary of a Part-Time Indian, *which won the National Book Award. Last year, the Front Section began with Alexie's "Sonnet, with Vengeance." This year, it begins with the following poem, which appeared in issue 52 of* Tin House.

Crazy Horse Boulevard

I.

During his lifetime, my big brother has chosen and been chosen by six best friends.

Five of them have died in car wrecks.

In Indian theology, there are Four Directions: east, west, north, and south. Sounds expansive, I guess, but it's really limited. What if I walked south for ten feet and then suddenly turned west and walked for two thousand miles? How would one theologically measure the difference between those two paths? Would those two thousand miles west be more sacred than those ten feet south? And what if I walked in a northwestern direction? Come on, come on, people, there are a hell of a lot more than four directions, even in a metaphorical sense.

And, really, there are maybe three Indians in the whole country who can say, "the Four Directions," without secretly giggling.

That might be only the second time that somebody has put "Indians" and "giggling" in the same sentence.

I've only been to one funeral for one of my brother's best friends. It was a highly traditional ceremony, so the mournful Indians spent a lot of time giggling.

2.

What if one is not the loneliest number?

What if two is actually the loneliest number? After all, how many times have you had your heart truly broken by a large group of people? You really have to be most wary of the other half of the couples you've created. Or been born into.

My friend says she's only been in romantic love three times. My other friend says he falls in love three times during his commute to work.

At the present moment, I have four dollars in my wallet. What if this were my only wealth? At times in my younger life, my entire wealth was less than four dollars. When it comes to love, is there a difference between four dollars and four million dollars? What did Lear say to his daughter Cordelia, who truly loved him, but was too tongue-tied to say anything other than "nothing" when he asked her what praise she had for him? He said, "Nothing comes from nothing." That fucker Lear disinherited his daughter because she was less articulate than her sisters. How's that for love?

I've served on the board of trustees for five different charitable organizations. I've lost count of the number of times a rich person would only give money if his or her name was publicly printed in bold type. Rich people want buildings to be named after them. Rich people want cities to be named for them. I think the saddest people in the world are rich. Maybe one *billion* is the loneliest number.

I worry that my big brother will soon lose the sixth best friend of his lifetime. I worry that my brother will outlive everybody. I worry that he'll be the last person on earth and spend his life wandering among innumerable gravestones. And I've just decided that the only structure that should bear anybody's name is a gravestone.

3.

I bet you all the money in my wallet that my brother is carrying about six dollars in his pocket. That would, indeed, be his entire wealth.

I love my big brother. I love my big brother. I love my big brother. I love my big brother. I love my big brother.

The fourth word in my copy of *Webster's Ninth New Collegiate Dictionary* (which I received in 1985 as a high school graduation gift from the Franson family) is *aardwolf,* a maned, striped mammal of southern and eastern Africa that resembles the related hyenas and feeds chiefly on carrion and insects. Have you ever heard of the aardwolf? It sounds like some mythical creature straight out of Dungeons & Dragons. I'm afraid to search for more information about the thing, though, because I'm sure it's extinct. One can't talk about Indians and death and genocide without magically discovering other dead and dying species.

Okay, I wait about three minutes before I type "aardwolf" into my search engine. And, hooray, the aardwolf is still alive! Though it's the only surviving species of the subfamily Protelinae (whatever that is). And what's more, this animal is a genocidal eater. According to Wikipedia, the aardwolf feeds mainly on termites and can eat more than 200,000 in a single night. Holy shit! Right now, in Africa, there's a termite shaman telling his people, "The aardwolf comes at us from every fucking direction."

It was around closing time, 2 a.m., when I saw Gail Franson in a grocery store in Spokane. This was maybe two years after I graduated from high school. Gail was a few years older, my big brother's age, and I'd always had a mad crush on her. And there she was. "Hey, that's Gail," I said to my big brother, who was stealing and eating food from the fruit department. He didn't care. But I shouted, "Hey, Gail, I love you! You have great legs!" She blushed and turned away. It probably doesn't surprise you that I haven't seen her since that moment. And, oh, just to remind you: it was Gail's family who gave me that dictionary as a graduation present. What does it say about me that I've kept this outmoded dictionary for twenty-seven years?

Like my big brother, I have also had six best friends in my life. All of them are still alive, though I only have contact with two of them.

4.

Who are the six greatest human beings who have ever lived? I bet you that most men would list six other men. And most women would list three women and three men.

Off the top of my head: Crazy Horse. Martin Luther King Jr. Michelangelo. Emily Dickinson. The person who invented the smallpox vaccine. That's five. I'll leave the last spot open because I'm sure I've forgotten somebody obvious. Four men and one woman. What does that say about me? Of course, I'm just assuming the inventor of the smallpox vaccine is a man. Isn't that sexist? Well, I look it up and discover that Edward Jenner invented the smallpox vaccine in 1796.

What? Do you know how many Indians died from smallpox *after* 1796? Millions! Just when you think the United States couldn't have been more genocidal, you discover more evidence.

I'm guessing there are four kids in each of my sons' classes who haven't been immunized against whooping cough, diphtheria, and polio. If my sons, Indian as they are, contract whooping cough, diphtheria, or polio from those organic, free-range white children and die, will it be legal for me to scalp and slaughter their white parents?

Three arrows: one in the head, one in the heart, and one in the crotch.

Two thoughts: Is there such a thing as Crazy Horse Boulevard? And if so, have white people built big houses there? In Seattle, when white folks first gentrified this neighborhood, they built big houses on Martin Luther King Jr. Way, but they turned the front doors of their homes so their street addresses would *not* be on MLK Jr. Way.

Among my immediate family, I'm the only one who doesn't live on the reservation. What does that say about me?

5.

Aardvark is the first word in my ancient dictionary. But *aardwolf* is a far more interesting word, animal, and concept. That's how poems get written.

Last week, my sister sent me two questions from her final exam in Native American Literature 101. Yes, my sister is studying my books in her class. And yes, she's unsure of the answers. I don't even want to think about the ramifications of this. Sometimes the poem doesn't need to be written.

Three ironies: I just included the discussion of what should be unwritten in this poem. Most of the people who read this poem will be white people. This poem doesn't use any form of rhyme or meter, so it's called a prose poem. It's called free verse. Yes, an Indian is using *free* verse to write about that rural concentration camp known as a reservation.

Okay, I think that was four ironies.

My big brother has helped carry five coffins from hearse to longhouse, longhouse back to hearse, hearse to graveside, and graveside to grave.

Here's a game: Grab a six-sided die. No, roll one red die and one white die together. Read the red die first and refer to the corresponding section of this poem; then read the white die and refer to the corresponding stanza of each numbered section. For example, if you rolled a red 4 and a white 6, you'd be reading this stanza. Now, roll the dice thirty-six times and reorder this poem. Do this as many times as you wish. No matter what happens, remember that my big brother, though he may not admit it, fully expects to bury his sixth best friend in the very near future.

6.

In the first six drafts of this poem, I placed the previous stanza at the end of the poem. But, for some ineffable reason, I decided that it wasn't correct. But who knows? When you write by instinct, you're going to get a whole lot of shit wrong.

We all live by instinct. We all live by instinct. We all live by instinct. We all live by instinct. We all live by instinct.

Ineffable. Ineffable. Ineffable. Ineffable.

My big brother's holy trinity: beer, pizza, and death songs.

Ah, big brother, when was the last time you and I sang together? What happened to our duet?

I've only got one birthmark. It's a heart-shaped mole on my right arm. It's next to a comet-shaped burn scar. What does this say about me?

Best American Term Paper Assignment

FROM *Kurt Vonnegut: Letters,* edited by Dan Wakefield

Kurt Vonnegut taught at the Iowa Writers' Workshop from 1965–1967. Vonnegut once suggested that he thought the students at the workshop were merely learning to play practical jokes. "If you make people laugh or cry about little black marks on sheets of white paper," he said in an interview with The Paris Review, *"what is that but a practical joke?" The following is a term paper assignment Vonnegut gave to his Form of Fiction class at the workshop. At the end of the assignment, Vonnegut signs as "Polonious," alluding to King Claudius's unreliable counselor in* Hamlet.

FORM OF FICTION TERM PAPER ASSIGNMENT
November 30, 1965

Beloved:

This course began as Form and Theory of Fiction, became Form of Fiction, then Form and Texture of Fiction, then Surface Criticism, or How to Talk out of the Corner of Your Mouth Like a Real Tough Pro. It will probably be Animal Husbandry 108 by the time Black February rolls around. As was said to me years ago by a dear, dear friend, "Keep your hat on. We may end up miles from here."

As for your term papers, I should like them to be both cynical and religious. I want you to adore the Universe, to be easily delighted, but to be prompt as well with impatience with those artists who offend your own deep notions of what the Universe is or should be. "This above all . . ."

I invite you to read the fifteen tales in *Masters of the Modern Short Story* (W. Havighurst, editor, 1955, Harcourt, Brace, $14.95 in paperback). Read them for pleasure and satisfaction, beginning each as though, only seven minutes before, you had swallowed two ounces of very good booze. "Except ye be as little children . . ."

Then reproduce on a single sheet of clean, white paper the table of contents of the book, omitting the page numbers, and substituting for each number a grade from A to F. The grades should be childishly selfish and impudent measures of your own joy or lack of it. I don't care what grades you give. I do insist that you like some stories better than others.

Proceed next to the hallucination that you are a minor but useful editor on a good literary magazine not connected with a university. Take three stories that please you most and three that please you least, six in all, and pretend that they have been offered for publication. Write a report on each to be submitted to a wise, respected, witty, and world-weary superior.

Do not do so as an academic critic, nor as a person drunk on art, nor as a barbarian in the literary market place. Do so as a sensitive person who has a few practical hunches about how stories can succeed or fail. Praise or damn as you please, but do so rather flatly, pragmatically, with cunning attention to annoying or gratifying details. Be yourself. Be unique. Be a good editor. The Universe needs more good editors, God knows.

Since there are eighty of you, and since I do not wish to go blind or kill somebody, about twenty pages from each of you should do neatly. Do not bubble. Do not spin your wheels. Use words I know.

poloniøus

Best American Anti-War Poetry Inspired by Kurt Vonnegut

FROM *So It Goes*

So It Goes is an annual literary journal founded by the Kurt Vonnegut Memorial Library, a nonprofit organization based in Indianapolis, Vonnegut's hometown. The journal prints newly published work alongside older, republished material. What follows are a few poems from their inaugural issue, "War and Peace."

Someone Warm, You Know Him

a friend of mine
a very gentle man
with laughing light blue eyes

we're at a bar
and he starts talking
tells me about Viet Nam
how he enlisted
so he wouldn't have to go there
went anyway
and became a star
the man who could shoot dimes
high in the air
automatically without thinking
the man who would shoot anything moving
clay bushes men
children

his eyes are laughing again
as he tells me
it took him six years
to break the reflex

now he can sometimes miss
when something moves in the woods

—*Katharyn Howd Machan*

"A soldier lives . . . "

A soldier lives a soldier dies
a military chaplain sighs

a flag is folded someone cries

a general tells the truth or lies
a politician simplifies
a voice vote echoes only ayes

reporters ask for hows and whys
a spokesman has to improvise

some doctrine somehow still applies
negotiators compromise

or don't as one more soldier dies.

—*Robert West*

Simon Pokagon and the Farmer

> In the 1870s, a well-educated Indian came to Lake County about twice
> each year to visit the graves of his ancestors.
>
> —Kankakee Valley Historical Society

From the way he squinted
I knew that farmer had no iota
of what to make of me—
a savage in a tailored suit
who quoted Shakespeare and Tecumseh,
spoke Potawatomi and Greek.

Near juniper, I prayed
for those who cradled me. I spoke
to steady their steps down slick ravines.
I sang that their days
might be pleasant among heaven's
herds of buffalo and elk.

One April, I found the mounded
graves plowed under, shin bones

stacked with fieldstones. I could have
splashed the kerosene of a curse
but, instead, turned to offer
my grief, a treeless prairie
without periphery. Those bones
could be mine or his.

My tribe's revered flower—
the trailing arbutus—
belongs to all who observe
its delicate white blossoms
on bended knee.

As my gaze caught his,
the farmer could only clear
his throat as if pushing
away dried leaves.

—*Shari Wagner*

Soldier on a Plane

The flight was overbooked,
the jet-belly packed tight
with tourists hurrying home,
travelers dreading home,
wanderers without a home
peacefully lost and content.
I found myself sitting by a
young soldier no more than twenty.
He was so quiet, looked so sad.
I suppose he had been on liberty,
and now, fresh from kisses goodbye,
he was going back to his unit.
He smiled at my hello,
then drifted into sleep,
his leg nestled against mine.

We flew that way for hours,
his leg always touching mine.
If I moved, he moved,
as if begging in his dreams
for the simple gift of human touch.
There was nothing sexual,
just a need for contact
with the mundane.

I remember when my grandmother was dying.
She lay in her bed touching things,
her gown, her sheets, her face and hair.
The doctor said he had seen this a lot,
it was common with the dying,
as if they knew life was ending
and they wanted to touch everything
just one last time.

—*Jim Wise*

Best American Consumer Report

EDW LYNCH

FROM *yelpingwithcormac.tumblr.com*

EDW Lynch is a San Francisco comedian and, according to his website, the world's first "corporate manglomerate." Lynch claims to have provided security for the Easter Bunny and brokered a historic treaty between kittens and puppies. What follows are a series of Yelp reviews in which Lynch impersonates acclaimed author Cormac McCarthy. Lynch's work can be found at edwlynch.com.

Red Lobster
Wichita, KS
Cormac M. | Author | Lost in the chaparral, NM
Two stars.

The manager sat tied to the chair in the corral, firelit on all sides by the torches of the townfolk. Dean stood next to him with a Colt army revolver pointed to the hardpacked earth. Who else will speak, he said.

A chorus of voices rose at once. From the din a miner hollered: The shrimp was rubberlike.

I believe Pastor Macabee already done spoke to that, said Dean. He looked around him. Ghastly amber faces staring back like funeral masks. Are there any other charges, he said.

A prostitute in dusty finery stepped forward. She spoke haltingly. I made a reservation for six persons. And we still had to wait 45 minutes to set down. Her face fell into her hands and she began weeping softly. We was on time, she said.

A drunk cowboy carrying a rusting hatchet lurched toward the manager. I'll tickle his neck with my axe so help me, he said.

Dean leveled the big revolver at the cowboy. The man regarded him wetly and melted back into the crowd. Dean spoke loudly so that all could hear. We will do this orderly or by God I'll send him to the capitol and to hell with the lot of you.

A little girl strode forward into the light and looked up at Dean and the manager with eyes shining and obsidian. Hang them, she said. Hang them both.

Chipotle Mexican Grill
SOMA - San Francisco, CA
Cormac M. | Author | Lost in the chaparral, NM
Three stars.

See that false burrito. See it swaddled in tinfoil on the desk in the bowels of that great tower, a bundle of meat and sauce in a place long ago ceded to silicone and copper. The stooped man eating that peasant food as if in consuming it he can escape to a farmfield in a verdant valley and look down and see blood running from his blisters and say, yes this is work. This is work. Instead his hands are clawlike and ruined by the keyboard and the mouse for he is a thing of bone and sinew in a sprawling contraption electric and of man's creation but not of man at all. And were he to saw his breast open with that plastic knife and soak the carpet black with his hot blood and were he to look ceilingward like some stigmatic enraptured and with the bellows of his lungs let forth a soaring wail in that subbasement his screams would be swallowed by the acoustic panels and repulsed by the good steel door as if he had made no sound and spilled no blood at all.

American Apparel
Haight Ashbury - San Francisco, CA
Cormac M. | Author | Lost in the chaparral, NM
Three stars.

Ballard sawed his brocklefaced mount around and faced the line of raiders. A stinking host clad in patchwork tunics of brightest cotton. As if their carnival colors could mask the blackness of their nature. For they rode as men of their kind have ridden for millenia on wasted steppes and beggared plains skylit by a dustveiled sun their implements glinting and in their hearts a hunger sated in blood.

Come on boys, Ballard said. Let's lay into these deadeyed hippites. Give no quarter but mind the cotton. Buffalo Exchange won't accept no sullied merchandise.

And from their number arose a cry ancient and of another world entire and the raiders spurred their mounts through the paneglass of the American Apparel and the souls within perished under the blade and the cudgel and their cotton hides were taken from them.

Urban Outfitters
Union Square - San Francisco, CA
Cormac M. | Author | Lost in the chaparral, NM
Three stars.

And they come there in great numbers shuffling into that mausoleum that was built for them like some monument to the slow death of their world and among those tokens and talismans of that faded empire they forage like scavengers their faces frozen in a rictus of worldweary their clothes preworn in some tropical factory and they shop and they hunt with dullbrown eyes through that cavalcade of false trinkets and those shrinkwrapped mockeries laying there in silent indictment and they reach out to touch those trite things and their faces are slack but in their gullets a scream lies stillborn for they are the kings and the queens reigning over the death of their people and the world is not theirs and never was and the suffering and the horrors are not their doing but the work of their bankrupt forbears and before them stretches an abyss beyond man's imagining and within their lifetime the promise of a coming reckoning measured in blood and in pestilence and they shuffle through that store near paralytic and finally they take a metal thing with a feather on it and they buy that thing.

Best American Advertisement for a Home Security System

TIM WIRKUS

FROM *Subtropics*

Subtropics *is the literary journal of the University of Florida. The following short story by Tim Wirkus was published in issue 14. Wirkus's writing has also appeared in* Gargoyle, Cream City Review, Sou'wester *and* Ruminate Magazine.

An Intrusion

This is what Mike Mitchell told me when I ran into him about a month ago. He said they found the first envelope after a weekend away visiting Julie's dying grandfather. It was pinned up on the wall above their TV, so when they sat down to watch the news that evening, after unpacking and grabbing a bite to eat, they couldn't miss it.

They had been living there about four months by that point, their first real house, bought with money from their first real jobs out of college—Mike working as a project manager for a company that developed accounting software, and Julie writing copy for a small advertising firm. Unfortunately, the advertising firm had folded unexpectedly a month after Julie had started there, and she was without a job. She and Mike were doing OK, though, making their house payments, with enough money left over for groceries and other essentials. Things were just a little tight.

Anyway, they got home from visiting Julie's grandfather, who had always been more like a father to her and was currently very, very ill, to find an envelope pinned above their TV. Mike noticed it first and asked Julie why she had pinned an envelope to their wall. Julie said she hadn't. Mike asked who else would have done it. They were the only ones with keys to the house. They didn't even have a spare key hidden outside yet; it was just one of those things they kept meaning to do.

Julie pulled the envelope down from the wall. Inside she found a dozen or so photographs. Mike looked over her shoulder as she flipped through them. The pictures showed a young couple engaged in a series of mundane domestic pursuits—standing together at a sink washing dishes, reading on a couch, playing cards at a dining room table, changing a light bulb in a floor lamp. The problem was that the couple—who were not Mike and Julie—were doing all these things inside Mike and Julie's house.

Mike grabbed the pictures from Julie and flipped through them again. None of the photographs revealed the face of either the man or the woman. In each picture, their backs were to the camera, or their heads were turned, or some object obscured their faces.

Mike called the police. They showed up quickly and were not very helpful. The police asked if anything was missing from the house. Nothing was missing, as far as Mike and Julie could tell. The police then asked if the pictures could have been taken before they moved in. Julie pointed out that the couch the couple was shown sitting on was Mike and Julie's couch, that the framed prints on the wall were Mike and Julie's framed prints, that the dishes in the couple's hands were Mike and Julie's dishes. The police asked who else had keys to the house. Mike said that nobody did. The police asked if the couple in the pictures resembled any friends or acquaintances of theirs, or if they knew anybody who was especially fond of pranks. Mike said no. The police said that they were sorry, but there wasn't much they could do. They told Mike and Julie to change the locks on their house and let them know if this happened again.

So Mike and Julie changed the locks on their doors and tried not to think about the strangers who had been inside their house. At work, Mike's team got a big new project from a prominent local gym that was unhappy with its current accounting software. At home, Julie searched for a new job, calling old acquaintances for leads, redesigning her résumé for the hundredth time, writing cover letters, scanning the classifieds section of the newspaper, and waiting for prospective employers to get back to her.

I stopped Mike at this point and asked him how they could just go about their lives like that. Didn't their house feel too weird to them? How could they sleep there? Mike shrugged. He said the pictures were upsetting, but what else could they do? He and Julie were a little jumpy for a week or two, but then they pretty much stopped thinking about it—it's surprising what you can get used to.

He went on with his story.

A few months later, they found some more pictures. Just three of them this time, in an envelope again, sitting on their dining room table. Julie had an interview that morning for a receptionist's position at a dentist's office—not ideal, but better than nothing—and found the envelope when she sat down to eat breakfast. The pictures showed the same faceless couple as before, the man tall and thin with pale, freckled skin, the woman shorter, nearly as thin as the man, with faded blond hair that reached halfway down her back.

While the previous set of pictures depicted scenes that, had they not been taking place in Mike and Julie's house, might be mistaken for innocent snapshots of the happy domestic life of a young, married couple, this second set of photos had an air of menace about it. In a picture taken in the living room, the couple seemed, at first glance, to be embracing. On closer inspection, however, something about the twisting posture of the woman and the tense, veiny grip of the man's arms suggested, respectively, resistance and restraint. The second photograph, taken from just behind the man, showed the woman leaning over, almost into, the kitchen sink, her hair pulled back from her face, which was turned away from the camera. The man watched from the doorway, hands on his hips. In the third picture, the husband lay face down in Mike and Julie's unmade bed, the sheets tangled and askew, while the woman knelt on the floor a few feet away, her face held in her hands.

The police were even less helpful this second time. They suggested that Mike and Julie install alarms in their house, or move. They said the relatively small magnitude of the crime didn't merit the kind of constant police surveillance it would require to find the perpetrators.

As they were leaving, one of the officers pulled Mike aside. The officer said that if this was a prank, it had gone far enough, and that Mike should stop trying to frighten his wife. Mike said he had nothing to do with any of it. The officer said that was fine, but if he did, it needed to stop.

At this point in his telling, Mike paused.

"So was that the end of it?" I asked.

"No," said Mike. "No."

It was just one picture the third time, in an envelope pinned to the sleeve of Mike's coat when he took it down from the rack in the corner to run to the store to pick up a head of lettuce for a salad that Julie was making. This was just a few weeks after the second set of pictures had turned up. Mike unpinned the envelope from the sleeve of his coat and handed the photo to Julie in the kitchen. She set down the knife with the bits of sliced radish clinging to it and held the picture with both hands.

In this photo, the man and the woman were posed in precisely the same positions that Julie and Mike had been in only moments before. The woman with the faded blond hair stood at the kitchen counter chopping radishes, while the wiry, pale-skinned man rummaged through the fridge for a head of lettuce that wasn't there.

Mike told me they moved out after that—sold the house at a big loss and were currently renting a tiny apartment across town. Mike and I used to be pretty close, but I wasn't sure what to say to him, how to react to all that, so I wished him good luck and said we should get together for dinner sometime. Like I said, this was about a month ago when he told me all this.

I've since heard that Mike and Julie are splitting up. Apparently she's already moved back in with her parents on the other side of the country and is filing for a divorce. Mike is living by himself in their little apartment and not talking to anybody. Not that I blame him—there are rumors floating around that Mike sent Julie to the hospital a couple of weeks ago with a broken nose and three cracked ribs, that this wasn't the first time, that maybe this kind of thing went on during their entire marriage. I've tried calling him several times, I've even stopped by his apartment once or twice, but he's never home and he doesn't return my calls.

Best American Apocryphal Discussion Between Our Nation's Founding Fathers

TEDDY WAYNE

FROM *The New Yorker*

This year, the United States' attention turned once again toward the debate surrounding gun control. Some argued that stricter gun control legislation would prevent gun violence, while others insisted that new legislation would impinge on Americans' constitutional right to bear arms. Teddy Wayne, author of The Love Song of Jonny Valentine *and* Kapitoil, *wrote the following piece in response to the latter argument.*

Second Thoughts

> The NRA is not going to let people lose the Second Amendment in this country.
>
> —NRA chief Wayne LaPierre

THOMAS JEFFERSON: Gentlemen, a thought has occurred to me regarding the Second Amendment.

JAMES MADISON: Fine amendment.

ALEXANDER HAMILTON: Superb amendment. Can't believe we left that out of the first draft.

JEFFERSON: Yes, my fellow land-owning framers, but are we perhaps not forward-thinking enough? What if, perchance, we someday develop a rifle that, instead of firing one bullet per sixty ticks of the clock's second hand, has the inverse effect—unloading sixty rounds per second through the power of machinery? Might it not fall into the hands of a town madman?

MADISON: Should such a potent "machinery gun" ever come into being and somehow not exceed the cost of an entire militia, a town madman would be refused sale from any responsible merchant because of his agitated demeanor.

HAMILTON: Hear, hear. Let us repair to the drawing room for a spirited game of dice. Who will roll the highest tally? Huzzah! Whoop! Fizzing! No more capital divertissement shall ever be created, just as my vernacular exclamations of joy will never become obsolete!

JEFFERSON: Not to flog a deceased equine, but let us suggest that man, with his infinite intellect, invents a series of machines, interconnected to one another, as if caught in a net, to purchase goods. Could our town madman procure arms more easily through clandestine means by buying them on this "interconnected net"?

MADISON: Nay, for this hypothetical "interconnected net" would not debase itself as a mercenary marketplace, but instead provide a forum for only the most enlightened minds of the day to comment on scholarly works, and on previous comments, in a virtuous cycle of belletristic discourse. The scenario you envision for the "interconnected net" is as unlikely as its serving as an emporium for free oil paintings of semi-nude portraiture!

HAMILTON: Moreover, our future physiognomists will surely improve at identifying those prone to madness, and they will be cured by our finest physicians with advances in leeches. Enough prattle; who desires to trade wigs?

JEFFERSON: But, two centuries from now, could not the tools of warfare progress so far beyond cavalry that arms will be woefully insufficient defense against a tyrant's militia, such that guns would simply be inflicted by the citizenry against itself?

HAMILTON: What, Jefferson, do you expect horses to be attached to some contraption that soars above the ground with the fearsome appendage of a cannon? Somebody send Revere to alert Franklin—he'll attempt to patent this chimera! William Dunlap shall pen a stage play entitled "Top Rider of a Mechanical Flying Warhorse That Bombards Enemies with Cannonballs"!

MADISON: Besides, such a firearm you describe would be employed solely by hunters to quintuple their productivity in acquiring healthful red meat along with beaver pelts for the increasingly cold winters.

. HAMILTON: And if there ever arises a need for an association to oversee our nation's rifles, I am certain it will be led by men like us, our country's most rational minds making sound arguments based on impeccable logic and selfless empathy.

MADISON: Remember, Jefferson: muskets don't kill colonists-turned-Americans; colonists-turned-Americans kill colonists-turned-Americans. If you wish to outlaw anything, it should be something an aggressor can easily and repeatedly employ in a rampage: the lethal bayonet.

HAMILTON: Not to mention the violence inspired by the daily broadsheets, children's wooden blocks, and sonnet cycles. Indeed, only town fools would seek to retroactively amend us. Who, for example, can imagine a civilized state whose disputes are resolved without gentlemen's duels?

JEFFERSON: Aye, I suppose you are correct. I am retiring for the night, secure in the knowledge that we have composed an unimpeachable document whose every directive will remain as relevant in the future as it is in 1789. Now, please send for my pipe, filled with our country's most important crop, which I, like all our yeoman-farmer statesmen, personally grow: glorious hemp. And then have my bed fluffed by that obedient sixteen-year-old girl, Sally.

Best American Yada Yada Yada

FROM @*seinfeldtoday*

After nine seasons, Seinfeld *stopped airing in 1998. This year, TV writer Jack Moore and comedian Josh Gondelman began to tweet new plot ideas for the sitcom that situate its characters in the present day. Within three days of launching, their handle @seinfeldtoday had 130,000 followers. Today it has over 600,000.*

Newman uses Jerry's photo for his online dating profile. George is disturbed when he learns the song he liked in a cab is by Justin Bieber.

George's boss fires him after misconstruing George's "sympathy like" on a Facebook post about his divorce. "I liked it but I didn't LIKE it."

Kramer starts an offline dating "site." KRAMER: It's like online dating . . . but at a place. JERRY: You're describing a bar! That's a bar!

Kramer pioneers an all-carb diet. A female TSA agent laughs at George's body scan.

Kramer becomes addicted to kombucha. George tries to sexually harass a co-worker to get fired. Instead she reciprocates his advances.

Elaine is late to a movie because her new boyfriend (James Wolk) will only get in hybrid cabs. Jerry's new gf cheats at Words With Friends.

George goes mad with power after writing some scathing Yelp reviews. Restaurants refuse him service. He makes Jerry bring him meals to go.

Elaine pretends to live in Brooklyn to date a cute, younger guy. Kramer becomes addicted to 5-Hour Energy. George's parents get Skype.

Elaine has a bad waiter at a nice restaurant. Her negative Yelp review goes viral, she gets banned. Kramer accidentally joins the Tea Party.

Kramer stockpiles honey when he hears that bees are disappearing, ends up on Hoarders. George tries to become a "hat guy," wears a fedora.

George "accidentally" sends a "reply all" e-mail in an attempt to get fired. He is promptly promoted for his gutsy attitude.

Jerry joins Twitter only to find that a Jerry parody account has 50k followers. It's run by Bania who will stop if Jerry buys him dinner.

Kramer is under investigation for heavy torrenting. Jerry's new girlfriend writes an extremely graphic blog. George discovers Banh Mi.

Best American Tattoo Stories

WENDY MACNAUGHTON AND ISAAC FITZGERALD

FROM *penandink.tumblr.com*

In 2012, artist Wendy MacNaughton and writer Isaac Fitzgerald set out to document tattoos and the stories behind them. Fitzgerald is a co-owner of the online magazine TheRumpus.net. MacNaughton is the illustrator of, most recently, Lost Cat: A True Story of Love, Desperation, and GPS Technology. *Their work together will be featured in the book* Pen and Ink, *which comes out in 2014.*

ANNA SCHOENBERGER, MANAGER at THRIFT STORE

WHEN I WAS 18 YEARS OLD I GOT THESE TATTOOS
as A TRIBUTE to MY GRANDMOTHER. I GREW UP
PLAYING VIDEO GAMES WITH HER. SHE HAD A COCKTAIL
TABLE WITH MS. PACMAN on IT WHERE WE WOULD PUT OUR
DRINKS as WE PLAYED for HOURS at A TIME. WE PLAYED
SUPER MARIO BROTHERS as WELL, but MS. PACMAN WAS
REALLY MY GRANDMOTHER'S GAME.

TO THIS DAY, WHENEVER I SEE MY GRANDMA, SHE
ALWAYS STARTS THE CONVERSATION by SAYING,
"PLEASE DON'T GET ANY MORE TATTOOS, ANNA." AND
EVERY TIME I RESPOND by POINTING at MY ARM and
SAYING, "I GOT THESE in HONOR of YOU, GRAMMIE
BEAR." AND THEN, EVERYTIME, SHE SAYS, "YOU'RE
SUCH A GOOD, GOOD GIRL," and SMILES.

JOSHUA MOHR, WRITER

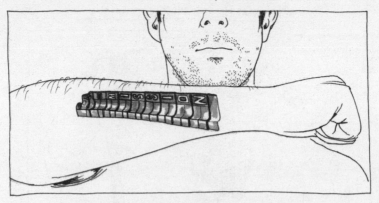

I GET A TATTOO COMMEMORATING EVERY NOVEL
I WRITE. THE ONE THAT MEANS THE MOST to ME
IS A PICTURE of THE NEW MISSION MARQUEE,
WHICH IS AN OLD, DILAPIDATED THEATRE on
MISSION STREET. WE USED IT for THE COVER of MY BOOK
"DAMASCUS." IT'S MORE THAN JUST A COMPELLING
IMAGE, THOUGH. IT'S MY LOVE LETTER to SAN FRAN-
CISCO, MY HOME SINCE I WAS 17. IT'S ALSO A
TRIBUTE to GETTING SOBER. A LOT of MISSION
DISTRICT ARTISTS FALL INTO THAT AGE OLD TRAP
DRINKING and DRUGGING SO HARD THAT YOU FORGET
THE WORLD IS IN COLOR. ANYWAY, I WAS WRITING
"DAMASCUS" and SUDDENLY AN OPTIMISM THAT
WASN'T IN MY FIRST TWO BOOKS STARTED to
CREEP IN. MY WORLD VIEW WAS MORPHING,
EVOLVING. THE TATTOO REMINDS ME of EMERGING
from THAT HIBERNATION, LOOKING AROUND and
LOVING THIS MAGICAL CITY.

RAYMOND "SHRIMP BOY" CHOW,
DRAGON HEAD of THE CHINESE FREEMASONS

← WRAPS
AROUND
THE BACK

I WAS SERVING ELEVEN YEARS in TEHACHAPI STATE PRISON
for RACKETEERING. REALLY ROUGH THAT PLACE, A LOT of GANGS,
BGF, AB, NORTHERN BOY, SOUTHERN BOY, CRIPS, BLOODS, TEXAS MOB.
ONE DAY A KID NAMED 007 WHO RAN DRUGS for ME GETS STABBED
in A RIOT. I CARRY 007 to THE PRISON HOSPITAL, but IT'S LOCKED
BECAUSE of THE RIOT. I BANG on THE DOOR and YELL and FINALLY
THEY DRAG HIM INSIDE.

007 COMES BACK and SAYS, RAYMOND, you SAVED MY LIFE,
LET ME MAKE you A TATTOO. SO I ASK for A DRAGON. YOU
KNOW HOW CHINESE LOVE DRAGONS. HE BREAKS A CASSETTE
PLAYER to GET THE MOTOR to MAKE A TATTOO GUN. THE NEEDLE
is A GUITAR STRING. FOR INK HE BURNS A BLACK PLASTIC
CHESS PIECE and COLLECTS THE SMOKY ASH and ADDS INDIA
INK and TOOTHPASTE. ARE YOU FUCKING SERIOUS, I SAY,
YOU'RE PUTTING THAT FUCKING SHIT in MY BODY? WHOLE
THING TAKES A MONTH. WITH A SINGLE NEEDLE you HAVE
to GO SLOW and DEEP, NOT LIKE A TATTOO SHOP with
MANY NEEDLES. THE PAIN WAS EVERYWHERE.

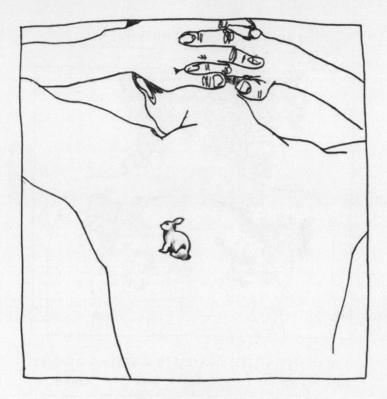

CHRIS COLIN, WRITER

I GOT THIS TATTOO BECAUSE I SUSPECTED ONE DAY
I WOULD THINK IT WOULD BE STUPID. I WANTED TO
MARK TIME, OR MARK THE ME THAT THOUGHT IT WAS
A GOOD IDEA. SEVENTEEN YEARS LATER, I HARDLY
REMEMBER IT'S THERE. BUT WHEN I DO, IT REMINDS ME
THAT WHATEVER I THINK NOW I PROBABLY WON'T
THINK LATER. WHY A BUNNY? IT SEEMED LIKE MOST
TOUGH TYPES WHO WERE GETTING TATTOOS AT THE TIME.
I WANTED SOMETHING THAT WASN'T THAT.

CASSY FRITZEN, BARTENDER

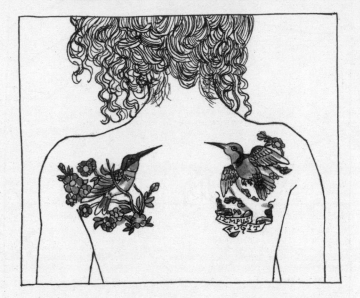

I HAD NEVER BEEN INTERESTED in GETTING A TATTOO
UNTIL AFTER MY FIANCÉ, STEVE, DIED from CANCER.
HE HAD SO MANY HIMSELF, and I WANTED to MEMORIALIZE
HIM. LATE into HIS DISEASE STEVE WAS BOUND to OUR
HOME, WHICH FORTUITOUSLY LOOKED OUT UPON A MEADOW.
I SET UP HUMMINGBIRD FEEDERS ALL OVER SO HE COULD
LAY ON OUR COUCH or SIT by THE SLIDING-GLASS DOOR
and WATCH THE SMALL BIRDS. WE ALWAYS GOT EXCITED
WHEN ONE WOULD COME DRINK THE SWEET SYRUP I MADE
RELIGIOUSLY to FILL THE FEEDERS. "HUMMINGBIRD," STEVE
WOULD CALL OUT to ME WHENEVER HE SAW ONE.

ERIC FLETCHER, PHOTOGRAPHER

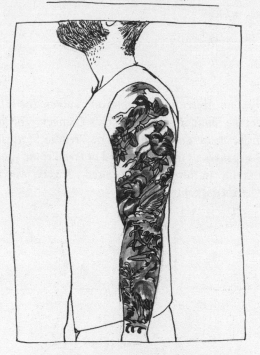

THIS TATTOO IS THE STORY of MY TWO HOMES.
I WAS BORN IN TALLAHASSEE, FLORIDA, and ADOPTED
FOUR DAYS AFTER MY BIRTH. THREE YEARS LATER
MY FAMILY and I MOVED NORTH to MASSACHUSETTS.
I HAD NO MEMORY of OUR LIFE in THE SUNSHINE STATE,
NO CONNECTION TO THE PLACE. FAST FORWARD 25 YEARS.
I RECEIVE A LETTER STATING THAT MY BIRTH MOTHER
WOULD LIKE TO CONTACT ME. WE MEET, WE BECOME FRIENDS,
AND QUESTIONS THAT I'D HAD MY ENTIRE LIFE START to BE
ANSWERED. THE FIRST TIME WE MET IN FLORIDA WE
WENT KAYAKING on THE WAKULLA RIVER, WHOSE SHORES
WERE LINED WITH GREAT BLUE HERONS. GROWING UP as
A CHILD IN MASSACHUSETTS, THE STREAM THAT RAN NEXT
TO OUR HOUSE HOSTED A FAMILY of MALLARD DUCKS EACH YEAR.
I PUT THESE BIRDS ALONG WITH OTHER SYMBOLS of
MY TWO HOME STATES (CHICKADEES and FALL FOLIAGE from MA.,
NORTHERN MOCKINGBIRDS and PALM TREES from FLORIDA) ON MY ARM,
WITH WATER, A CENTRAL THEME TO BOTH MY STORIES,
RUNNING THROUGHOUT. I'M NOT SURE IF ANY MEMBERS
of MY FAMILY, NORTH or SOUTH, ACTUALLY KNOW
WHAT THIS TATTOO MEANS. BUT I DO.

Best American Comic That Ends in Arson

LYNDA BARRY

FROM *The Freddie Stories*

Lynda Barry is an American cartoonist and author. She is best known as the creator of the comic strip Ernie Pook's Comeek. *The following is an excerpt from her latest graphic novel,* The Freddie Stories. *Throughout the book, Barry takes us inside the mind of Freddie, the youngest child in the Mullen family. In this particular episode, Freddie is accused of a heinous crime he did not commit.*

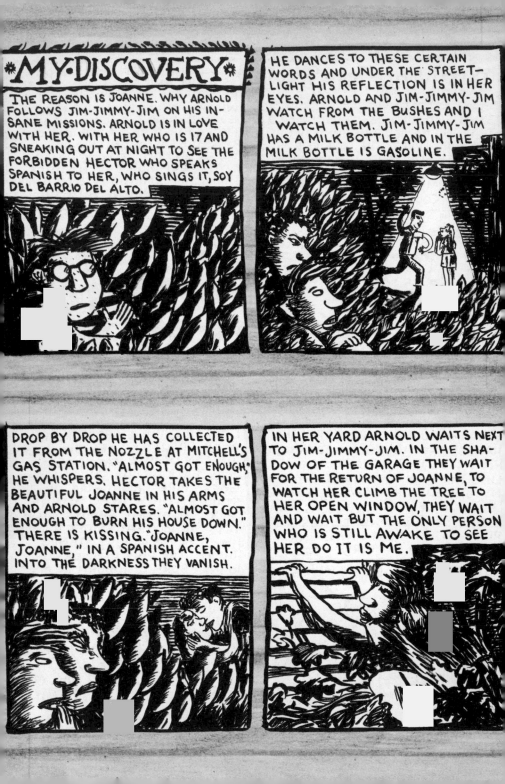

MY·DISCOVERY

THE REASON IS JOANNE. WHY ARNOLD FOLLOWS JIM-JIMMY-JIM ON HIS INSANE MISSIONS. ARNOLD IS IN LOVE WITH HER. WITH HER WHO IS 17 AND SNEAKING OUT AT NIGHT TO SEE THE FORBIDDEN HECTOR WHO SPEAKS SPANISH TO HER, WHO SINGS IT, SOY DEL BARRIO DEL ALTO.

HE DANCES TO THESE CERTAIN WORDS AND UNDER THE STREET-LIGHT HIS REFLECTION IS IN HER EYES. ARNOLD AND JIM-JIMMY-JIM WATCH FROM THE BUSHES AND I WATCH THEM. JIM-JIMMY-JIM HAS A MILK BOTTLE AND IN THE MILK BOTTLE IS GASOLINE.

DROP BY DROP HE HAS COLLECTED IT FROM THE NOZZLE AT MITCHELL'S GAS STATION. "ALMOST GOT ENOUGH," HE WHISPERS. HECTOR TAKES THE BEAUTIFUL JOANNE IN HIS ARMS AND ARNOLD STARES. "ALMOST GOT ENOUGH TO BURN HIS HOUSE DOWN." THERE IS KISSING. "JOANNE, JOANNE," IN A SPANISH ACCENT. INTO THE DARKNESS THEY VANISH.

IN HER YARD ARNOLD WAITS NEXT TO JIM-JIMMY-JIM. IN THE SHADOW OF THE GARAGE THEY WAIT FOR THE RETURN OF JOANNE, TO WATCH HER CLIMB THE TREE TO HER OPEN WINDOW, THEY WAIT AND WAIT BUT THE ONLY PERSON WHO IS STILL AWAKE TO SEE HER DO IT IS ME.

HECTOR

SO MUSIC IS COMING OUT OF HECTOR'S HOUSE, IT'S WARM AND THE WINDOWS ARE OPEN AND ARNOLD AND JIM-JIMMY-JIM ARE SPYING FROM THEIR USUAL SPOT AND I AM SPYING FROM MINE. THEY ARE WATCHING AN OLD LADY WITH BRAIDS BRING HECTOR FOOD.

IN THE YELLOW-LIT WINDOW, HECTOR AND THE GRANDMA ARE LAUGHING. JIM-JIMMY-JIM SOCKS ARNOLD, SAYS, "KEEP YOUR HEAD DOWN." AND THAT HE HAS ENOUGH NOW, ENOUGH GASOLINE. JIM-JIMMY JIM CHECKS HIS MATCHES.

TONIGHT IS JUST PRACTICE. TONIGHT IS PRACTICE FOR THE REVENGE, FOR WHEN JIM-JIMMY-JIM PAYS HECTOR BACK FOR TOUCHING THE BEAUTIFUL JOANNE. "HECTOR," HE WHISPERS AND LIGHTS A MATCH. "HECTOR, HECTOR." THE LIGHTS GO OFF. THE HOUSE IS DARK. "WHAT TIME?" HE SAYS. "11:57," SAYS ARNOLD. JIM-JIMMY-JIM WRITES IT IN A RED NOTEBOOK. HE HAS BEEN WATCHING MANY DAYS.

"LET'S GO," SAYS HE. BUT FROM UP THE STREET COMES SOMEONE WALKING FAST. THE SOUND OF GIRL FEET MOVING TOWARD THE HOUSE. "HECTOR, HECTOR," SHE WHISPERS. "I WILL KILL HIM," SAYS JIM-JIMMY-JIM. "JOANNE," ARNOLD WHISPERS. AND THEN HECTOR'S FRONT DOOR OPENS. JOANNE GOES INSIDE. "TOMORROW," SAYS JIM-JIMMY-JIM. "TOMORROW."

The Morning

EXCUSE ME, EXCUSE ME, YOUR NAME IS HECTOR, RIGHT? — HE LOOKS AT ME — YOU'RE THE BOYFRIEND OF JOANNE, RIGHT? — HE REALLY LOOKS AT ME. WE'RE AT THE BUS STOP. HE'S GOING TO WORK. JANITOR. BAKER HOSPITAL. THE STITCHED NAME ON HIS UNIFORM POCKET SAYS "NICK."

EXCUSE ME, IT'S IMPORTANT. AND I TELL HIM. ALL OF IT. EVERYTHING. TONIGHT, I SAY. "THIS NIGHT?" HE SAYS. YES. YES. YOU SHOULD CALL THE POLICE. "NO POLICE." HE WAVES HIS HANDS. "NO POLICE." WHEN HIS BUS COMES, HE SHAKES MY HAND AND SAYS IT AGAIN. "NO POLICE."

> WHAT WERE YOU DOING UP SO EARLY?

> WENT FOR A WALK.

> LORD GOD, MY HEAD HURTS. I'M GETTING OLD. 3 BEERS IS MY LIMIT.

AT DINNER-TIME THE LONG SHADOW OF JIM-JIMMY-JIM CROSSES THE PORCH. MY AUNT YELLS, "WE'RE STILL EATING!" THE SHADOW SAYS, "I'LL WAIT." THE PLAN WAS A SLEEP OVER BUT ARNOLD DIDN'T WANT TO GO. IN A SOFT VOICE HE SAID, "I'M SICK, MOM. MY STOMACH, MOM. TELL HIM, MOM. HOW YOU'RE MAKING ME STAY HOME TONIGHT." MY AUNT SQUINTED.

> WHAT SICK?

> UM. YOU SAID YOU COULD ONLY DRINK 3 BEERS BUT NOW YOU'RE ON NUMBER FIVE.

> I NEVER SAID THAT.

"SICK?!" SHE SAID. "WHAT KIND OF BALONEY IS THIS? SICK? YOU'RE UP TO SOMETHING." HER VOICE WAS VERY LOUD. "GO TELL HIM YOURSELF. I'M NOT LYING FOR YOU." ARNOLD STOOD UP. "I'M ABOUT TO BARF." I SAID "IT'S OK. I'LL TELL HIM," AND I WENT TO THE SCREEN DOOR. I LOOKED LEFT AND I LOOKED RIGHT. THE SHADOW WAS GONE.

> GONE?

> YUH-HUH

> I THINK I MIGHT BE DEAD.

> I THINK I POSSIBLY JUST DIED.

RED SPARKS FLY

I HEAR FIRE TRUCKS. DID HE DO IT? IS HECTOR'S HOUSE ON FIRE? I HEAR SIRENS SCREAMING IN THAT DIRECTION. MY COUSIN SAYS, "WHAT ARE YOU DOING? FREDDY! FREDDY!" I CLIMB OUT THE BEDROOM WINDOW AND RUN ACROSS THE DARK YARD.

THE STARS ARE BRIGHT AND POWERFUL THROUGH THE BERZERK BLACK BRANCHES OF TREES. I'M RUNNING TO WHERE THE RED SPARKS ARE FLYING. TO THE CHOKING SMOKE. AND I WAS CONCENTRATING ON THAT. THEN BLAM! I GET BASHED ON THE HEAD AND EVERYTHING GOES WHITE. JIM-JIMMY-JIM IS THERE SCREAMING HE KNOWS IT WAS ME. KICKING HARD SHOES INTO MY SIDE AND SAYING I MUST DIE FOR MY CRIME OF WARNING HECTOR

CRACK

AFTER THAT, I DON'T KNOW. THE SMELL OF SMOKE, THE SMELL OF BURNING AND THEN FILL-IN-THE BLANK. IT WAS 16 STITCHES ON THE BACK OF MY HEAD. THE HOUSE THAT BURNED DOWN WASN'T HECTOR'S. HIM AND HIS FRIENDS WERE WAITING FOR JIM-JIMMY-JIM IN A CIRCLE SO JIM-JIMMY-JIM BURNED A DIFFERENT HOUSE INSTEAD.

AND THE HOUSE HAD A LADY IN IT AND THAT LADY DIED. AND THE POLICE CAME KNOCKING AND ASKING FOR MY COUSIN BECAUSE JIM-JIMMY-JIM TOLD THEM ARNOLD PLANNED IT ALL OUT. SAID ARNOLD WAS THE MASTER MIND, HE WAS JUST OBEYING ARNOLD AND INTO THE POLICE CAR WENT ARNOLD AND MY AUNT SAID I WAS NEVER ALLOWED TO COME THERE AGAIN. MY INFLUENCE IS SOMETHING TERRIBLE.

Best American Story About a Hazardous, Symbolical Cesspool

PETER ORNER

FROM *The Paris Review*

Peter Orner is a writer and professor of creative writing at San Francisco State University. His most recent book was Love and Shame and Love. *The following short story is a part of his new collection* Last Car over the Sagamore Bridge.

Foley's Pond

Nate Zamost took that week off school. We wondered what he did those long days other than the funeral, which didn't take more than a few hours. The Zamosts lived in one of those houses just across the fence from Foley's Pond. Nate's sister, Barbara—they called her Babs—slid under the chain-link and waddled down to the water. This was in 1983. She was two and a half.

The day Nate came back to school, we refrained from playing Kill the Guy with the Ball at recess. We stood around in a ragged circle on the edge of the basketball court and spoke to each other in polite murmurs. We were a group of guys in junior high who hung out together. It wasn't like we weren't capable of understanding. Some of us even had sisters. But instinctively we seemed to get it that our role was not to understand or even to console but, in the spirit of funerals, to act. So we stood there and looked at our shoes and kicked at loose asphalt. Nate went along with it. He played chief mourner by nodding his head slowly. I remember Stu Rothstein finally trying to say something.

"Look, it's not like it's your fault," Stu said. "I mean how could you have known she knew how to slide under the fence?"

Nate looked up from his shoes.

"I taught her."

What could anybody say to that? Stu took a stab. He'd always been decent like that.

"Well, it's not like you told her to do it when you weren't looking."

"I didn't?"

Stu didn't say anything after that. Nobody else did, either. We let Nate's question hang there, and to this day I don't know whether he meant it or whether, out of grief, he was assuming even more guilt than he needed to. Like Stu Rothstein, Nate Zamost was a gentle guy. During Kill the Guy with the Ball, he never went for your head; he'd always go for your ankles and take you down easy. It was the rest of us who were more interested in blood than the ball itself. But who's to say what goes on behind closed doors, between siblings? Nate, like all of us, was thirteen that year. His parents went out for a couple of hours and left him in charge of his little sister.

Remembering it all now, what comes to me most vividly is my private anger toward Nate. Foley's Pond had always been a secret place and now everybody in town knew all about it. It was wedged inside a small patch of woods, between where Bob-O-Link Avenue ended and the public golf course began. The pond was said to have been created by runoff from the golf course, that it was nothing but a cesspool of chemicals. Proof of this theory was embodied by the large, corrugated drainpipe that hung out over the edge of the pond. Whatever it was that flowed from it didn't look like water. Once, Ross Berger dove into Foley's and came up with green hair and leeches on his thighs. Someone shouted, "The sludge supports life!" We all jumped in. It was like swimming in crude oil. A fantastic place, Foley's—scragged, infested, overgrown, and gloomed long before Nate Zamost's sister wrecked it. How many mob hits, feet tied to bricks, bobbed and swayed at the bottom of that fetid swamp? All the missing kids in Chicago, milk-carton phantom faces, all, all were dumped into Foley's.

After school we'd go down there and talk down the waterlogged afternoons. There is something overripe about spring in the Midwest, the wet and green world, the ground itself rotten, oozing, dripping. Foley's was protected by a canopy of trees. The sun only crept through in speckles. There was nothing beautiful about that pond, even in April, except that it was ours. Foley's in the rain, the rain smacking the leaves, how hidden we were, talking and talking and talking about God only knows what. Had we been a little older we may have drunk beers or smoked dope or brought girls so they could scream about not wanting to go anywhere near that disgusting water. We were thirteen and conspiratorial and what was said is now out of reach, as it should be.

It took them eleven hours to find her. Foley's was a lot deeper than anybody had thought. The fire department's charts turned out to be inaccurate. Police divers had to come up from Chicago. And something else that by now most people may have forgotten and newcomers would have no way of knowing. When they laid Babs on the grass in the dark, Nate Zamost's mother refused to acknowledge that the mottle of bloated flesh lit up by high-powered flashlights was her daughter, anybody's daughter. Mrs. Zamost didn't know Foley's. Ross Berger was down there twelve seconds, and he came up looking like an alien. She wouldn't even touch it. I was there, just outside the ring of lights. Mrs. Zamost didn't scream, just shook her head, and stepped backward into the dark.

Foley's is a real park now. The Park District manicured it. The trees have been trimmed. There's a wide, wood-chip path off Bob-O-Link that leads right to it. And they've installed tall bird feeders, long poles topped with small yellow houses.

Best American Poem About a Particle Accelerator

BRENDAN TODT

FROM *Ninth Letter*

One of the scientific highlights of the year was the pursuit of the Higgs boson, an elementary particle that could be responsible for all of the mass in the universe. Although it still has not been seen, researchers at the Large Hadron Collider near Geneva, Switzerland tentatively confirmed its existence in March 2013. The following poem tells the story of a similar but fictional particle accelerator in Siberia.

At the Particle Accelerator at Krasnoyarsk

The Belgian physicist sits with the Flemish physicist as the journalist
    from Denmark writes everything down.
Inside, the married couples spin by at velocities just shy of the speed
    of light.
At any time now, the Belgian explains, one couple will collide with
    another and shatter into its constituent parts.
And it all seems simple enough for the journalist who feels obliged
    to ask what exactly the point is of this kind of science
when you know you will observe afterward the man and the woman
    whirling wildly around separately.

But the Belgian and the Fleming exclaim *NoNoNo,*
The man and woman disappear entirely from the eight hundred and
    forty-two mile accelerator
and what they have observed and hope to capture are the colorful
    corpuscles of fury, envy, lust, capriciousness, tenderness,
    tardiness, punctuality, sexuality, fortitude, temperance, malice,
    disobedience, loyalty,
and any of the other quark-sized emoticons that may appear and
    adhere to the accelerator walls
chilled nearly to absolute zero eighty-seven stories below ground in
    Siberia.

And when it happens, there is no sound, no moan of discomfort or
    pleasure,
as the Brazilian couple smashes into the Filipino couple and a red
    flashing light above the console begins flashing and rotating
and all of the instrumentation goes berserk,
and the Danish journalist begins writing something down though he
    understands nothing,
and he watches on the monitors as the accelerator fills with a gas that
    was previously explained to him
to facilitate the condensation of the quark-size emoticons into
    particles with just enough mass to cause them to drop to the floor
which is constructed, much like a microscope slide is constructed, so

that they can be instantaneously illuminated and documented and
    studied,
and if the receptacles are fast enough—and to date they have not
    been—captured and stored and possibly even reproduced and
    patented and sold above ground by the Science Ministries of the
    United Nations, et cetera.
And so the journalist returns to Denmark and publishes his front-
    page feature on the purpose of the science in Siberia
and its practical applications to marriage counselors and perfume
    salespersons at Macy's and the ad-men and -women of Madison
    Avenue in New York.
And it is read widely across Denmark where a representative in
    Parliament proposes a bill to provide greater funding for the
    particle accelerator at Krasnoyarsk.
And when the bill passes and the story is picked up on the wire, it is
    agreed to in Washington
that we should support sciences like these that have clear and
    identifiable purposes in mind,
and so the Americans offer three times the assistance of the Danish
in exchange for more slots for their scientists, and more shares of the
    patents, and more real estate to erect department stores and so on.

Meanwhile the physicists are trying to catch those tricky little
    buggers—fortitude, fury, and the newly discovered benevolence—
in little compartments that can withstand both the cold of the
    accelerator walls and the immeasurably quick vibrations of its
    particles.
And the chemists are hard at work cloning punctuality and
    temperance, which are the heaviest and least mobile elements.
And the lawyers are arguing over patent law and intellectual property.
And husbands and wives are predicting their concentrations of
    discontent, valor, antagonism.
And on the six o'clock news, national anchors are charting the
    inequities between Europeans and North Americans in their
    concentration of loyalty, capriciousness, and envy.
And it is postulated in the Cabinet that North Korea is constructing
    its own accelerator, although no one can be sure.

And the President delivers speeches condemning his predecessor for permitting Siberia to spearhead such a grand scientific endeavor.

And there are a couple of factories in the Great Plains manufacturing underground shelters in case of an attack.

And there are people in all corners of the country buying them.

And there is a child in Idaho writing MALICE with a Sharpie on his passed-out-father's forehead

because he has learned the word from the television and walks around the house reciting it.

And on October first *Punctuality* goes on sale and is immediately sold out.

And when the perfume industry declines the President delivers more speeches about that.

And by February it becomes clear who his opponent will be in the general election.

And in the wake of such incredible scientific discovery, everyone knows he will be reelected and he is.

And funding increases and taxes increase and airlines begin to offer direct flights from Little Rock and Gary and Atlantic City to Norilsk in the Krasnoyarsk Region of Siberia.

And the airlines advertise no fees for checked luggage because there are generally no checked bags accompanying married American couples flying into Siberia.

And for two weeks the United Family Counselors of Nebraska picket the accelerator.

And because of the exoduses of married couples in Indiana, Oklahoma, Utah, and Maryland, massive redistricting takes place and three-quarters of their representatives in Congress are defeated in primary challenges.

And the House Minority Whip has lost his parents to the particle accelerator in Krasnoyarsk

and there is a public memorial held on the Mall in Washington.

And flower sales spike as red, white, and artificially-blue-dyed roses accumulate against a fence erected in memoriam of the Minority Whip's mother and father.

And one Mall groundskeeper is fired for taking a blue rose, which he

has never seen in his life, home to his wife who has promised him
to never fly into Siberia.
and his face is adopted as the new symbol of the destructive nature of
modern science.
And the Parliamentarian who originally proposed the increased
funding for the particle accelerator in Krasnoyarsk is defeated
and the funding is allowed to expire and Denmark loses its allocation
of physicists.

And the following April *Temperance* is released by Calvin Klein and
does not sell out.
And the Vice President of Quantum Fragrances is fired and departs
with a generous severance package.
And he moves his wife and his daughter and his live-in cook to
Aspen.
And the cook is overjoyed to walk the streets of Aspen during the
Food and Wine Classic.
And the sous chefs at the accelerator in Krasnoyarsk talk quietly
between meals about what the next discovery will be
and how they will pair their house wines with opportunism,
temptation, and generosity.
And on the basketball court at lunch a physicist from Norway elbows
a physicist from Ecuador
and in the locker room afterward the biochemist from Belarus asks
if anyone else saw the drop of blood pause in its descent before
hitting the ground
and six months later imagination is discovered.
And in Texas the state school board is obstructing the inclusion of a
new periodic table in the nation's textbooks.
And in four years a good-old-boy is elected President and the
American funds expire and the British funds expire
and in a conference room at what was once known as the particle
accelerator at Krasnoyarsk
the maintenance staff will watch a World Cup quarterfinal match and
cheer
as skinny men in shorts run around and smash into each other
while the fates of their countries hang in the balance.

Best American Account of Tragedy and Nationality

SIBYLLA BRODZINSKY, CATALINA HOYOS,
AND MAX SCHOENING

FROM *Throwing Stones at the Moon*

For nearly half a century, there has been an ongoing armed conflict in Colombia between paramilitary groups, guerrilla groups, and the government's armed forces. As a result of this strife, thousands of civilians have been displaced, and many others have been kidnapped, killed, or raped. The following narrative is an excerpt from a book of oral histories that seeks to trace the history of this conflict. The book, called Throwing Stones at the Moon, *was produced by Voice of Witness, a nonprofit organization that records oral histories of contemporary human rights crises. Names in this narrative have been changed at the request of the narrator.*

An Oral History of Catalina Hoyos

I was born in Tolima province but grew up in Bogotá. I come from a well-off family, but mine was never a normal family that sat down to meals together. My dad was always studying, traveling. He wanted to help make a better society, and his missions included helping children of the Indians of Vaupés province and the poor black communities in Chocó province. He was also a film buff, and he helped found the film school at the National University. He was never one of those fathers who plays with his children, but he was loving with me, my sisters Verónica and Angélica, and my brother Alberto. My mom, on the other hand, is a very tough woman. She was a criminal prosecutor.

My parents separated when I was fourteen years old, and it was around that time that I decided I wanted to be an actress. I'd go see a movie and for the whole week I'd pretend I was the leading lady.

When I was fifteen, a friend from school won a beauty pageant in a town called Pacho, about eighty kilometers from Bogotá. She invited all her friends to go to the party where she was going to receive her sash. Pacho was this small town, and I remember when we arrived at the town hall, the police chief was there with all the municipal authorities. This was a real backwater!

Then this fat, little, dark-skinned guy came up to me. With the big hat and the jewelry, he had all the look of a *traqueto*, a drug trafficker. He looked at the cowboy boots I was wearing and asked me where I'd got them. I told him the name of the store in Bogotá, and right there he told one of his people to go to Bogotá and buy a pair for him. I thought it was funny, but the whole scene was sort of sleazy. Those people were so arrogant, with all the money they had.

I phoned my mother after that, because she'd told me to call her once I'd arrived. She asked me who was at the party, so I asked some of the people for their names and I started telling her. Then she said, "Get in a taxi and tell them I'll pay the fare here," so I left the party right away. It turned out that the guy who'd asked me about the boots was a drug trafficker named Gonzalo Rodríguez Gacha. The place was filled with *traquetos*. I didn't really know who they were at the time, but since my mom was a prosecutor who dealt with drug trafficking cases, she knew.

When my brother and sisters and I were growing up, my mom would tell us that when she took on cases against drug traffickers, plane tickets to Disney World would arrive at her office with the names of all us kids. It was a bribe, but at the same time it was a threat, showing that they knew our names. She'd also get envelopes stuffed with cash. But my mother never accepted a bribe in her life.

I finished high school in 1982, when I was sixteen, and started studying at an acting academy. When I was seventeen I got my first modeling contract, which was for a local clothing store. After that I was on television and in magazines, and I could make maybe 400,000 pesos in a single photo shoot. From one moment to the next I was suddenly part of the elite, the twenty or so professional models that were working in Colombia back then. I'd travel around the country to runway shows, and at one point I was in about fifteen different television commercials at the same time. I would see myself on T.V. and say, "That's me!"

It was a life of parties. In Bogotá, cocaine was passed around like hors d'oeuvres. At any party in Colombia you'd go into the bathroom and there would be lines on the sink counter. I tried it once at the Keops discotheque, which was all the rage then. It was one of the most anxiety-producing experiences of my life. My heart started racing, and I thought I was going to die! I managed to get home, but I sat outside on the steps until the effect wore off because inside the house I felt like a caged animal.

There were always *traquetos* at the parties. I've sometimes thought that, if I hadn't had the education my parents gave me, I would have ended up the wife of one of those *traquetos*, like all my counterparts did. Why would I be any different? But I saw these people differently. I mean, if I went to a party and it was filled with *traquetos* I didn't say, "Uy! I'm not going because I don't mix with those people." I went, but I kept them at a distance.

My father never really approved of my career choice. He was an intellectual, and he thought the telenovelas I acted in were trash. But we had a good relationship.

In 1989, when I was twenty, my dad was working in New York at a development organization. He came back to Bogotá one Sunday in November and we got together at my sister Verónica's house. My brother Alberto wasn't there at the time because he was studying at the Naval Academy in Cartagena. At the get-together, my dad, my sisters and I all started planning a vacation together. My dad was going to be lecturing at the Universidad del Valle in Cali for three or four days, and we were making plans to all go to the beach afterward to Cartagena or San Andrés. It was the first time in six months that we'd seen him. By that time, I had moved out of my mom's house and was living in a big house in La Calera, a wealthy suburb in the mountains above Bogotá.

During the meal my dad began to speak to each of us sisters about our lives. He also talked to me about each one of my sisters and my brother, telling me to take care of all of them. He said, "You have to take care of Alberto, he's still young. Take care of Vero." Vero is Verónica, my little sister who he thought had married too young. He told me to believe in myself and to believe in my instinct. I remember I got a cold shiver; I had the feeling my dad was saying goodbye. I remember thinking, What's going to happen? Why is he telling me this now and not in Cartagena while we sunbathe and have a few drinks?

The next day, November 27, 1989, I went to the gym early like I always did. I always called my mom early in the morning but that day I called my godfather first. He asked me if I'd spoken to my mom and when I told him I hadn't he said, "Call your mother." I asked him, "What happened?" and he just insisted, "Call your mother." I called my mom and she told me the news. The plane my dad had taken to Cali had exploded over Soacha. The plane had taken off at 7:10 a.m., and five minutes later it blew up, killing 110 people.

I got in my car and rushed to my mom's house. In the car, I turned on the radio, and the announcer was reading out the passenger list. The presidential candidate César Gaviria was apparently supposed to be on that flight. The radio announcer said a bomb had blown up the plane, and that Pablo Escobar and Rodríguez Gacha were suspected of ordering the attack. At that moment, I remembered that I'd met Rodríguez Gacha at the party in Pacho years before. I had met my dad's executioner.

I went to my mom's house and my two sisters were already there. It was chaotic. Everyone screaming, crying. I spoke again with my godfather. He had an air transport company that chartered planes and helicopters for oil companies and he asked me if I wanted a helicopter to fly over the crash site. But I said no. I wanted to be on the ground to see what happened. I grabbed my two sisters and we set out in the car through Monday morning traffic toward Soacha. I told them, "Do you want to live with the doubt? Not me." We could have waited quietly at home to get the notification of my dad's death but I needed to see. When we got to Soacha, the residents there guided us to the crash site because the plane had fallen in a mountainous part of Soacha, not in the town center.

It was about nine in the morning when we got to the crash site, and we saw that it had been cordoned off by the army. They weren't supposed to let anyone into the site but I said to one of the soldiers, "What would you do if it were your dad on that plane?" He saw us three girls—I was twenty, Verónica was nineteen and Angélica was twenty-one—and he took pity on us. He asked me, "What did he look like?"

I told him, "My dad always wore a turtleneck and corduroy pants." The soldier said, "I know where he is." We walked uphill about a kilometer and saw pieces of clothing on the ground, a briefcase and body parts. There were body parts everywhere; we walked among heads, limbs, and guts. I have never forgotten the scent.

After a long while, the soldiers came up to us with a huge black bag and they shook a body out. I almost fainted. My dad was a handsome man; he looked like Jack Nicholson. But the face of the dead person was frozen in a scream that he must have let out from way up there. His mouth was completely open, and the expression of distress on his face was clear. His skull was open and his brains had exploded. I looked at my sister Angélica. She was a beautiful woman, like a Colombian Pocahontas, but when she saw the body fall out of the bag she became disconnected from the planet and she didn't speak.

I couldn't believe it. Eight or ten hours earlier we'd been with him. At three in the afternoon the day before it had been all about planning a vacation, the beach, laughter, delicious food, wine. At 7:45 a.m. the next day: death.

The soldiers asked us, "Is it your father?" It looked like him, but my sisters and I began to doubt it, especially my little sister Verónica. She said, "I don't think it's him." It was very difficult. I felt that it was him, but I wanted to be absolutely sure. Verónica said, "Look at his hands. They don't look like his hands." My dad's hands had been very pretty. He was a vain person, and his hands were spotless. This man who fell from three thousand meters, his skin was intact, but every inch of bone in his body must have been broken to pieces because his hand was like rubber; it bent this way and that.

I thought, What do we remember about my dad that was unique? And it was his feet. When he was little his mother made him lace up his boots really tight and it deformed his instep; it was really high. So in the end we recognized him from his feet.

The whole time Angélica was silent. She just looked at us and said nothing. She was completely gone. Through all of this process I was the one who stayed completely sane. My dad had always said that I was the crazy one—his nickname for me was "La Loquita." I was the one who drove really fast, I was the model, I did what I wanted. He thought the sane one was Angélica, but no. I realized then that I had to take the reins because no one else would.

Then a doctor came, and without saying a word, he knelt down and sliced my dad open. He looked at the organs and then he said, "Okay, let's close him up." He took a needle and thread and sewed four big stitches. Then he handed us a little piece of paper with a number, like the kind you pull at a butcher shop to wait your turn. The piece of paper had "438" written on it. The doctor said we could use that to claim our dad's body at the Forensic Medicine Institute in Bogotá.

My sisters and I stayed and watched as the rescuers threw the body bags into a muddy dump truck. The relatives of other passengers had also shown up at the site, and the rescuers were piecing bodies together to present to them. We were lucky to have a full body; others were content with just an arm or a leg. We stayed for five hours in the hot sun, watching, because I wanted to make sure that they put my dad in the dump truck, that they weren't going to leave him. We finally left at about two in the afternoon and went to my mom's house. She was hysterical, screaming. Even though my parents had separated, my mother was still in love with my dad. A fortune teller had once told her that my dad would come back to her, so she was waiting for him. We got to her house and we gave her medicine to calm her down.

It was raining when my sisters and I went to the Forensic Medicine Institute at about five in the afternoon. But when we got there we were told that the bodies hadn't arrived yet. We said we'd wait. We finally left at ten, after the officials at the Forensic Medicine Institute told us they wouldn't hand over the bodies that night. It was still raining.

I took my sisters home and went to my house. It was something like two or three in the morning. I was crying as I drove up the hill because that's when I said to myself, Now I can cry. I got home, went into my bedroom and built a fire in the fireplace. I sat in front of it and I said to my dad, "I'm not going to sleep until you tell me what happened." I stayed up all night; I was struggling to understand what had happened.

My little brother Alberto arrived from Cartagena early the next morning, and I went with him and my sisters to the Forensic Medicine Institute at seven. I told the person in charge there, "I've come for my father," and he said, "Look, there's been a problem. The body bags broke, and all the bodies have been mixed up, so you'll have to go in and ID him." The little number I'd been given was useless.

My brother said, "I don't think I can do this." And I said, "You're the man of this family now. Grab onto my arm as tight as you can and we'll go together, but you can't live with the doubt of whether it really was Dad or not." So we went into a muddy, open-air court-yard filled with body bags. We had to walk among the dead, among the severed limbs, as an official from the Forensic Medicine Institute opened the bags and asked, "Is this him?" The decomposition pro-cess, after sitting out in the sun and then in the rain overnight, was incredible. When we finally found our dad, it was horrible, because his body was slimy; his skin had sort of melted.

We took his body and held a funeral a few days later. We couldn't have an open casket because of the state he was in. Lots of people sent flowers, and there were nice eulogies. I fell into a sort of limbo; I was there but I wasn't. I didn't eat. In that week, I lost something like eleven kilos from the anxiety, from not sleeping. Then, two weeks after my father was killed, my sister Angélica started doing heavy drugs. She's never gotten over it. She's been in and out of rehabilita-tion clinics seven times.

After the funeral, my family hired a well-respected lawyer to sue the state for the bombing, because the airport security controls had failed. In the days following the bombing, investigators determined that someone had walked onto the plane, left the bomb in a briefcase un-der a seat, and walked off. The lawyer was also handling the cases of several of the other families from the plane. However, three days after we hired him, the lawyer was gunned down at the door to his building.

About a month after my dad was killed, I was riding in a taxi in Bogotá. I was chatting with the taxi driver because I like to do that. He was listening to the radio when the announcer said that the drug trafficker Rodríguez Gacha had just been killed.

I said, "Stop, please, please stop." The driver said, "Why, what happened?" I said, "Do you have a minute?" He stopped, and I got out, looked up to heaven and gave thanks to God. "One down," I said.

By that time I felt I couldn't live in this country any more. I was

incensed by everything that was happening with the drug traffickers trying to take over the country, the war they had declared. So on
February 11, 1990, I left Colombia for New York on a temporary visitor's visa. I lived in a tiny apartment on 58th Street between Fifth and
Sixth Avenues, but I wasn't exactly struggling. I started working at an
art gallery, and I studied language and literature at Columbia University to improve my English. I then started studying film direction.

I met my husband Pedro on a trip back to Colombia in March
1990. I was there for an event in my dad's memory. Pedro is Spanish and he worked at a bank there. He would fly up to New York on
the weekends to see me, and a year later we got married and moved
to Spain. We had two children, Juan Carlos and Pilar. Now we live in
southern Florida.

For many years I was embarrassed to admit that I was a victim of
my country. And I was afraid to remember, to face all that again. I
never spoke about how my dad died. You try to forget because that's
your medicine. I only started facing it in 2011. I've lived outside of
Colombia for more than twenty years and I go back for visits, but I
wouldn't live there. Drug trafficking has been a cancer on this country. It's contaminated everything, it's penetrated everywhere. And I
never want my kids to think that's normal.

ANA ARANA AND SEBASTIAN ROTELLA

■

Finding Oscar: Massacre, Memory, and Justice in Guatemala

FROM *ProPublica*

Chapter 1: "You Don't Know Me"

THE CALL FROM GUATEMALA put Oscar on edge.

Prosecutors came looking for you, relatives in his rural hometown told him. Big shots from Guatemala City. They want to talk to you.

Oscar Alfredo Ramírez Castañeda had plenty to lose. Although he was living in the United States illegally, the 31-year-old had built a solid life. He worked two full-time jobs to support his three children and their mother, Nidia. They had settled in a small but cheerful townhouse in Framingham, Mass., a blue-collar suburb of Boston.

Oscar usually did his best to avoid contact with the authorities. But he decided to call the prosecutor in Guatemala City. She said it was a sensitive matter about his childhood and a massacre in the country's civil war long ago. She promised to explain in an email.

Days later, Oscar sat at his computer in a living room full of toys, school trophies, family photos, a crucifix and souvenirs of his native land. He had arrived home from work late at night, as usual. Nidia, seven months pregnant, rested on a couch nearby. The children slept upstairs.

Oscar's green eyes scanned the screen. The email had arrived. He took a breath and clicked.

"You don't know me," it began.

The prosecutor said she was investigating a savage episode of the war, a case that had deeply affected her. In 1982, a squad of army commandos had stormed the village of Dos Erres and slaughtered more than 250 men, women and children.

Two small boys who survived were taken away by the commandos. Twenty-nine years later, 15 years after she had started hunting the killers, the prosecutor had reached an inescapable conclusion: Oscar was one of the boys who had been abducted.

"I know that you were much loved and well treated by the family in which you grew up," the prosecutor wrote. "I hope you have the maturity to absorb everything I am telling you."

"The point is, Oscar Alfredo, that although you don't know it, you were a victim of this sad event I mentioned, just like the other child I told you that we found, and the families of the people who died in that place."

By now, Nidia was reading over his shoulder. The prosecutor said she could arrange a DNA test to confirm her theory. She offered an incentive: help with Oscar's immigration status in the United States.

"This is a decision you must make," she wrote.

Oscar's mind raced through images of his childhood. He struggled to reconcile the prosecutor's words with his memories. He had never known his mother. He did not remember his father, who had never married. Lt. Oscar Ovidio Ramírez Ramos had died in an accident when he was just four. Oscar's grandmother and aunts had raised him to revere his father.

As the family told it, the lieutenant was a hero. He graduated at the top of his academy class, became an elite commando and won medals in combat. Oscar treasured the soldier's red beret, his aging photo album. He liked to leaf through the pictures showing an officer with a bantam build and youthful smile, riding in a tank, carrying the flag.

The lieutenant's nickname, a diminutive of Oscar, was Cocorico. Oscar called himself Cocorico the Second.

"You don't know me."

If the prosecutor's suspicions were correct, Oscar didn't know himself. He was not the son of an honorable soldier. He was a kidnapping victim, a battlefield trophy, living proof of mass murder.

Yet, as overwhelming as the revelation was, Oscar had to admit it was not completely new. A decade earlier, someone had sent him a Guatemalan newspaper article about Dos Erres. It mentioned his name and the supposed abduction. But his family back home convinced him the idea was preposterous, a leftist fabrication.

Far from the harsh realities of Guatemala, Oscar put the story out of his mind. The country he had left was among the most desperate and violent in the Americas. About 200,000 people died in the civil war that had ended in 1996. The right-wing military, accused of genocide in the conflict, remained powerful.

Now, the case was pulling Oscar into Guatemala's struggle with its own tragic history. If he took the DNA test and the results were positive, it would transform his life in dangerous ways. He would become flesh-and-blood evidence in the quest to find justice for the victims of Dos Erres. He would have to accept that his identity, his whole world, had been based on a lie. And he would be a potential target for powerful forces that wanted to keep Guatemala's secrets buried.

Guatemalans wrestled with a similar dilemma. They were divided over how much effort to devote to punish the crimes of the past in a society overwhelmed by lawlessness. The uniformed killers and torturers of the 1980s had helped spawn the mafias, corruption and crime that assail Central America's small and weak states. The Dos Erres investigation was part of the battle against impunity, a fight for the future. But small victories had big potential costs: retaliation, political strife.

Like his country, Oscar would have to choose whether to confront painful truths.

Chapter 2: "We're Not Dogs For You to Kill"

The fall of 1982 was tense in Petén, Guatemala's northern panhandle near Mexico.

Government troops in the region battled a guerrilla group known as the Fuerzas Armadas Rebeldes (Rebel Armed Forces), or FAR. The nationwide counterinsurgency campaign was methodical and brutal. Dictator Efraín Ríos Montt, a general who had taken power after a coup in March, unleashed search-and-destroy missions on rural villages suspected of sheltering guerrillas.

Although there had been fighting near Dos Erres, the remote

jungle hamlet was comparatively calm. It had been founded only four years earlier in a government land redistribution program. Unlike areas where rebels recruited aggressively among the country's indigenous peoples, the residents of Dos Erres were mainly *ladinos*—Guatemalans of mixed white and indigenous descent. The 60 families who lived in the lush terrain grew beans, corn and pineapples. There were dirt roads, a school and two churches, one Catholic and one evangelical. The village name, which meant "Two R's," was a tribute to the founders, Federico Aquino Ruano and Marcos Reyes.

The area army commander, Lt. Carlos Antonio Carias, wanted the men of Dos Erres to join an armed civil-defense patrol at his base in the town of Las Cruces, about seven miles away. The men resisted, saying they would only patrol their own community. Lt. Carias turned hostile, accusing the people of Dos Erres of harboring guerrillas. He barred residents from flag-raising ceremonies. As evidence of their supposed treachery, he showed his superiors a harvesting sack that bore the initials FAR, claiming it was the insignia of the rebel group. In reality, the sack belonged to the hamlet's cofounder Ruano and was inscribed with his initials.

In October, the army suffered a humiliating defeat in which guerrillas killed a group of soldiers and made off with about 20 rifles. By early December, intelligence indicated the rifles were in the area of Dos Erres. The army decided to send its crack commandos, the Kaibiles, to recover the weapons and teach the villagers a lesson.

The commandos were the point of the spear in an anti-guerrilla offensive that had already drawn international condemnation. Kaibil means "having the strength and astuteness of two tigers" in the Mam indigenous language. With a notoriously harsh training regime in survival skills, counterinsurgency and psychological warfare, the Kaibil commandos were viewed as Latin America's most brutal special forces. Their motto: "If I advance, follow me; if I stop, urge me on; if I retreat, kill me."

The plan was to conceal the identity of the raiders. On Dec. 6, 1982, a 20-man Kaibil squad assembled at a base in Petén and disguised themselves as guerrillas, replacing their uniforms with green T-shirts, civilian pants and red armbands. The 40 uniformed troops who joined them had orders to provide perimeter support and prevent anyone from entering or leaving. Whatever happened in Dos Erres would be blamed on the leftists.

The troops departed at 10 p.m. in two unmarked trucks. They drove until midnight, then hiked for two hours into the dense humid jungle. They were guided by a captive guerrilla who had been forced into the mission.

On the outskirts of the hamlet, the attack squad deployed in the usual configuration of groups: assault, perimeter, combat support and command.

The command group had a radio operator who would communicate with army brass throughout the operation. The assault group consisted of specialists in interrogation and close-quarters, hands-on killing. Even fellow commandos in the squad kept their distance from the marauders of the assault group, whom they viewed as psychopaths.

The Kaibiles chosen for the secret mission were considered the elite of the elite. At 28, Lt. Ramírez was the most experienced of them all.

Known as Cocorico and El Indio (The Indian), Ramírez had graduated at the top of his class in 1975. He had won a scholarship for advanced training in Colombia, but got in trouble for partying and misspending funds. Suspended by the army for six months, he fought in Nicaragua as a mercenary in 1978 for the forces of the dictator Anastasio Somoza Debayle, a U.S. ally. Leftist guerrillas toppled Somoza the next year, raising fears of a domino effect and reinforcing Guatemala's role as a strategic bastion for Washington's fight against communism in Central America.

Ramírez returned to Guatemala and joined an artillery unit. Wounded and decorated in November 1981, he engaged in covert operations against guerrillas, often in civilian dress, and developed a reputation for cruelty and thievery. A fellow soldier who served with him considered him "a criminal in uniform."

Other veterans, however, admired his battlefield prowess and loyalty to his troops. Ramírez was a dutiful son, wiring money to his mother each month. The mother complained frequently that the unmarried lieutenant hadn't given her a grandchild.

Ramírez became an instructor at the commando training school in Petén. In 1982, the Ríos Montt regime closed the school and created a roving squad of instructors who were skilled combatants: lieutenants, sergeants, corporals. Ramírez was deputy commander of the unit, which could be deployed rapidly as a strike force in rebel strongholds.

The squad stormed Dos Erres at 2 a.m.

Commandos kicked in doors and rounded up families. Although the soldiers had been ready for a firefight, there was no resistance. They did not find any of the stolen rifles.

The commandos herded the men into a school and the women and children into a church. The violence began before dawn. One of the soldiers, César Ibañez, heard the screams of girls begging for help. Several soldiers watched as Lt. César Adán Rosales Batres raped a girl in front of her family. Following their superior officer, other commandos started raping girls and women.

At midday, the commandos ordered the women they had abused to prepare food at a small ranch. The soldiers ate in shifts, five at a time. Young women cried as they served Ibañez and the others. Returning to his post, Ibañez saw a sergeant leading a girl down an alley.

The sergeant told him the "vaccinations" had started.

The commandos brought the villagers one by one to the center of the hamlet, near a dry well about 40 feet deep. Favio Pinzón Jerez, the squad's cook, and other soldiers reassured the captives that everything would be all right. They were going to be vaccinated. It was a routine health precaution, nothing to worry about.

Commando Gilberto Jordán drew first blood. He carried a baby to the well and hurled it to its death. Jordán wept as he killed the infant. Yet he and another soldier, Manuel Pop Sun, kept throwing children down the well.

The commandos blindfolded the adults and made them kneel, one at a time. They interrogated them about the rifles, aliases, guerrilla leaders. When the villagers protested that they knew nothing, soldiers hit them on the head with a metal sledgehammer. Then they threw them into the well.

"Malditos!" the villagers screamed at their executioners. "Accursed ones."

"Hijos de la gran puta, van a morir!" the soldiers yelled back. "Sons of the great whore, you are going to die!"

Ibañez dumped a woman in the well. Pinzón, the cook, dragged victims there alongside a sub-lieutenant named Jorge Vinicio Sosa

Orantes. When the well was half-filled, a man who was still alive atop the pile of bodies managed to get his blindfold off. He shouted curses up at the commandos.

"Kill me!" the man said.

"Your mother," Sosa retorted.

"Your mother, you son of the great whore!"

Pinzón watched as the infuriated Sosa shot the man with his rifle and, for good measure, threw a grenade into the pile. By the end of the afternoon, the well overflowed with corpses.

The carnage continued elsewhere. Salome Armando Hernández, 11, lived in another hamlet near Dos Erres. Early that morning he had traveled on horseback with his 22-year-old brother to buy medicine in Las Cruces. When they arrived in Dos Erres at about 10 a.m. to visit an uncle, commandos put Hernández in the church with the women and children.

Peeping between wood slats, the boy saw commandos beat and shoot people. His brother and uncle were killed.

In the afternoon, the raiders gathered about 50 women and children from the church and marched them toward the hills. Hernández positioned himself in the front of the line. He knew they were being taken to their deaths. So did the others.

"We're not dogs for you to kill us in the field," a woman declared. "We know that you are going to kill us, why don't you kill us right here?"

A soldier near the front charged among the prisoners to grab the woman by the hair. Hernández saw his chance and bolted off the path, gunfire echoing behind him. The boy hid in the vegetation and listened.

One by one, the soldiers killed the prisoners. Hernández heard the groans of the dying, a boy crying for his mother. The soldiers executed them with single shots from their rifles, one after another, 40 or 50 shots in total.

By nightfall, only corpses, animals and commandos inhabited the village. The squad bunked for the night in looted homes. Rain fell. Hernández crept back into town through the dark and mud. He passed the cadavers of his neighbors lying in streets and clearings. Huddled in tall grass, the boy heard the soldiers laughing.

"We finished them off, bro," a commando said. "And we are going to keep hunting."

Hernández eventually made his way back to Las Cruces.

Five prisoners had also survived the annihilating fury of the Kaibiles. It was a fluke: The three teenage girls and two small boys had apparently been hiding somewhere. They wandered into the center of the hamlet at sunset, when most of the villagers were dead. Commandos took them to a house that had been converted into the command post. The lieutenants decided not to kill the newcomers right away.

On the morning of Dec. 8, the squad set off on foot into the jungle hills, captives in tow. The commandos dressed the girls in military uniforms. Lt. Ramírez took charge of the 3-year-old boy; Santos Lopez Alonzo, the squad's baker, carried the 5-year-old.

That night, three commandos took the teenage girls into the brush and raped them. In the morning, they strangled and shot them.

The squad spared both little boys. Both were light-skinned and had green eyes, prized features in a society stratified along racial lines.

Lt. Ramírez told Pinzón and the others that he was going to bring the younger boy to his hometown of Zacapa, in eastern Guatemala, and outfit him in the style of the region.

"I'm going to dress him up sharp, like a cowboy," Ramírez said. "Cowboy boots, pants and shirt."

Days later, a helicopter set down in a clearing. It was there to pick up Pedro Pimentel Rios for his next assignment. He went to Panama to serve as an instructor at the School of the Americas, the U.S. military base that trained many Latin American officers implicated in atrocities. The two boys were loaded aboard the helicopter and flown back to the Kaibil base.

In the jungle, the squad hiked on. They relied on the directions of the captive guerrilla they used as a guide. The prisoner was bound to a long rope, like a leash.

The commandos were low on provisions by now. While they sat around a fire on the side of the trail, Lt. Ramírez told a subordinate, Fredy Samayoa Tobar, that he felt like eating meat.

"Where am I supposed to get some meat?" Samayoa said.

"Go take a piece out of that guide and bring it to me," Ramírez answered.

Samayoa drew his bayonet. He sliced a piece of skin about a foot long from the back of the captive guide. He brought the chunk of flesh to the lieutenant.

"Here's your meat."

"Oh no, no, no, you've got to execute him," Ramírez said. "He's suffering."

The commando killed the guide. The lieutenant did not eat the meat.

The rampage ended near the town of Bethel, where the commandos plundered a grocery, stealing beers, cigars and water. They ran across some peasants and decapitated them.

By the time the squad returned to base, more than 250 people were dead. The Kaibiles christened the mission "Operation Brushcutter." They had mowed down everyone they had encountered.

Four days after the massacre, Lt. Carias, the commander in Las Cruces, led troops on trucks and tractors into Dos Erres. They looted vehicles, animals and property, then burned and razed the hamlet.

Carias met with terrified relatives of the missing. Some had been away from Dos Erres that day. Others lived in villages nearby. He blamed the guerrillas for the incident.

Anyone who asked too many questions, Carias warned, was going to die.

Chapter 3: Living Proof

Within just a few weeks, the U.S. Embassy in Guatemala had figured out what happened in Dos Erres.

A "trusted source" told embassy officials that soldiers posing as rebels had killed more than 200 people. It was the latest in a stream of reports to the embassy blaming the military for massacres around the country. On Dec. 30, three U.S. officials went to Las Cruces, where interviews with local residents raised further suspicions.

The team flew over Dos Erres in a helicopter. Although the Guatemalan Air Force pilot refused to land, the evidence of an atrocity—burned houses, abandoned fields—was clear enough. In an unusually blunt cable to Washington, diplomats stated that "the party most likely responsible for this incident is the Guatemalan Army."

The U.S. government kept that conclusion secret until 1998. No action was taken against the army or the commando squad. The United States continued to support Central America's repressive but avowedly anti-communist governments.

It would be 14 years before anyone tried to bring the killers of Dos Erres to justice.

In 1996, more than three decades of civil war ended with a peace treaty between the rebels and Guatemalan military. Both sides agreed to an amnesty that exempted combatants, but allowed for prosecution of atrocities.

There was considerable doubt about whether the new government would succeed in bringing such cases. The perpetrators of some of the worst war crimes retained power in the armed forces or in rapidly growing criminal mafias. Drug cartels recruited ex-Kaibiles as triggermen and trainers.

An unlikely sleuth who challenged those dangerous forces was Sara Romero.

Romero was short and soft-spoken, her black hair parted in the middle. She looked more like a schoolteacher or a clerk than a frontline crime-fighter. At 35, she was a rookie prosecutor. She had graduated from law school the year before and been assigned to a special human rights unit in Guatemala City. Although the crimes of the war had gone unpunished for years, she was determined to pursue the investigations no matter the odds. If not, she thought, impunity would remain entrenched in Guatemalan society.

Romero was assigned the Dos Erres case. There had been hundreds of massacres during the conflict. United Nations investigators would eventually conclude that 93 percent of the casualties came at the hands of the military, and that the systematic slaughter of indigenous people constituted genocide.

Romero had little to go on. The military still insisted that the Dos Erres incident had been the work of the guerrillas. Because of the eyewitness account of Hernández, the 11-year-old survivor, the prosecutor was convinced of the army's involvement. But she needed more.

Romero traveled to the scene, a rattling eight-hour bus ride north to the remote region. A pall of silence hung over the ruins. She interviewed survivors who had been away from the hamlet on the day of the slaughter. Many were afraid to talk. They whispered that they feared the wrath of Lt. Carias, who was still the area commander in Las Cruces. They suspected he masterminded the massacre because he had clashed with the residents of Dos Erres.

Romero found it hard to establish basic facts, such as the identities of victims. Trying to assemble a kind of census, she asked a former teacher in Dos Erres to list the names of all the children and their relatives she could remember.

Without confirmed victims and strong witnesses, Romero might never make a case. But she found a providential ally: Aura Elena Farfán.

Dignified and grandmotherly, Farfán had thick gray hair and a disposition that mixed sweet and steely. She led a human rights association in Guatemala City for victims of the conflict. Despite intimidation and threats, she had filed a criminal complaint accusing the army of mass murder in Dos Erres. In 1994, she had brought in a team of volunteer forensic anthropologists from Argentina to exhume the remains.

The Argentines—their skills honed by investigating their own nation's "dirty war"—worked quickly and in risky conditions. The army battalion in Las Cruces harassed them by playing loud military music and following them around. The exhumation initially identified the remains of at least 162 bodies, many babies and children retrieved from the well.

Farfán handed prosecutors a major breakthrough. She gave frequent radio interviews in the area urging witnesses to come forward. After one broadcast, U.N. officials told her a former soldier wanted to talk about Dos Erres. Farfán traveled to the man's home. The activist took precautions, concealing her identity with sunglasses, a red hat and a shawl. A Spanish U.N. official followed from a distance to help ensure her safety.

The door opened. The tipster was Pinzón, the chubby, mustachioed former cook for the roving Kaibil squad. He was having breakfast with his children. After his initial surprise, he welcomed Farfán.

Pinzón told her he had left the military and worked as a driver at a hospital. He had never been a full-fledged commando because he had washed out of training. As a lowly cook, he had been mistreated by the other soldiers. He was an outsider, a weak link in the warrior code of silence. Dos Erres haunted him.

"I wanted to talk to you because what I have right here in my heart, I cannot stand it anymore," Pinzón said to Farfán.

Pinzón told the story of the massacre and named the members of the squad. The conversation lasted four hours. Farfán was overcome by a mix of disgust and gratitude. She couldn't bring herself to shake the soldier's hand. But his repentance struck her as genuine.

Pinzón soon introduced Farfán to another repentant veteran: Ibañez. She convinced both men to give statements to Romero. They recounted their stories coldly, without emotion. It would have been impossible to know the details of the massacre if the two had not testified. Because their information was fundamental, prosecutors granted them immunity and relocated them as protected witnesses. From the start, investigators had encountered obstruction and threats from the military. Now they had explosive firsthand testimony implicating the Kaibil rapid reaction squad.

They also had a startling new lead: the abduction of the two boys by Lt. Ramírez and Alonzo, the squad's former baker.

Romero thought it was a miracle. Finding the boys was critical. They had to know the truth—they were living with the people who'd killed their parents. No other atrocity case had this kind of evidence.

In 1999, Romero and another prosecutor went to Alonzo's home, near the city of Retalhuleu. Because her office had only meager resources, there was no police backup, no weapons. Romero was apprehensive about confronting a commando with such grave allegations. She knew the Kaibiles prided themselves on being killing machines.

When she saw the soldier resting in a hammock in front of his tumbledown house, her fear faded. He's just a simple man, a humble peasant, she thought.

Family pictures in Alonzo's home confirmed her suspicions that she was in the right place. Alonzo was a dark-skinned Maya. Five of his children resembled him. The sixth, a boy named Ramiro, had light skin and green eyes.

"My oldest son has a sad story," Alonzo told the prosecutor.

Alonzo confessed. After the massacre, he had kept Ramiro at the commando school for three months. He brought the child home and told his wife he'd been abandoned. Alonzo said he had enlisted Ramiro, by now 22, in the army. He refused to disclose the youth's location. When the prosecutor's office inquired, the Defense Ministry asked Ramiro if he had a problem with law enforcement. Rather than cooperate, the ministry moved him from base to base.

Investigators worried that Ramiro would be in grave danger if the military knew he was living proof of an atrocity. Eventually, prosecutors found him and spirited him away. Ramiro told them he had memories of the massacre and the murders of his family. The Alonzo family had treated him badly, he said, beating him and using him as a near slave. During a drunken rage, Alonzo had once fired a rifle at him. Authorities convinced Ramiro to leave the army and got him political asylum in Canada.

The search for the other youth foundered.

Prosecutors learned that the boy's name was Oscar Alfredo Ramírez Castañeda. His suspected abductor, Lt. Ramírez, had died eight months after the massacre. He had been using a truck to transport wood for a house he was building. The truck overturned as Ramírez rode in the bed, killing him instantly.

Questioned in Zacapa in 1999, a sister of the lieutenant disclosed that he had brought home the boy in early 1983, claiming Oscar was his son with an unmarried woman. Prosecutors found a birth certificate for him, but no sign that the mother actually existed. The sister admitted that she had heard the boy was from Dos Erres.

Oscar had left the country for the United States. His family did not want to help the investigators find him. Romero decided to call off the search.

Investigators made headway on other leads. They had identified numerous perpetrators from the commando squad. In 2000, a judge issued arrest warrants for 17 suspects in the massacre.

In the suffocating reality of Guatemala, however, the results were anticlimactic. Police failed to execute most of the warrants. Defense lawyers bombarded courts with paperwork, appealing to the Supreme Court. They argued that their clients were protected by amnesty laws, a claim that was inaccurate but effectively stalled the prosecution.

Romero had run up against the might of the military. It looked as if justice would elude her, just as Oscar had.

Chapter 4: Strange News from Home

In the summer of 2000, Oscar was living near Boston when he received a perplexing letter.

A cousin in Zacapa sent him a copy of an article published in a Guatemala City newspaper. It described Romero's search for two young boys who had survived the massacre and had been raised by military families.

"AG Looks for Abducted of Dos Erres," the headline declared. "They Survived The Massacre."

The story went on to explain that prosecutors had identified both young men. Prosecutors believed that one of them, Oscar Ramírez Castañeda, was living somewhere in the United States. It was quite possible that he had been too young to remember anything about the massacre or his abduction by the lieutenant, the prosecutors said.

The newspaper ran a family photo showing Oscar as an 8-year-old. The article reported more information about Ramiro than about Oscar because prosecutors had succeeded in finding and questioning the older boy before helping him win asylum in Canada.

There was a recent snapshot of Ramiro as a military cadet, holding a rifle and wearing the uniform of the army that had slaughtered his family. The story mentioned the investigators' suspicion that the two boys, who both had light skin and green eyes, were brothers.

"The order was to finish off all the inhabitants of Dos Erres," the article said. "No one can explain why Lt. Ramírez Ramos and Sgt. Lopez Alonzo made the decision to take the boys."

Oscar was mystified. He called an aunt in Zacapa.

"What is this all about?" he asked. "Why is my photo in the paper?"

The aunt had seen the article. She told him she didn't know what to make of the allegations, except that they were false. She insisted that the lieutenant was Oscar's father, period. The story struck her as an attempt by leftists to smear the name of an honorable soldier.

In the persistent ideological strife of Guatemala, that was plausible.

Many families affiliated with the military and right-wing political parties felt that the left had distorted the narrative of the civil war. They complained that Guatemalan and foreign critics exaggerated the abuses of the armed forces while playing down the violence by guerrillas.

Oscar's aunt convinced him that the allegations were too bizarre to be credible.

"If I really have a brother like they are claiming, let him find me," he told her. "He'll know if he's my brother or not."

Oscar's memories of his early childhood were hazy. He had never known anything about his mother. He had no real memories of the lieutenant. The boy grew up in a two-room house on an idyllic farm in the hot and dry region of Zacapa, where his family raised cows and grew tobacco. The family matriarch was Oscar's grandmother, Rosalina. She had taken charge of his upbringing after the death of Lt. Ramírez. Oscar considered her his mother.

Rosalina was affectionate and strict. Oscar always had chores. He milked the cows at 5 a.m., worked in the fields after school, tried to make cigars—though he never quite got the hang of it. He loved life on the farm, riding horses, roaming the countryside. His aunts made sure he was clean and neat for school.

The Ramírezes were strivers. One of Oscar's uncles was a prominent local doctor. Two aunts were nurses. The family and their neighbors and friends idolized Oscar's father, the lieutenant, for his battlefield exploits and his generosity. He had helped pay for the education of his siblings. He had brought fellow fighters from his mercenary days in Nicaragua to settle in Zacapa. The community had even named a soccer field at a military school in Ramírez's honor.

Curiously, though, Oscar had shown no interest in following in the lieutenant's footsteps. His aunts urged him to go to military school, but he had an independent streak. He didn't like taking orders.

Oscar got a vocational high school degree in accounting. It was hard to find work. After his grandmother died, he skirmished with relatives over an inheritance. He decided to seek his fortune in the United States. So in late 1998, Oscar made his way north like so many fellow Guatemalans. He flew to Mexico and slipped illegally across the border into Texas.

After a brief stay in Arlington, Va., Oscar settled in Framingham, Mass. The suburb west of Boston had a growing community of Central Americans and Brazilians. He found a job in the produce section of a supermarket. The pay and benefits were solid, and nobody bothered him about his immigration status.

Oscar's new life soon consumed him. He reunited with Nidia, his teenage sweetheart, who had arrived from Guatemala. In 2005, they moved into a small duplex in a weathered residential complex.

Nidia gave birth to two girls and a boy, smart and energetic kids who slid easily between English and Spanish. The family kept Oscar busy: church, swimming lessons, cookouts on the outdoor grill. He rose to assistant manager at the supermarket but lost the job in an immigration crackdown in 2009. He found new jobs as a supervisor: mornings at a cleaning company, evenings at a fast-food restaurant.

Oscar was polite and poised and spoke English well. Some of the regulars at the Mexican burrito place that he managed even mistook him for the owner.

Despite the precarious nature of life as an illegal immigrant, Oscar was healthy and putting food on the table. He considered himself a happy man.

The newspaper article had stirred doubts. But he came from a part of the world where mysteries abounded, where allegations and suspicions outnumbered facts.

As the years went on, he thought about the episode less and less.

Chapter 5: The Hunt Moves North

Frustrated that the Dos Erres case had ended up in limbo, Guatemalan activists sued their own government in international court.

The legal action resulted in public disclosure of the list of suspects. A few had died, but the rest were at large. And then help came from an unexpected quarter: a special unit of U.S. Immigration and Customs Enforcement in Washington that tracks down war criminals.

The unit forwarded a lead to Jon Longo, an ICE agent in West Palm Beach, Fla. A compact Italian-American from Boston with a goatee, Longo, 39, had only two years on the job. But he had experience persuading criminals to talk. He held a master's degree in psychology and had worked for eight years as a prison therapist.

Analysts at ICE headquarters suspected that one of the Kaibil commandos on the Dos Erres list, Gilberto Jordán, was living in Delray Beach, about a half-hour drive from Longo's office. Jordán worked as a cook at two country clubs. Longo's orders were to determine if he had taken part in the massacre and, if so, to build a case under U.S. law.

It wasn't going to be a murder case. Because Jordán had become a U.S. citizen, he could not be deported to Guatemala for trial. Nor could he be prosecuted in U.S. courts for a crime committed many years earlier in a foreign country.

Longo focused instead on U.S. immigration statutes. Jordán, who was 53, had stated on naturalization forms that he hadn't served in the military or committed crimes in Guatemala. If he had been in the army or participated in the Dos Erres attack, his statements would violate laws against lying to obtain citizenship. Longo wanted to approach the case as simply as possible. He asked himself: "How do I prove these crimes?"

The agent immersed himself in the case file, circling his target. Jordán had left Guatemala soon after the massacre and crossed into Arizona illegally. Thanks to the 1986 immigration amnesty, he became a legal resident. He obtained U.S. citizenship in 1999. He had three grown children—one of them a U.S. Marine and Iraq vet.

Longo obtained Jordán's army file from the Guatemalan government and confirmed he had been a commando. Separately, agents in Houston caught another Dos Erres suspect: Alonzo, the squad's baker, who had taken 5-year-old Ramiro. Alonzo had been deported once before. ICE charged him with breaking U.S. laws against re-entering the United States.

In early 2010, Agent Longo interviewed Alonzo about Dos Erres. He also questioned the repentant soldiers-turned-witnesses, Pinzón and Ibañez, who described Jordán's actions during the massacre. By May, Longo was ready to arrest Jordán. But U.S. prosecutors told Longo he needed more proof that Jordán had participated in the massacre and lied about it. Without direct evidence, such as a confession, they would not indict.

Longo and his bosses decided to knock on Jordán's door. It was a long shot. Murderers tend to confess more readily on television than in real-life. Especially veteran commandos versed in stealth and psychological warfare.

Longo planned carefully for the confrontation. He was dealing with a highly trained soldier who might own weapons. To help build rapport, Longo enlisted a Latino agent—a military special operations veteran—to approach Jordán with him.

As permitted by law, the ICE team concocted a ruse. Because Jordán had served in the presidential guard, they would tell him they were interested in the recent U.S. arrest of a former Guatemalan president accused of corruption. Then they would ask about Dos Erres. If Jordán refused to talk, they would have to walk away.

On the morning of the operation, Longo deployed agents to tail Jordán's wife as she worked cleaning homes in the area. The agents planned to confront Jordán at work, but he called in sick. Wearing raid jackets, the agents went to his home in a modest, multiethnic subdivision with narrow streets. Jordán's truck was parked in the driveway of his well-kept, one-story house, which sits behind a row of tropical trees. The garage door was open when the agents cruised by, but closed when they came back.

Longo called Jordán on his cell phone and identified himself. Jordán politely told him to come over. When the team knocked on his door, though, no one answered. Longo called again. No response. Minutes ticked by. The agents had their hands on their guns.

"We don't have a warrant," Longo thought. "He could be getting a cannon ready in there, for all we know."

Longo directed the agents shadowing Jordán's wife to stop her and explain the situation. She agreed to call her husband. He reacted like a hunted man.

"They are here to kill me," Jordán told his wife.

"No, they are the Americans," she said.

"They have guns," he replied.

The tension subsided, and Jordán invited the agents into his home. He was short and stolid, with close-cropped gray hair and a lined face. He wore puttering-around clothes: baseball cap, T-shirt, jeans. They sat at a rustic wood kitchen table, photos of Jordán's children on the walls, and made small talk in Spanish and English. Soon his wife joined them.

Jordán agreed to answer questions, signing a Miranda form after Longo read him his rights. He admitted he had been a commando. He said he did not display military memorabilia in his house because his wife had heard of former soldiers attacked by Guatemalans with grudges against the military.

Longo had dealt with plenty of murderers in his career. Jordán didn't have the look of a killer. Although calm and guarded, he seemed somewhat eager to talk. He's throwing out breadcrumbs, Longo thought.

"I had problems in Guatemala," Jordán said. "They say I did things. There was a massacre."

"Where?" Longo asked.

"At a place called Dos Erres."

Longo bided his time. The conversation eventually returned to the massacre. Jordán took a deep breath. He told the story of Dos Erres. He described the slaughter at the well.

"*Todos* (everyone)," Jordán said, making a gesture to depict victims falling into the well. He began to cry. He said: "I threw a baby into the well."

Jordán told the agents that he had wept as he killed the infant. He denied raping anyone. His wife listened morosely. She knew all about Dos Erres, Jordán explained.

"I knew this day would come," Jordán said. He looked relieved. Longo felt Jordán had been dying to get it off his chest.

After about 45 minutes, Longo thanked Jordán for his candor. Heart pounding, he went out to the driveway and called a federal prosecutor to report Jordán's admissions. The prosecutor knew Longo wanted to handcuff Jordán on the spot. She told him to hold off, saying she wanted to create a clear record that the confession was voluntary.

Tell him to come to your office tomorrow morning for a formal appointment, she said.

The next day, agents arrested Jordán when he showed up with a lawyer. Within weeks, he had agreed to plead guilty to concealing facts and willful misrepresentation on his immigration application.

Prosecutors pushed for the maximum sentence. At a hearing in a Florida courtroom, they called Ramiro Cristales, who had traveled from Canada, where he lived as a refugee. Longo expected Ramiro to be a shell of a man. Instead, the 33-year-old Guatemalan impressed the agent with his courage and maturity.

In his testimony, Ramiro described commandos storming into the house where he lived with his parents and six siblings, and beating and terrorizing the family.

"We started praying because they was saying [to] us, if you believe in God, pray, because nobody will save you," Ramiro testified.

Though it is not clear how precise his memories are, Ramiro told the court he spent most of the massacre in the church with the women and children. He said the soldiers threw his younger siblings in the well.

Jordán's immigration crime rarely results in a prison term of more than six months. But U.S. District Judge William J. Zloch was disgusted by what he heard in court. He grew even angrier when Jordán's lawyer argued that her client was not a danger to the community.

"After these allegations?" Judge Zloch demanded. "How many more does he have to commit after this incident? How many more heads have to be smashed in? How many more women need to be raped? How many more people shot? How many?"

In September 2010, the judge sentenced Jordán to the maximum possible term: 10 years in federal prison.

Across the United States, ICE investigators sifted the list of suspects for leads. Agents in Orange County, Calif., arrested Pimentel, the commando who had left for the U.S. military academy in Panama weeks after killing and raping at Dos Erres. In 1985, the U.S. military had awarded Pimentel an Army Commendation Medal for his service. He was found living illegally as a maintenance worker in the United States. Authorities deported him to Guatemala to stand trial.

Federal investigators learned that Sosa, the sub-lieutenant who had allegedly thrown a grenade into the well in Dos Erres, was a U.S. citizen and prominent martial arts instructor in Orange County. Sosa moved to Canada, where he was jailed pending extradition for trial in California on charges of falsifying his U.S. immigration application. Alonzo, Ramiro's abductor, pleaded guilty in Houston. He agreed to testify against Sosa, his former superior officer.

Chapter 6: Cocorico2

The U.S. arrests helped jolt Romero's investigation back to life.

The Guatemalan military had been more responsive to requests from U.S. authorities than its own prosecutors, turning over documents about the fugitive commandos caught by ICE. American investigators sent the material to counterparts in Guatemala, where Jordán's confession and other evidence strengthened the cases against about a dozen suspects still at large.

The atmosphere in Guatemala had changed. In late 2010, a new attorney general, Claudia Paz y Paz, was appointed by President Álvaro Colom. Guatemala's first female attorney general launched an unprecedented campaign against human rights abusers, charging former dictator Ríos Montt with genocide and crimes against humanity.

In addition, the Inter-American Court of Human Rights in Costa Rica had ruled in favor of the lawsuit by Guatemalan activists, forcing Guatemala's Supreme Court to order the Dos Erres prosecution to resume.

Fifteen years into the case, prosecutor Romero ordered a new round of arrests in 2011. Police were able to capture three of the commandos and Carias, the former local commander.

Investigators faced danger and hostility. A witness in another atrocity case was murdered. Military families in the Guatemala City neighborhoods where suspects lived threatened to lynch police who were hunting for war criminals. Col. Roberto Aníbal Rivera Martínez, the former lieutenant in charge of the Dos Erres unit, had escaped when the arrest team arrived at his home, which was equipped with a tunnel connected to another building. Prosecutors suspected that some of the fugitives were hiding on army bases or in areas dominated by the military.

During questioning in Guatemala City, a captured commando described the abduction of the two boys. The judge supervising the case ordered Romero to redouble her efforts to find Oscar. Years before, she had been thwarted by the resistance of Oscar's family. The newspaper story about her investigation had not helped.

But once again, in May 2011, Romero returned to Zacapa, where Oscar had been raised. Again she sat down with Oscar's uncle, the prominent doctor. During her previous visit, he had accused her of slandering the lieutenant's honor with her questions about the boy. This time, the doctor was a bit more cooperative. He disclosed that Oscar was living in the United States and now had a family. He said he did not know their phone number.

"His wife's nickname is *La Flaca* (The Skinny Girl)," the doctor said.

Armed with that lead, investigators located a merchant who helped them identify Nidia and track down her family in a nearby town. The prosecutor interviewed Nidia's parents. They gave her Oscar's email address, which incorporated the word Cocorico2. Romero realized that Oscar used the same nickname as Lt. Ramírez.

A few days later, after hearing about her visit, Oscar called Romero. She kept the conversation brief, not wanting to deliver a bombshell over the phone.

Then she sat down to compose an email. She struggled to find the best words to explain that his entire life had been based on a lie. Romero knew Oscar was an illegal immigrant. She imagined his existence far from home. She thought about the impact the email might have. How would he take the news? Would he need psychological counseling?

She pushed ahead. It had to be done. She began with the phrase: "You don't know me."

In the moments after he read her message in Framingham, Oscar whirled through convoluted thoughts and emotions. The prosecutor was claiming that he had lived a completely different life until the age of three. He found it hard to believe. He could summon no mental picture of Dos Erres. The people he knew as blood relatives in Zacapa had treated him as a full-fledged member of the family.

Then he thought back to the newspaper article about him and Ramiro from a decade before—the story that his relatives had dismissed as unthinkable. The doubts flooded back.

Oscar called Romero and agreed to take a DNA test. Last June 20, a Guatemalan human rights investigator named Fredy Peccerelli arrived in Framingham to collect the evidence that would determine Oscar's true identity once and for all.

The two men hit it off. With his shaved head, weightlifter's physique and Bensonhurst accent, Peccerelli seemed more like an action hero than a scientist and human rights crusader.

Born in Guatemala and raised in Brooklyn, N.Y., the 41-year-old Peccerelli was one of the top forensic anthropologists in Latin America. His private, internationally funded Guatemalan Forensic Anthropology Foundation supported state investigations of atrocities and high-profile crimes, exhumed remains at massacre sites and clandestine cemeteries, and performed DNA tests at a state-of-the-art lab behind high walls in Guatemala City.

In 2010, Peccerelli's foundation had analyzed the Dos Erres remains recovered years earlier by the Argentine team. The forensic investigators used sophisticated technology to take DNA from relatives of the victims and look for matches.

When they met, Peccerelli tried to imagine what Oscar had gone through as a boy. Had he seen his entire family being killed?

Peccerelli felt protective toward Oscar. The young man was wary at first. Peccerelli told him he knew what it was like to be an immigrant in the shadows. His father had been a lawyer in Guatemala, and when Peccerelli was a boy, the family had fled death threats by rushing to the United States.

Gradually, Oscar opened up, telling the story of his own clandestine odyssey from Guatemala. After the Guatemalan visitors took the DNA sample, Oscar and Nidia cooked a big meal for Peccerelli and a fellow investigator in the kitchen of their townhouse.

Peccerelli had spent years piecing together the secrets of shattered skeletons. Now, for the first time, he was face to face with living evidence. He had a rare chance to ask important questions. In past cases, children who had been abducted by soldiers had been raised abusively, like Ramiro, forced to sleep in barns and work 20 hours a day. Peccerelli was fascinated to hear about a firsthand experience.

"How did they treat you?" Peccerelli asked Oscar.

"Where I was raised, I was raised well," Oscar said in his serene, laconic way. "I wasn't treated differently than any other kid."

Peccerelli returned to Guatemala to complete the tests. He had the impression that Oscar was deeply curious, but also ambivalent.

At some level, he thought, Oscar hoped the whole thing might not be true.

Chapter 7: "Sorrows Can Swim"

Oscar waited about six weeks for the DNA results.

On Aug. 7, Peccerelli called from Guatemala City. He explained that the tests had conclusively ruled out one of the prosecution's theories: that Oscar and the other abducted boy, Ramiro, might be brothers.

"Thank you," Oscar said. "I'm not surprised."

Peccerelli paused. There was more.

"We found your biological father," he told Oscar. "He's a gentleman named Tranquilino."

Oscar turned to Nidia. He said the words he still found hard to believe: "They found my father."

Tranquilino Castañeda had been a farmer in Dos Erres. He had escaped the massacre because he was working in the fields in another town. For nearly 30 years, he thought the commandos had killed his wife and all nine of his children.

Oscar was his youngest son: His real name was Alfredo Castañeda.

Peccerelli, Aura Elena Farfán and other investigators set up a video conversation between the two survivors.

Oscar saw his father appear on the computer screen. Castañeda was a lanky, rugged 70-year-old in a cowboy hat, his craggy face etched by decades of work, solitude and sadness.

Investigators had taken Castañeda's DNA and talked to him for months without disclosing their suspicions about Oscar's true identity. When they were certain and decided to tell Castañeda, they brought a doctor along just in case. One of the human rights investigators pulled Castañeda's chair next to hers and leaned close.

"I'm going to tell you something," she said. "Do you know that person, that young man on the screen?"

"No, I don't know who that is," Castañeda said.

"It's your son."

Castañeda was staggered. His reaction was more sad and bewildered than joyful. The group gathered around to comfort him. He downed a shot of liquor to clear his head.

The father peered in disbelief at the screen. He tried to compare the face of the grown man two thousand miles away with the chubby toddler he remembered. As the people around him watched, tears in their eyes, Castañeda addressed his son by his real name.

"Alfredito," he said. "How are you?"

The conversation was emotional and uncomfortable. Oscar did not know what to say. Castañeda asked if Oscar remembered that he had been missing his front teeth when he was little. Oscar said he did remember that. Mainly, they spent a lot of time looking at each other.

Father and son spoke again by phone and Skype. Soon they were talking every day, getting to know each other, filling in three missing decades.

The lieutenant's family was equally stunned. But there was no apparent rancor. They promptly invited Castañeda to visit them in Zacapa. They marveled at the resemblance between Castañeda and the man they knew as Oscar. Castañeda joined the Ramírez family for a festive outdoor meal. In photos the family sent to Oscar, his father looked years younger.

Castañeda had been destroyed by the loss of his family. After the massacre, he holed up in a shack in the jungle. He never remarried. He became an alcoholic. He drank as much as a person can.

"I thought I would drown my sorrows, but you can't," Castañeda said. "Sorrows can swim."

Oscar's deepening relationship with his father propelled him into a new world. He did a lot of thinking. Though talkative about some topics—work, soccer, life as an illegal immigrant—it took effort for him to open up about the miracles and traumas of the past year.

The one person he found easy to talk to was Ramiro, the other abducted survivor. They had long phone conversations. They asked unanswerable questions. Why did the soldiers spare them? What kind of man slaughters families, yet decides to save and raise a boy?

During the dictatorships in Argentina and El Salvador, abduction of infants from leftist families became an organized and sometimes profitable racket. On an ideological level, the kidnappers wanted to eliminate a generation of future subversives by giving or selling them to right-wing families.

In Guatemala, such crimes were more haphazard and opportunistic. Government investigators estimated the military had kidnapped more than 300 children during the civil war. In a poor and rural society, Ramiro's story of forced labor and abuse tended to be typical.

Oscar's experience stood out because he was treated with care and affection. Investigators think the lieutenant brought him home to please his mother because of her complaints about not him not giving her grandchildren.

Oscar now understood that his "adoptive" father oversaw the murders of his mother and siblings. He read about the medieval horrors of the massacre. He realized that a stark photo in the lieutenant's album—of soldiers posing with an apparent prisoner tethered to a rope—perhaps showed a scene like the "guide" who was tortured and killed after Dos Erres.

Oscar sat at his kitchen table, examining the photo album. He returned, quietly and adamantly, to two facts. The lieutenant saved him. And the Ramírez family treated him as one of their own.

"He's still a hero for me," Oscar said. "I see him the same way I did before."

And then: "He was in the army. And in the army they tell you things, and you have to do things. Especially in times of war. Even if someone doesn't want to."

For the investigators, Oscar had become a powerful new witness. He had to be protected. Peccerelli helped him find a high-powered American lawyer. R. Scott Greathead, a partner in the New York office of the firm Wiggin and Dana, had been active in human rights work across Latin America for three decades. Among other major cases, Greathead represented the families of U.S. nuns who were raped and murdered by Salvadoran soldiers in 1980.

Greathead and fellow pro bono lawyers in Boston filed a claim seeking political asylum in the United States for Oscar on the grounds that he would be a high-profile target if he had to return to Guatemala.

"There are people," Oscar said, "who don't want to dig up the past."

Chapter 8: Two Guatemalas

Last August, a Guatemalan court found three former commandos of the Dos Erres squad guilty of murder and human rights violations. The defendants each received sentences of 6,060 years in prison, or 30 years for every one of the 201 identified victims plus 30 more for crimes against humanity.

The court convicted and sentenced Col. Carias, the former lieutenant and local commander who helped plan and cover up the raid, for the same crimes. He received an additional six years for aggravated robbery for looting the hamlet.

Two months ago, another Guatemala court handed a sentence of 6,060 years to Pimentel, the former School of the Americas instructor arrested by ICE agents in California and deported. During this trial, prosecutors used Oscar's story for the first time, introducing his DNA test into evidence.

Attorney General Paz said the convictions sent an unprecedented message.

"It's very important because of the gravity of the facts," Paz said in an interview. "Before it seemed impossible."

The case is by no means over. Seven suspects remain at large, including two of the squad's top officers. Authorities think they could be in the United States or at home in Guatemala, sheltered by powerful networks linking the military and organized crime.

The convictions have stirred resentment. Critics argue that the left's focus on historic human rights cases is out of touch with the realities of life. Most Guatemalans under 30 are more concerned with crime, poverty and unemployment, according to recently elected President Otto Pérez Molina, a former general and one-time commander of the Kaibil school.

When it comes to the prosecutions of atrocities, the president walks a narrow line. The silver-haired 61-year-old ran on a tough-on-crime platform. During the peace talks of the 1990s he played a leading role, and he has cultivated the profile of a moderate military man since then. After initial uncertainty about his intentions, he has expressed support for Attorney General Paz and a special U.N. team investigating corruption.

On the other hand, Pérez Molina accuses the left of exaggerating the abuses by the military and failing to acknowledge the historical context for atrocities. He says Guatemala, and all of Central America, face more immediate challenges.

"There are emblematic cases, like Dos Erres," Pérez Molina said in an interview. "I believe the courts are the ones that have to respond and the ones that have to provide answers. Emblematic cases should be known, but it's not the path or the route that Guatemala should follow, should get stuck in, this fight in the courts."

This week, there was another judicial breakthrough in the Dos Erres case that has wider political repercussions for Guatemala. A judge ordered former dictator Ríos Montt to stand trial as the alleged mastermind of the Dos Erres massacre. Ríos Montt, already being prosecuted in a separate case for genocide and crimes against humanity, told the judge that he is innocent under military law.

Central America has become a front line in the drug war spreading south from Mexico. The Obama administration is battling the rise of mafias in Guatemala, Honduras and El Salvador, all hubs for smuggling cocaine and immigrants north. The onslaught threatens to overwhelm the region. The 38 homicides per 100,000 citizens in Guatemala is about 10 times the rate in the U.S. It combines with an impunity rate (cases with no convictions) of about 96 percent. The numbers in Honduras and El Salvador are even worse.

In response, Pérez Molina wants more regional teamwork and U.S. assistance and a bigger role for the military. He wants to deploy Kaibil commandos on surgical missions, as opposed to the all-out combat with traffickers launched by Mexico's army.

U.S. legislators and human rights advocates worry that enlisting the military in the drug war, especially the Kaibiles, could lead to new abuses of civilians. But Pérez Molina said critics are behind the times. "Thinking that this army, now in 2012, is from the '70s or the '80s is a major mistake," he said.

Military officials insist that the armed forces have reformed. They deny allegations that officers have interfered with the Dos Erres prosecution or others.

Investigators say they believe the military—or factions within it—still plays a sinister role.

Days after the Dos Erres verdict last August, Peccerelli saw a car pull up alongside him as he was driving in Guatemala City with an American anthropologist. A man leaned out and stabbed at one of Peccerelli's wheels. Fearing an ambush, the burly Peccerelli sped away on the punctured tire.

Days later, a threatening note arrived at the home of his sister. It described the recent movements of Peccerelli, whose forensic work provided key evidence in the trial, and promised revenge for the prison sentences.

"Because of you, ours will suffer," the note said. "The tire was nothing. The next time it will be your face . . . Son of a bitch, we have you all under surveillance with your kids, your cars, your pickups, the house, schools . . . When you least expect it, you will die. Then revolutionaries, your DNA won't be good for anything."

Prosecutors say threats will not deter them.

"We are doing this precisely so that there will not be two Guatemalas," said Attorney General Paz, "so that there is not a Guatemala that has access to justice and another Guatemala of citizens who do not have access to justice."

Oscar knows both Guatemalas now. He is still trying to decipher the larger meaning. Dos Erres was one of more than 600 mass killings during the war. The pattern recurred across the map: Women raped, children slaughtered, entire villages erased. Oscar is ready to testify at future trials.

"For me, yes, it's important to investigate Dos Erres, because I am connected to this," he said. "Probably if this hadn't happened to me, I would have said, 'Look at the violence in Guatemala right now, this other stuff already is past us.'

"Before, I thought the guerrillas and the army killed each other in the war. But I didn't know that they massacred innocent people. I imagine there is a connection between the violence of the past and the present. If you don't catch these people, it keeps spreading. People do whatever they want."

Oscar's father is not much for political introspection. Castañeda's new mission in life is to meet Oscar in person. Peccerelli and human rights activist Farfán plan to bring him to the United States soon. The waiting makes him anxious. He still wrestles with his drinking problem. Sometimes he has trouble with his memory.

But some things he hasn't forgotten. During a conversation in Guatemala City, Castañeda made a sudden request.

"Can I give the names of my children?" he said.

He recited the list. Esther, Etelvina, Enma, Maribel, Luz Antonio, César, Odilia, Rosalba.

And Alfredo, the youngest. Now known as Oscar.

"I believe it is my duty to mention them by name because they were my children," the father said. "Out of the nine, one is still living. But all of the rest are dead."

PAMELA COLLOFF

■

Hannah and Andrew

FROM *Texas Monthly*

WHAT LITTLE IS KNOWN about Andrew Burd's early life is contained in a slim Child Protective Services case file that chronicles the boy's descent into the child welfare system. His mother was just sixteen, the file shows, when she gave birth to him in Corpus Christi on July 28, 2002. She would later admit, according to one report, "to using alcohol, methamphetamines, cocaine and crack cocaine, LSD, marijuana, cigarettes, and taking prescription Xanax." His father was seventeen and worked for a traveling carnival. CPS launched its initial investigation into Andrew's well-being shortly after his first birthday, when his mother took him to a local hospital with a broken arm. Four subsequent investigations were triggered by reports of abuse or neglect, including one allegation that both his mother and maternal grandmother were incapable of properly caring for him because they used methamphetamines. When Andrew was two-and-a-half years old, CPS determined that he was in "immediate danger," according to an affidavit, and he was put in foster care. His mother's and father's parental rights were terminated soon after he turned three.

If not for a Corpus Christi couple named Larry and Hannah Overton, Andrew might have lingered in state custody, shuffled from one foster home to another. The Overtons already had four children, and Larry's income—he installed landscape lighting—was barely enough to make ends meet. But as devoted Christians, their desire to adopt a foster child was rooted in faith more than in practicality. Both Larry and Hannah had done missionary work, and as a teenager, Hannah had spent holidays volunteering at an orphanage across the border, in Reynosa, where she had fed, bathed, and ministered to kids who had been living on the streets. The experience had affected her deeply, and she told Larry that she was willing to adopt a child with disabilities or an older child who had been unable to find a permanent home. As a former private-duty nurse, Hannah felt equipped to handle the challenges of a foster child; she had spent several years caring for special-needs children, some of whom were profoundly disabled. In 2005 the Overtons began to pursue the idea seriously. They considered adopting a nine-year-old girl who was deaf, but when, after much prayer and deliberation, they decided to move forward with the adoption, they learned that the girl had been placed with another family.

Not long afterward, Larry and Hannah heard about Andrew at their church, Calvary Chapel of the Coastlands, which Andrew's foster mother also attended. The nondenominational church, on the south side of Corpus Christi, drew many young evangelicals with its emphasis on a verse-by-verse understanding of the Bible, and Larry and Hannah were well-regarded members. Larry taught Sunday school, Hannah led a Bible study, and their children, whom Hannah homeschooled, attended youth group and socialized with other members' kids. Andrew accompanied his foster mother to services every Sunday, and with his thatch of blond hair and beaming grin, he was hard to miss. He had a speech delay and spoke haltingly, sometimes with a stutter, but every week, when his Sunday school classmates went around in a circle to say their prayer requests, he made the same wish aloud: that he would be adopted. The Overtons' daughters, four-year-old Isabel and three-year-old Ally, reported back to their parents that the new boy in their class needed a family. "Can Andrew be our brother?" the girls pleaded.

A church elder, who was himself an adoptive parent, invited the Overtons to dinner one night and encouraged them to consider bringing Andrew into their home. Andrew's foster mother, who had provided refuge to roughly three hundred children over three decades, was also supportive. But others at Calvary Chapel expressed their concern. The church's pastor, Rod Carver, and his wife, Noreen, had initially considered taking in Andrew but ultimately decided he was more than they could handle. More outspoken was Andrew's

Sunday school teacher, who sat Hannah and Larry down and told them that he was a troubled kid. He hoarded food and sometimes ate from the trash, she warned, and he threw intense temper tantrums, which could be tamed only by holding and rocking him. On several occasions his fits had grown so extreme that she had resorted to asking a male parishioner to physically remove him from the classroom until he could regain self-control. "Think of your other children," she urged the couple.

Yet if anyone was up to the task, most everyone agreed, it was the Overtons, and Hannah in particular. She was unflappable and unfailingly patient with children. Hannah shrugged off the teacher's warnings, certain that Andrew would improve once he had the stability of a permanent home. "All he needs is lots of love and attention," she told Larry.

The Overtons moved forward with the adoption process, and in the spring of 2006, they received word that Andrew would be coming to live with them for a six-month trial period before the adoption was finalized. In anticipation of his arrival, Larry built a three-tiered bunk bed for Andrew and the two Overton boys: Isaac, who was seven years old, and Sebastian, who was two. Larry and Hannah knew that Andrew loved Spider-Man, so they made sure to have all manner of Spider-Man-themed necessities for him: sheets, pajamas, a toothbrush, a towel, a swimsuit, and even a plate embossed with the superhero's image.

Andrew spent his first night at the Overtons' modest ranch-style house on Mother's Day, when he was two months shy of his fourth birthday, and he seemed to quickly grow attached to his new family. He called Hannah and Larry "Mommy" and "Daddy," and he followed Larry everywhere he went, often stepping on Larry's heels as he trailed after him. At Sunday school, he became more expressive, stringing words into sentences and holding hands with his new sister Ally. "The Overtons are nurturing, loving, patient, and very family-oriented," an adoption supervisor noted in her paperwork. "Andrew seems very happy in this home."

Four months later, on October 2, 2006, Andrew fell suddenly and acutely ill while he was alone with Hannah. Larry hurried home to help, but Andrew, who had been vomiting, only grew worse. The

Overtons rushed him to a nearby urgent care clinic after his breathing became labored and he stopped responding to their questions, but by the time they arrived, he had fallen unconscious. The following evening, Andrew was dead. The cause of death was determined to be salt poisoning, an extremely rare occurrence that, in children, results from either a child inadvertently ingesting too much salt or a caretaker deliberately forcing the child to do so. People who knew the Overtons were certain that Andrew's bewildering death was accidental. But law enforcement and emergency medical personnel who treated Andrew thought otherwise. The following week, Hannah—who had no history with CPS and no previous arrests, and had never had so much as a parking ticket—was charged with capital murder.

Before Hannah got married, when she was still Hannah Saenz, she knew she wanted a large family—"at least six kids," she used to tell people. Standing just five feet tall, with wide-set brown eyes, a girlish laugh, and a warm, easy manner, Hannah was almost childlike herself. The daughter of a pastor and a homemaker, she had grown up longing for the companionship and boisterous energy of the big, churchgoing families she saw around her. She had only one sibling, a brother who was seven years her junior, and a father who was largely absent from her life.

Hannah's father was the Reverend Bennie Saenz, an evangelical preacher in Corpus Christi whose fall from grace profoundly altered the course of her childhood. Hannah was seven when Saenz was arrested in 1984 and charged with a singularly horrific crime: the bludgeoning death of a sixteen-year-old girl whose nude body was discovered at the water's edge on Padre Island. Until his arrest, Saenz had led a seemingly normal life: in addition to leading his nondenominational congregation, he worked as an office-machine mechanic while his wife, Lane, stayed home with their two children. He delivered sermons to a small but devoted following that met every Sunday, and during services he also played guitar. (Larry's parents, who were friends of the Saenzes', were parishioners.) But Saenz's account of his whereabouts on the evening of the murder did not jibe with the evidence, and blood that matched the victim's type was discovered inside his van. After a week-long trial, he was convicted of murder and sentenced to 23 years in prison. The congregation quickly dissolved. Hannah understood little of what had taken place except that she, her mother, and her brother had to leave Corpus Christi behind.

Lane and her children moved to the East Texas town of Lindale, where a missionary organization, the Calvary Commission, allowed them to live in a modest apartment on its grounds free of charge. Lane earned her college degree and became an elementary school teacher, while Hannah played with, and later babysat, the children of missionaries who used the campus as a home base between trips abroad. "She looked after dozens of children, including my grandchildren, and in all the years she was here, I can't recall one negative thing being said about her," the commission's founder, Joe Fauss, told me. "Kids loved her. She was always smiling, always laughing." As a teenager, she was captivated by missionaries' stories of serving in far-flung places, and she began going on group mission trips herself, once venturing as far as Romania. Every Easter and Christmas holiday was spent at the Reynosa orphanage, whose wards were primarily the unwanted children of prostitutes who worked the nearby red-light district. Though the kids were in poor health, Hannah was unreserved in her affection. She hugged them and let them climb onto her lap, often returning to Lindale with head lice. "Some people love stray animals," remembered her mother, now remarried. "Hannah was always drawn to stray people."

When she was fifteen, Hannah returned to Corpus Christi with her family to visit, and Larry, who had not seen her since they were kids, was immediately smitten. Hannah was less impressed, given that Larry—who, at sixteen, was an enthusiastic fan of Christian punk rock—was sporting a nose ring and a blue mohawk. Despite appearances, however, he was hardly a reprobate. A committed Christian, he had gone on mission trips with his family since he was a child, including a fourteen-month stint in Papua New Guinea and several treks across Mexico. He didn't drink or smoke, and the bands he listened to sang about glorifying God. He struck up a correspondence with Hannah, but she did not warm to him until their paths crossed again at a year-long missionary training school outside Tyler, when she was nineteen and he was a more clean-cut twenty. Hannah liked the tall, serious-minded student who shared the same hopes she had of creating a life centered on children and Christian outreach. They wed a year later and moved to Corpus Christi. On their honeymoon, they stopped at the orphanage in Reynosa, where Hannah wanted Larry to meet some of the children she had told him so much about.

Before they started a family, Hannah worked as a private-duty nurse for disabled children, and her longest assignment—with a four-year-old named Michael Subialdea—became as absorbing to her as her time in Reynosa. Michael, who had been born prematurely, was severely impaired; he had cerebral palsy, was blind, and could not walk or talk. Rather than let him remain in his wheelchair most of the day, as previous caretakers had done, Hannah kept him moving; she took him into his family's pool to stretch and used massage to loosen his contracted muscles. He felt at ease around her; his favorite thing to do was sit on her lap and rest his mouth on her cheek, and she gladly obliged. "She had a way with Michael that even my wife and I didn't completely understand," his father, Richard, told me. He recalled how Michael used to chew on his fingers, a chronic problem that left his skin bloody and raw. Richard and his wife had tried all sorts of tactics to deter him: redirecting his attention, putting gloves on him, even restraining his hands. Only Hannah had been able to break through. "When Michael put his fingers in his mouth, she would call his name softly—there was no anger in her voice—and he would smile and slowly slide his fingers out," Richard said. "We were in awe."

Hannah went into labor with her first child, Isaac, at the Subialdeas' house, and though she had planned to come back to work after her son's birth, she found the separation from him too wrenching. She left nursing behind, channeling her energy instead into raising the large family she had always wanted. "I'm a pretty easygoing guy, but I remember thinking, 'Six kids?'" Larry told me. "Hannah was sure I would eventually come around. I figured, 'Well, we've got to start with one, so let's see how far we get.'" Isabel, and then Ally, followed. Each pregnancy felt extraordinarily fortunate; after Isaac, Hannah had suffered two miscarriages and been advised that she might not be able to have more children. But after the girls, the Overtons conceived their fourth child, Sebastian. Early in the pregnancy, Hannah and Larry were informed that the boy would likely have Down syndrome. They declined to do any further chromosomal testing and turned to prayer instead. "If he had Down's, that was the blessing that God had chosen to give us," Larry said. Not until Sebastian was born did doctors discover that his only impairment was a hole in his heart, which healed on its own.

Two years later, the Overtons learned that their adoption application had been approved and that Andrew would be joining their family. They also discovered that Hannah was pregnant again. Just as she had hoped, they would have six children. It was, Hannah and Larry would later remember, one of the happiest times in their lives.

At first, the transition with Andrew went smoothly. He seemed to enjoy having brothers and sisters to play with, and the Overton kids—especially the girls, who doted on him—were enthralled by the new arrival. Although he hung back when his siblings embraced their parents in group hugs, Larry and Hannah learned that if they asked Andrew to join in, he would do so enthusiastically, throwing his arms around them. Whenever he got scared—and there was a long list of things that petrified him, from swimming to large crowds to the sound of balloons popping—the Overtons worked to help him overcome his fears, reassuring him that they loved him and that he was in safe surroundings. "I can do all things through Christ who strengthens me," Hannah would remind him, quoting Philippians.

Andrew's standard answer whenever he was asked to perform a simple task was "Sorry, I can't," but Hannah was heartened one day that summer when he deviated from the script. "Sorry, I—" he began, when she asked him to put on his shoes. Then he corrected himself. Reaching for his shoes, he announced, "I can do all things." Larry remembered, "We felt like we were really making headway with him."

Although the adoption agency that had worked with CPS to find Andrew a home had described him as "developmentally on target" except for his speech delay, Larry and Hannah observed otherwise. He acted more like a toddler than a preschooler, they noted; if he wanted an object, he pointed to it and grunted. At four, he spent most of his time playing with Sebastian, who was two, rather than Ally, who was his own age, and his motor skills lagged far behind those of his peers. He moved unsteadily, and he was so clumsy that Hannah had him wear a life jacket whenever he splashed around in their inflatable kiddie pool. Most striking to the Overtons, and to their neighbors and friends, was his preoccupation with eating. Regardless of how much food he consumed, he complained that he was hungry. If he was denied a second or third helping, he would routinely throw a tantrum or get down on his hands and knees to scavenge the floor for crumbs. Larry and Hannah caught him trying to eat cat food, crayons, toothpaste, glow sticks, tufts of carpeting—anything he could get his hands on. When they took him along on errands, they had to keep him from eating the old gum and cigarette butts he found on the ground.

Yet the Overtons were not too concerned. In the classes they had been required to take by CPS to become adoptive parents, they had been warned that foster children often hoarded food and were more likely to have eating disorders. And given that abuse and neglect during the first year of life can profoundly affect behavioral development, they were not surprised that Andrew was different. "We had been told to expect a lot of the things we were seeing with Andrew," Larry told me. His foster mother had taken him to a pediatrician for an adoption screening shortly before he had come to live with them, and the checkup had raised no red flags. "We truly thought his obsession with food was a behavioral issue, not a medical one," Larry said. "We thought that he would stop turning to food for comfort when he learned that he could trust us." To try and curtail Andrew's compulsive eating, they put him in time-outs, though to little effect. Other couples they knew who had adopted foster children assured them that their kids had outgrown similar eating issues, and the Overtons assumed that, with time, Andrew would outgrow his as well.

Andrew's behavior worsened that September, after the family was involved in a car accident. The Overtons were returning from a visit to the obstetrician's office, where they had brought the children to find out whether the baby they were expecting was a boy or a girl. The mood in the car was giddy; the kids were excitedly discussing the news that they would have a baby sister when Larry, distracted, ran a stop sign and collided with another car. The passenger side of their old Ford van was not equipped with an air bag, and Hannah, who had pulled down her seat belt so she could turn to talk to the kids, was jolted forward, her face hitting the dashboard. Afterward, she instinctively looked back to check on the children, not realizing that her face was covered in blood. In the midst of the chaos that followed, no one recognized how distressed Andrew was by the sight of Hannah's bloodied face. Hannah and the girls, who complained of feeling achy, were taken to the hospital in an ambulance while Larry's parents picked up the rest of the family and, after dropping Larry off at the hospital, took the boys to a nearby Whataburger. Throughout the meal, Andrew repeatedly asked, "Is my mom okay?" He also kept requesting more food.

Hannah, who was left with whiplash and a severely swollen jaw, spent the next several weeks immobilized by a neck brace, mostly confined to bed. Financially, the accident had come at a precarious time; Larry had recently purchased his boss's landscape lighting business, and he needed to put in long hours just to make ends meet. Relatives, neighbors, and members of the Overtons' church pitched in to look after the kids during Hannah's recovery, but the revolving door of caregivers proved to be difficult for Andrew, who began acting out on a scale they had not seen before. He picked at mosquito bites on his body incessantly, prompting Larry to put socks on his hands; still, Andrew would not stop scratching and eventually developed a staph infection on his arm. His tantrums grew longer and more extreme, and he often banged his head against the floor. Sometimes he cried inconsolably for hours.

Overwhelmed, the Overtons sought guidance in prayer. Fellow church member Anita Miotti remembers their telling her and her husband, Rich, that they were struggling. "They said Andrew was going through a very difficult time," she said. "They asked us, 'Can you pray that we have discernment and wisdom in helping him through this?'"

Andrew's preoccupation with eating intensified, and he began getting out of bed at night to forage for food in the kitchen. Hoping to show him that his behavior was self-destructive, Larry told Andrew one morning that he could have as much as he wanted for breakfast. "I knew it would probably make him sick, but I wanted him to understand why we were setting limits," Larry explained. At Andrew's request, he made a plate of sausage and more than a dozen eggs, all of which the boy eagerly devoured. Andrew continued eating until he threw up. Then he asked for more.

Perplexed, Larry installed a baby monitor equipped with a video camera in the boys' room so that he and Hannah could observe if Andrew was wandering into the kitchen at night. It was while watching the monitor that Hannah saw him trying to eat part of his foam mattress and paint off the wall. She reported Andrew's unusual eating habits to his adoption supervisor when she visited the Overton home on September 25. The supervisor suggested that Andrew might have an eating disorder called pica, which is characterized by a desire to consume things that have no nutritional value, and she recommended that he be evaluated by a specialist if his behavior continued.

That Sunday, October 1, Larry took the other kids to church while Hannah devoted some extra attention to Andrew. Before the family returned home, Andrew asked if he could have lunch, and Hannah told him that he needed to wait; Larry was bringing them something to eat, she explained, and he would be back in a few minutes. Andrew flew into a rage. He defecated on the floor of his bedroom, then smeared feces on the bed, the dresser, and the walls.

Larry attempted to restore order upon his return, putting Andrew's soiled sheets in the garbage and hosing off the boy and his foam mattress in the backyard. While Larry tried to scrub down the bedroom, Andrew pulled his sheets out of the trash several times, despite repeated warnings not to do so. Losing his patience, Larry took the sheets to the family's fire pit and burned them. "Not the brightest thing to do," Larry conceded. "But I was frustrated. The sheets were filthy, and he was getting poop everywhere. I made sure that he saw that we had an identical set of Spider-Man sheets so he would calm down."

That evening Larry laid a sleeping bag on top of Andrew's plywood bed frame, where, he told the boy, he would have to spend the night while his mattress finished drying. The three oldest Overton children had gone to their aunt's house to see their cousins, who were visiting from out of town, and Andrew grew increasingly agitated and restless, throwing a tantrum at three o'clock in the morning. "Before we ever tried to adopt, we had been warned that this was going to be difficult, that this was not going to be the *Little Orphan Annie* story,"

Larry told me. "We were having a hard time, but we knew it was going to pass. We were in it for the long haul."

Larry left for work the following morning, and Hannah, who was still in considerable pain from the car accident, gave Andrew and Sebastian breakfast before bringing them into bed with her to watch cartoons. Exhausted from the previous night, she briefly dozed off, then awoke to discover that Andrew had slipped out of the room. She found him standing on a stool in the pantry, near the baking ingredients, having pulled something off the shelf. She could not recall later what, exactly, he had been holding in his hand.

According to Hannah, Andrew once again asked for an early lunch, and once again, when she told him that he would have to wait, he defecated and smeared feces across the floor. Hannah managed to clean him up, but when she reiterated that he would have to wait until lunchtime to eat, he defecated on the floor again. Finally she relented, heating up what she had on hand: leftover vegetable-beef soup flavored with Zatarain's Creole Seasoning. Shortly after noon, Larry picked her and the boys up and took them to a McDonald's drive-through, and then the chiropractor, before returning to work. (Andrew was told that he could not have any food at McDonald's, since he had already eaten.) When Andrew complained of being hungry that afternoon, Hannah gave him more of the leftover soup. When she refused to give him a second helping, he threw a tantrum and shouted, "I hate you!" Finally, Hannah resorted to sprinkling some Zatarain's into a sippy cup of water, hoping that the taste alone would appease him. After drinking a little, he threw another tantrum that continued unabated for twenty minutes.

Then, abruptly, Andrew grew quiet and stumbled to the floor. "Mommy, I'm cold," he said, and threw up. Shortly afterward, at three-thirty, Hannah called Larry and asked him to come home since Andrew was vomiting and she needed his help. The boy's symptoms that afternoon—vomiting, chills, and lethargy—initially suggested to the Overtons that he had a routine ailment, like a stomach bug. But as the afternoon wore on, his symptoms grew troubling; his breathing became congested, and he became less and less responsive. Just after five o'clock, the Overtons put him in their car and rushed him to a nearby urgent care clinic. A block away from the clinic, as they waited at a red light, Andrew stopped breathing. Frantic, Hannah began administering CPR in the backseat. At the clinic, she continued giving him mouth-to-mouth and chest compressions until paramedics took over, but the four-year-old lay motionless. He soon lapsed into a coma.

The next morning, Corpus Christi police detective Michael Hess paid a visit to Kathi Haller, the Overtons' next-door neighbor, who knew the family well. Like Hannah, Haller homeschooled her children, and the two mothers split teaching duties; the Haller children went to the Overton home for instruction for part of the day and vice versa. The families shared an unofficial open-door policy, and when Andrew had begun acting up the previous afternoon, Hannah had called Haller for help, asking if she could look after Sebastian for a little while. Then, as always, Hannah had been composed, despite the strain she was under. "We had known each other for ten years, and I don't think I'd ever seen her mad," Haller told me.

Hess, who investigated child abuse cases for the police force's family violence unit, had a very different impression of Hannah. The detective had been alerted to Andrew's grave condition when the boy was transported to a nearby hospital the previous afternoon and, as was protocol, had begun looking into the circumstances surrounding the boy's unusual and rapid decline. Haller, who took notes documenting her conversation with Hess and later testified about it under oath, recalled the detective's certainty that Hannah had tried to kill Andrew. According to Haller, he told her, "Look, she's pregnant and she has all these kids, but it was just too much for her. So she had to find a way out." (Hess did not respond to interview requests for this article but has previously denied Haller's version of events.) Haller was stunned by the accusation. "I kept denying that Hannah could do such a thing," she told me. "Hannah would never harm a child." Even setting aside her loyalty to her friend, the detective's theory made no sense to her. "Andrew's adoption hadn't been finalized," Haller said. "If Hannah had been looking for a 'way out,' she would have called the adoption agency and told them that she and Larry couldn't go through with it." Hess was unmoved. Before he left, Haller recalled his saying, "You might want to prepare for the media."

Hess' suspicions had developed the previous evening during an interview with Hannah, who had consented to talk to him without an attorney present. The medical staff at Driscoll Children's Hospital had determined that Andrew had nearly twice the normal level of sodium in his blood—a highly abnormal finding—as well as bleeding in the brain, and as Hess questioned her, he tried to ascertain what had happened. But Hannah, who was bewildered by Andrew's condition, had no ready answers. Impatient to return to the boy's bedside, she gave a hurried, disjointed account of the day that omitted critical details, such as how she had found Andrew in the pantry unattended, and she made only fleeting mention of his unusual eating habits. Hess became exasperated. "I don't see what caused the trauma to the brain," he said. "I don't see what caused the high salt content. That's what I'm trying to get you to tell me." With no obvious explanations to consider, he focused his attention on Hannah. "Did you at any time strike him?" Hess asked. "Push him?" Throughout the interrogation, which spanned more than two hours, Hannah insisted that she had never harmed Andrew.

Hannah did describe how she and Larry had at first tried to treat the boy's symptoms themselves, often volunteering more information than the detective had asked for. When Andrew started "breathing funny," she told Hess, she had administered asthma medication with a nebulizer, hoping to open up his airways. And when he became "less responsive," she had pulled out her old EMT books to assess what was wrong. Larry had also tried to rouse him by giving him a warm bath. "I wasn't thinking, obviously, or I would have just taken him to the hospital," Hannah told the detective. She had studied years earlier to be an EMT, she explained, and although she had never worked as a paramedic, she had felt confident in her training. "I was just trying to fix it—to do anything I could to fix my baby," she said. When Andrew's condition worsened, she and Larry had debated whether to call 911 or go to the nearby urgent care clinic, a concern because Andrew lacked health insurance. (CPS had not yet sent them his Social Security card, which they needed to get him insured.) She and Larry were under tremendous financial strain, she admitted, but she stressed that they had rushed for help as soon as they realized how critical Andrew's condition was.

Hess remained skeptical of Hannah's account. "It should be noted that during the entire conversation, Hannah Overton showed almost no emotion," he later wrote in his police report. In the context of a criminal investigation, the calm that she had always exhibited in the midst of crisis was suddenly a liability—an indication, perhaps, that she was cold-blooded enough to have killed a child.

A pediatric critical care specialist who treated Andrew at Driscoll, Alexandre Rotta, grew equally troubled. EMS records show that the boy was admitted with no more than a bruised knee and sores on his right elbow, but during his hospitalization, other significant black-and-blue marks emerged—in particular, on his trunk and nose. EMTs and hospital staff had vigorously poked and prodded the boy as they attempted to revive him, first at the clinic, then in an ambulance, then at Christus Spohn Hospital, where he was initially taken, and finally at Driscoll, where he was transferred to the intensive care unit. CPR had also been performed for an extended period by Hannah and later by medical personnel, who had squeezed the boy's nose and administered chest compressions for 35 minutes. But Rotta was alarmed by his overall appearance. "This was not a child that came into the office looking well, with a story of, you know, 'He's just a tomboy, and he falls and hits himself,'" Rotta would later testify. "This is a child that came in [to the emergency room] in cardiopulmonary arrest and was dying. So it is the context and the totality of the injuries that worried me . . . I was convinced that we were in the presence of a crime."

Within hours of Andrew's arrival at the hospital, the Overtons' home had been searched, and soon more facts seemed to bolster the notion of abuse. There was Andrew's bed—just a bare piece of plywood, with no mattress—and a "security camera," as the baby monitor was later called at trial, trained on it. There were the charred remnants of his Spider-Man sheets in the fire pit. And then there was the abnormally high sodium level, coupled with Hannah's account of feeding him Creole seasoning after he had misbehaved. Taken together, the disparate details formed a disturbing picture. It did not matter that Haller, who had seen Andrew in the days leading up to his hospitalization and who was frequently in the Overton home, had never observed any suspicious bruises or indications of abuse. In the eyes of law enforcement, Hannah and Larry were not grieving parents but perpetrators of an appalling crime. As Andrew's condition deteriorated, CPS barred the Overtons from visiting their son. They were not allowed to be at Andrew's bedside on the evening of October 3, when he experienced massive organ failure. He died at 9:30 p.m.

The death of a child—particularly a sudden, unexplained death in which abuse is suspected—evokes strong emotions, even among seasoned investigators, doctors, forensics experts, and prosecutors. A more thorough investigation would have uncovered ample evidence to suggest that Andrew had an undiagnosed eating disorder, raising the possibility that he had unintentionally consumed too much salt on his own. But law enforcement officials are accustomed to handling child abuse cases, not medical mysteries, and salt poisoning is rare enough that most emergency room doctors will never encounter a case during their careers. Against the backdrop of possible abuse, authorities wasted little time. Larry was charged with injury to a child for failing to get Andrew timely medical attention. The onus for the boy's death fell on Hannah, who was charged with capital murder.

The state's case would be predicated in part on the findings of Ray Fernandez, the Nueces County medical examiner, who ruled Andrew's death to be a homicide. Fernandez determined that the boy had died as a result of acute sodium toxicity, with "blunt force head trauma" as a contributing factor. That Andrew had sustained a head injury was based on the presence of a half-inch area of hemorrhaging under the scalp. There was no evidence of external bleeding or injuries to Andrew's head, however, and at a pre-trial hearing, Fernandez conceded that the hemorrhaging could have been related to elevated sodium in the blood. State district judge Jose Longoria, who would oversee Hannah's trial the following fall, would later rule Fernandez's finding of blunt force trauma to be inadmissible because it was not based on sufficient data or reliable methodology. Nevertheless, the idea that Andrew had sustained a head injury propelled the case forward, further casting Hannah as an abuser.

That perception would throw her other children into the investigation as well. During a wide-ranging interview with a social worker to determine if he had ever been abused, Isaac mentioned that he and his siblings had been given pepper, which he described as "spicy stuff," as a punishment for lying. (A former pastor of Hannah's had advocated reprimanding children when they were dishonest by putting a single red pepper flake on their tongues.) Given that Hannah was suspected of poisoning Andrew with Creole seasoning, the suggestion that the Overtons had used pepper to discipline their children raised immediate concerns. On October 3, while Andrew was still hospitalized, the agency removed Isaac, Isabel, Ally, and Sebastian from their parents' custody, placing them in two separate foster homes in Beeville, sixty miles away. The following day, family court judge Carl Lewis awarded temporary custody to Hannah's mother and stepfather. Larry and Hannah were granted supervised visits. Once reunited with their children—who were terrified by the ordeal—Larry and Hannah had to break the awful news to them about Andrew. Weeping, they told the children that their brother had gone to be with Jesus.

A funeral for Andrew followed at Seaside Memorial Park, alongside Corpus Christi Bay, at which Pastor Rod Carver officiated. He and Noreen had recently lost their own son, who had been stillborn, making his grief particularly acute. As he grasped for the right words to convey the depth of pain a parent feels over the loss of a child, he noticed a row of unfamiliar faces. "Hess and a group of CPS workers were standing in the back with dark glasses on, their arms crossed, scowls on their faces," Carver said. "That was the most uncomfortable service I have ever done. It was very tense. By that point, Hannah had completely broken down emotionally."

Corpus Christi's introduction to Hannah came the following week, when she and Larry were arrested and led past a bank of TV cameras outside the Nueces County jail. News reports that followed, prominently featuring their grim-faced mug shots, cast the Overton home as a house of horrors. ("More shocking details on abuse suffered by four-year-old before death," began one breathless report.) Veteran defense attorney John Gilmore, whom the Overtons had retained using funds raised by their church, was stunned to learn of the arrests from reporters, who called asking for comment. "Channel Three,

Channel Six, Channel Ten, the *Caller-Times*—they all knew ahead of time," Gilmore said. "Hess had given me his word that he would tell me if and when warrants were going to be issued, so that Hannah and Larry could turn themselves in." Instead, law enforcement officials had apprehended the Overtons by making a felony traffic stop, a practice usually reserved for suspects believed to be armed and dangerous. With guns drawn, police officers had surrounded Hannah and Larry's car as they returned from an errand, forcing them to the ground and handcuffing them. "It was like they were arresting Bonnie and Clyde," Gilmore said.

The media coverage of the case stirred widespread outrage. The *Corpus Christi Caller-Times*'s online comments section filled with the vitriol of readers, some of whom called for Hannah to receive the death penalty. ("You can just tell by looking at her how evil she is," one wrote.) Fueling the public's antipathy was an affidavit written by a CPS child abuse investigator named Jesse Garcia, who claimed that Hannah had admitted to forcing Andrew to drink two cupfuls of "chili with water" and quoted her as saying that she then "beat the shit out of him." Garcia never produced any documentation or witnesses to corroborate his claim, and internal police memos show that law enforcement officials doubted the veracity of his story. Hess disavowed Garcia's account at a court hearing regarding the Overton children, and prosecutors never entered Garcia's affidavit into evidence or called him to testify at Hannah's trial. (He was subsequently fired by CPS after having three car accidents on the job in less than six months.) But the damage was done: that Hannah had confessed to force-feeding Andrew and beating him was repeated, uncorrected, on the local news.

Even more devastating to Hannah were the actions that CPS took that January. Days after she gave birth to her daughter Emma, CPS took the newborn into protective custody. At a subsequent family court hearing, in which Hannah's civil attorney argued that she should be given access to the infant so that she could continue nursing her, Judge Lewis returned Emma to her parents, but with conditions. The Overtons had to remain at the Carvers' home, where they had been staying to avoid the camera crews that were camped out on their own doorstep, and they were never to be left alone with the baby. Hannah—who had already lost a child and was now living apart from her four older ones—was in a fragile state of mind. "There were days I had to remind her to eat, to brush her teeth, to get out of bed," Noreen told me.

The Carvers, like most members of Calvary Chapel, never doubted her innocence. "Knowing Hannah, it was inconceivable that she would ever hurt a child," said Noreen. Hannah's supporters included a young churchgoer named Dawn Werkhoven, who had lived with the Overtons the year leading up to Andrew's death. Hannah and Larry had taken her in after her marriage ended in divorce, giving her their extra bedroom while she got back on her feet. "I never saw Hannah be anything but patient and loving with all the kids," the now-married mother of two told me. Being in the Overtons' home had afforded Werkhoven an intimate view of the family. Her bedroom was just a few feet away from the children's rooms, which were always open; their doors had been removed so that the kids could easily come and go as they pleased. The children liked to hang out in her room and talk to her, particularly Andrew, who always visited her for an extra hug before bedtime. "If anything had been wrong, I would have known it," she insisted. "Would I really have stayed with a family that would abuse a child?"

The most unsettling aspect of *The State of Texas v. Hannah Ruth Overton*, which got under way in August 2007, was how effectively a woman who had spent most of her life as a do-gooder could be recast as a monster. The particulars of her crime, as sketched out by the prosecution, were vague; assistant district attorney Sandra Eastwood, a passionate child advocate, conceded in opening arguments that she was not sure how Hannah had made Andrew eat so much salt. "We don't know precisely how she got it down Andrew, but we know that he was very, very obedient," Eastwood told the jury, standing before the TV news cameras that Judge Longoria had allowed inside the courtroom. "And we do have some evidence of bruising to his nose [which could indicate] his nostrils were squeezed and he was made to drink it."

Over the course of the three-week-long trial, Eastwood sought to convince jurors that a mother with no history of violence or mental illness had force-fed her child to death—a scenario that each prosecution witness helped, incrementally, to suggest was possible. Patricia

Gonzalez, a nurse at the urgent care clinic, told the jury that Hannah had not behaved like a panic-stricken parent and had "had a smile on her face" as she performed CPR on the boy. Another nurse, Dina Zapata, remembered Hannah smirking as she tried to resuscitate him. Both women's accounts were problematic; Gonzalez had never made a statement to police and was testifying from memory after nearly a year's worth of negative media coverage, while Zapata had failed to mention anything about Hannah smirking when she wrote her initial report about the incident. Yet the image they conjured—of a woman grinning at the sight of a comatose four-year-old—was devastating. Gemma Mitchell, a phlebotomist, recalled overhearing Hannah tell medical staff that Andrew had stopped breathing after he was "punished." No one could corroborate her story, and under cross-examination, she admitted that she had never told anyone this fact until taking the stand. Still, the overall impression was a damning one.

Other witnesses testified that they had detected signs of abuse. One paramedic recounted how he had seen two sores on Andrew "that looked to me like cigarette burns because they were round." Another paramedic also believed the sores were cigarette burns, though he admitted he had only looked at them "from a distance." Fernandez, the medical examiner, said he had observed "burnlike scarring" on Andrew's arm that had likely been caused by "contact with a hot surface." But neither Larry nor Hannah smoked. Not until shortly before closing arguments did jurors hear from the defense's expert witness, a Harvard-educated pathologist and assistant medical examiner in San Francisco, Judy Melinek, who offered her opinion that the sores were consistent with mosquito bites that had been scratched and picked at.

The prosecution's most persuasive testimony came from Rotta, the pediatric critical care specialist who had originally expressed concern that Andrew had been mistreated. "A comment someone made was that it appeared that this child had been in a fight with a porcupine," the physician stated. "There were so many bruises and scratches that it would be difficult to describe them all." Rotta allowed that the appearance of Andrew's body may have been due in part to the fact that he was coagulopathic, or not able to clot blood properly, a condition that occurs after a person has gone into cardiac arrest and can cause excessive bleeding and bruising. But he was adamant that the boy's death had not been accidental. Andrew had never been diagnosed with pica, Rotta reminded jurors. "We have a child that was well until that afternoon, that had behavioral issues, that was having temper tantrums, that was then given something . . . probably to punish his behavior, that then goes into cardiorespiratory arrest."

Rotta stopped short of describing the manner in which he believed Andrew had been made to eat a lethal amount of salt—a dose that, after analyzing Andrew's blood, he determined would have consisted of 23 teaspoons of Zatarain's Creole Seasoning or 6 teaspoons of salt. The physician only said that the scratch marks he had noticed on the boy's neck had been caused, he believed, by another person. The marks "could be consistent with many things, including a fight, an altercation, someone trying to hold this child's neck forcefully," he said.

Andrew's former foster mother, Sharon Hamil, who was devastated by the boy's death, testified that Andrew had not exhibited significant developmental or behavioral problems, aside from his speech delay, during the time that he lived with her—a characterization that was rebutted by numerous members of Calvary Chapel later in the trial but that cast Hannah's credibility into doubt. "He was always happy," Hamil testified. She believed that Andrew's eating habits were not the stuff of pathology but those of a growing boy. "Andrew liked to eat every day, all day, any time," she said.

By the time Hannah took the stand, jurors appeared to have made up their minds. Several crossed their arms; others looked away. By that point, they had already been shown numerous photos of Andrew's small, bruised body postmortem. They had also watched the video of Hess questioning Hannah, during which she described calling a paramedic friend in Oklahoma for guidance when the boy's condition deteriorated, and even using her camera's flash to check if his pupils were reactive, but never calling for an ambulance. Sitting in the courtroom, she tried to explain how she had failed to recognize that Andrew's condition was life-threatening. "I realized that it was something serious . . . a few minutes before we actually took him in," she testified. Until then, she said, Andrew "was doing nothing that my other kids hadn't done with the flu . . . There wasn't anything that

I thought was dangerously wrong with him at that point. I didn't realize the seriousness of the situation." Eastwood questioned how Andrew had come to have scratches on his neck. "Could it be that you held his nose, held his neck, and made him drink this horrible concoction?" the prosecutor challenged her during a withering cross-examination. "Absolutely not," Hannah shot back.

Despite Eastwood's zeal, there were still basic questions that the prosecution could not explain. How had Hannah, who was six months pregnant and recovering from whiplash, managed to overpower Andrew? How had she known how much salt would kill him? And how had she forced him to choke down the lethal slurry through a sippy cup—a drinking container that is, by design, able to release its contents only when sucked on? Yet according to the unusual wording of the jury charge, jurors had to believe just one of two scenarios to find Hannah guilty: that she deliberately made Andrew ingest a lethal amount of salt or that she purposely neglected to get timely medical attention, knowing that this would kill him. In other words, if the jury could not agree conclusively that she had poisoned Andrew, it could still rule that she was guilty of capital murder "by omission," or by failure to act.

Gilmore and his defense team, which included two civil attorneys versed in the intricacies of medical testimony, tried to counter the prosecution's claims that Hannah had poisoned Andrew and purposely delayed medical treatment. (In his 32 years of practicing law, Gilmore told me, he has never run across the charge of "capital murder by omission" before or since.) Melinek, the defense's expert witness, testified about pica and an array of factors that could have contributed to Andrew's death, including undiagnosed diabetes. And a succession of witnesses, nearly all of them members of Calvary Chapel, recounted Andrew's unusual eating habits and Hannah's attentive parenting. During closing arguments, Gilmore emphasized that Hannah had no motive to kill Andrew and that the state had failed to prove that she had intentionally caused the boy's death.

But just as the prosecution could not show exactly how Hannah had forced Andrew to ingest a lethal dose of salt, neither could the defense give precise details for how the four-year-old had come to have so much sodium in his body. Prosecutors exploited that uncertainty in final arguments, asserting that Andrew did not have pica. Throughout the trial, Eastwood had suggested that the Overtons had withheld food as part of a larger pattern of abuse, and as she addressed the jury, she insisted that Andrew had scavenged for food because he was hungry. "The defendant has portrayed herself as a nurturing Christian woman," Eastwood proclaimed. "Does God want a child to go to bed hurting, in pain, fearful, being looked at by closed-circuit television? Any God, Christian or not, would have wanted a better mother for Andrew."

The burden on the state to prove its case beyond a reasonable doubt was, Gilmore told me, perhaps less than it should have been. "There was a dead child," he observed. "The jury was not just going to let her walk." Capital murder carries two possible punishments in Texas—the death penalty or life without parole—and the district attorney's office had already decided not to seek death. If convicted, Hannah would receive an automatic life sentence. However, Judge Longoria could allow the jury to consider a lesser charge if he felt that the evidence did not support capital murder, and after hearing the state's case, he did so, telling both the prosecution and the defense that he was willing to let the jury consider manslaughter or criminally negligent homicide. (Both carry shorter sentences and differ from capital murder on the issue of intent; a motorist who hits and kills someone while driving too fast is often deemed to be criminally negligent in that he did not set out to take a life but was aware of the danger of speeding.) Gilmore urged Hannah more than once to agree to have the jury consider a lesser charge, but she was uneasy with what she perceived as an underlying suggestion of wrongdoing. She could not consent to a lesser charge, she told her attorneys, because she felt it would mean she was admitting fault.

It was a catastrophic decision. After nearly eleven hours of deliberation—during which jurors sent out thirteen notes to the judge, primarily seeking to clarify medical testimony—the jury found her guilty of capital murder. As the verdict was read, Hannah looked horror-struck. Larry, who was sitting behind her, broke down. Before she was led away in handcuffs, the couple embraced for several minutes, overcome with emotion.

But had jurors fully understood the decision they had been asked to make? When Gilmore polled the jury afterward, all twelve members stated that they had found Hannah guilty of capital murder by omission for not acting quickly enough to save Andrew; none believed that she had poisoned him. Yet to find her guilty, they'd had to believe that she knew he would die if she did not get him immediate medical attention. According to juror number three, a high school English teacher named Margaret Warfield, that was not the case. "The jury found that Mrs. Overton failed to procure medical care within a reasonable time frame," she wrote in an affidavit that was later filed with Hannah's appeal. "It seemed to me, based upon the wording of the charge, that we had no choice but to find her guilty of capital murder." But, Warfield added, "I do not believe that Mrs. Overton knew that her actions (or lack thereof) would kill Andrew Byrd [*sic*]. Although I believe that Mrs. Overton was remiss in seeking timely medical care for Andrew Byrd, I do not believe that she intended or knew that this would result in his death." The wording of the jury charge, she added, had been "ambiguous and confusing." Ultimately, Warfield wrote, "I do not feel that justice has been served."

Two days after Hannah was sentenced to life in prison without the possibility of parole, a pediatrician named Edgar Cortes took the unusual step of contacting Gilmore. The doctor had been the on-call emergency medicine physician at Driscoll the day that Andrew arrived, and he had resuscitated the boy as he was transported to the intensive care unit. Although Cortes had been scheduled to testify for the prosecution, he was never put on the witness stand. (During the third week of the trial, moments before the case was sent to the jury, Eastwood had asked Judge Longoria if she could call Cortes as a rebuttal witness, but the judge, who had grown impatient with the length of the trial, denied her request.) As a frequent witness for the state in child abuse cases, Cortes was not in the habit of reaching out to defense attorneys, but he was so angered by the verdict that he picked up the phone. "I have mitigating testimony that I think would have been very useful to your client," he said in a voice mail he left for Gilmore. "Please call me at your earliest convenience."

Unlike the three physicians who had testified for the prosecution, Cortes was the only doctor who had seen Andrew before his hospitalization; he had evaluated the boy during a routine checkup when Andrew was three years old and still living with Hamil. "Andrew was not a normal child," Cortes explained to me. "A colleague of mine who attended the trial told me that the prosecution described Andrew again and again as a normal child, and that is a great distortion of the truth. Andrew was a sweet boy who had significant neurological and developmental disorders. He had a speech disorder called echolalia, which is one of the things we see typically in children who have autism spectrum disorders. He displayed hyperactive behavior and possibly had some cognitive delays as well." The doctor's assessment of Andrew as developmentally delayed was significant because it dovetailed with Hannah's testimony. She had told the jury of the boy's unusual habits—the inappropriate eating, the obsessive picking and scratching, the head banging—but her version of events had been tainted by the specter of abuse.

Cortes believed that Andrew's death was accidental. "The intentional poisoning of a child is usually perpetrated with sedatives, anticonvulsants, or medications like injectable insulin, not food," he told me. "The sodium content of Zatarain's is not listed on its packaging. How do you poison someone with a substance you don't know the contents of?" That Hannah had not sought immediate medical attention did not change his view. "Benign conditions and life-threatening conditions look the same in the beginning," he said. "You can ask, 'Why didn't she go to the hospital sooner?' but in hindsight, everything is obvious. If she had taken Andrew to the hospital earlier, what would she have taken him in for? Because he was vomiting? Because he felt cold?" He suspected that as the boy's condition worsened, Hannah had fallen victim to what he calls "stress blindness," a phenomenon he had witnessed many times during his 42 years of practicing medicine. "I've seen doctors and nurses freeze up when a patient comes in convulsing or in extremis," he said. "When people are under severe stress, their judgment becomes poor."

Cortes's perspective was revelatory. "He would have been witness number one for the defense," Gilmore told me. "The key issues in this case were knowledge and intent, and his opinion went directly to those issues." Hannah's attorneys would later argue on appeal that the doctor's opinion—that Hannah had never intended for the boy to die—amounted to exculpatory evidence that the state had withheld from the defense. But at a hearing on the defense's motion for a new trial, Eastwood stated under oath that Cortes had always been a passionate advocate for the prosecution; he had even remarked to her that he thought Hannah should "fry." Cortes does not dispute that story. "When I first learned Andrew had died, I was angry," he explained to me. "But I told prosecutors five months before the trial that I believed Hannah had no intent to kill him and that this was not a capital murder case. I was assured that they would be seeking lesser charges." During the trial, he said, "I sat at the courthouse for five days, waiting to testify. I came in the morning, and I left in the evening. To never have been produced—it was very strange."

Hannah's conviction was upheld in 2009 by the Thirteenth Court of Appeals. "It is unclear," read the court's ruling, "whether the state actually knew of Dr. Cortes's opinion." The court also ruled that the wording of the jury charge was "free from error." The Texas Court of Criminal Appeals declined the opportunity to reconsider the decision.

Then, in the spring of 2010, Hannah's appellate attorney, Cynthia Orr, made a startling discovery. Orr—a formidable legal mind whose work recently helped exonerate Michael Morton, a Williamson County man who was wrongly convicted of his wife's 1986 murder—had begun preparing a writ of habeas corpus, a last-ditch effort to persuade the courts to review Hannah's case. The writ is the final opportunity a defendant has to introduce new evidence into the record. Looking for any information that might bolster the appeal, Orr requested access to the prosecution's case file. Sifting through it one afternoon, Orr came across documents she had never seen before, which showed that Andrew's stomach contents did not have an elevated amount of salt when he arrived at the urgent care clinic. Orr forwarded the paperwork to a leading expert on salt poisoning, Michael Moritz, and asked him to explain its significance.

Moritz is the clinical director of pediatric nephrology at the Children's Hospital of Pittsburgh, where he specializes in children's kidney diseases. In 2007 he published a seminal paper on salt poisoning, in which he examined, among other things, documented cases of children who had accidentally ingested excessive quantities of salt.

He found that they fit a narrow profile: they were between the ages of one and six, they had been in the foster system or were from abusive homes, and they had pica. Moritz, in fact, had been asked to testify as an expert witness for Hannah's defense at her trial. After examining Andrew's medical records, he had determined that the boy's death was likely accidental. Yet the jury had never heard from him. Short on time as the trial drew to a close, the defense had asked Moritz—who needed to return to Pittsburgh—to sit for a videotaped deposition; when the deposition ran long and could not be completed, the defense was unable to enter it as testimony.

The paperwork Orr now forwarded to him, which showed that Andrew's stomach contained a great deal of water, only confirmed the clinical director's initial conclusion. "If someone was trying to murder Andrew, they would have restrained him and prevented him from drinking water," Moritz subsequently wrote in an affidavit. "The very dilute gastric sodium contents suggest . . . that he had unrestricted access to water." Given these facts, he explained, "There is not a single piece of evidence which suggests that Hannah Overton salt-poisoned Andrew." Instead, Moritz added, the most likely scenario was that Andrew "accidentally salt-poisoned himself."

In light of this information, Moritz felt certain that Andrew's prognosis would have been the same whether or not Hannah had called an ambulance. "It is unlikely that any intervention would have made a significant difference as Andrew had already taken the most critical step to save himself [by consuming] copious amounts of fluid," he wrote. The newly discovered documents, Moritz later told me, were "a monumentally important piece of evidence."

The discovery soon exposed strains among the prosecution team. Former prosecutor Anna Jimenez, who had assisted Eastwood as second chair at Hannah's trial, subsequently wrote a letter to Orr claiming that a sheaf of medical records that Eastwood had asked her to fax to an expert witness before trial had not included the documents that Orr had uncovered. "I fear she may have purposely withheld evidence that may have been favorable to Hannah Overton's defense," Jimenez wrote in her letter, which Orr would include in the writ. She also described her unease with Eastwood's "trial strategy," claiming the prosecutor had told her that they would not be calling Cortes because a record in his file indicated that Andrew had behavioral problems. Finally, Jimenez stated, "I do not believe that there was sufficient evidence to indicate that Hannah Overton intentionally killed Andrew Burd." In response, Eastwood penned an affidavit, asserting that she did not engage in any misconduct. "[I] fully disclosed the DA's office's case file to the defense," she wrote in the lengthy statement. "If I failed in my duties of disclosure before the Hannah Overton trial (which the record corroborates I did not), then so did Ms. Jimenez."

Orr filed the writ in April 2011, and soon afterward *San Antonio Express-News* reporter John MacCormack—whose reporting has raised questions about the fairness of Hannah's conviction—made a routine call to the office to gauge the reaction to the recent developments in the case. He reached Doug Norman, who was part of the prosecution team at Hannah's trial and who is now responsible for fighting her appeal. (Like Eastwood, neither Norman nor Jimenez would comment for this article.) Norman's remarks were hardly the stuff of a cocksure prosecutor. "I may harbor doubts, but a jury heard this case and made a decision, and everyone has to respect that decision," he told the *Express-News*. "I'll put it this way. My job requires me to be an advocate for the state. As long as I can make a nonfrivolous argument, I'll make it, but nothing in my job prevents me from praying for a more just outcome."

Every Saturday for the past several years, Larry has ridden his motorcycle from Corpus Christi to the Murray Unit, the maximum-security women's prison west of Waco where Hannah is incarcerated: a squat, concrete building walled off from the world with cyclone fencing and coils of razor wire. He and Hannah are allotted two hours, during which they sit together in the dayroom, flanked by other inmates and their families. Once a month, Larry loads the kids into his van and they make the trip together, although on those visits, no contact is allowed. Hannah must sit on the opposite side of a metal divider, behind Plexiglas. There are two phones that the kids can speak into, and they eagerly pass the receivers back and forth, recounting the month's events in stereo. "They get to see her for two hours, once a month—twenty-four hours in a year," Larry said. He and the kids return home the same day so that he can teach Sunday school the next morning. Round-trip, the journey is 632 miles.

That Larry is able to be with the children at all, much less raise them, is "a huge blessing," he told me. Not long after his arrest, a grand jury upgraded the charges against him to capital murder, and he feared that he too might face life in prison. But after Hannah's conviction, the DA's office offered him several plea deals, each of which required him to acknowledge that he had intentionally caused Andrew's death. Larry turned them down. Finally he agreed to plead no contest to criminally negligent homicide. "The way it was explained to me, that's how I would be charged if I accidentally ran a stoplight and hit somebody," he said. "Pleading out to that was much better than having my children grow up without a mother or a father." In exchange for his plea, Larry was given five years' probation and a $5,000 fine. (Hannah's mother and stepfather—whom the courts had named "managing conservators" of the children—were then able to return them to Larry's custody.) While he was relieved not to have to serve prison time, the discrepancy between his wife's punishment and his own left him stupefied. "How can one person get probation and another get life without parole for the same thing?" Larry said.

I visited Hannah at the Murray Unit one bright, cloudless afternoon, when the warden granted her a few hours to speak with me. She was even slighter in person than I had expected, and as she related the events of the past five years in her soft voice, she looked hopelessly out of place in her white prison jumpsuit. Yet her life behind bars, however incongruous, has taken on its own rhythm. She is awakened every morning at 2:45 a.m., rarely sleeping well; the overhead light above her bed never shuts off, and announcements blare throughout the night over the loudspeaker. At 4 a.m., she reports to the laundry, where she folds shirts and hands out clean clothes to inmates. After her shift ends in the late morning, there are letters to write home, in which she tries to stay present in her children's lives by choreographing what she can from a distance. "I plan their birthday parties from here," she told me. "I pick out the games and I make the decorations, if I can." She devotes most of her evenings to Bible studies, leading groups of inmates through careful examinations of Scripture. One of her favorite books to revisit is Ruth. "It's about trusting God and seeing how he is a god of redemption and restoration," she said.

As we sat across from each other in the dayroom, Hannah and I discussed her case and the anguish that had consumed her following Andrew's death. "I spent many nights beating myself up over 'Could I have done this or could I have done that?'" Hannah told me, staring at her hands. "I regret that I didn't push harder from the beginning to find out what was wrong with him—that I believed his problems were just due to his previous abuse and neglect, and that, when I finally decided he needed to see a doctor about his pica, we didn't get him in quicker." When I pressed her to explain why she and Larry had not called 911, she leaned forward, as if pleading with me to understand. "Because we were not thinking we were in a life-or-death situation," she insisted. "For us to go to [the clinic] was a lot faster than it would have been had we called, at that point."

As we talked about Andrew, she had to stop several times to compose herself. "I'm supposed to be done crying," she said apologetically at one point, brushing away tears. Despite all the pain, she told me that if she could do it over again, she would not change their decision to bring Andrew into their home. "It's not even a consideration," she said. "I wouldn't give up that time we had with him and that he had with us."

I asked Hannah if her faith had been shaken by Andrew's loss and the suffering that she and her family had experienced. "There was a time when I questioned how God could allow this to happen," she said. "But what I've realized is that I can trust his heart, even though I don't understand his plan." The reality that Hannah, who is 34, may spend the rest of her life in prison for capital murder—a sentence usually reserved for violent criminals who pose a continuing threat to society—is one she is still struggling to understand; even harder to grasp is the possibility that she might never be reunited with her children. "I miss everything," she later wrote to me. "Good-night kisses, bedtime stories, playing in the yard, birthdays, loose teeth, Christmas plays . . . movie nights, waking up to their beautiful faces." The Court of Criminal Appeals is currently reviewing her writ, which contends that the information about Andrew's gastric contents are grounds for a new trial. The court, which could rule imminently or years from now, could send the case back to Judge Longoria for a hearing or—far less likely—overturn her conviction. Because the court has not been inclined to intercede so far, members of Calvary Chapel have begun a letter-writing campaign to the Texas Board of Pardons and Paroles in hopes of securing a pardon or a commutation.

Meanwhile, those who once pursued Hannah with such certainty have undergone their own trials. Detective Hess was put on administrative leave in 2008 after it came to light that he had disclosed confidential information to the suspect in an ongoing investigation for indecency with a child. Hess was allowed to return to the force and is now a patrol sergeant. And Eastwood was fired from the DA's office in 2010. Then–district attorney Jimenez did not publicly disclose the reasons for the termination, but it occurred one week after Eastwood informed her superiors that she had been romantically involved in the past with a sex offender; she reported that she feared the information had been used by the offender's defense attorney to get him probation in a criminal case. (A subsequent investigation by the attorney general's office found that no crimes had been committed.)

As the Overtons wait on the appellate courts, Larry goes about the task of raising their five children, while also trying to rebuild his business. (After his arrest, he lost most of his clients. "One woman said she didn't want to work with a child killer," Larry told me.) In his role as single dad, he is aided by his extended family and his many friends from Calvary Chapel, who pitch in to do cleaning, grocery shopping, laundry, and babysitting. A church member who homeschools her daughters educates the Overton children, using lesson plans Hannah sends her. (Haller, their next-door neighbor, has since moved to Houston.) The kids now range in age from four to twelve, and when I visited them late one afternoon, not long after I had seen Hannah, they seemed unencumbered by the tragedy that had engulfed their family. They were no different from other children their age: exuberant, funny, guileless. As Larry stood in the kitchen and peeled potatoes, the kids—excited to have a visitor—showed me around their house, pointing out their favorite hiding places and the plaster cast of their footprints in the hallway, which includes the letter A for Andrew. The absence of their mother and their late brother was quietly acknowledged. "This is where Andrew used to sleep," Isaac told me softly as he led me into the boys' room. "There have been a few tear-filled nights because one of the kids misses Andrew," Larry told me later. "I remind them that the Lord loves him more than anyone could and he is with Him now and we will see him again someday."

The kids took me out back, where they jumped on the trampoline and played hide-and-seek in the salt grass. Emma, the youngest, trailed behind them with a doll, occasionally running inside to bang on the piano. It was Emma whom Hannah was pregnant with when Andrew died, and she is the child Hannah knows least. When Emma took her first steps, Larry brought her to the parking lot outside the county jail so that Hannah could watch from her cell above.

Larry called out that dinner was ready, and we gathered inside around a rough-hewn oak table he had made years ago. Dinner was potato soup—"It's good and filling, and it's cheap," Larry told me—which the kids dived into after saying grace. They chattered about an upcoming birthday party and discussed the merits of their favorite colors, finishing each other's sentences between slurps of soup. Had Andrew sat among them, I realized, he would have been nine years old.

After dinner the kids settled down in front of the TV to watch a movie that was Isabel's pick: a Japanese animated film that her brothers and sisters showed less enthusiasm for, fidgeting as they lay next to each other on the carpet. Before they headed to bed, Larry turned up the lights for their nightly devotions. Isaac read John 9 aloud while Larry helped him sound out the difficult words ("synagogue," "Pharisees"). A short discussion followed about the passage, in which Jesus heals a blind man, and then Larry closed his Bible and said, "Okay, guys, let's pray." One by one, the kids spoke their prayers, each of which ended with the same wish.

"Dear God, thank you for the soup," Isaac said, his head bowed, his eyes closed tightly. "And thanks for the movie, even though it was kind of weird. I pray that you will bring Mom home soon."

JENNIFER EGAN

■

Black Box

FROM *The New Yorker*

1

PEOPLE RARELY LOOK the way you expect them to, even when you've seen pictures.

The first thirty seconds in a person's presence are the most important.

If you're having trouble perceiving and projecting, focus on projecting.

Necessary ingredients for a successful projection: giggles; bare legs; shyness.

The goal is to be both irresistible and invisible.

When you succeed, a certain sharpness will go out of his eyes.

2

Some powerful men actually call their beauties "Beauty."

Counter to reputation, there is a deep camaraderie among beauties.

If your Designated Mate is widely feared, the beauties at the house party where you've gone undercover to meet him will be especially kind.

Kindness feels good, even when it's based on a false notion of your identity and purpose.

3

Posing as a beauty means not reading what you would like to

read on a rocky shore in the South of France.

Sunlight on bare skin can be as nourishing as food.

Even a powerful man will be briefly self-conscious when he first disrobes to his bathing suit.

It is technically impossible for a man to look better in a Speedo than in swim trunks.

If you love someone with dark skin, white skin looks drained of something vital.

4

When you know that a person is violent and ruthless, you will see violent ruthlessness in such basic things as his swim stroke.

"What are you doing?" from your Designated Mate amid choppy waves after he has followed you into the sea may or may not betray suspicion.

Your reply—"Swimming"—may or may not be perceived as sarcasm.

"Shall we swim together toward those rocks?" may or may not be a question.

"All that way?" will, if spoken correctly, sound ingenuous.

"We'll have privacy there" may sound unexpectedly ominous.

5

A hundred feet of blue-black Mediterranean will allow you ample time to deliver a strong self-lecture.

At such moments, it may be useful to explicitly recall your training:

"You will be infiltrating the lives of criminals.

"You will be in constant danger.

"Some of you will not survive, but those who do will be heroes.

"A few of you will save lives and even change the course of history.

"We ask of you an impossible combination of traits: ironclad scruples and a willingness to violate them;

"An abiding love for your country and a willingness to consort with individuals who are working actively to destroy it;

"The instincts and intuition of experts, and the blank records and true freshness of ingénues.

"You will each perform this service only once, after which you will return to your lives.

"We cannot promise that your lives will be exactly the same when you go back to them."

6

Eagerness and pliability can be expressed even in the way you climb from the sea onto chalky yellow rocks.

"You're a very fast swimmer," uttered by a man who is still submerged, may not be intended as praise.

Giggling is sometimes better than answering.

"You are a lovely girl" may be meant straightforwardly.

Ditto "I want to fuck you now."

"Well? What do you think about that?" suggests a preference for direct verbal responses over giggling.

"I like it" must be uttered with enough gusto to compensate for a lack of declarative color.

"You don't sound sure" indicates insufficient gusto.

"I'm not sure" is acceptable only when followed, coyly, with "You'll have to convince me."

Throwing back your head and closing your eyes allows you to give the appearance of sexual readiness while concealing revulsion.

7

Being alone with a violent and ruthless man, surrounded by water, can make the shore seem very far away.

You may feel solidarity, at such a time, with the beauties just visible there in their bright bikinis.

You may appreciate, at such a time, why you aren't being paid for this work.

Your voluntary service is the highest form of patriotism.

Remind yourself that you aren't being paid when he climbs out of the water and lumbers toward you.

Remind yourself that you aren't being paid when he leads you behind a boulder and pulls you onto his lap.

The Dissociation Technique is like a parachute—you must pull the cord at the correct time.

Too soon, and you may hinder your ability to function at a crucial moment;

Too late, and you will be lodged too deeply inside the action to wriggle free.

You will be tempted to pull the cord when he surrounds you with arms whose bulky strength reminds you, fleetingly, of your husband's.

You will be tempted to pull it when you feel him start to move against you from below.

You will be tempted to pull it when his smell envelops you: metallic, like a warm hand clutching pennies.

The directive "Relax" suggests that your discomfort is palpable.

"No one can see us" suggests that your discomfort has been understood as fear of physical exposure.

"Relax, relax," uttered in rhythmic, throaty tones, suggests that your discomfort is not unwelcome.

8

Begin the Dissociation Technique only when physical violation is imminent.

Close your eyes and slowly count backward from ten.

With each number, imagine yourself rising out of your body and moving one step farther away from it.

By eight, you should be hovering just outside your skin.

By five, you should be floating a foot or two above your body, feeling only vague anxiety over what is about to happen to it.

By three, you should feel fully detached from your physical self.

By two, your body should be able to act and react without your participation.

By one, your mind should drift so free that you lose track of what is happening below.

White clouds spin and curl.

A blue sky is as depthless as the sea.

The sound of waves against rocks existed millennia before there were creatures who could hear it.

Spurs and gashes of stone narrate a violence that the earth itself has long forgotten.

Your mind will rejoin your body when it is safe to do so.

9

Return to your body carefully,

as if you were reentering your home after a hurricane.

Resist the impulse to reconstruct what has just happened.

Focus instead on gauging your Designated Mate's reaction to the new intimacy between you.

In some men, intimacy will prompt a more callous, indifferent attitude.

In others, intimacy may awaken problematic curiosity about you.

"Where did you learn to swim like that?," uttered lazily, while supine, with two fingers in your hair, indicates curiosity.

Tell the truth without precision.

"I grew up near a lake" is both true and vague.

"Where was the lake?" conveys dissatisfaction with your vagueness.

"Columbia County, New York" suggests precision while avoiding it.

"Manhattan?" betrays unfamiliarity with the geography of New York State.

Never contradict your Designated Mate.

"Where did you grow up?," asked of a man who has just asked you the same thing, is known as "mirroring."

Mirror your Designated Mate's attitudes, interests, desires, and tastes.

Your goal is to become part of his atmosphere: a source of comfort and ease.

Only then will he drop his guard when you are near.

Only then will he have significant conversations within your earshot.

Only then will he leave his possessions in a porous and unattended state.

Only then can you begin to gather information systematically.

10

"Come. Let's go back," uttered

brusquely, suggests that your Designated Mate has no more wish to talk about himself than you do.

Avoid the temptation to analyze his moods and whims.

Salt water has a cleansing effect.

11

You will see knowledge of your new intimacy with your Designated Mate in the eyes of every beauty on shore.

"We saved lunch for you" may or may not be an allusion to the reason for your absence.

Cold fish is unappealing, even when served in a good lemon sauce.

Be friendly to other beauties, but not solicitous.

When you are in conversation with a beauty, it is essential that you be perceived as no more or less than she is.

Be truthful about every aspect of your life except marriage (if any).

If married, say that you and your spouse have divorced, to give an impression of unfettered freedom.

"Oh, that's sad!" suggests that the beauty you're chatting with would like to marry.

12

If your Designated Mate abruptly veers toward the villa, follow him.

Taking his hand and smiling congenially can create a sense of low-key accompaniment.

An abstracted smile in return, as if he'd forgotten who you are, may be a sign of pressing concerns.

The concerns of your Designated Mate are your concerns.

The room assigned to a powerful man will be more lavish than the one you slept in while awaiting his arrival.

Never look for hidden cameras: the fact that you're looking will give you away.

Determine whether your Des-

ignated Mate seeks physical intimacy; if not, feign the wish for a nap.

Your pretense of sleep will allow him to feel that he is alone.

Curling up under bedclothes, even those belonging to an enemy subject, may be soothing.

You're more likely to hear his handset vibrate if your eyes are closed.

13

A door sliding open signals his wish to take the call on the balcony.

Your Designated Mate's important conversations will take place outdoors.

If you are within earshot of his conversation, record it.

Since beauties carry neither pocketbooks nor timepieces, you cannot credibly transport recording devices.

A microphone has been implanted just beyond the first turn of your right ear canal.

Activate the microphone by pressing the triangle of cartilage across your ear opening.

You will hear a faint whine as recording begins.

In extreme quiet, or to a person whose head is adjacent to yours, this whine may be audible.

Should the whine be detected, swat your ear as if to deflect a mosquito, hitting the on/off cartilage to deactivate the mike.

You need not identify or comprehend the language your subject is using.

Your job is proximity; if you are near your Designated Mate, recording his private speech, you are succeeding.

Profanity sounds the same in every language.

An angry subject will guard his words less carefully.

14

If your subject is angry, you may leave your camouflage po-

sition and move as close to him as possible to improve recording quality.

You may feel afraid as you do this.

Your pounding heartbeat will not be recorded.

If your Designated Mate is standing on a balcony, hover in the doorway just behind him.

If he pivots and discovers you, pretend that you were on the verge of approaching him.

Anger usually trumps suspicion.

If your subject brushes past you and storms out of the room, slamming the door, you have eluded detection.

15

If your Designated Mate leaves your company a second time, don't follow him again.

Deactivate your ear mike and resume your "nap."

A moment of repose may be

a good time to reassure your loved ones.

Nuanced communication is too easily monitored by the enemy.

Your Subcutaneous Pulse System issues pings so generic that detection would reveal neither source nor intent.

A button is embedded behind the inside ligament of your right knee (if right-handed).

Depress twice to indicate to loved ones that you are well and thinking of them.

You may send this signal only once each day.

A continuous depression of the button indicates an emergency.

You will debate, each day, the best time to send your signal.

You will reflect on the fact that your husband, coming from a culture of tribal allegiance, understands and applauds your patriotism.

You will reflect on the enclosed and joyful life that the two of you have shared since graduate school.

You will reflect on the fact that America is your husband's chosen country, and that he loves it.

You will reflect on the fact that your husband's rise to prominence would have been unimaginable in any other nation.

You will reflect on your joint conviction that your service had to be undertaken before you had children.

You will reflect on the fact that you are thirty-three, and have spent your professional life fomenting musical trends.

You will reflect on the fact that you must return home the same person you were when you left.

You will reflect on the fact that you've been guaranteed you will not be the same person.

You will reflect on the fact that you had stopped being that person even before leaving.

You will reflect on the fact that too much reflection is pointless.

You will reflect on the fact that

these "instructions" are becoming less and less instructive.

Your Field Instructions, stored in a chip beneath your hairline, will serve as both a mission log and a guide for others undertaking this work.

Pressing your left thumb (if right-handed) against your left middle fingertip begins recording.

For clearest results, mentally speak the thought, as if talking to yourself.

Always filter your observations and experience through the lens of their didactic value.

Your training is ongoing; you must learn from each step you take.

When your mission is complete, you may view the results of the download before adding your Field Instructions to your mission file.

Where stray or personal thoughts have intruded, you may delete them.

16

Pretend sleep can lead to actual sleep. Sleep is restorative in almost every circumstance. The sound of showering likely indicates the return of your Designated Mate.

As a beauty, you will be expected to return to your room and change clothes often; a fresh appearance at mealtimes is essential.

The goal is to be a lovely, innocuous, evolving surprise.

A crisp white sundress against tanned skin is widely viewed as attractive.

Avoid overbright colors; they are attention-seeking and hinder camouflage.

White is not, technically speaking, a bright color.

White is, nevertheless, bright.

Gold spike-heeled sandals may compromise your ability to run or jump, but they look good on tanned feet.

Thirty-three is still young enough to register as "young."

Registering as "young" is especially welcome to those who may not register as "young" much longer.

If your Designated Mate leads you to dinner with an arm at your waist, assume that your attire change was successful.

17

When men begin serious talk, beauties are left to themselves.

"How long have you been divorced?" suggests the wish to resume a prior conversation.

"A few months," when untrue, should be uttered without eye contact.

"What was he like, your husband?" may be answered honestly.

"From Africa. Kenya" will satisfy your wish to talk about your husband.

"Black?," with eyebrows raised, may indicate racism.

"Yes. Black," in measured tones, should deliver a gentle reprimand.

"How black?" suggests that it did not.

"Very black" is somewhat less gentle, especially when accompanied by a pointed stare.

"Nice" hints at personal experience.

"Yes. It is nice" contradicts one's alleged divorce. "Was nice" is a reasonable correction.

"But not nice enough?," with laughter, indicates friendly intimacy. Especially when followed by "Or too nice!"

18

House-party hosts are universally eager to make guests eat.

For most beauties, the lure of food is a hazard; as a beauty of limited tenure, you may eat what you want.

Squab can be consumed by ripping the bird apart with your hands and sucking the meat from the bones.

A stunned expression reveals that your host expected the use of utensils.

A host who caters to violent guests will understand implicitly the need for discretion.

The adjacency of your host's chair to your own may presage a confidence.

If your job is to appear simpleminded, a confidence may mean that you have failed.

Everyone should brush his teeth before dinner.

Turning your ear toward your host's mouth will prevent you from having to smell the breath coming from it.

Ears must be kept clean at all times.

If your host warns you that your Designated Mate may pose an immediate danger to you, assume that your Designated Mate has left the room.

19

Going to the rest room is the most efficient means of self-jettisoning.

Never betray urgency, not even in an empty hallway.

If you have no idea in which direction your Designated Mate has gone, hold still.

If you find yourself hovering beside a pair of glass doors, you may open them and step outside.

Nights in the South of France are a strange, dark, piercing blue.

A bright moon can astonish, no matter how many times you have seen it.

If you were a child who loved the moon, looking at the moon will forever remind you of childhood.

Fatherless girls may invest the moon with a certain paternal promise.

Everyone has a father.

A vague story like "Your father died before you were born" may satisfy a curious child for an unlikely number of years.

The truth of your paternity, discovered in adulthood, will make the lie seem retroactively ludicrous.

Publicists occasionally have

flings with their movie-star clients.

Discovering that you are a movie star's daughter is not necessarily a comfort.

It is especially not a comfort when the star in question has seven other children from three different marriages.

Discovering that you are a movie star's daughter may prompt you to watch upward of sixty movies, dating from the beginning of his career.

You may think, watching said movies, You don't know about me, but I am here.

You may think, watching said movies, I'm invisible to you, but I am here.

A sudden reconfiguration of your past can change the fit and feel of your adulthood.

It may cleave you, irreparably, from the mother whose single goal has been your happiness.

If your husband has transformed greatly in his own life, he will understand your transformation.

Avoid excessive self-reflection; your job is to look out, not in.

20

"There you are," whispered from behind by your Designated Mate, suggests that he has been looking for you.

Holding still can sometimes prove more effective than actively searching.

"Come," uttered softly, may communicate a renewed wish for intimate contact.

The moon's calm face can make you feel, in advance, that you are understood and forgiven.

The sea is audible against the rocks well before you see it.

Even at night, the Mediterranean is more blue than black.

If you wish to avoid physical intimacy, the sight of a speedboat will bring relief, despite the myriad new problems it presents.

If no words are exchanged between your Designated Mate

and the speedboat's captain, their meeting was likely prearranged.

A man known for his cruelty may still show great care in guiding his beauty into a rocking speedboat.

He may interpret her hesitation to board as a fear of falling in.

Resist the impulse to ask where you are going.

Try, when anxious, to summon up a goofy giggle.

Locate your Personal Calming Source and use it.

If your Personal Calming Source is the moon, be grateful that it is dark and that the moon is especially bright.

Reflect on the many reasons you can't yet die:

You need to see your husband.

You need to have children.

You need to tell the movie star that he has an eighth child, and that she is a hero.

21

The moon may appear to move, but really it is you who are moving.

At high velocity, a speedboat slams along the tops of waves. Fear and excitement are sometimes indistinguishable.

When the captain of a boat adjusts his course in response to commands from your Designated Mate, he may not know where he is taking you.

If your Designated Mate keeps looking up, he's probably using the stars for navigation.

The Mediterranean is vast enough to have once seemed infinite.

A beauty should require no more context than the presence of her Designated Mate.

A beauty must appear to enjoy any journey he initiates.

Simulate said enjoyment by putting an affectionate arm around him and nestling your head close to his.

A beauty whose head is aligned

with her Designated Mate's can share in his navigation and thus calculate the route.

At night, far from shore, stars pulse with a strength that is impossible to conceive of in the proximity of light.

Your whereabouts will never be a mystery; you will be visible at all times as a dot of light on the screens of those watching over you.

You are one of hundreds, each a potential hero.

Technology has afforded ordinary people a chance to glow in the cosmos of human achievement.

Your lack of espionage and language training is what makes your record clean and neutral.

You are an ordinary person undertaking an extraordinary task.

You need not be remarkable for your credentials or skill sets, only for your bravery and equilibrium.

Knowing that you are one of hundreds shouldn't feel belittling.

In the new heroism, the goal is to merge with something larger than yourself.

In the new heroism, the goal is to throw off generations of self-involvement.

In the new heroism, the goal is to renounce the American fixation with being seen and recognized.

In the new heroism, the goal is to dig beneath your shiny persona.

You'll be surprised by what lies under it: a rich, deep crawl space of possibilities.

Some liken this discovery to a dream in which a familiar home acquires new wings and rooms.

The power of individual magnetism is nothing against the power of combined selfless effort.

You may accomplish astonishing personal feats, but citizen agents rarely seek individual credit.

They liken the need for personal glory to cigarette addiction: a habit that feels life-sustaining even as it kills you.

Childish attention-seeking is usually satisfied at the expense of real power.

An enemy of the state could not have connived a better way to declaw and distract us.

Now our notorious narcissism is our camouflage.

22

After a juddering ride of several hours, you may not notice at first that the boat is approaching a shore.

A single lighted structure stands out strongly on a deserted coastline.

Silence after a roaring motor is a sound of its own.

The speedboat's immediate departure signals that you won't be making a return trip anytime soon.

Knowing your latitude and longitude is not the same as knowing where you are.

A new remote and unfamiliar place can make the prior remote and unfamiliar place seem like home.

Imagining yourself as a dot of light on a screen is oddly reassuring.

Because your husband is a visionary in the realm of national security, he occasionally has access to that screen.

If it calms you to imagine your husband tracking your dot of light, then imagine it.

Do not, however, close your eyes while ascending a rocky path in darkness.

At Latitude X, Longitude Y, the flora is dry and crumbles under your feet.

A voice overhead suggests that your arrival was expected and observed.

An empty shore is not necessarily unpatrolled.

The best patrols are imperceptible.

23

A formal handshake between your new host and your Designated Mate implies that this is their first meeting.

A formal handshake followed by a complex and stylized hand gesture implies a shared allegiance.

So does the immediate use of a language you don't recognize.

In certain rich, powerful men, physical slightness will seem a source of strength.

The failure of your new host to acknowledge you may indicate that women do not register in his field of vision.

Being invisible means that you won't be closely watched.

Your job is to be forgotten yet still present.

A white, sparkling villa amid so much scrabbly darkness will appear miragelike.

A man to whom women are invisible may still have many beauties in his domain.

These neglected beauties will vie for his scant attention.

Among neglected beauties, there is often an alpha beauty who assumes leadership.

As you enter the house, her cool scrutiny will ripple through the other beauties and surround you.

The sensation will remind you of going as a child with your mother to visit families with two parents and multiple children.

At first, the knot of unfamiliar kids would seem impenetrable.

You would wish, keenly, that you had a sibling who could be your ally.

Feeling at the mercy of those around you prompted a seismic internal response.

The will to dominate was deeper than yourself.

You were never childish, even as a child.

Your unchildishness is something your husband has always loved in you.

Once the new children were under your control, it was crushing to leave their midst.

24

A small table and chairs carved into a spindly clifftop promontory are doubtless designed for private conversation.

If your Designated Mate brings you with him to this place, it may mean that he feels less than perfectly at ease with your new host.

When your new host dismisses his own alpha beauty, important business may be under way.

An alpha beauty will not tolerate her own exclusion if another beauty is included.

If your new host makes a motion of dismissal at you, look to your Designated Mate.

Take orders from no one but your Designated Mate.

If your Designated Mate keeps an arm around you in the face of your new host's dismissal, you have become the object of a power play.

If your new host moves close to your face and speaks directly into it, he is likely testing your ignorance of his language.

If your Designated Mate stiffens beside you, your new host's words are probably offensive.

When you become an object of contention, try to neutralize the conflict.

A giggle and a look of incomprehension are a beauty's most reliable tools.

If the men relax into their chairs, neutralization has been successful.

Your new host has insulted you and, by extension, your Designated Mate.

Your Designated Mate has prevailed in his claim that you're too harmless to bother sending away.

Congratulate yourself on preserving your adjacency and activate your ear mike.

25

In the presence of business conversation, project an utter lack of interest or curiosity.

Notice where you are at all times.

On a high, narrow promontory at Latitude X, Longitude Y, the ocean and heavens shimmer in all directions.

There will be moments in your mission, perhaps very few, when you'll sense the imminence of critical information.

It may come in the form of a rush of joy.

This joy may arise from your discovery that the moon, hard and radiant, is still aloft.

It may arise from the knowledge that, when your task is complete, you will return to the husband you adore.

It may arise from the extremity of the natural beauty around you, and the recognition that you are alive in this moment.

It may arise from your knowledge that you have accom-plished every goal you've set for yourself since childhood.

It may arise from the knowledge that at long last you've found a goal worthy of your considerable energies.

It may arise from the knowledge that, by accomplishing this goal, you'll have helped to perpetuate American life as you know it.

A wave of joy can make it difficult to sit still.

Beware of internal states—positive or negative—that obscure what is happening around you.

When two subjects begin making sketches, concrete planning may have commenced.

The camera implanted in your left eye is operated by pressing your left tear duct.

In poor light, a flash may be activated by pressing the outside tip of your left eyebrow.

When using the flash, always cover your non-camera eye to shield it from temporary blindness occasioned by the flash.

Never deploy flash photography in the presence of other people.

26

Springing from your seat with a gasp and peering toward the house will focus the attention of others in that direction.

Having heard something inaudible to others puts you in an immediate position of authority.

"What? What did you hear?," uttered close to your face by your Designated Mate, means that your diversion was successful.

Wait until their eagerness to know verges on anger, evidenced by the shaking of your shoulders.

Then tell them, faintly, "I heard screaming."

Men with a history of violence live in fear of retribution.

Your new host will be the first to depart in the direction of alleged screaming.

Your Designated Mate's glance toward the dock, far below, may reveal that his interests are not fully aligned with your new host's.

His attention to his handset may portend that your diversion has run amok, undermining the transaction you meant to capture.

Among the violent, there is always a plan for escape.

27

It is reasonable to hope that a backlit screen will distract its user from a camera flash at some slight distance.

Move close to the sketches you wish to photograph, allowing them to fill your field of vision.

Hold very still.

A flash is far more dramatic in total darkness.

An epithet in another language, followed by "What the fuck was that?," means you overestimated your Designated Mate's handset absorption.

A bright, throbbing total blindness means that you neglected to cover your non-camera eye.

Distance yourself from agency in the flash by crying out, truthfully, "I can't see!"

It is hard to safely navigate a clifftop promontory at high speed while blind.

It is hard to defer said navigation when your Designated Mate is forcefully yanking your hand.

A distant buzz presages an approaching speedboat.

Cooler air and a downward slope indicate that you are now below the cliff's edge.

Trying to negotiate a crumbling wooded path in a state of blindness (and heels) will soon lead to tripping and collapsing.

Receding downhill footfalls indicate that you've overtaxed your limited value to your Designated Mate.

A sense of helpless disorientation may prevent you from doing much more than sitting there in the dirt.

28

Variegation in the textures around you is a first sign that your temporary blindness has begun to fade.

Temporary blindness sharpens one's appreciation for not being blind.

In the aftermath of blindness, the accretion of objects around you may have an almost sensual quality.

A boat departing at high speed will send a vibration trembling up through the soil.

The knowledge that you are alone, without your Designated Mate, will settle upon you slowly and coldly.

Each new phase of aloneness reveals that you were previously less alone than you thought.

This more profound isolation may register, at first, as paralysis.

If it soothes you to lie back in the dirt, then lie back.

The moon shines everywhere.

The moon can seem as expressive as a face.

Human beings are fiercely, primordially resilient.

In uneasy times, draw on the resilience you carry inside you.

Recall that the mythical feats you loved to read about as a child are puny beside the accomplishments of human beings on earth.

29

The presence of another person can be sensed, even when not directly perceived.

The discovery of another person at close range, when you thought you were alone, may occasion fear.

Leaping from a supine into a standing posture will induce a head rush.

"I see you. Come out" must be uttered calmly, from the Readiness Position.

If you show fear, make sure that it isn't the fear you actually feel.

When you've expected a man, the appearance of a woman may be shocking.

Despite all that you know and are, you may experience that shock as a relief.

"Why are you here?," uttered by your new host's alpha beauty, is likely hostile.

Respond to abstract questions on the most literal level: "He left without me."

"Bastard," muttered bitterly, suggests familiarity with the phenomenon of being left behind.

Sympathy from an unexpected source can prompt a swell of emotion.

Measure the potential liability of shedding tears before you let them fall.

The perfumed arm of a beauty may pour strength and hope directly into your skin.

30

A lavish clifftop villa may look even more miragelike on a second approach.

Sustaining an atmosphere of luxury in a remote place requires an enormous amount of money.

So does coordinated violence.

Your job is to follow money to its source.

A powerful man whose associate has fled the premises after a false alarm is unlikely to be cheerful.

The reappearance of the vanished associate's stranded beauty will likely startle him.

Astonishment is satisfying to witness on any face.

"Where the fuck did he go?" is remarkably easy to decipher, even in a language you don't recognize.

A shrug is comprehensible to everyone.

An alpha beauty's complete indifference to the consternation of her mate may mean that he's easily moved to consternation.

It may also mean that he's not her mate.

As a beauty, you will sometimes be expected to change hands.

Generally, you will pass from the hands of a less powerful man to those of a more powerful man.

Greater proximity to the source of money and control is progress.

Your job is identical regardless of whose hands you are in.

If your vulnerability and helplessness have drawn the interest of an enemy subject, accentuate them.

Scraped and dirty legs may accentuate your vulnerability to the point of disgust.

They might get you a hot shower, though.

31

Homes of the violent rich have excellent first-aid cabinets.

If, after tending to your scrapes, you are shown to a bathing area with a stone-encrusted waterfall, assume you won't be alone for long.

The fact that a man has ignored and then insulted you does not mean that he won't want to fuck you.

Slim, powerful men often move with catlike swiftness.

Begin your countdown early—as he lowers himself into the tub.

By the time he seizes your arm, you should be at five.

By the time your forehead is jammed against a rock, you should perceive your body only vaguely, from above.

32

If you feel, on returning to your body, that much time has passed, don't dwell on how much.

If your limbs are sore and your forehead scraped and raw, don't dwell on why.

When you emerge from a warm, churning bath where you've spent an indeterminate period of time, expect to feel shaky and weak.

Remind yourself that you are receiving no payment, in currency or kind, for this or any act you have engaged in.

These acts are forms of sacrifice.

An abundance of diaphanous bathrobes suggests that the occupants of this bathroom are often female.

A soiled and tattered white sundress can seem oddly precious when it's all you have.

Keep with you the things that matter—you won't come back for them later.

The stationing of a male attendant outside the bathroom means that you haven't been forgotten.

If he shows you to a tiny room containing a very large bed, your utility to your new host may not have been exhausted.

A tray containing a meat pie, grapes, and a pitcher of water suggests that visits such as yours are routine.

At times, you may wish to avoid the moon.

At times, the moon may appear like a surveillance device, tracking your movements.

The ability to sleep in stressful conditions is essential to this work.

Sleep whenever you can safely do so.

33

Your abrupt awakening may feel like a reaction to a sound.

In moments of extreme solitude, you may believe you've heard your name.

We reassure ourselves by summoning, in our dreams, those we love and miss.

Having awakened to find them absent, we may be left with a sense of having spoken with them.

Even the most secure houses achieve, in deep night, a state of relative unconsciousness.

A beauty in a diaphanous lavender bathrobe can go any-

where, as long as she appears to be delivering herself to someone.

34

A universal principle of home construction makes it possible to guess which door will lead to the master bedroom.

Linen closets, with doors closed, can resemble master bedrooms.

So can bathrooms.

Bare feet are virtually soundless on a stone floor.

Even a slim, catlike man may snore.

When trespassing in a sleeping man's bedroom, go straight to his bed, as if you were seeking him out.

An alpha beauty who has appeared to have no tie to your new host may turn out to be his intimate, after all.

Their sleeping entanglement may contradict everything you have witnessed between them.

A small crib near the bed may indicate the presence of a baby.

Avoid indulging your own amazement; it wastes time.

Master bedrooms in lavish homes often divide into "his" and "hers" areas.

A beauty's closet is unmistakable, like a quiver of bright arrows.

The closet of a slight, catlike man will usually be compact.

Having penetrated a man's personal space, immediately seek out his Sweet Spot.

The Sweet Spot is where he empties his pockets at the end of the day and stores the essentials he needs to begin the next.

The Sweet Spot of a secretive, catlike man will most often be inside a cupboard or a drawer.

When you find it, consider using a Data Surge to capture the contents of his handset.

A Data Surge must be deployed with extreme caution, and only if you feel confident of an exceptional yield.

The quantity of information captured will require an enormous amount of manpower to tease apart.

Its transmission will register on any monitoring device.

We can guarantee its effectiveness only once.

35

Reach between your right fourth and pinky toes (if right-handed) and remove the Data Plug from your Universal Port.

Attached to the plug is a cable with a connection pin at one end for insertion into the handset's data port.

Sit on the floor, away from sharp surfaces, and brace your back against a wall.

A red ribbon has been tucked inside your Universal Port; enclose this in one of your palms.

Spread apart your toes and gently reinsert the plug, now

fused to your subject's handset, into your Universal Port.

You will feel the surge as the data flood your body.

The surge may contain feeling, memory, heat, cold, longing, pain, even joy.

Although the data are alien, the memories dislodged will be your own:

Peeling an orange for your husband in bed on a Sunday, sunlight splashing the sheets;

The smoky earthen smell of the fur of your childhood cat;

The flavor of the peppermints your mother kept for you inside her desk.

The impact of a Data Surge may prompt unconsciousness or short-term memory loss.

The purpose of the red ribbon is to orient you; if you awaken to find yourself clutching one, look to your foot.

When your body is quiet, unplug the handset and return it to its original location.

36

A Data Surge leaves a ringing in your ears that may obscure the sound of another person's arrival.

A face that brought you relief once may trigger relief a second time.

When an alpha beauty accosts you at high volume in an unfamiliar language, it may mean she's too sleepy to remember who you are.

It may also mean she's calling someone else.

Beauty status will not excuse, for another beauty, your appearance where you are not supposed to be.

Should you be perceived as an enemy, prepare to defend yourself at the first sign of physical encroachment.

Your new host lunging at you, shouting, "What the fuck are you doing?," constitutes physical encroachment.

Thrust your elbow upward into the tender socket underneath

his jaw, sending him backward onto the floor.

The wails of a newborn will lure its mother away from almost anything, including the physical travails of her mate.

A man disabled by an elbow blow will have little reaction to infant cries.

37

At the revelation of martial-arts expertise, a man who has perceived you as merely a beauty will recalculate your identity and purpose.

Watch his eyes: he'll be measuring the distance to his nearest firearm.

An immediate exit is advisable.

A slim, catlike man may well rebound before a hasty exit can be made.

Obstructing the path of a violent man to his firearm will nearly always result in another encroachment.

Kicking him in the foreneck, even barefoot, will temporarily occlude his windpipe.

The alpha beauty of a violent man will know where his firearm is kept, and how to use it.

A woman holding a gun and a baby no longer qualifies as a beauty.

No beauty is really a beauty.

Disabling a gun holder is likely to hurt the baby she is holding, too.

When self-preservation requires that you harm the innocent, we can provide no more than guidelines.

As Americans, we value human rights above all else and cannot sanction their violation.

When someone threatens our human rights, however, a wider leeway becomes necessary.

Follow your instincts while bearing in mind that we must, and will, hew to our principles.

A woman holding a thrashing baby in one arm may have trouble aiming a firearm with the other.

Bullets do actually whistle in an enclosed space.

If a person has shot at you and missed, incapacitate her before she can fire again.

We are most reluctant to hurt those who remind us of ourselves.

38

A lag time exists between getting shot and knowing that you have been shot.

Assuming there is no artery involvement, wounds to the upper limbs are preferable.

Bony, tendony body parts bleed less, but are harder to reconstruct if shattered.

The right shoulder is a bony, tendony part.

When shots have been fired in a powerful man's home, you have minutes, if not seconds, before the arrival of security.

Your physical person is our Black Box; without it, we have no record of what has happened on your mission.

It is imperative that you re-

move yourself from enemy possession.

When you find yourself cornered and outnumbered, you may unleash, as a last resort, your Primal Roar.

The Primal Roar is the human equivalent of an explosion, a sound that combines screaming, shrieking, and howling.

The Roar must be accompanied by facial contortions and frenetic body movement, suggesting a feral, unhinged state.

The Primal Roar must transform you from a beauty into a monster.

The goal is to horrify your opponent, the way trusted figures, turned evil, are horrifying in movies and in nightmares.

Deploy your camera flash repeatedly while Roaring.

When approached by a howling, spasmodic, flashing monster, most women holding newborns will step aside.

Discontinue Roaring the instant you're free from immediate danger.

Those stampeding to the aid of a powerful man will barely notice a dishevelled beauty they pass in a hallway.

If you're lucky, this will buy you time to flee his house.

Resume your beauty role while running: smooth your hair and cover your bleeding wound with the sundress scrunched in your pocket.

The fact that you can't hear alarms doesn't mean you haven't set them off.

39

After violence in a closed room, cool night air will have a clarifying effect.

Get to the bottom of a hill any way you can, including sliding and rolling.

In residences of the violent rich, there will be at least one guard at each port of egress.

In deep night, if you are extremely lucky (and quiet), that guard will be asleep.

Assume, as well as you can, the air

of a beauty larkishly gambolling.

If running barefoot onto a dock transports you back to your childhood, pain may be making you hallucinate.

Lying with girlfriends on a still-warm dock in upstate New York, watching shooting stars, is a sensation you remember after many years.

Hindsight creates the illusion that your life has led you inevitably to the present moment.

It's easier to believe in a foregone conclusion than to accept that our lives are governed by chance.

Showing up for a robotics course by accident, because of a classroom mixup, is chance.

Finding an empty seat beside a boy with very dark skin and beautiful hands is chance.

When someone has become essential to you, you will marvel that you could have lain on a warm dock and not have known him yet.

Expect reimmersion in your old life to be difficult.

Experience leaves a mark, regardless of the reasons and principles behind it.

What our citizen agents most often require is simply for time to pass.

Our counsellors are available around the clock for the first two weeks of your reimmersion and during business hours thereafter.

We ask that you allow our Therapeutic Agents, rather than those in the general population, to address your needs.

Secrecy is the basis of what we do, and we require your extreme discretion.

40

Even preternatural swimming strength cannot propel you across a blue-black sea.

Staring with yearning ferocity from the end of a dock cannot propel you across a blue-black sea.

When your body has been granted exceptional powers, it is jarring to encounter a gulf between your desires and your abilities.

For millennia, engineers have empowered human beings to accomplish mythical feats.

Your husband is an engineer.

Children raised among wild animals learn to detect irregular movements in their landscape.

That particular awareness, coupled with scientific genius, has made your husband a national-security hero.

Intimacy with another human can allow you to scrutinize your surroundings as he would.

Along a rocky, moonlit shore, the irregular movement is the one that is lurching in time with the water beneath an overhang of brush.

A speedboat has most likely been hidden by your new host as a means of emergency escape.

The key will be inside it.

41

Slither between branches

and board the boat; untie it and lower its motor into the water.

Be grateful for the lakes in upstate New York where you learned to pilot motorboats.

Fluff up your hair with your functional arm and essay a wide, carefree smile.

A smile is like a shield; it freezes your face into a mask of muscle that you can hide behind.

A smile is like a door that is both open and closed.

Turn the key and gun the motor once before aiming into the blue-black sea and jamming the accelerator.

Wave and giggle loudly at the stunned, sleepy guard.

Steer in a zigzag motion until you are out of gunshot range.

42

The exultation of escape will be followed almost immediately by a crushing onslaught of pain.

The house, its occupants, even the gunshots will seem like phantoms beside this clanging immediacy.

If the pain makes thought impossible, concentrate solely on navigation.

Only in specific Geographic Hotspots can we intervene.

While navigating toward a Hotspot, indicate an emergency by pressing the button behind your knee for sixty continuous seconds.

You must remain conscious.

If it helps, imagine yourself in the arms of your husband.

If it helps, imagine yourself in your apartment, where his grandfather's hunting knife is displayed inside a Plexiglas box.

If it helps, imagine harvesting the small tomatoes you grow on your fire escape in summer.

If it helps, imagine that the contents of the Data Surge will help thwart an attack in which thousands of American lives would have been lost.

Even without enhancements, you can pilot a boat in a semi-conscious state.

Human beings are superhuman.

Let the moon and the stars direct you.

43

When you reach the approximate location of a Hotspot, cut the engine.

You will be in total darkness, in total silence.

If you wish, you may lie down at the bottom of the boat.

The fact that you feel like you're dying doesn't mean that you will die.

Remember that, should you die, your body will yield a crucial trove of information.

Remember that, should you die, your Field Instructions will provide a record of your mission and lessons for those who follow.

Remember that, should you die, you will have triumphed merely by delivering your physical person into our hands.

The boat's movement on the sea will remind you of a cradle.

You'll recall your mother rocking you in her arms when you were a baby.

You'll recall that she has always loved you fiercely and entirely.

You'll discover that you have forgiven her.

You'll understand that she concealed your paternity out of faith that her own inexhaustible love would be enough.

The wish to tell your mother that you forgive her is yet another reason you must make it home alive.

You will not be able to wait, but you will have to wait.

We can't tell you in advance what direction relief will come from.

We can only reassure you that we have never yet failed to recover a citizen agent, dead or alive, who managed to reach a Hotspot.

44

Hotspots are not hot.

Even a warm night turns frigid at the bottom of a wet boat.

The stars are always there, scattered and blinking.

Looking up at the sky from below can feel like floating, suspended, and looking down.

The universe will seem to hang beneath you in its milky glittering mystery.

Only when you notice a woman like yourself, crumpled and bleeding at the bottom of a boat, will you realize what has happened.

You've deployed the Dissociation Technique without meaning to.

There is no harm in this.

Released from pain, you can waft free in the night sky.

Released from pain, you can enact the fantasy of flying that you nurtured as a child.

Keep your body in view at all times; if your mind loses track of your body, it may be hard—even impossible—to reunite the two.

As you waft free in the night sky, you may notice a steady rhythmic churning in the gusting wind.

Helicopter noise is inherently menacing.

A helicopter without lights is like a mixture of bat, bird, and monstrous insect.

Resist the urge to flee this apparition; it has come to save you.

45

Know that in returning to your body you are consenting to be racked, once again, by physical pain.

Know that in returning to your body you are consenting to undertake a jarring reimmersion into an altered life.

Some citizen agents have chosen not to return.

They have left their bodies be-

hind, and now they shimmer
sublimely in the heavens.

In the new heroism, the goal
is to transcend individual life,
with its petty pains and loves, in
favor of the dazzling collective.

You may picture the pulsing
stars as the heroic spirits of former agent beauties.

You may imagine Heaven as a
vast screen crowded with their
dots of light.

46

If you wish to return to your
body, it is essential that you
reach it before the helicopter
does.

If it helps, count backward.
By eight, you should be close
enough to see your bare and
dirty feet.

By five, you should be close
enough to see the bloody dress
wrapped around your shoulder.

By three, you should be close
enough to see the dimples you
were praised for as a child.

By two, you should hear the
shallow bleating of your
breath.

47

Having returned to your body,
witness the chopper's slow,
throbbing descent.

It may appear to be the instru-
ment of a purely mechanical
realm.

It may look as if it had come to
wipe you out.

It may be hard to believe
that there are human beings
inside it.

You won't know for sure until
you see them crouching above
you, their faces taut with hope,

JIM GAVIN

■

Bewildered Decisions in Times of Mercantile Terror

FROM *The Paris Review*

BOBBY'S OFFICE, for the time being, was the Berkeley Public Library. On a Thursday afternoon in August, with sunlight pouring through the arched windows of the reading room, he closed his book and quietly observed the homeless man sitting across from him. The man was bald and sunburned, and he had grimy strips of duct tape wrapped around his fingertips. With a chewed-up pencil in his hand, he scrawled notes in the margins of an old physics textbook that was crawling with ants. Bobby couldn't take his eyes off the ants; he watched them moving in clusters across equations and diagrams, and it occurred to him that the ants were messengers, reading the book for this infernal professor, and when they were done they would crawl up the man's arm and into his ear, burrowing directly into his brain.

Bobby hadn't slept in two or three days.

He looked around for another table, but the reading room was packed with the elderly and the unemployed. Some people seemed hard at work, or at least pleasantly engaged, but most were either asleep or staring out the windows, as if waiting for something. It felt more like a bus terminal than a library. Bobby wore a Cal T-shirt and a pair of boardshorts. He was trying to read a reference manual on patent law, but it was boring and his eyes kept slipping off the page. The hours were melting together. Last night, after *Conan,* he had fallen into a vortex of infomercials, and then, at some point, he snuck off with his roommate's laptop and sent another pleading e-mail to his cousin, Nora. When the sun came up, he left his apartment in the Berkeley Flats and rode his bike up University Avenue. He ate breakfast at McDonald's, and when he got to the library at nine o'clock, a crowd was already waiting to get inside. He struggled with his work all day—he kept taking long breaks to read magazines—but his lack of concentration, he knew, had more to do with excitement than fatigue. If anything, he worried that he was too awake.

It was three o'clock. Far up the hill, on campus, the tower bells were ringing. Bobby closed his eyes and listened. As a student, he had always loved the swirling bronze melody of the carillon. Ten years ago, he had gone to Cal on a swimming scholarship. He majored in business, pledged a fraternity, and flunked out his junior year.

"See you later," he said, standing up and collecting his things, but the homeless man ignored him. In his own pungent way, this guy was a snob, and Bobby could respect that. It was a snobbery well earned. When he died alone in a gutter, in a puddle of his own piss, he would take with him a crazed and singular form of expertise. Bobby ran his fingers through his buzz cut. He wished he had a nice hat to doff, a bowler cap or fedora. He hated belonging to such a crude and hatless generation.

He sat down at a computer. His Yahoo! mailbox was filled, almost exclusively, with undeleted spam. Some day, Bobby imagined, a single pill would grow hair, restore virility, and consolidate debt, but until then the market was wide open and he still had a chance to capitalize on his terrible idea. With this in mind, he scrolled down and was relieved to find a response from Nora. He had been trying to reach her all week, to get her advice on how he should go about branding the Man Handle, but she wouldn't answer her phone or reply to his e-mails. This happened sometimes. She was director of marketing for a company that sold investment-management software. When she was on the road, she closed ranks and forgot about everybody in her life who wasn't a client or prospect. He would go weeks without hearing from her. Then she would come back to the city, haggard and lonely and claiming that she was sick of her job, that she was ready to meet a decent man and go into full suburban lockdown. Nora was tall and pale, and because of her stylish pixie haircut and listless expression men often asked her if she was a model. She had actually paid her way through college doing catalogue work, posing in cardigans next to duck ponds, but she liked to tell men that she was dying of consumption. Bobby and Nora had always shared a certain ghoulishness. At his father's funeral, when they were both seniors in high school, she met him on the front steps of St. Bonaventure in Huntington Beach and said, "Your eulogy sucked." They rode together from the church, passing a bottle of Jameson back and forth, and when they got to the gravesite Nora took off her heels and ran across the expansive lawn, scattering crows like a burst of black confetti.

Now and then she met a guy who appreciated these qualities in her, but it would never last. They either got frustrated with the demands of her career, or she got bored with them. Bobby despised most of the men she dated. She had a weakness for solvent hipsters—architects, creative directors at advertising agencies, and other lieutenants in the corduroy mafia. They all supported progressive causes, not in any active or financial way, but just in general, as they walked around the city in vintage Japanese tennis shoes. And yet, in some ways, Bobby understood the plight of these slender princelings. Nora had a unique gift for turning cold on people.

The last time he saw her was three months ago, in May, when she asked him to accompany her to Geneva Software's Annual Client Appreciation Party. The latest staff restructuring had decimated marketing and direct sales, so her boss, Dave Grant, executive vice president and general manager of global accounts, had encouraged the survivors to bring guests, because the clients would feel more at ease in a full room. "There's free food for you," Nora told Bobby. "Just look presentable and keep me entertained." He got a haircut, wore a gray suit that he found in a roommate's closet, and in a hotel bar overlooking Union Square he shook hands with Nora's colleagues, mostly men, who seemed weirdly impressed by the fact that Bobby was stuck doing plumbing work. He used to work summers with his dad, doing repair and remodel jobs, so he knew what he was doing most of the time, but he didn't have a license and he was getting paid under the table by a shady house flipper in Castro Valley who had posted an ad on Craigslist. But still, the men from Geneva Software expressed wonder and delight, as if they were shaking hands with a sea captain or gunslinger. When Bobby asked what they did, most seemed vaguely ashamed that they were marketing associates or software engineers; in parting, they all shook his hand with a firmer grip than they did before.

Nora introduced him to Dave Grant, who, despite being the boss, seemed nervous around her. "That fucker's in love with you," said Bobby, as soon as Dave left, and Nora feigned vomiting. They were having a great time. Someone handed Bobby a drink; someone else, mistaking him for a client, handed him a gift bag filled with coffee mugs and key chains emblazoned with the Geneva logo. He watched a stray red balloon wedge itself in the crystal arm of a chandelier. Bobby told Nora that he wanted a job with her company—"I have sales experience," he reminded her, crushing a lime into his vodka—but then one of her company's actual clients found her and said hello. Nora turned her back on Bobby and began speaking in tongues. Bobby heard the word *functionality* repeated over and over. She made no attempt to introduce Bobby, and for a long time he hovered behind her, feeling invisible. When the client finally left, she turned around like nothing had happened. Later, in the cab, Bobby screamed at her. "You *literally* turned your back on me."

"It was client-appreciation night, not Bobby-appreciation night," said Nora, offering him a sip from the bottle of champagne she had stolen on the way out. When they stopped at a light, he grabbed the champagne bottle and threw it out the window. It smashed against the curb, and for moment they both sat there in silence; then Bobby jumped out of the cab.

He hated Nora for a couple weeks, but kept hoping for her to call and apologize to him. When his cell phone got shut off, he checked his e-mail obsessively, but there was nothing. Since they were kids, growing up a few blocks from each other, they had always fought and made up, and the time in between was pure desolation. But he never heard from her, and he realized that he was being overly sensitive and a little self-righteous. He envied Nora's ability to turn herself on and off, to indulge in vile misanthropy one minute and false pleasantry the next. This golden switch guaranteed her future. She had a great place in the Richmond, and on more than one occasion she had loaned him money, though both knew it was a donation. He didn't have the on-off switch, and he understood now, with thrilling clarity, that Nora's path to success—corporate, dignified, incremental—would never work for him. Bobby required a bonanza.

In the e-mail he sent last night, or early this morning, he told her he would be in the city tonight, ready to show her the prototype. He encouraged her, only half joking, to bring along some of her venture-capital friends. The Man Handle, he explained, would appeal to the very men who had the power to invest in it. Indeed, it was a tool that no depraved capitalist could do without. He sketched out his business plan, which had evolved over the last few days from a few bullet points of satirical bombast to something that actually seemed plausible and real, and then he took some time to tell her how things had been going for him, personally, since they last spoke that night in the cab. In June, the house flipper had disappeared without paying Bobby for his last month of work. After that, he answered a Craigslist ad—"$$$$ Sales Pros Needed $$$$"—and got hired to sell ad space for an East Bay newspaper conglomerate. It was horrible, and he discovered, once again, how much he hated sales. At some point he stopped going to work, and by now he was pretty sure they had fired him. He was broke and the walls were closing in, but in this moment of darkness he had found inspiration. Cometh the Hour, Cometh the Man Handle: the thing pretty much marketed itself. However, his sudden lack of income and increase in free time was causing friction with his latest batch of roommates. The guy farthest down the hall, a programmer from Lahore, had caught Bobby using his laptop a few times, and Bobby knew that it was only a matter of time before the guy slit his throat with a bejeweled dagger. Looking back, it was a pretty macabre e-mail and it worried Bobby that her response was so short. Nora usually wrote back in a tone that was as equally paranoid and macabre, but this time she just said that if he was around, she could meet him for a drink in the city at eight o'clock, and she named her favorite Irish pub. Even worse, she had signed her name without the usual "love."

As he left the library, the alarm went off. A security guard asked to see his duffel bag. Bobby complied and watched the guard remove a book.

"I forgot to check it out," Bobby admitted.

The guard pulled out a twelve-inch length of brass pipe that had been wrapped in black grip tape, the kind that went on skateboards.

"What's this?" he asked.

"It's a prototype."

"Of what?"

"The dumbest thing ever invented."

Bobby grabbed the bag from the guard and brought his book to the front desk.

"Please get in line," said the young librarian, a cute and supremely archetypal librarian—shy, bespectacled, and wearing a green cardigan, the kind Nora used to model. Bobby had wanted to talk to this librarian for the last couple weeks, but it seemed that whenever he had a book to check out, the desk was occupied by some miserable crone who would give him grief about his fines. Now, with a clear-cut opportunity, Bobby felt suddenly embarrassed by his appearance; he wished he had shaved, but all of his roommates' razor blades were dull.

The librarian stood a few feet back from the desk.

"This will only take a minute," said Bobby, putting his book on the counter.

"You can't check out reference books," said the librarian.

"Just me, or everybody?"

"Everybody."

"I'm joking!" Bobby handed her the book. "What's your name?"

"Catherine."

"I'm Bobby."

She nodded, and Bobby felt good when he got outside. He finally knew her name, at least. In the distance he could hear the final movement of the carillon. Before he got on his bike, he turned back to the library, a block of dusty green marble reposing in the milky afternoon light. It looked like the palace of a Babylonian king.

Earlier that morning, on her flight back from Los Angeles, Nora examined a laminated safety card that depicted plucky cartoon figures surviving a series of airborne catastrophes. Whenever she got on a plane, some part of her hoped for a crash landing. She was interested in her own reaction to mortal danger—would she act stoically or just shit herself?—but more than anything, she thought about how fun it would be, afterward, going down one of those big, yellow, inflatable slides.

They were somewhere over the central coast. She could see brown hills, the ruffle of breaking waves. A few clouds dotted the sky, but otherwise it would be a pure, blue drop. Members of the Geneva marketing team were spread throughout the cabin, sipping coffee and staring at their laptops. In the next seat, Nora's assistant, Jill, scrolled through her iPod. Nora ordered a gin and tonic, and when the drink came she asked the stewardess if she ever had the chance to go down the rescue slide.

"No," whispered the stewardess, a cheerful, older woman with gorgeous silver hair. "And I hope I never do!"

She patted Nora on the shoulder, and, feeling her touch, Nora almost melted with gratitude. She wanted to follow the stewardess down the aisle and sit with her on the jump seats. She wanted to ask for a job application.

This year's CTI Media B2B Software Development Conference & Expo had been, as Nora feared, a brutal dry hump. Geneva had dropped ten grand for their booth, five grand for collateral inserts in the official conference backpacks, fifteen grand to have the Geneva logo placed on water coolers and cups spread throughout the exhibit hall, and twenty-five grand to sponsor a luncheon that featured, as entertainment, a sullen stand-up performance by a former cast member of *Saturday Night Live*. The carpet-bombing strategy had come down from Dave Grant, and with another staff restructuring on the way, Nora had asked him how he could justify this kind of spending. Dave felt confident that the risk would pay off, not so much in the short term, for staff, but down the road, for the company. "I'm sorry," he said, "but that's the reality of the situation." He showed some discretion, however, by staying in San Francisco and sending Nora to Los Angeles to handle the conference. That way, when she came back with a meager list of new prospects to hand over to sales, her name would be tarnished, not his. It was a suicide mission. Nora, who had always taken great comfort in the endless sorrow of Irish history, thought of de Valera sending Michael Collins to sign the Anglo-Irish Treaty.

For three days the pipe-and-curtain corridors were empty; the only people she really talked to were other software exhibitors. The asset managers and hedge-fund reps who did show up to sample the goods were greeted as liberators; they nodded their heads, shook hands, exchanged cards, and left each booth laden with spoil. Yesterday was especially bleak, and after packing up their booth, the Geneva marketing team ran up a huge tab at a trendy tapas bar. Nora considered tapas a scam, so she left early and walked by herself through the barren maze of downtown Los Angeles, hoping to get mugged. Then she hailed a cab and instructed the driver to take her to the nearest Del Taco, which was the only thing she missed about SoCal. At the Bonaventure Hotel she ate her number-six combo in a concrete alcove above the main lobby and spent an hour riding the glass elevators, feeling more relaxed than she had all week. Later, curled happily in bed, with a full stomach, she turned off her Blackberry and finished rereading O'Flaherty's *Famine*.

"Are you okay?" Jill asked.

"Yes."

"You're just staring out the window."

"I can see the ocean."

"If you're bored," she said, offering her iPod, "I have some NPR podcasts."

"I'm not a lesbian."

Jill laughed, mechanically, and reinserted her headphones. She had no time for the curdled sarcasm of her elders. A year removed from Stanford undergrad, Jill embodied the kind of blond, forthright striving that Nora associated with Viking oarsmen. Nora amused herself with visions of what would happen after the next restructuring. Jill weeping at her desk; Jill throwing herself off the roof; Jill running amok with a shotgun. But these were only fantasies; in the end Jill would use her severance to travel through Asia or South America, and then she would write about her experience in her business-school application.

The plane landed safely, and Nora and Jill got in a cab together. As they swerved onto the 101, Jill called her mom. She talked loudly and without embarrassment. Nora could never get over this—it was as if Jill and her mom were friends. Nora felt obliged, finally, to turn on her Blackberry. It was only ten o'clock, and she already had six e-mails from Dave Grant. There was a meeting at three o'clock in "The Golden Gate Room," which was actually just conference room B. Two years ago, when Dave became executive vice president and general manager of global accounts, he renamed all the conference rooms after local landmarks.

She scrolled down farther and saw another message from Bobby. He had a "business" idea, apparently, but she couldn't tell if it was a joke or not, which gave her a sinking feeling that she hadn't wanted to deal with in the middle of the conference. Now, as she opened his latest message, the sinking feeling came back. The first paragraph didn't seem to end. She kept scrolling, and the paragraph went on for another three or four pages. Entire sections were set off in parentheses. She went back to the top of the e-mail and saw that he had sent it at four o'clock in the morning.

They drove past Candlestick Park and through the gloomy hills of South San Francisco. The peninsula was shrouded in fog, but across the bay Nora could see the bright green hills of Berkeley and Oakland. He was somewhere over there, marauding in sunlight. She wrote back quickly, telling him she could meet for a drink. She would have to collect him, get him drunk in a friendly atmosphere, and bring him back to her place and slip him a Valium. It had worked before. Then she would call his mom, who was now remarried to a blackjack dealer and living in a trailer outside Las Vegas. She would be very worried but in the end offer no real help. Nora's parents had always been there to bail out Bobby's parents—Bobby's father, an independent contractor, had been a better plumber than businessman—and this arrangement had been passed down to the next generation. Six years ago, when Nora announced that she gotten her dream job in San Francisco, everyone on both sides of the family, instead of congratulating her, said with great relief, "You'll be near Bobby!" So now she would collect him, again, and then he would end up sleeping on her couch for a month or two, eating all her food and generously offering to move in full-time, to help her out. The worst part was this: they would have a great time together, staying up late, watching crap on TV, and she would miss him when he was gone.

With a few hours to kill, Bobby decided to have a swim at the Claremont, a luxury hotel and country club in the Oakland Hills. He rode his bike through campus and down Telegraph Avenue. He saw people on the sidewalk selling tie-dyed shirts, and he smelled vomit waft-ing down from People's Park. As a rule, he believed in the extermi-nation of hippies, but here he was, ten years on, still hanging around Berkeley. After he flunked out of school, Bobby thought he would re-turn to SoCal, but his mom wasn't there anymore, and neither were any of his high school friends. He kept trying to leave Berkeley, but then he would find a job or a new girlfriend. He paid cheap rent in the flats, and he stayed in good shape riding his bike everywhere. Nora, on one of her rare visits to the East Bay, told him that he might as well learn how to play the sitar.

By the time he got across town and up the hill, he was soaked in sweat. He locked up his bike and took a path that led to the back of the hotel. Three years ago he got a job at the Claremont's poolside café. During his orientation, as he sat between two Senegalese na-tionals, the hotel's operations manager said that if anyone took more than fifteen minutes for their breaks, they were stealing from the ho-tel. Bobby didn't mind the job. He walked around the pool all day, de-livering gourmet sandwiches. The sprawling patio offered panoramic views of the East Bay, and on clear days you could see the Golden Gate Bridge. For a while he dated another server, who had just grad-uated from high school. One afternoon she stole a pass key from a maid, and they fucked for fifteen minutes in the tower suite. In the fall, she left for college, and shortly after, Bobby got fired for stealing avocados from the kitchen.

Café employees used to take their smoke breaks on a balcony overlooking the tennis courts, but members complained and so management set aside a designated smoking area behind the hotel, next to the Dumpsters. This was where Bobby found a high school kid in a café uniform. He asked him to get Salif, who, after three years, was still working as a cashier. "Tell him Bobby's here," he said. "We're old friends."

A few minutes later, Salif arrived. He was fifty years old, tall and spindly, with yellow teeth and gray hair. Bobby once asked him what he did in Senegal, before coming to the United States, and Salif told him that he had worked in a hotel.

"This is the last time," said Salif.

Bobby laughed. "You always say that."

At the pool gate, Salif told the guard that Bobby was a hotel guest who had lost his key card. They walked in together and Bobby threw himself on a lounge chair.

"I want an eggplant sandwich," he said, "and a glass of Chardonnay."

"Fuck you," said Salif, in his sharp French accent.

It was warm and sunny, but across the bay Bobby could see fog rolling over the city. The guy in the next lounge chair was snoring. All around him, women shuffled around in white robes, on their way to spa treatments. Bobby once bought Nora a treatment for her birthday—he got an employee discount—but when she came she ended up getting drunk in the hotel bar and never made it to her massage.

Bobby jumped into the water and for a long time did an easy breaststroke, so he wouldn't splash anybody. He lost track of his laps. At some point, a bunch of kids dragged him into an epic game of Marco Polo. Volunteering to be all-time "it," Bobby torpedoed through the crystal-blue depths, hearing muffled screams on the surface. Every time he popped out of the water, he shouted "Marco" as loud as he could. He could hear his voice echoing across the patio. The kids loved it and answered in kind. All his victims sat along the side of the pool, cheering on the last two kids in the water. Bobby trapped one of them in a corner, and then heard footsteps on the pavement. "Fish out of water!" he yelled, right before he heard a thud and a collective gasp. Opening his eyes, he saw a boy crying and holding his head. A few moms in white robes ran to him and started calling for hotel staff. Bobby ducked underwater and swam to the other side of the pool. He grabbed his bag and left without drying off.

Coasting down Ashby Avenue, he kept seeing colorful flags out of the corner of his eye. It was like riding past a row of embassies, but when he turned to look, the flags were gone. At the BART station, Bobby walked to the end of the platform and stood by the tunnel, bracing himself for the rush of wind. Inside the train he concentrated on the BART map, its routes marked by elementary bars of red, yellow, and blue. It kept his mind off the black watery abyss waiting above him.

He got off at Powell, emerging into cold, gray twilight. In his T-shirt and damp boardshorts, he thought he might freeze to death waiting for the 38 bus, so he did jumping jacks until it arrived. He sat next to the window, looking down on Geary Boulevard. At one stop, in the heart of the Tenderloin, an old drunk staggered up the steps and offered the driver a bouquet of dead transfers. The driver motioned for him to take a seat, but instead the guy walked down the aisle to the exit doors, threw his transfers in the air, and hopped off. Bobby laughed, but no one else on the bus seemed to notice the man's performance.

The pub was in the Richmond. It was nice and warm inside, and the walls were decorated with portraits of poets and rebels. He had been here a few times before with Nora, who described it as "a proper pub." Now that she had money, Nora spent all of her vacations in Ireland. It was her bizarre way of establishing legitimacy, like some derelict countess tracing her bloodline to an ancient king. Bobby didn't understand why someone who was born and raised in Southern California cared so much about a wet, miserable country she had no real connection to; but she always came back from her trips seeming refreshed, like she had gone home.

The girl tending bar looked underage. He asked if he could make a local call.

"I'll let you dial the number," he offered.

Her face was pale and freckled, like Nora's, and once again Bobby wished he had shaved. She handed him the portable phone and walked down to the other end of the bar. When Nora didn't answer her work phone, he quickly hung up and tried her cell. She didn't answer, so he left a message:

"Hey, it's Bobby. I hope you're having a proactive day, adding value and so forth. I'm at the bar. I got here early. I'm going to run a tab and let you pay for it when you get here. I'll probably need to stay at your place tonight. Also, my cell phone got turned off. And I need a new kidney. And the mob wants to kill me. And I've got the stigmata, again. Hurry up and get here."

He gave back the phone and asked for a menu.

"They're doing a pork chop tonight," the bartender said. She had an Irish accent.

"That sounds great. I'll start a tab."

"I can't run a tab without a credit card."

"Where in Ireland are you from?"

"A small place. You've never heard of it."

"I bet my cousin's been there. You two should talk. She'll be here soon. Do you know her? Nora Sullivan. She's in here a lot."

"I do know her," she said. "She always puts 'Fairytale of New York' on the jukebox."

"She said to go ahead and start a tab for her. She's on her way."

"I need a card."

Bobby handed her a credit card. "This one's expired, but just barely."

Her face was blank, but somehow a friendly blank. She took the card, and he ordered a Guinness and a pork chop.

A few men in the bar were wearing suits. One gentleman, grinning warmly at the bartender as he ordered a drink, had on a paisley tie and a sharp-looking vest. In this den of brass and mahogany, Bobby felt a sudden kinship, and once again, he wished for a hat, something he could remove in their presence, as a sign of respect. He pictured himself sitting in a top-floor office, with papers spread neatly before him, awaiting his signature, and he saw on the far side of the polished table, cast in silhouette against the window, a row of faceless investors, nodding silently to one another, communicating annualized return rates through some sinister form of clairvoyance. Bobby was excited to shake hands with these fragrant and shadowy men. Once they felt the rugged texture of his hand, they would instantly understand the physical and psychological advantages provided by the Man Handle, and they would have no choice but to furnish Bobby with grotesque sums of money.

His pork chop was dry, but he enjoyed it, gristle and all, and ordered another Guinness and a basket of fries. He finished those, ordered another Guinness, and at some point John, Paul, George, and Ringo walked through the front door. Four guys wearing Beatles wigs and dark, high-button suits. They were lugging instruments. Bobby called over to the bartender, and she said it was Beatles night. A bunch of cover bands were going to play.

"Why are you making concessions to the British?" he asked.

"It's just some locals playing music."

"Why not a U2 night?"

"Because I'd fucking gag," she said, taking his empty glass.

In walked four Sgt. Peppers, arrayed in full Edwardian pomp.

"Who the fuck *are* these guys!" said Bobby, but the bartender was helping other customers. The pub was getting crowded. One of the mop-top Beatles, a short husky guy in his forties with a red, pock-marked nose, came up to the bar to order drinks. He had meaty hands, and he was holding a scuffed pair of drumsticks.

"Ringo!" said Bobby, slapping him on the back.

Ringo looked startled, but smiled.

"You guys are really going for it," said Bobby.

"That's what we do," said Ringo. "We always go for it on the second Thursday of every month." He tapped the brass bar rail with his sticks. "How's your night going?"

"Me?" Bobby was taken off guard. He couldn't remember the last time somebody had asked him a question about himself. "I'm meeting my cousin. She's late. It's already nine o'clock. I'm worried she's not coming. She's in here all the time. Do you know her?"

Bobby described Nora, and as it turned out, Ringo did know her. He pointed across the bar to the band's John Lennon and said the poor guy had tried asking her out, without success.

"What's Lennon's day job?" Bobby asked.

"He doesn't have one at the moment."

"Then he doesn't have a chance," Bobby laughed. "Nora tries to slum, but she doesn't have the heart for it. She's going to marry somebody rich and boring."

"I thought she was very nice when I talked to her."

"I don't think she's coming."

"That's too bad."

"No, no! That's the thing. I should be in a bad mood, but I'm excited to hear you guys play."

"Are you a big Beatles fan?"

"Can you guys play 'Paperback Writer'?"

"We can definitely do that."

The bartender brought over four bottles of beer, and Bobby, with a gallant flourish of his hand, indicated that this round was on him.

"I hope you guys had fun at the conference. I want to hear all about it, but first a few things. Now keep in mind, this isn't me talking, this is everybody, and the reality is we need a back-up strategy for wealth creation."

Dave Grant picked up his juggle balls. Once they were in flight, he paced back and forth in front of a window that looked down on the bright streets of SoMa. The Geneva offices were next door to the birthplace of Jack London. A plaque commemorated the site, and whenever Nora walked past it at lunch, she liked to imagine the old waterfront, a proper sink of iniquity, crawling with proper scoundrels and proper whores. She now sat on one side of the conference table, next to Jill and the rest of the marketing team. Mike LaBrocca, head of sales, sat on the other side of the table with his team, a pack of hyenas from third-tier M.B.A. programs who spent their days quoting *Old School* and refreshing ESPN.com. A star-shaped conferencing unit at the center of the table transmitted the meeting to satellite offices in Chicago and New York. These people could hear Dave, but they couldn't watch him juggle. In spite of herself, Nora liked watching Dave juggle. It was soothing and hypnotic. He was only thirty-two, a wunderkind who decorated his office with memorabilia from his lacrosse days at Princeton and his stint in Guatemala with the Peace Corps. He spoke Spanish to the cleaning staff, expressing gratitude for their hard work. This annoyed Nora, and even worse was the fact that most of the janitors seemed to genuinely like Dave, often seeking him out to say hello. They never said hello to her. Dave worked insane hours, and yet somehow he made time to participate in a lot of expensive outdoor hobbies—kayaking, rock climbing, action kites. He had a nice tan and a nice family, too; his wife and three boys were installed in a Noe Valley town house. One of his boys had survived leukemia.

"I want to emphasize that we're not being reactive here, just opportunistic."

"I want to hear about the conference," said Mike.

"You bet. Nora can give us a rundown in a minute. But first I'd like to say a few things to get us started."

"Did you talk to anyone from Pinnacle?" said Mike quickly, ignoring Dave. "I've been priming them for months."

"No," said Nora.

"So you guys basically went down to L.A., passed out some hats and water bottles, and then went to the beach."

"Pretty much. I spent the whole week snorting coke off George Clooney's ass."

"Okay, okay," said Dave, with a nervous laugh. "Let's try not to have a tone here."

"Did you talk to *anybody*?" Mike continued, rising up in his chair. "I haven't heard a word from you guys all week."

"As a lover, George is both tender and thorough."

"That's great. Thanks, Nora. My guys are in the trenches all day, trying to sell . . . "

"*Trenches*? Is that a bar in the Marina?"

"No, I'm talking about actual trenches."

"Like World War I?"

"No, of course not," said Mike, rolling his eyes. "I don't mean *actual* trenches."

"Like *All Quiet on the Western Front*?"

"Look, I would never compare myself to a soldier. I'm just saying that right now all the pressure's on us. On sales."

"There's a passage where one character is trapped down in the trenches, and the only way he can get out is to take a knife and tunnel his way through the corpse of a dead comrade. He literally digs his way through the guy's intestines."

Dave put down his juggle balls.

"Actually, Mike, I did talk to Pinnacle. Did you know they changed their name to the Randers Capital Group? Did you even know that? They want to upgrade their multicurrency capabilities."

"That's great," said Dave, "but from a business-justification perspective you guys need to understand the role you play. Right now there's a disconnect between them and us about what *commitment* means."

The room went quiet. Mike, with his eyes closed, said, "Who's 'them,' Dave?"

"'Them' is everyone."

"Let Nora talk. I want to hear about the conference."

"Who said that?"

"It's Gabe in Chicago. I want to hear about the conference."

"Hi, Gabe! While I'm thinking about it, I have a question on the finance side of things. And I'm throwing this out there to everyone, but mainly finance. What is the process in the event that cost-basis information is not available when the action becomes effective? Do we get notified and reprocess internally, or does the corporate-action service prepare cancellation and rebook transactions to the blotter?"

"It goes both ways."

"Is that still you, Gabe?"

"Yes, it's me. It goes both ways. The door swings both ways."

Dave resumed juggling. "What's so funny?"

"That's *Ghostbusters*," said one of the sales guys. "He's talking about Gozer the Gozerian."

"Who?" said Dave.

"John Belushi was supposed to be in that, but he died," said a mysterious voice in either Chicago or New York. "Bill Murray took his place."

Another voice said, "Eddie Murphy was supposed to be in it, too. He was going to play the African American guy."

"Winston Zeddemore."

Gabe's voice said, "So Nora was going to tell us about the conference."

"Let Nora talk," said several voices all at once.

Nora's presentation didn't last long. She handed over a very small list of "promising potential prospects"—that's how she phrased it—and Mike and his sales team walked out in disgust. Afterward, Jill followed Nora back to her office. The brick corridors were dim and quiet. There wasn't a single phone ringing anywhere in the world.

"Are you okay?" Jill asked.

"Please stop asking me that."

"What's Mike's problem?"

"He needs prospects. That's our job."

"What about Randers?"

"Who?"

"The guys who used to be Pinnacle."

"I made that up. I wasn't going to let Mike ambush me like that."

Jill leaned against the door frame. "I'm not sure that was the best idea."

"It doesn't matter. We're fucked."

"What do you mean? Do you know something?"

"Go call your mom," said Nora. "Tell her to fluff the pillows on your bed."

Jill looked at Nora with a sudden and superior calm. "I know you're upset right now, and I know you don't like me. But there's no reason for you to talk to me like that. It's totally unprofessional."

"Fuck off."

Nora's screen saver was a picture she had taken last winter at the Cliffs of Moher. She went late in the day and had them all to herself, except for a group of young Russians, who hopped over the safety rail and pranced right along the edge, goofing around with one another, daring the wind to blow them into the ocean. A seven-hundred-foot drop, jagged rocks, and crashing waves, but these Russians carried on, brave and merry in the face of death. She checked her e-mail and in the minute that had passed since the meeting ended, Dave had managed to schedule another meeting with her at the end of the day.

There was a brief note from Bobby, saying he was excited to see her tonight. For a while she tried reading his previous e-mail, the six-thousand-page epic. Parts of it made her laugh—what the hell was the Man Handle?—but most of it didn't make any sense. The worse part was that he seemed to know which parts didn't make any sense. She knew where this was going. The first time it happened, in college, campus security found him in the life-sciences building, throwing pinecones at the giant skeleton of the *Tyrannosaurus rex*. A couple of his fraternity brothers brought him to the emergency room. He told the doctors he couldn't sleep. His grades were terrible, his girlfriend had broken up with him, he didn't know what he wanted to do with his life—the same stuff everybody worries about, but he couldn't get a handle on it, and everything snowballed. It happened again four years later, after he got fired from his hotel job. Nora saw this one coming. As his situation got worse, he became more and more cheerful, and his phone calls started coming later and later. She brought him to her apartment and got him to sleep, and later demanded that this time he get on some regular medications, or at least get some regular therapy. Bobby told her he was fine, and for a couple years he was, but then he broke up with another girl, lost another job, and it happened all over again. He didn't have health insurance, and Nora paid his emergency-room bill. Three months ago, when he threw the champagne bottle out the window, she probably should've seen it coming, but even if she did, she no longer felt any power to do anything about it.

She closed her office door, thinking she was about to cry. But she didn't. Something rattled in her chest, but she didn't cry.

At six o'clock, she walked down to Dave's office. When he saw her at the door, he stopped juggling and reached for his jacket.

"Do you want to get out of here?"

They went down the street to a sports bar. The Giants were playing, so they had to fight their way through crowds moving toward the waterfront stadium. Dave kept looking back, as if he might lose her, and Nora realized she had never been alone with him. Here, in public, the veneer of dynamism fell away, and he seemed pensive and unsure of himself. When he brought over their pitcher, he spilled some on the table and got flustered as he looked for napkins.

"I'm sorry," he said, and carefully wiped down the table, sopping up every drop. Then he sat down, took a sip of beer, and Nora knew what he was going to say.

"At this point in time, Nora, we need to start thinking about migrating some of our resources to an outside vendor."

"Do I still have a job?"

"Yes! God, I'm sorry!" He almost spit out his beer. "I mean, that's the good news. For you, I mean. I'm not explaining this very well. Listen, we've decided to make some major...in a couple weeks. Direct mail, prospect management, customer analytics—we can't justify those costs right now."

"Are you leaving anything in-house?"

"Like I said, we can't justify . . ."

"Who's left?"

"You, mostly. The plan is to shift you into more of a liaison role with sales."

Nora leaned forward, slowly, and rested her forehead on the edge of the table.

"I want you to know that I fought for you and your team. But mostly you. That's why I wanted to maximize our profile at the conference. I was hoping something good might happen."

"That was a great plan, Dave. Thanks."

"I know this isn't ideal for you, but I did—I really fought for you."

"I heard you," she said, lifting her head, "and I said, 'Thanks.'"

"But you were being sarcastic. Which is okay. I understand. That's how some people cope with challenging situations. It's something I've always liked about you, the way you're kind of . . . Everyone in the office enjoys your sense of humor. But listen, I fought for you and, going forward, I think you'll be in a good position. As Geneva evolves, you'll be right there, with me, delivering the . . ." Dave stopped for a moment and stared at his beer. Finally, he cleared his throat. "Basically, the kind of mission-critical solutions that address the needs of our clients."

Outside the window a scalper was yelling and waving tickets. Nora asked in a sour tone if Geneva was going to sacrifice their luxury box at the ball park. Dave looked hurt, as if she had failed to understand something obvious, and said, "I fought for you."

Nora suddenly understood the evening's shape and direction. It was like floating on a river and hearing a waterfall in the distance. She signaled the waitress for another pitcher, and for the next hour she watched Dave get drunk. He couldn't handle his liquor, but that seemed part of whatever clumsy plan he had set in motion. By the time they got to the third pitcher, Dave was trying to pet Nora's arm. She lightly removed it, and he looked ashamed. She got the feeling that he had never tried anything like this before. It was almost touching. Eventually, his seduction devolved into a series of whimpering confessions about his family life and the pressures he was under at Geneva. He and his wife were constantly at odds, and he got the feeling that if the next restructuring didn't work out, he might get the ax himself.

"It's been a difficult time for me," he said.

Nora, still relatively sober, figured that if she offered him a choice, right now, between fucking her or crying like a little boy on her shoulder, he would choose to cry.

Dave paid the tab, and they started walking towards Market, without any real destination in mind. At a crosswalk, he tried to kiss her, but she pushed him away.

"I saw something the other day," he said, as they kept walking. "We took the boys to Golden Gate Park for a picnic. We're sitting there and a kid walks out of the bushes. She's a punk-looking kid. She could've been twelve years old or nineteen. I have no idea. But she's in ratty clothes, and I swear to God she's got a homemade bow and arrow slung over one shoulder and a dead cat over the other.

She walked right past us, like we weren't even there."

"I want another drink," said Nora.

Dave stepped away and made a phone call. They walked down Kearny and into North Beach. On the way, Nora's phone rang. It was Bobby. She let it go to voice mail and listened to the message.

"What's so funny?" Dave asked.

"Nothing," she said, and when they finished their second round of cocktails at nine o'clock, she turned off her phone and said, "Let's get dinner."

"Next time Nora's in, she'll take care of it. I swear."

"It's fine. Do you want your credit card back?"

"No, keep it. As a token of my affection."

The bar backs were wiping down counters and turning off the lights. A fat Beatle was onstage, whistling to himself and unplugging his amps. Bobby picked up his bag and followed the bartender out the front door, where a few other Beatles were smoking. Ringo smiled and waved to Bobby.

Geary Boulevard was a cold, misty hollow, tilting toward the ocean. Bobby saw the bartender getting in a cab and ran after her.

"Where are you going?" he said.

"Home."

"You should stick around."

"Let go the door, you fuck!"

He heard voices behind him. A pair of John Lennons were moving toward him saying, "Hey, hey, hey . . ."

"Hold on," he said, turning back to her. "I want to show you my Man Handle."

He reached into his bag, and she started to scream. Before he could show it to her, someone grabbed him around the waist. Bobby tumbled to the ground. He watched the cab's red taillights disappear down the street. Slowly, the Fabs dispersed. Ringo helped him up.

"What the hell?" said Bobby.

"They thought you were about to do something."

"Do what?"

"Hit her."

"I'd never hit a pretty girl."

Bobby grabbed his bag and started walking down the sidewalk. Ringo caught up with him and asked if he was all right.

"Which way is the ocean?" Bobby asked. "I'm freezing out here."

"Do you want a ride?"

"Can you take me to Nora's house? It's around here somewhere."

As they turned and walked past the bar, one of Ringo's bandmates said, "What are you doing, man?"

"I'm giving him a ride."

"Tell him to take a cab."

"He bought us drinks all night."

Ringo had somehow packed his drum kit into the trunk of his Honda Civic. The trunk didn't close all the way, but he had everything secured with bungee cord.

"I'm glad Nora flaked," said Bobby, as they drove off. "I had a blast tonight. You guys are unbelievable. Where'd you get the wig?"

"It's not a wig."

"Bullshit!"

"It's not. I swear."

"Do you go to work like that?"

"I teach music. No one cares what I look like."

"That's lucky."

The avenues were washed out in an orange, syrupy light. It was like driving around inside a pharmacy bottle. All the houses looked the same. Bobby told Ringo to stop.

"I think this is it."

He rang the bell several times. Inside a dog started to bark, which was a bad sign, because Nora didn't have a dog. He heard footsteps in the hall, and the door opened. Behind the metal security screen, an old woman in a bathrobe was looking at him.

"Who are you?" she said.

Bobby turned around and was glad to see Ringo still there, with the engine running. He ran down the steps and got back in the car.

"I thought that was it," Bobby said. He tried calling her with Ringo's cell phone. She didn't answer. They drove around some more, but Bobby had no idea where to go. BART had stopped running and so without any other choice, he asked Ringo if he would mind driving him downtown, so he could catch the Transbay bus.

"I took it once a few years ago," said Bobby. "It was all junkies and janitors."

Ringo puffed out his ruddy cheeks and tapped a beat on his steering wheel. Finally, he offered to let Bobby crash on his couch.

"You're a soft touch," Bobby said. "That's what Nora says whenever she loans me money. She says, 'Lucky for you, I'm a soft touch.' "

"My wife will be asleep," Ringo said. "So we have to be quiet."

They drove somewhere in the vicinity of Eddy and Divisadero and parked in the underground garage of a drab apartment building.

"What neighborhood is this?"

"I don't know. It's kind of a non-neighborhood. My wife calls it NoSo."

"What's that?"

"North of South."

"How long have you lived here?"

"Fifteen years."

When they entered his apartment, Ringo shushed him and went down the hall to change out of his suit. The furniture looked dingy and second-hand, but the walls were resplendent with Beatles memorabilia. Ringo came back out in sweatpants and asked Bobby if he wanted some tea.

"Nora drinks tea," said Bobby, absently, and walked over to the small strip of linoleum that marked off the kitchen. "Let me see your hands. Hold them out like this."

Ringo put out his hands, and Bobby grabbed them. "Now these are hands. This is what I'm talking about."

"What are you talking about?"

"There's texture here. Strength. Is that from drumming?"

"And guitar. I can play anything, really." Ringo dropped his head a little. "Jack of all, master of none. As they say."

"You look like a master to me."

Bobby grabbed his bag and handed Ringo the prototype. "This is the Man Handle. It gives your hands strength and texture."

Ringo looked at it and said, "I don't get it."

"Right now it's just some pipe and grip tape. But when you're sitting around, doing nothing, you squeeze it and roll it in your hands. That's all. After a while you get calluses."

Ringo started to roll it in his hands. "Okay. But I still don't get it."

"We're going to market it toward managers and executives, so they don't feel bad when they shake hands with plumbers and other righteous members of the working class. It puts everybody on equal terms."

"Why would they feel bad?"

"I don't know. It's psychological. Bankers want to be cowboys."

The kettle whistled. Ringo made two cups and brought them over to the couch.

"It sounds dumb when I say it out loud," said Bobby.

"I don't think it's any dumber than half the infomercials I see."

"Thank you! The bigger the lie, right? Well, the dumber the idea, the more people will buy it. These are standard marketing concepts. What's your real name, anyway?"

"Alex."

Bobby picked up his teacup and looked around the room. "Nora missed out. She should be here. Do you think something happened to her?"

"Are you worried?"

Bobby stood up and started to pace back and forth behind the couch.

"She was a fuckup in high school. She went to junior college, and now she makes six figures, easy. Easy." He sat down on the couch and got back up. "She hasn't been picking up her phone. I don't know if I should be worried. I think she's just mad at me. What part of town is this?"

"We can call the police," said Ringo. "If that would make you feel better."

Bobby sat back down. "No. I'm getting worked up over nothing. I had fun tonight. I've been talking and talking, but what about you? Are you good? Some of these guys Nora dates, they don't have any manners. They go on and on and by the end of the night I know everything about them and they don't know anything about me." Bobby looked out the window. "What floor are we on?"

"Third floor."

Ringo moved toward the hallway. He came back with a neatly folded blanket and placed it on the coffee table. "I'm going to bed. Will you be all right out here?"

"Don't go. There's probably something on TV."

Ringo declined with a polite smile and moved into the hallway.

"Have you ever been in a fancy hotel lobby, with all the clocks set to different times around the world?"

Ringo didn't answer. There seemed to be some invisible force dragging him toward the shadows.

"All of us should hang out sometime," Bobby called after him.

He watched *SportsCenter* on mute for a while and then brought a chair to the window. He stared at a street lamp farther down the street. He stared too hard and it flickered. All the street lamps flickered, one by one. Bobby wondered how many units were in the building. He closed his eyes, trying to hear how many. But the place was silent.

Ants were crawling on the tiles above the kitchen sink. He looked through the cabinets, but couldn't find any snacks. Then he was standing in front of the bathroom mirror, shaving, first his face, and then his head. In college, he used to shave his head before every swim meet. He ran the razor through sticky mounds of Barbasol, giving himself little nicks on the top of the skull. Halfway through he stopped and looked at himself. He suddenly wished he hadn't told Ringo about the Man Handle. It seemed to break the spell. Tomorrow he'd be back in the sunny East Bay, without any ideas. He wiped his head off and walked down the hall to the bedroom.

The door opened with a squeak, and there was Ringo, sleeping alone on a futon mattress. He was on his side, with his back to the door and a sheet pulled tightly to his chin.

"I can't sleep," said Bobby, walking into the room.

Ringo jerked awake. "What are you doing?"

"Scoot over, man," said Bobby. "I can't sleep."

Ringo reached for the bedside lamp, but Bobby jumped on the bed and knocked his hand away. Ringo rolled against the wall, with his back to Bobby. "Don't," he said, weakly, covering his head.

Bobby slid toward Ringo and put his arms around him, burying his face in the back of Ringo's neck. For a long time they didn't move.

"Let me turn on the light," said Ringo, finally, slinking down the bed. "Just for a second. Can I do that?"

"I can't sleep."

"I have something you can take."

"Don't go."

"I won't," he said, and the room filled with light.

Nora woke up right before her alarm went off. Halfway through her shower, she remembered that Dave was in the other room, sleeping peacefully on the couch. Only a few a hours ago, he had announced with a sense of triumph that he couldn't go through with the act it-self. Nora had shrugged and made coffee; then she listened to Dave talk about his family, the heartbreak and joy. "I'd be a fool to throw all that away," he said. She was impressed. By some miracle he had transformed the most despicable moment of his life into an opportu-nity to celebrate his own virtue. Now he would return home a better and more loving husband. Nora had fulfilled her role in his personal quest, just not in the way she imagined—this chaste and redemptive version, somehow, was even more hollow—and he thanked her for understanding what he was going through. "I quit," she said, and for a while he tried meekly to talk her out of it, strongly advising her to wait for the next restructuring, so she could collect severance. Nora, con-fused, said, "But I thought I was moving to a liaison role with sales." Dave admitted that he hadn't totally worked out the specifics on that.

Later, in bed, she thought of Bobby swimming the butterfly, the way his head would pop out of the water, in perfect rhythms, and the way he would suck in the air, as if every breath was going to be his last.

It was a bright, gray morning. Nora finished dressing and came out to the front room. Dave had already left. The down comforter she had given him was piled on the floor between the couch and coffee table. She folded it and left for work.

Jill was waiting for her when she got out of the elevator. She was her normal chipper self, having already forgotten the horrible way Nora had treated her yesterday. Nora found this deeply annoying; she had no patience for people who didn't hold grudges.

"Are you okay?"

"I'm hungover."

"There's a funny-looking guy in your office."

She recognized him from Beatles night at the pub. It was absurd seeing him now, in this context. He wore jeans and a ratty fleece, but the mop-top remained, crowning his pudgy, red face.

"I'm Alex," he said. "Bobby's asleep at my place."

Somehow this made total sense. Alex drove her to his apartment. The car's ashtray was overflowing, and he used T-shirts for seat covers.

"He thinks the world of you," he said.

"Why'd you take him back to your place?"

He looked at her, as if he didn't quite understand the question. "He was stuck out here."

Back at the apartment, Alex warned her that Bobby had tried to shave his head.

"Wonderful," she said. Alex made tea while Nora went to check on Bobby. When she sat at the edge of the bed, he looked at her with groggy eyes. He smiled and ran a finger along one of his bald streaks.

"How do I look?"

"Come on," she said. "I'll fix it."

She brought him into the bathroom. He kneeled in front of the sink, staring at himself, while she quietly shaved his head. He smelled like chlorine. When Nora finished, she sprayed a wad of cream into her hand and ran it through her hair.

"What are you doing?" said Bobby.

Nora didn't say anything. She just handed him the razor.

CYNTHIA GORNEY

∎

Cuba's New Now

FROM *National Geographic*

"I WANT TO SHOW YOU WHERE WE'RE HIDING IT," Eduardo said.

Bad idea, I said. Someone will notice the foreigner and wreck the plan.

"No, I figured it out," Eduardo said. "You won't get out of the car. I'll drive by, slowly, not so slow that we attract attention. I'll tell you when to look. Be discreet."

He had borrowed a friend's *máquina,* which means "machine" but is also what Cubans call the old American cars that are ubiquitous in the Havana souvenir postcards. This one was a 1956 Plymouth of a lurid color that I teased him about, but I pulled the passenger door shut gently, the way Cubans always remind you to, out of respect for their máquinas' advanced age. Now we were driving along the coast, some distance from Havana, into the coastal town where Eduardo and nine other men had paid a guy, in secret, to build a boat sturdy enough to motor them all out of Cuba at once.

"There," Eduardo said, and slowed the Plymouth. Between two peeling-paint buildings, on the inland side of the street, a narrow alley ended in a windowless structure the size of a one-car garage. "We'll have to carry it out and wheel it up the alley," he said. "Then it's a whole block along this main street, toward that gravel that leads into the water. We'll wait until after midnight. But navy helicopters patrol offshore."

He peered into his rearview mirror at the empty street behind him, concentrating, so I shut up. Eduardo is 35, a light-skinned Cuban with short brown hair and a wrestler's build, and in the months since we first met last winter—he's a former construction worker but that day was driving a borrowed Korean sedan and trying to earn money as an off-the-books cabdriver—we had taken to yelling good-naturedly and interrupting each other as we drove around La Habana Province, arguing about the New Changing Cuba. He said there was no such thing. I said people insisted there was. I invoked the many reports I was reading, with names like "Change in Post-Fidel Cuba" and "Cuba's New Resolve." Eduardo would gaze heavenward in exasperation. I invoked the much vaunted new rules opening up the controlled economy of socialist Cuba—the laws allowing people to buy and sell houses and cars openly, obtain bank loans, and work legally for themselves in a variety of small businesses rather than being obliged to work for the state.

But no. More eye rolling. "All that is for the benefit of these guys," Eduardo said to me once, and tapped his own shoulder, the discreet Cuban signal for a person with military hardware and inner-circle political pull.

What about Fidel Castro having permanently left the presidency four years ago, formally yielding the office of commander in chief to his more flexible and pragmatic younger brother, Raúl?

"Viva Cuba Libre," Eduardo muttered, mimicking a revolutionary exhortation we'd seen emblazoned high on an outdoor wall. Long live free Cuba. "Free from both of them," he said. "That's when there might be real change."

If there is in fact a Cuba under serious transformation—and you can find Cubans all over the country engaging now in their own versions of this same debate—Eduardo is a crucial component of it, although not for the reasons you might think. "Dissident" is the right label for a subset of politically vocal Cubans, notably the bloggers whose critical online missives have gained big followings outside the country, but Eduardo is no sort of dissident. He's not fleeing persecution by the state. He's just young, energetic, and frustrated, a description that applies to a great many of his countrymen. Ever since he was a teenager in high school, Eduardo told me, it had been evident to him that adulthood in revolutionary Cuba offered exactly nothing by way of personal advancement and material comfort to anybody except the *peces gordos.* The big fish. (Well, literally translated, the fat fish—the tap-on-the-shoulder parties.) Nothing *works* here, Eduardo would cry, pounding the steering wheel of whatever car he'd hustled on loan for the day: The economic model is broken, state employees survive on their tiny salaries only by stealing from the jobsite, the national news outlets are an embarrassment of self-censored boosterism, the government makes people crazy by circulating two national currencies at once.

"I love my country," Eduardo kept saying. "But there is no future for me here."

Over nine weeks of traveling around Cuba this year and last, I heard this particular sequence of complaints so often, and from so many different kinds of people, that it began to form a kind of collective national lamentation: I love my country and it doesn't work. There were loyal optimists among the complainers, to be sure, and after a while, whenever I encountered one, I found myself marshaling ammunition to bring Eduardo. I wanted to hear how he'd respond, but when I was being honest with myself, I realized that I also wanted to talk him out of the boat. (Sharks swim in those Cuba-to-Florida waters. The currents are dangerous. There are drownings, people never heard from again.)

Optimist: Roberto Pérez, a shaggy-haired environmental biologist, filled with enthusiasm about the progress of Cuba's extensive urban agriculture and organic farming projects. Pérez is six years older than Eduardo. Eighty percent of his own high school graduating class, Pérez told me, has left the country. "But things are changing," he said. "Very fast. And there are so many good things here that people take for granted, because they were born with them. You tell me another place where a kid can grow up so safe, get his vaccinations, get his education, not be involved in gangs or drugs. I can see people crossing the river north from Mexico, to get away from that. But from here? To face the Florida strait? I fail to see it."

Still no? OK. Optimist: Josué López, exactly Eduardo's age, just immigrated back to Cuba after six years in Florida and a growing disenchantment with the values of some of his hyper-acquisitive Cuban émigré neighbors in Miami. López and his wife are going into business for themselves, taking advantage of the new self-employment laws and new flexibility in agricultural land use, and developing a bed-and-breakfast resort on a few acres they've acquired outside Havana. "I'm telling my friends who went to the States," López told me, in his practiced slangy English, "Dude! If you want to start something, the place to be is Cuba."

Eduardo would listen, interested, his face sober. He would shake his head. We were arguing in a café one morning, a rooftop spot in the historic part of Havana, and Eduardo grabbed a glass saltshaker from the table. "My whole *life*, the government has been telling us, Look! I'm giving you this nice full saltshaker!" he said. "But it's never full."

This one wasn't either. A half inch of salt, maybe. Eduardo put the shaker down and told me he had gotten hold of some oars. The men would have to row for a while, before they could risk motor noise that might alert authorities; the departure itself would violate Cuban law, since none of them had a *tarjeta blanca*, a white card, the government permission required of all citizens before they may leave the country, even temporarily. Cubans hate the tarjeta blanca, and the government subsequently hinted at doing away with it entirely—but on this early spring morning Eduardo hadn't even applied for one, since he assumed the tarjeta would be denied, as they sometimes are, with no explanation beyond the bland, omnipresent *No está autorizado*—It is not authorized. Besides, a Cuban applying for a tarjeta blanca is supposed to have a visa from the destination country. Just to secure a spot on the consideration list for a U.S. visa, a Cuban must pay $160 and produce a written invitation from some actual person living in the United States.

Eduardo had neither. I had expected him to solicit help from me, the money or the invite, but he never did; he just blurted out the boat plan one day in the middle of a long, talky car ride, as though he'd been desperate for a non-Cuban confessor, and now here we were staring at a saltshaker and brooding about Eduardo's son, who was nine and didn't know his father was going.

"I don't know if it will be better to tell him or worse," he said.

At least the money he'd send home would buy his son new shoes, Eduardo said. "Everything has a risk in life," he said. "I'm not worried. Use my real name. I've told you this before. Use it! I'm not afraid of anybody!" He spread his arms wide, trying to look unworried, and repeated his name the Latin American way: first name, paternal surname, maternal surname. I told him to quit being foolish, that he still lived in a one-party state in which people get roughed up or arrested or excoriated as mercenaries for criticizing their leaders too vigorously, and that we were talking about this in public only because the café waiter was a friend of his and nobody else was nearby. So forget it, I said. Sorry. No real name. We were quiet. Beneath us spread the most famous district in Cuba, the streets the tourists want to see first. There were shining 19th-century tile work, the filigreed top of a Corinthian column, a glimpse of the turquoise sea.

The whole city seemed to be shining, that morning with Eduardo, even though there'd been a *derrumbe* in the neighborhood where I was staying. That's a building collapse, a thing that occurs with some regularity, especially in Havana. Buildings that were once beautiful and grand are rotting now in the tropical air, and the country has no money to repair them, so they cave in, partially or all at once, a giant rumbling roar followed by rubble and grief. This derrumbe killed four people, three of them teenage girls; the building had been designated unsafe, but Cubans are inventive about their living space in Havana, where parts of the city are so crowded that multiple families and generations wedge into residences that in more decadent eras served as single-family homes. Eduardo had the idea that the number of deaths in my neighborhood derrumbe was 21—he had heard this via *radio bemba,* the radio of lips, which is what Cubans call the word on the street, the only censor-free method for the dissemination of discouraging domestic news. But I had been reading *Granma,* the national Communist Party daily, which to the surprise of many people had actually run articles about this derrumbe rather than pretending it had never occurred and was steadfast about the death toll of four. Anyway, the city looked shiny. The tourists were charging all over by the busload, maps in hand, and from what I could see they appeared to be having a great time, sipping their rum-and-mint *mojitos,* following their multilingual Cuban guides, and applauding the happy cacophony of rumba and *son* that spilled out into the plazas from restaurants and street corners and bars.

Unmistakably, and provocatively, unusual things were transpiring in the streets. In some neighborhoods half the buildings' doorways seemed to have been taken over by new self-employed vendors, the men and women sitting hopefully alongside makeshift displays of hair accessories or homemade pastries or DVDs of movies and television shows. "For Sale" signs, prohibited during the decades when it was legal to exchange residences but not to sell them, now appeared in house windows. In a few weeks Pope Benedict XVI was due to arrive, the first papal visit to Cuba in 14 years. Along the route the papal cortege would follow, state workers were cleaning and painting house facades so assiduously that I heard people joke that they wished the Holy Father would show up more often, just for the urban cleanup.

Hefty half-built structures stuck out here and there—the anti-der-rumbes, as I came to think of them, into which the country's sparse investment resources were being directed. High cranes and scaffolding delineated the rehabilitation of historic buildings, the gussying up of tourist destinations, the construction of new port facilities. From certain spots along the shoreline, you could make out the shape of the huge deepwater rig exploring the Cuban seabed, believed to contain billions of barrels' worth of oil. If large-scale oil production is merited, the possibilities for the country's economic future are profound.

Most of the Cubans I talked to seemed consumed, in fact, by this whole idea of possibility. Not permanent transformation, most would say, not yet; the Cuban government has a history of switching signals on its citizens, encouraging private enterprise and then pronouncing it counterrevolutionary and shutting it down again. But Raúl Castro is not his brother, and there's a particularly Cuban combination of excitement, wariness, calculation, black humor, and anxiety that accompanies even the possibility of real change—the suggestion that after a half century under Fidel, something big may truly be happening to the way Cubans live day to day. "The rebuilding of the house of Cuba," an ecclesiastical lawyer and editor named Roberto Veiga said gravely, pronouncing the Spanish words with the elegance of a pastor at the pulpit: *La reconstrucción de la casa Cuba.*

Careful, though: The rebuilding metaphor implies a blueprint. Those outside Cuba who imagine that this blueprint is agreed to by some clear Cuban consensus are deluding themselves. The unconstrained individualism of the United States, where neither health care nor a college education are free? The showy wealth and envi-

ronmental havoc of modern China? The economic woes and internal tensions of Europe? The narco wars of Mexico? "This is our great
challenge," Veiga told me. He helps run a publication of the Archdi-
ocese of Havana, *Espacio Laical* (literally, *Secular Space*), which, like
the Cuban Roman Catholic Church itself, has become one of the
few venues in which semicritical debate about the country's future
is aired in public. "What will it be like, this house of Cuba?" Veiga
asked. "These are changes that should have begun two decades ago.
But they didn't. And now we are a nation trying to define itself."

Eleven million people live in Cuba, less than the population of
central Tokyo. It's the biggest island in the Caribbean, and famously
only 90 miles from United States territory, but Cuba still grips the
international imagination mostly because the dueling narratives of
its history are so exaggerated by myth. Either a ruthless revolutionary took power in 1959, seized American corporate property, forced
out his country's own professional classes, and silenced all opposi-
tion by creating a totalitarian police state (that's the version audible
to this day on Miami's Radio Mambí, the broadcast voice of Florida's
most vehement anti-Castro community); or a brilliant revolutionary
led the overthrow of a corrupt dictatorship, shook off the colonialism
of foreign companies and the Mafia, brought literacy and health care
and egalitarian values to a mobilized people, and created a university-
educated bastion of socialism in spite of a half century of U.S. efforts
to destroy it by prohibiting Americans from doing business with or
spending tourist money in Cuba.

Both narratives contain substantial truth, both at the same time.
This is why Cuba fascinates and makes people's heads hurt. The
place is exhausting in its complexity and paradoxes—Cubans are the
first to tell you that—and the questions modern Cuba sets off in a
visitor are big, serious, unwieldy. What is the definition of freedom?
What do human beings need? What do they owe to each other? What
do they want, beyond what they need? "We've all been the subjects
of an experiment," a 58-year-old university-educated woman who
works in the arts told me thoughtfully one evening, chopping sweet
peppers in her kitchen for supper. She lives in an airy place, with a
fenced front lawn and a backyard patio, in a leafy part of Havana; the
home has belonged to her family since before the Triunfo, the Tri-

umph of the Revolution, as Cubans generally refer to the events of 1959. Her lightbulbs are compact fluorescents, the woman pointed out—one legacy of an ambitious national project a few years back, directing all Cubans to switch to lower watt fixtures in the interests of energy independence and the environment.

"They'd come to check," she said. "They would break your old bulbs, in front of you, to make sure you didn't sneak any back into your lamps." She smiled and looked over her glasses at me to make sure I was listening closely enough. She has one child, a son a decade younger than Eduardo—gone now, having bailed out on Cuba and obtained a therapy credential in Spain. "The idea was marvelous, to change all the lightbulbs," she said. "The problem is how they did it."

In its headline version, the rebuilding of the house of Cuba looks like this: Capitalism intrudes, around the edges, small bits at a time. Since 2010 more than 150,000 Cuban workers have left or been laid off from their state jobs, a concept previously unimaginable in a system that was supposed to provide all the work and all the social benefits. President Castro himself has said that the state apparatus is bloated and too conducive to dependence and corruption, and that the state must trim a half million workers. State agricultural land is now being leased in pieces to private farmers and cooperatives, and other kinds of legal self-employment are being gingerly promoted as well. Over the past two years the government has authorized 181 job-specific categories of *cuentapropismo*, as it's called—the keeping of one's own account.

Even the ration book—the *libreta* issued to all Cuban households, with its check-off columns for the state-subsidized basic foods every citizen is supposed to get each month—may be an artifact near the end of its time, Raúl Castro has said. The libreta! This is big. Nothing is more evocative of the bewildering Cuban economy, and Cubans' complicated reaction to it, than the baseball card-size libreta, each one stapled together from thin cardboard and white paper and listing the items the holder may buy at artificially low prices: rice, sugar, and milk, if the family includes children under eight. There are squares to be checked off by hand. The pages look like the accounting ledgers of Dickensian clerks.

Here are things I have watched Cubans do with the libreta:

Reinforce its fraying cover carefully with decorative paper and tape.

Hold it in one hand, a plastic shopping bag in the other, while sweating in the moist heat, gossiping with neighbors, waiting for subsidized bread.

Whip it from their purses or off kitchen shelves, shoving the opened pages at me, exclaiming simultaneously that it demonstrates Cubans' care for each other and that the allotments have been so cut back the government might as well be trying to starve them all.

Once I was in the home of a priest of Santería, the Afro-Cuban religious practice that is the faith even of many professed Cuban Catholics. I was still trying to compose myself because the priest had just completed an initiation ceremony that included slitting the necks of pigeons and chickens and bleeding their corpses into sacred dishes and praying in Yoruba. But what the priest really wanted to talk about was his libreta. "Look at this!" he cried. "Eight ounces of oil, per person, for a month! Ten ounces of beans! One package of pasta maybe every three months!"

There's a term Cuban housewives use as they make their rounds in search of the day's family food: *pollo por pescado*. It means "chicken for fish": You have promised fish for dinner, but in the stores there is no fish, so you get a little chicken and pretend it's your fish. Cuba is surrounded by seawater, of course. Where is all the fish? Ah, any Cuban will tell you, leaning in close, a merry gleam in his eye: glad you asked, *mi amor*. The fish is in the restaurants. The fish is in the hotel buffets, a popular amenity for tourists, where long counters are piled high with varieties and quantities of food no ordinary Cuban ever sees. The fish is being sold out of private homes, if you know which doorbell to ring.

In many of these locales the fish—like nearly every desirable product in Cuba, from nightclub admission to hair dye and plasma TVs and acid-washed blue jeans—is being sold in CUCs.

Now we come to that aspect of present-day Cuba that causes the *yuma* (that's the grammatically adaptable slang for "American," "foreigner," and also "the general outside world to the north and east") to reach for a calculator and some aspirin and a crash course in recent Cuban history. The CUC, which is shorthand for Cuban convertible peso, is one of the two official currencies of Cuba. Like the libreta, the double-currency system is in theory destined for extinction; things are so fluid in Cuba that by the time you read this, it's conceivable the government will have begun ending it. But to appreciate fully the elaborate survival negotiations that have dominated so many Cubans' daily lives in recent years, you have to come to grips with the essential weirdness of the CUC.

It's a recently invented currency, introduced a decade ago as a replacement for the dollars and other foreign money that began flooding and disrupting the country after the Soviet Union collapsed in 1991, thus ending the big-socialists-to-little-socialists financial support that had been holding up the Cuban economy. The multiyear Cuban depression that followed the Soviet breakup was catastrophic (fuel shortages, 14-hour blackouts, widespread hunger), and the government set out to counter it by throwing the island open to international tourism. This was all done rather fiercely, with a flurry of beach hotel building that continues to this day—current plans include multiple golf courses and jet-capacity airports—while anti-capitalist admonishments still declaim from highway billboards and urban walls:

SOCIALISM OR DEATH!
THE CHANGES MEAN MORE SOCIALISM!

In its purest concept the CUC is used for goods and services somehow connected to foreignness: hotel bills, international transactions, Fidel T-shirts in the souvenir shops, and so on. One CUC is worth about one U.S. dollar, and it's simple to obtain them; whether you're a yuma or a Cuban, state employees at exchange centers will take whatever currency you hand them and count out your reciprocal CUCs, wishing you a pleasant day when they're done.

These employees, like the rest of the Cubans who work for the state—currently about 80 percent of the country's labor force—are not paid in CUCs. They're paid in the other currency, the Cuban national peso. One national peso is worth 1/24 of a CUC, or just over four cents, and in socialist Cuba state salaries are fixed; the range as of mid-2012 was between about 250 and 900 pesos a month. Some workers now receive a CUC stimulus to augment their peso wages, and recent changes are lifting top-end salary limits and linking pay more to productivity than to preset increments. But it was Cubans who taught me the national comic line about public workplace philosophy: "They pretend to pay us, while we pretend to work."

In the city of Santa Clara, where the principal attraction is a massive monument to revolutionary martyr Ernesto "Che" Guevara (fought with Fidel, died trying to foment insurrection in Bolivia), I spent an afternoon with a visiting emergency physician whose medical salary was fixed at 785.35 national pesos per month. That works out to CUC$32.72. Like so much about Cuba, this isn't straightforward; Dr. M owes nothing for his professional education and his own family's medical care. His son's lifetime schooling is free. Produce and certain other basic foods not on the family libreta can be purchased in pesos, as can Cuban books, baseball game tickets, fares on the crowded public buses, and admission to museums and movie theaters and the ballet. The currency in which he is paid as a doctor will buy Dr. M the very kind of 1960s ascetic nationalism Che Guevara liked to espouse—in other words, as long as Señora M uses only the poor-quality peso soap, the M family brews only the peso coffee that comes with fillers ground in, and nobody ever buys deodorant.

"The toy truck I wanted for my son, with the little motor and remote control?" Dr. M said, as we stood side by side beneath the gigantic monument pedestal, craning our necks up at Che. "Forty CUCs."

Forty CUCs in a state store, that is. Cubans maintain a robust black market—por la izquierda, they call it, "over to the left"—in which anything can be obtained. But the most surrealistic aspect of life in Cuba 2012 is the vigor with which the government, the same entity paying Cubans in pesos, sells goods to Cubans in CUCs. Retail stores, like pharmaceutical factories and nickel mines, are national enterprises, run by the state. Clerks often don't bother specifying "CUC" on the pricing of merchandise either; if a thing whirs or glitters or comes in good packaging, Cubans know the currency in which it is being sold, and regardless of whatever the ghost of Che may be whispering in their ear, they want it.

By the time I met Dr. M, I had done so much confounded window-shopping that there were numbers all over my notebooks: Pepsodent toothpaste, CUC$1.50 per tube. Electric blender, CUC$113.60.

Upholstered loveseat-and-armchair living room set, CUC$597.35. Multistory malls, with cafés and video game halls and clothing stores, all functioning exclusively in CUCs.

The cell phones Cubans depend upon—pre-Raúl they were prohibited; now they're everywhere—are sold, both the device and the per-minute fees, in CUCs. Even a Bucanero Fuerte, one of the good Cuban beers, is likely to be sold in CUCs. The Bucanero price of one CUC, not an unreasonable sum in many countries for a bottle of beer, constitutes a full day's medical pay for Dr. M. You see the problem with the toy truck. This is why for four days a week, when he's supposed to be recuperating from his 24-hour emergency shifts, Dr. M drives a cab.

Technically, he drives his own car, the aged Russian beater he inherited from his father. But he picks up tourists in it, because tourists pay in CUCs. Over one high-season month Dr. M's cabbie days earn him the CUC equivalent of 15 times his salary as a physician. In Cuba there's nothing remarkable about this. The taxi fleet, like the rest of the tourist industry, is replete with splendidly educated Cubans no longer practicing their professions because their years of study to be of service to the nation—in engineering, medicine, psychology—produced salaries in "the money that's worthless," as a kindly Cuban bank teller once remarked to me. The phenomenon is referred to as the "inverted pyramid." Every Cuban who repeated that term to me did so in a tone of despair, as in: This, you see, is why the ambitious young keep leaving.

Dr. M and I studied the object Che was holding in his giant fist above us, determined that it was a hand grenade, and went into the museum. Che Guevara was an Argentine medical school graduate when he met Fidel Castro, and as we walked past the glass-encased displays of the Che medical journals and the Che lab coat, I glanced over at Dr. M. In the 15 years since Che's ashes were delivered to Santa Clara, Dr. M told me, this was the first time he had visited the museum. But he was silent and impassive, and when we came out, all he said was, "I don't get this about us now—how a taxi driver can make so much more than a doctor." The expression on his face made it clear that Che Guevara was not a topic he wished to continue exploring. "I don't get it," he said.

*   *   *

Eduardo told me the boat's departure date was set, depending on what the men could learn about tide and weather predictions, for the days just after the pope's visit ended. When I was away from Havana, in the island's interior, text messages from his number showed up every so often on my temporary Cuban phone: "hi my friend am going soon on vacation."

I was doing a lot of walking, or strapping on flimsy passenger helmets and climbing (imprudently) onto the backs of unlicensed motorcycle taxis. To my outsider's eye, the New Changing Cuba looked both real and raggedy, as though an enormous flea market had been busted up and scattered the length of the country. Young men sat in stairwells, offering to repair cell phones or refill cigarette lighters. Families lined their front porches with display tables of used kitchen merchandise or thermoses of coffee and chipped plates of wrapped ham-and-cheese sandwiches.

Here were small corner businesses that used to be run by the state but now, experimentally, were not: barbershops and snack bars, for example, in which management was being transferred to the employees. Here was a former high school math teacher, a soft-spoken 42-year-old who had learned to speak Russian fluently back in the comfortable days of life support from the U.S.S.R. Now he was selling baby clothes for CUCs from one corner of a rented streetfront foyer in the central city of Camagüey. "My wife does the sewing," the former math teacher said. "She used to be a teacher too."

And here, in the middle of one residential block back in Havana, was a chic new restaurant called Le Chansonnier. No signage marked the entrance; Le Chansonnier is a *paladar*, a privately run restaurant inside a home, and people with money—correction, people with CUCs—know where it is. Paladares have been legal for years in Cuba but used to be strictly contained, under the pretense that they were all tiny family operations siphoning no business from state restaurants. Since 2011, though, they've been allowed to expand and hire staff, and like the guest rooms Cubans may rent to foreigners inside their own homes and apartments, some of the popular paladares have basically turned into busy CUC cash registers for their owners. "I always dreamed of having my own business," the co-owner, a 39-year-old named Héctor Higuera Martínez, told me the afternoon

I stopped by. "I used to think I'd be an engineer. But I saw that there was a living in working with tourists."

Higuera waved a hand at somebody and in short order produced an amazing salad for me, with beautiful butter lettuce, shaved chicken, and a dusting of chocolate. He was trying to figure out how to manage the evening's multiple parties of ten; dinner at Le Chansonnier, which draws foreigners and Cubans alike, runs about 40 CUCs per person. His business partner, Laura Fernández Córdoba, who's run the restaurant with him since they opened in fall 2011 with the help of French investors, was approving a tableware purchase in the next room. It was easy to envision money flying in and out of the building, in a New Changing Cuba sort of way, and part of what had been flummoxing me during my early weeks in Cuba was starting to come clear. Not every Cuban drives a taxi or tends bar for tourist tips, right? So how on Earth, I had wondered every time I examined all the nonpeso merchandise being hawked at Cubans from every direction, were they accumulating these CUCs?

Part of the answer is remittances, the dollars and euros sent from relatives abroad. The amount of money sent to Cuba annually is hard to track, but some economists estimate the number may surpass $2 billion this year. That means the modern Cuban state is being nourished partly by people who've left it. And because both the U.S. and Cuban governments have eased restrictions on émigrés returning to visit family, the Cuban Americans who arrive to weepy reunion embraces at the Havana airport are usually carrying both money and goods: televisions, appliances, duffel bags full of clothing, and anything else their relatives can resell por la izquierda for CUCs.

There's stealing too, which during the post-Soviet-collapse depression years emerged as a nationwide mechanism for family survival. The verb *luchar*, which means "fight," also translates loosely in Cuba to "transfer workplace items into one's personal possession, which the system impels us to do because our salaries won't cover a lousy Bucanero." The standard lucha involves eating, drinking, using, bartering, or selling the items in question. Reform campaigns pushed by Raúl Castro have produced scores of high-level corruption arrests, but one defining quality of any attractive workplace, still, is the nature of the lucha. ("If you can't look around and find things you can take home or resell," a woman in her forties from a working-class neighborhood outside Havana told me firmly, "then it's not a good job.")

Nothing about this combination, remittances plus pilfering, is unusual in a small tropical country without abundant raw material for export. Neither is the third important way CUCs arrive in Cubans' pockets: legal commerce, of any sort, that directly or indirectly procures foreigners' money. But the government of the Cuban *proyecto socialista*, or socialist project—in official dispatches that remains the preferred term—has tried for a half century to wall off much of the country from the very buy-sell system that generated that money in the first place. Watching Cubans grapple, as they consider just how many of those walls ought now to be dismantled, is a sobering experience. Take Higuera and Fernández: Their private, for-profit business and their ten employees are legal under the new self-employment laws, as long as they pay their taxes.

But business taxes, in themselves a relatively new concept in Cuba, increase sharply as employers hire more people. The system is weighted against much private expansion while Cubans experiment with new tax and regulation policies, and this question of limits—of just how successful individual entrepreneurs should aspire to become—is a matter of great philosophical and political contention in the New Changing Cuba. Last year, after months of discussions around the country, a remarkable official document called "Guidelines for the Economic and Social Policy of the Party and the Revolution" was published—313 guidelines, to be exact, each one addressing a specific subject, like land use or the civic importance of sports. Guideline number three declares that the "concentration of property" by individuals, as opposed to the state, "will not be permitted."

What does that mean, exactly? The guidelines don't say. The cynical will tell you it means the government shall countenance no threat, no real business competition, to the bureaucracies and personal fiefdoms of government companies. The less cynical will tell you that it means Cuba must manage this move toward privatization carefully, while trying to protect the services Cubans have come to expect—that there remains some genuine national conviction in Cuba, no matter how exhausted the SOCIALISM OR DEATH! slogans may now appear to the young, that it's deeply wrong for certain citizens of a nation to make themselves thousands of times wealthier than others.

"We just don't know yet," a veteran University of Havana economist named Juan Triana Cordoví told me, when I asked about guideline number three. "You can do this big bang style, as Russia did, but I don't think that worked very well. Or you can do it step-by-step, watching what will happen. I am one of the ones who prefer step-by-step. I think of it as testing the stones of the river, one foot at a time, to see if each stone will hold."

I could see how the guidelines, which were released to great fanfare, might look from a certain perspective like one more saltshaker only a quarter full. This is why so many young people spend a lot of time talking to their peers about their futures in Cuba, about whether to stay or go. There are multiple routes away now, most much safer than little boats pushed out to sea in the dark. Family members wait out the long delays for visas to join relatives abroad. Professionals overseas on Cuban service missions, like the thousands of medical professionals and sports trainers now working in Venezuela, sometimes decline to return home. "You're always trying to convince people not to leave," Higuera said. "Always. I have a friend in Madrid now. He got there just in time for the crash."

What might he and Fernández say, I wondered, if they could talk directly to a Cuban I knew, halfway between their two ages, buying canned tuna this very week for an illegal departure into the Straits of Florida?

Higuera sighed. "I'd say to him, If you're going to do this thing, do it," he said.

I had heard this before, after asking other Cubans the same question, and it still surprised me a little; I expected to hear the word *gusano*, worm, which in an earlier era was the famous public castigation for anybody who abandoned the revolution. But I never did. People would nod and say they understood. Or they'd point to a framed picture—on a wall, hanging from a rearview mirror—of a relative who'd already done the same thing. "But I'd tell him to make sure he's doing it for himself, not somebody else's expectation of him," Higuera said. "And I'd ask him to look hard at what he sees in other places. I really do have hope that things are improving here."

A week later I went home, and I waited for Eduardo to call me collect, as we'd both arranged, from somewhere in South Florida. Two weeks passed without a call. Then another week, and then another. I tried the Havana cell phone Eduardo had been using, but there was no answer, and finally I called his brother, who immigrated to Mexico a few years ago to marry a Mexican woman he had met in Cuba.

The phone connection was bad, and I wasn't sure how much was safe to say. I was an American who had befriended Eduardo in Havana, I said, and I just wondered—how he was, that was all. I said he had spoken of an impending vacation. His brother became very excited. "He didn't make it," he said in Spanish. He was shouting into the phone. "There was a problem with the boat. *El timón*. They didn't make it."

I didn't have my dictionary in reach, and I didn't know what a timón was, and all I could think was that it was like *tiburón*, which means shark. *"Tell me what that means,"* I said urgently, and Eduardo's brother said he didn't know how to describe it exactly but that it was a boat part, a thing that had failed before they were too far out, and it was all right, they had used the oars, they were back in Cuba. No one was arrested. He was going to wait a while, Eduardo's brother said, and stay in their mother's apartment with his wife while he saved some more money.

After we hung up I got the dictionary. A timón is a rudder. I had a picture in my mind now, what had happened to Eduardo: Floating in the sea, the rudder broken, he and his companions had surely discussed it for a time, what would happen if they tried to motor on, toward a landfall they couldn't see, with nothing beneath them to keep the direction true. Then they turned the boat around, back into the piece of the ocean they already knew, and rowed home.

PETER HESSLER

■

All Due Respect

FROM *The New Yorker*

ONE OF THE FOREMOST EXPERTS on Japanese organized crime is Jake Adelstein, who grew up on a farm in Missouri, worked as the only American on the crime beat for Japan's largest newspaper, and currently lives in central Tokyo under police protection. Japanese police protection means that the cops make daily visits to Adelstein's home, where they leave yellow notes that say, "There was nothing out of the ordinary." The notes feature the Tokyo police mascot, Pipo-kun, a smiling cartoon figure with big mouse ears and an antenna jutting out of its forehead. Some people in town have trouble taking Adelstein seriously. They dismiss him as a crank, a paranoid foreigner who talks obsessively about death threats from the gangsters known as yakuza. Others react with suspicion; a number of people in Japan claim that his journalism is a front for C.I.A. work. Adelstein does little to dismiss such rumors, apart from maintaining an image so flamboyant that it would shame any actual agency man. He's in his early forties, and he wears a trenchcoat and a porkpie hat, and he chain-smokes clove cigarettes from Indonesia. For a while, he dyed his hair bright red, claiming that this disguise would foil would-be assassins. He employs a bodyguard who doubles as a chauffeur, an ex-yakuza who cut off his pinkie finger years ago as a gesture of apology to a gang superior. Adelstein says he needs a car and a nine-fingered driver in order to avoid the subway, where a hit man might shove him in front of a train.

Japan is not a dangerous country. Each year, approximately one murder is committed for every two hundred thousand people. This is among the lowest rates in the world, on a par with Iceland and Switzerland; the odds of being murdered in the United States are ten times higher. In Japan, it's a crime to own a gun, another crime to own a bullet, and a third crime to pull the trigger: three charges before you even think about a target. Yakuza are notoriously bad shots, because practice is hard to come by, but somehow they have gained enormous influence. The police estimate that there are nearly eighty thousand members of yakuza organizations, whereas in America the Mafia had only five thousand in its heyday. The economic collapse of the nineteen-nineties is sometimes called "the yakuza recession," because organized crime played such a significant role.

"I can't think of a similar major civilized country where you have this kind of criminal influence," an American lawyer who handles risk assessment on behalf of a major financial firm told me recently, in Tokyo. He has a background in intelligence, and extensive experience reviewing potential investments to make sure they aren't connected to organized crime. "Every month, we turn away about a dozen companies that want to do business with us, because they have ties to the yakuza," he said. He told me that during the crash of 2008 Lehman Brothers lost three hundred and fifty million dollars in bad loans to yakuza front companies, while Citibank lost more than seven hundred million.

The lawyer didn't want me to use his name or identify his firm. He was familiar with Adelstein's work, and he noted that Adelstein took a completely different approach. "Jake has got a high profile," he said. "That's his style." He laughed about the clove cigarettes and the porkpie hat, but then he said, "If I were to learn that he was murdered this evening, it wouldn't surprise me."

Adelstein and I both grew up in Columbia, Missouri, and although I met him only a few times, he was the kind of kid that you don't forget. Back then, his name was Josh, and he was tall and thin, with a spindly frame. He was so cross-eyed that he had to have corrective surgery. Even after the procedure, his expression remained slightly off-kilter, and you could never tell exactly what he was looking at. Years later, he was given a diagnosis of Marfan syndrome, a rare disorder of connective tissue that often causes serious problems for the eyes, the heart, and other major organs. But as a boy he simply seemed odd. His vision and coordination were so poor that he didn't get a driver's license, an essential possession for any high-school male in mid-Missouri, and he had to have classmates chauffeur him around town. He loved theatre, which also qualified as a rare disorder in a sports-mad school. The jocks teased and bullied him, until a teacher suggested that he take up martial arts. Karate led to a freshman-year course in Japanese at the University of Missouri, which went well until Josh fell down an elevator shaft while working at a local bookstore. Even this was a sort of distinction—there aren't all that many elevators in Columbia, Missouri. Josh spent a week in the hospital with a bad head injury, and although he recovered, he couldn't remember any Japanese. But the head trauma also erased many memories of high school, so it may have been a good trade. He could always learn the Japanese again.

He spent his sophomore year in Tokyo and never came back. He transferred to a Japanese university, and as a student he lived in a Zen Buddhist temple for three years. Somewhere along the way, he abandoned plans to become an actor, and he changed his name to Jake, for reasons that seemed to vary depending on when you asked him about it. He learned Japanese so quickly that within five years of studying the language he had passed the three-part exam to become a police reporter for Tokyo's *Yomiuri Shimbun*. Adelstein is believed to be the first American ever to make it through the newspaper's rigorous exam system.

The *Yomiuri* is the largest daily in the world. It prints two editions every day, and the total circulation is thirteen and a half million, more than ten times higher than that of the *Times*. Most stories are covered by teams of journalists. At the *Yomiuri*, rookie police reporters are assigned to cover high-school baseball, because the sport is supposed to be good training for crime journalists—the teamwork, the statistics, the attention to detail. Adelstein told me that he spent his training period longing for a major crime to be committed. "In the middle of the high-school baseball season, we were saved by the murder of this really beautiful girl who was killed and her body was found in a barrel," he said. "It's terrible to say, but I was happy to be doing something different."

In 2004, when I was living in China, I made a trip to Tokyo and contacted Adelstein. One evening, he gave me a tour of the red-light district in Kabukicho, telling outlandish stories about yakuza pimps. As part of his job, the *Yomiuri* provided a car and a full-time driver. Adelstein sat in back, dressed in a suit and tie; periodically, he instructed the chauffeur to stop so he could meet a contact at a pachinko parlor or a dodgy massage joint. The last time I had seen him, a high-school buddy was driving him around mid-Missouri in a station wagon, because his vision was so bad, but now he had transformed back-seat status into a mark of prestige. A Missouri friend named Willoughby Johnson once said that Adelstein was still essentially an actor. "There's a degree to which anybody who becomes a character does so through self-fashioning," Johnson told me recently. He had been Adelstein's most faithful chauffeur in high school, and he still called him Josh. "I think of Josh in this way," he continued. "He decided that he wanted to become this international man of mystery."

In Japan, yakuza sometimes speak of themselves in terms of acting. "It's an atmosphere, a presence," an ex-gang member once told me. As a young criminal, he had been given valuable advice by his *oyabun,* the "foster parent" within his gang. "My *oyabun* told me that when you're a yakuza people are always watching you," he said. "Think of yourself as being onstage all the time. It's a performance. If you're bad at playing the role of a yakuza, then you're a bad yakuza."

The name refers to an unlucky hand at cards—*yakuza* means "eight-nine-three"—and bluffing has always been part of the image. Many gangsters are Korean-Japanese or members of other minority groups that traditionally have been scorned. These outsiders proved to be nimble after Japan's defeat in the Second World War, an era that is explored in "Tokyo Underworld," by Robert Whiting. During this period, organized-crime groups established black markets where citizens could acquire necessities, and they were skilled at dealing with the occupying Americans. As Japan rebuilt, the yakuza got involved in real estate and in public-works projects.

For the most part, the yakuza eschewed violence against civilians, because the image of criminality was effective enough in an orderly society. Gangsters decorated their backs and arms with elaborate tattoos, and they permed their hair in tight curls that stood out among the Japanese. If a yakuza displeased a superior, he chopped off his own pinkie finger as a sign of apology. Gang members excelled at loan-sharking, extortion, and blackmail, and they found creative ways to terrorize banks. A few months ago, I accompanied Adelstein on a visit to the home of an aging mid-level gang member, who, along with a former colleague, reminisced about extorting banks in the nineteen-eighties.

"Sometimes we'd send three guys with cats, and they would twirl the cats around by the tail in front of the bank," one said, with Adelstein translating. "They'd do that until the bank finally gave them a loan. Or we'd have a hundred yakuza line up outside a bank. Each would go in and open an account for one yen, which was the lowest amount allowed. It would take all day, until finally the bank would agree to give some loans, to get rid of us." He said they wouldn't pay the loans back. "But we'd give the bank some protection, as well as help with collecting other bad loans," he said. "So it wasn't a terrible deal for them."

Both men were heavyset, with broad noses that looked to have been broken in the past. Their eyes were incredibly expressive—they had high arched brows, as fine as manga brushstrokes, that fluttered whenever they got excited. One had had his shoulders and arms tattooed with chrysanthemums, a patriotic symbol of imperial Japan. The men believed that true yakuza do honorable work: they go after deadbeats who don't repay loans, and they allow people to solve problems without wasting money on lawyers. Yakuza groups also engage in charity, especially after earthquakes or other disasters.

Many yakuza became rich during the bubble economy of the eighties and nineties, and they developed extensive corporate structures. (There's never been a law that bans the gangs, which are fully registered.) Nowadays, yakuza run hedge funds. They speculate in real estate. The Inagawa-kai, one of the three biggest gangs, keeps its main office across the street from the Ritz-Carlton Hotel in midtown Tokyo. At least one Japanese Prime Minister has been documented socializing with yakuza, and politicians have the kind of contact with criminal groups that would destroy a career elsewhere. In the mid-nineties, Shizuka Kamei, who was the minister of exports, admitted that he had accepted substantial donations from a yakuza front company, though he denied being aware of the criminal links. This did so little damage to his reputation that he eventually became minister of the agency that regulates Japan's finance industry.

As a foreigner, Adelstein moves easily between the yakuza and the police, playing the flamboyant outsider with both. Yet he follows strict rules: Information that comes from cops can be taken to other law-enforcement officials, but it cannot be passed to yakuza. In contrast, if a yakuza tells Adelstein something, the goal is usually to expose a rival group, so this information can be passed on to the cops. Adelstein says that the key to his work is the Japanese concept of *giri*, or reciprocity. His typical routine involves exchanging small favors with contacts, collecting bits of information that can be leveraged elsewhere.

One afternoon last spring, I accompanied Adelstein to a Mexican restaurant in the neighborhood of Roppongi, to meet with a gangster who had a favor to ask. He was around forty years old—I'll call him Miyamoto—and he was college-educated, with perfect English. During his pre-yakuza days, he had worked for a public-relations firm in Tokyo. Back then, one of the agency's clients was an American auto manufacturer that regularly sent high-level management to Japan. In the evenings, it was Miyamoto's task to escort the gaijin to the massage parlors known as "soapland," where customers can enjoy a bath, a massage, and sex. Eventually, some yakuza extorted the public-relations firm, threatening to go to the tabloids with stories about American auto execs at soapland. Miyamoto handled the payoff, and then the next shakedown, and soon he became the firm's de-facto yakuza liaison. The gangsters liked what they saw and recruited him away from the agency.

Since then, Miyamoto had become a full gang member, although his *oyabun* had told him to avoid tattoos, because they would be a liability in the corporate world. He had kept all his fingers for the same reason. Nowadays, he helped his gang manage three hedge funds. At the restaurant, he handed Adelstein a new business card. "Be really careful with this card, because it's my legitimate business," he said, in English. "If this gets out, we won't get listed on the stock market."

The favor he needed was personal. His wife had left him after he became a yakuza, and he hadn't seen his child for years. The recent tsunami, which had occurred less than two months earlier, made him want to get back in touch. He asked Adelstein to contact his estranged wife and tell her that he wasn't a yakuza anymore.

"I can't lie to her," Adelstein said. "I can say you're doing legitimate business. But I can't say you're not a yakuza."

Miyamoto agreed, and then he talked about other corporate gangsters, mentioning a well-known gang. "They now have a guy who worked for Deutsche Bank," he said.

Adelstein remarked that Miyamoto had posted his gang symbol online, and he warned him to be careful. "You need to back off on Twitter."

"Man, I've got a thousand followers!"

"You shouldn't say that stuff on Twitter about your bitches giving you money."

"The police won't read it. People think it's fake, anyway."

"Well, there's a new law going on the books in October, and if you're talking about taking protection money you could get arrested," Adelstein said.

There was never any mention of what Miyamoto might do in exchange for Adelstein's contacting his wife. But after a while the yakuza leaned forward and spoke in a low voice about the Tokyo Electric Power Company, or TEPCO, which owns and manages the Fukushima nuclear reactors that had been damaged by the tsunami. There had been accusations of mismanagement, and Miyamoto suggested that Adelstein research potential links between TEPCO and the Matsuba-kai, a criminal organization. "You know what's really interesting?" he said. "The Matsuba-kai guys play golf with the waste-disposal guys for TEPCO. That's what you need to look into." He also named a yakuza from another gang who had supposedly made a million-dollar profit from supplying workers and construction materials to the reactors.

During the following weeks, Adelstein took pieces of information about the reactors to various contacts. Over the summer, he published a number of articles in *The Atlantic* online, the London *Independent*, and some Japanese publications, exposing criminal links at TEPCO. He described how yakuza front companies had supplied equipment and contract workers, and he quoted an engineer who had noticed something strange when he saw some cleanup crews change clothes: beneath the white hazmat suits, their bodies were covered with tattoos.

When Adelstein worked for the *Yomiuri,* he says there was a tacit understanding that investigative reporting on the yakuza shouldn't go too far. Media companies, like many big Japanese corporations, often had links to criminal groups, and even the police tried not to be too combative. For one thing, tools were limited: Japanese authorities can't engage in plea bargaining or witness relocation, and wiretapping is almost never allowed. In the past, yakuza were rarely violent, and if they did attack somebody it was usually another gang member, which wasn't considered a problem. One officer in the organized-crime-prevention unit told me that, in the nineteen-eighties, if a yakuza killed a rival he often turned himself in. "The guilty person would appear the next day at the police station with the gun and say, 'I did it,'" the cop said. "He'd be in jail for only two or three years. It wasn't like killing a real person."

Even the police officer believed that yakuza serve some useful functions. "Japanese society doesn't really have any place for juvenile delinquents," he said. "That's one role the yakuza play. Traditionally, it's a place where people can send juvenile delinquents." The fact that these delinquents are subsequently raised to become yakuza didn't seem to bother the cop too much. When I asked if he had ever fired his gun, he said that he hadn't even used his nightstick. His business card identified his specialty as "Violent Crime Investigation," and it featured the smiling Pipo-kun with his antenna, which symbolized how police can sense things happening everywhere in society. The officer explained that until recently the cops would notify yakuza before making a bust, out of respect, which allowed gangsters to hide any particularly damning evidence. "Now we don't do that anymore," he said.

He lamented a loss of civility among a new generation of yakuza. "It used to be that they didn't do theft or robbery," he said. "It was considered shameful." He blamed greed: when the bubble economy collapsed, in the nineties, many wealthy yakuza had trouble adjusting. After years of adopting the façade of dangerous sociopaths, some began to live up to the image. The officer identified a gangster named Tadamasa Goto as an example of the new breed. "He's much more ruthless than yakuza were in the past," he said. "He'll go after civilians. Unfortunately, more yakuza have become like that."

Six days before our conversation, one of Goto's former underlings had been shot dead in Thailand. For years, he had been on the run, a suspect in the murder of a man who had stood in Goto's way in a real-estate deal. The cop said that Goto was cleaning up potential witnesses, and he reminded me that the gangster had also issued death threats against Adelstein. The most recent had been made last year, when Goto published his autobiography. "We suspect Goto of being involved in the killing of seventeen people," the cop said.

The criminal autobiography is a perverse genre anywhere, but this is especially true in Japan, where Goto's book appeared with the title *Habakarinagara,* a polite phrase that means "with all due respect." At the time of publication, the author announced that all royalties would be dedicated to a charity for the disabled in Cambodia and to a Buddhist temple in Burma. The book begins in a David Copperfield vein: As a boy, Goto lacked shoes, and he ate barley instead of rice. ("Those years were extremely tough, with an alcoholic bum for a father.") He describes the rise from juvenile delinquency to the yakuza with a nice baseball metaphor. ("I felt as though we had been playing neighborhood baseball in a weedy field then suddenly got scouted to play in the major leagues.") Crimes are mentioned breezily, with few details, although even the offhand ones tend to be memorable. ("My third brother, Yasutaka, was one of the guys who threw leaflets and excrement around Suruga Bank, and he went to prison for that.") Goto emphasizes his sense of honor; if nothing else, he has the courage of his convictions. ("I couldn't go apologize and beg forgiveness. I am not cut out that way. I have pride. So instead I chopped off one of my fingers and brought it to Kawauchi.")

For years, this auto-amputee was one of the largest shareholders of Japan Airlines. According to police estimates, Goto's assets are worth about a billion dollars, and he controlled his own faction within the Yamaguchi-gumi, the top criminal organization in the country. He is notorious for an attack on Juzo Itami, one of Japan's greatest filmmakers. In May of 1992, Itami released *Minbo, or the Gentle Art of Japanese Extortion,* a movie that portrayed yakuza as fakes who don't live up to their tough-guy image. Days later, five members of Goto's organization attacked the filmmaker in front of his home, slashing his face and neck with knives.

Afterward, Itami became even more outspoken. Five years later, he apparently committed suicide, leaping from the roof of his office building. He left a note explaining that he was distraught over an alleged love affair. But Adelstein, citing an unnamed yakuza source, subsequently reported that the filmmaker had been forced to sign the note and jump, and the police have treated the case as a possible homicide. The American lawyer who researches organized crime told me that some yakuza groups specialize in murders that look like suicide. "I used to think they committed suicide out of shame, because the Japanese do that, culturally," he said. "But nowadays when I hear that somebody killed himself I often doubt that's what happened."

At the *Yomiuri,* Adelstein started investigating Goto. He had been making progress when one of his sources, a foreign prostitute, disappeared. Adelstein was convinced that she had been murdered, and soon he became obsessed with the case. He was married to a Japanese journalist named Sunao, and they had two small children. But Adelstein rarely made it home before midnight, because Japanese crime reporters are expected to smoke and drink heavily with cops and other contacts. Sometimes he was threatened by yakuza; once he was badly beaten and suffered damage to his knee and spine. Like many people with Marfan syndrome, he took daily medication for his heart, and there were signs that his life style was becoming self-destructive. He had always had a tendency to dramatize his health problems—this was part of his image—but now he seemed to be growing into the role of the troubled crime reporter.

Years later, both Adelstein and his wife said that this period destroyed their marriage. It also finished his career at the *Yomiuri.* After a certain point, he says, the paper balked at publishing more stories about Goto, and Adelstein quit. To this day, nobody at the paper will speak on the record about him; some reporters told me that he was a liar, while others said that the *Yomiuri* had been frustrated by his obsession. A couple of people alleged that he worked for the C.I.A.

Staff from competing papers seemed more likely to praise his work, and a number of people indicated that the Japanese media tended to shy away from stories that would anger powerful yakuza figures like Goto. They also said that people at the *Yomiuri* were angry about Adelstein's departure because it violated traditional corporate loyalty.

After leaving the *Yomiuri*, Adelstein kept investigating, until finally he homed in on Goto's liver. For yakuza, the liver is a crucial body part, a target of self-abuse on a par with the pinkie finger. Many gangsters inject methamphetamines, and dirty needles can spread hepatitis C, which is also a risk of the big tattoos. In addition, there's a lot of drinking and smoking. In the yakuza community, a sick liver is a badge of honor, something that a proud samurai like Goto brags about in his memoirs. ("I drank enough to destroy three livers.") But it also means that yakuza often need transplants, and a criminal source told Adelstein that Goto had received a new liver in the United States, where his extensive record would make him ineligible for a visa. After months of investigation, Adelstein discovered that Goto and three other yakuza had been patients at the U.C.L.A. Medical Center, one of the nation's premier transplant facilities. Goto had been granted a visa because of a deal with the F.B.I.—he had agreed to rat out other yakuza.

Adelstein broke the story in May of 2008, first in the *Washington Post* and then with details that he gave to reporters at the *Los Angeles Times*. Jim Stern, a retired head of the F.B.I.'s Asian criminal-enterprise unit, confirmed the deal, although he told the *L.A. Times*, "I don't think Goto gave the bureau anything of significance." (Stern was not involved in the deal.) According to Adelstein's Japanese police sources, the U.C.L.A. Medical Center received donations in excess of a million dollars from yakuza. An investigation at U.C.L.A. found no wrongdoing, and the medical center reported only two hundred thousand dollars in donations, although it acknowledged other signs of *giri*—for example, one yakuza gave his doctor a case of wine, a watch, and ten thousand dollars. The year that Goto received his liver, a hundred and eighty-six Americans in the Los Angeles area died while waiting for a transplant. Long before the articles appeared, Goto's men had contacted Adelstein. He says that they threatened to kill him, while another gang leader offered him half a million dollars to drop the story. After that, Adelstein was placed under Tokyo police protection, and the F.B.I. monitored his wife and children, who had moved to the United States.

In 2008, the Yamaguchi-gumi officially expelled Goto. He undertook the training necessary to be certified as a Buddhist priest, a step that's not uncommon for ex-yakuza who fear retribution from former colleagues. It's bad karma to kill a priest, even if he's a former crime boss who reportedly still commands many loyal followers. And Goto is the type of Buddhist priest who uses his autobiography to issue oblique threats. "Just because I've retired from the business, doesn't mean I have the time to track down this American novelist," he says in *With All Due Respect*. "If I did meet him it would be a serious matter. He'd have to write, 'Goto is after me' instead of 'Goto may come after me.'"

In 2010, Adelstein hired a lawyer named Toshiro Igari to sue Goto's publisher and force the retraction of this threat. Igari was involved in many anti-yakuza cases, including investigations into fixing sumo matches and professional baseball games. In August, the lawyer went on vacation to the Philippines, where he was found dead in a room with a cup of sleeping pills, a set of box cutters, a glass of wine, and a shallow cut on his wrist. The Philippine police report was inconclusive, although most Japanese newspapers reported the death as a suicide. In Japan, Goto's book has sold more than two hundred thousand copies, and, since the earthquake in March, all royalties have been dedicated to tsunami relief.

During the spring, I visited Adelstein in Tokyo, and the first thing he told me was that a week earlier he had been given a diagnosis of liver cancer. He had also nearly completed training to become a Zen Buddhist priest. Adelstein figured that if Goto could do it for protection he could, too. He considered himself a Buddhist, and he liked the concept of karma, although he had told the priest who was training him that he didn't believe in reincarnation. "He said you don't have to believe," Adelstein said. "In Buddhism, it's not about faith. It's about doing."

He seemed neither surprised nor upset about the cancer diagnosis. The disease had been discovered in the early stages, and doctors at a clinic in Tokyo were treating it with injections of ethanol. They had told Adelstein that the cancer might be connected to diet, or to years of drinking and smoking, or even to Marfan syndrome. Regardless, his tranquillity probably had less to do with Zen than it did with operating in a milieu where everybody knows something about liver problems. One afternoon, we stopped by the neighborhood police station, where Adelstein mentioned the diagnosis to a detective friend. "Wow, you're just like a yakuza!" the cop said. "Are you actually covered with tattoos?" When we met with one of Adelstein's criminal contacts, he talked about how his gang boss had originally hoped to get a U.C.L.A. liver, but after Adelstein's exposé he had been forced to settle for an Australian organ instead. (He eventually went through two Aussie livers, and then died.) Periodically, Adelstein's driver gave updates on a mutual acquaintance whose liver hadn't responded to ethanol and was currently being zapped with radio-wave treatment. The driver himself had a lucky liver—his hepatitis C had been successfully treated with interferon.

The driver's name was Teruo Mochizuki, and he had a long criminal history. As a teen-ager, he had been a delinquent, until finally his parents, in frustration, passed him off to a local yakuza. Mochizuki joined the Inagawa-kai, and he became addicted to methamphetamines. He had gone to prison four times on drug-related charges. Now in his fifties, he said he had been clean for more than two decades. He was powerfully built, with broad shoulders, no neck, and a bullet-shaped head. Like other yakuza I met, he had expressive eyes, although even the manga brows remained still when I asked about his left hand. He said quietly, "There was some trouble and I had to lose the finger." He had done it in front of his boss at the gang's office. A doctor stopped the bleeding, but Mochizuki had declined treatment of the nerve endings. "To repair the finger would be to take back the apology," he explained. He said that the yakuza tradition is connected to the way that samurai warriors ritually sliced their own stomachs in ancient times. He also remarked that Japanese law grants disability status to a nine-fingered person, but Mochizuki refused to apply, out of respect for his digital apology.

He had known Adelstein for more than fifteen years. When I asked how they had first met, he told the story casually, as if these were the details of an everyday personal encounter. In 1993, an associate of Mochizuki's was blackmailing the criminal owner of a pet store, so the owner murdered the yakuza, and, according to rumor, carved up the body and fed it to his dogs. Adelstein, who was single at the time, covered the story and interviewed the dead yakuza's meth-head girlfriend; almost immediately, they began sleeping together. One day, Mochizuki went to the girlfriend's house to pay his condolences, and Adelstein answered the door, postcoital.

I had lots of possible questions but decided to go with the most obvious: "What was your first impression of Jake-san?"

"My first impression was 'What an idiot!'" Mochizuki said. "You can look all over Japan and you won't find a reporter willing to do these things. I was surprised that he was fearless. He was just so strange."

Over the years, Adelstein and Mochizuki became friends. In 2007, Mochizuki was expelled from the Inagawa-kai, after an internal conflict that he didn't want to talk about. The following year, Adelstein offered Mochizuki a job as his bodyguard and driver. "I didn't want to do it," Mochizuki told me. "Goto is one of the most influential guys in Japan, and nobody would want a job like that. But I felt like I had no other choice." He explained that Tokyo job prospects are poor for an uneducated middle-aged man with nine fingers and tattoos that show beneath a dress shirt. He now earns about thirty-five hundred dollars a month for driving Adelstein around Tokyo in a black Mercedes S600, which is a common yakuza car model. Adelstein had bought it cheap from a gang contact who was retiring and no longer needed a statement vehicle.

Mochizuki told me that Adelstein behaved differently from typical Japanese journalists, who are careful not to cross certain lines. "He has no regard for those taboos or restrictions," he said. "If he were Japanese, he wouldn't be around right now." Mochizuki explained that some yakuza dislike Adelstein's stories, but he is widely recognized as a man of his word. "He has a heart," Mochizuki said. "People appreciate him for that. It's not common for somebody who is not Japanese to have this feeling of obligation."

Adelstein has published a book about his adventures on the police beat, *Tokyo Vice,* and is working on two more. A few years ago, he researched human trafficking for the U.S. State Department, and now he serves as a board member for the Polaris Project Japan, a nonprofit that combats the sex trade. Periodically, he does investigations for corporations. The American lawyer who researches organized crime told me that when he first met Adelstein his image was off-putting. But he had become deeply impressed by his work. "He's a craftsman," he said. "He takes pride in doing the kind of research he does correctly." He continued, "It's this odd thing where you have this white guy who is as close to that part of Japanese society as a person can get."

Adelstein follows his strict rules of reciprocity and protection of sources, but otherwise he is willing to do nearly anything to get a story. He said that once, after his marriage had fallen apart, a lonely female cop offered access to a file on Goto if he slept with her, so he did. In the red-light district, he relies on foreign strippers for information, and on a few occasions when they have run into visa problems he has introduced them to gay salarymen who need wives in order to rise at their conservative Japanese companies. Adelstein says he never breaks the law—he puts these people in touch and tells them that they are free to fall in love and get married, and then they are also free to apply for spousal visas and to show up at corporate events together. But he acknowledges that a journalist in America would be appalled. "I've slept with sources," he told me. "I've done hard negotiations that are probably tantamount to blackmail. I've ransacked rubbish bins for information. I'm willing to get information from organized crime or antisocial forces if the information is good."

By now, he's played the stereotypical role of the crime reporter for so long that he can't shake the life style. Whenever I went out with him, we always seemed to end up having drinks with some beautiful, bright woman. For five years, he has rented a house in a quiet neighborhood, but it was as if he had just moved in: at night, he dragged a futon out of a closet and slept on the floor of his office. For breakfast, he microwaved instant meals from a convenience store and served them on paper plates. In the kitchen, I counted five bottles of whiskey, four bottles of vodka, and three spoons. There was no table; he ate takeout meals on the couch. He marked his hand with a pen every time he lit a clove cigarette, supposedly to cut back, although once I watched him accumulate six marks while we were en route to a cancer treatment. On that particular day, the doctor decided to postpone the injection of ethanol, but I wasn't sure that Adelstein's body noticed the difference. We went straight from the appointment to dinner at a shabu-shabu restaurant, where he ordered two bottles of *sake* and finished them while waiting for an elegant Japanese-American woman to join us. After that, he had five more drinks at three different bars, and he was still going strong at two in the morning.

In the farmland of southern Boone County, atop the last line of hills that overlook the Missouri River, stands a six-sided pagoda. The structure has three tiers marked by upturned eaves. "It was my impression of what a Japanese house should be," Eddie Adelstein told me, when I visited in April. He said that he didn't know much about Japan, having travelled there only once to see his son, but he had always liked the idea of an Asian house. He had a friend in Kansas who specialized in designing six-sided buildings, so they combined their interests. Since 2005, the pagoda has been home to Sunao Adelstein and her two children. Eddie and his wife, Willa, live in another building on the property.

The neighbors are mostly farmers and people who moved to the countryside for the quiet, but they've picked up certain ideas about the yakuza and Tadamasa Goto. "When it started, somebody from the F.B.I. came by and talked to everybody," Heidi Branaugh, a nurse who lives on a small farm nearby, told me. "It was just odd. The first night I was here, after the sheriff came by, there was a helicopter overhead." Branaugh keeps a donkey, forty chickens, ten goats, and a dog named Bessie. She said that for a year Bessie barked at the car that the sheriff's department parked near the pagoda every evening. "They'd sit right up there on the drive, watching. Once, they chased some guys who were looking for mushrooms."

Sunao Adelstein told me that she was tired of thinking about Goto. In 2008, the F.B.I. had advised the family to install an alarm system and buy some guns, because it wouldn't be too hard for a hit man to track down a pagoda near the Missouri River. Since then, the authorities believed that the local risk had passed, although at the time of my visit Sunao had not returned to Japan for two years, because the Tokyo police were still concerned about Goto's threat. Sunao used to work as a business reporter in Tokyo, but now she was studying accounting and trying to adjust to life in rural Missouri. She liked the pagoda, although she complained that there was almost no closet space, because the designer had been so obsessed with the Japanese exterior. Who would have imagined that a pagoda needed closets? "Very often I think, Why am I living here?" she said. "I grew up in Saitama. It's not a big city, but it's a suburb of Tokyo. I never dealt with ticks, with bugs. I hate ticks!"

Sunao is a slender, pretty woman, and she took me for a walk in the countryside with the children. She wore a short red skirt and black leggings; periodically, she stopped to check for ticks. After years of living apart, she and Jake had finally decided to file for legal separation. She said that her husband had changed after his research took him deep into the criminal underworld. "He was beaten by somebody, so he was wary. He was not goofy Jake anymore," she said. "He would use words the yakuza way." She continued, "It has to do with the facial expression, the way they speak. When he got angry, he was like this. We argued once and he said, *'Omae niwa kankeine! Kono Bakayaro!'* I thought, Oh, he knows bad Japanese now."

She said that at one time she had hoped he would find a different career, but now she realized that it would never happen. Some of Adelstein's friends and family told me that he was addicted to the excitement, while others mentioned that he was too attached to the character that he had created. But beneath the chaotic personal life there was also something deeply moralistic about his outlook. He seemed to have more faith in giri than he did in any system of justice, and he could respect even a criminal as long as the man kept his word. "He expects people to be fair and honest," his father told me.

Eddie Adelstein said that his own experiences with crime had influenced his son. He worked as a pathologist at the V.A. hospital in Columbia, and had served as the county medical examiner for more than twenty years. In the early nineteen-nineties, patients suddenly began dying at a high rate, and there were rumors about a nurse named Richard Williams. Finally, Dr. Adelstein commissioned an epidemiologist, who performed a study and said that there was evidence of foul play: it was ten times more likely that a patient would die during one of Williams's shifts than under another nurse's care. Some believed that the nurse might be killing patients by injecting codeine, but nobody knew for certain. When Dr. Adelstein approached hospital administrators, their first response was to hide the findings. "Everybody who took part in the coverup was promoted, and everybody who tried to expose it was punished," he said.

Williams eventually left the hospital, but the director gave him a letter of recommendation that helped him find a job at a rural nursing home. During Williams's first year at the nursing home, there was a sudden increase in deaths over the preceding year. Dr. Adelstein and others took the story to the F.B.I., Congress, and "ABC News." The F.B.I. investigated, but forensic results were incomplete, in part because labs were too busy with tests related to the O. J. Simpson trial. Williams was charged, but the case was dismissed when prosecutors could not determine the cause of death. At last report, he was living quietly in suburban St. Louis. He is suspected of murdering as many as forty-two people, many of them war veterans—more victims than are attributed to Ted Bundy, John Wayne Gacy, or Tadamasa Goto.

All that had happened while Jake Adelstein was starting his career in Japan. "It made me extremely distrustful of everyone," he told me. "The biggest lesson I took was that even when you're in the right, when you're doing something good, you won't be rewarded." And it occurred to me that the darkest element of his life wasn't the image he projected of the tormented reporter, or even the crazy yakuza stories. Beneath all the exoticism, it was actually the normalcy of crime that was most disturbing. Whether you're in Missouri or Tokyo, things aren't always what they seem—the nurse might be a murderer, and the gangster might run a hedge fund.

During one of my trips to Japan, I contacted Tadamasa Goto's publicist, who said that his client wasn't accepting interviews. So I got in touch with Tomohiko Suzuki, a journalist who has written for yakuza fanzines, which cover criminals as celebrities. Recently, there had been rumors that Suzuki was channelling messages from Goto.

We met at a Tokyo coffeehouse. Suzuki wore blue work clothes and heavy boots, because he had just returned from a charity event in a town called Minamisoma, which was still suffering from the effects of the tsunami. In recent weeks, yakuza had been donating aid, and Goto had pitched in by sponsoring the day's charity event, which was called With All Due Respect. When I asked if any famous yakuza had attended, Suzuki named one and said, "He's the guy who stabbed the cult member in front of the media." I didn't pursue the details; by now I understood that the blandly offhand tone of such statements was basically the point.

Suzuki said that Adelstein's status as a foreigner had protected him from Goto. People in law enforcement and in diplomatic circles had told me that they still took the threats seriously, but Suzuki said that their caution wasn't necessary anymore. "Those are the kinds of things that yakuza say all the time," he said. "It's kind of like saying 'Hello' for a yakuza."

A few months later, though, there were reports that Goto had become formally active again in organized crime. Not long after that, new laws went into effect that finally made it illegal to pay off yakuza. It was unclear how rigorously such regulations would be enforced, but they seemed to reflect a growing desire to control criminal groups. Suzuki hadn't said anything about Goto's plans during our meeting. He had visited the crime boss just a week earlier. "I didn't notice anything wrong with him—he looked very healthy," Suzuki said. "I think U.C.L.A. did a good job."

On the morning of my departure, Mochizuki drove Adelstein and me to Narita Airport. Adelstein had heard that somebody had recently smuggled a Marine-issued rifle through customs. "I have a contact in customs that I'll talk to about it," he said. "There might be a story." Afterward, he planned to go to a press conference downtown, and he was dressed in black suit pants, a pin-striped shirt, and a black trenchcoat with red silk lining. He wore his porkpie hat. We had been on the road for a few minutes before he realized that he had forgotten his shoes. He laughed hysterically at his bulky house slippers and said that he'd have to buy a pair of loafers at an airport shop.

He was scheduled to undergo a chemotherapy treatment in about a week. At seven-twenty-five, he lit the day's first clove cigarette, and he chain-smoked during the long drive to the airport. (A few months later, he would finally succeed in quitting cigarettes.) On the way, Mochizuki asked Adelstein if he'd like to go on a beach vacation with him. "We should do this before one of us has bad health," the driver said. A couple of nights earlier, I had been in the car when Adelstein asked Mochizuki if he had ever killed a person. The driver paused, as if choosing his words carefully. "I've never killed anybody who wasn't a yakuza," he said at last, laughing.

Stories tended to tumble out of Adelstein, full of crazy yakuza details, and today he told a new one. He said that during his period of obsessive research he had conducted an affair with one of Goto's mistresses. The gangster reportedly kept more than a dozen women in Tokyo and other cities, and Adelstein slept with one who gave him useful information. Eventually, he helped her escape Goto by introducing her to a gay salaryman who needed a wife and was about to be posted overseas. He said that the couple still shared an address in Europe. I asked what the mistress was like.

"We had this lovely conversation once in bed," Adelstein said. "She said, 'Do you love me?' I said, 'No, but I like you.' She said, 'I like you, too. You're a lot of fun.' Then she said, 'Are you sleeping with me to get information about Goto?' I said, 'Pretty much. What about you?' She said, 'Well, I hate the motherfucker and every time I sleep with you it's like I'm stabbing him in the face.' She was into astronomy. Once, we went to a planetarium in Sunshine City. I think that was the only time we ever went out in public together. That was our only date." He continued, "It was nice. Another time, I gave her a gift—I bought an expensive planetarium set that Sega makes. She cried."

He lit another cigarette. He had told me once that he didn't expect to have a long life, but in Tokyo he always seemed happy and full of energy. I liked the image from his story: the odd couple at the planetarium, the Japanese gangster's mistress and the cross-eyed kid from Missouri, both of them staring up at the stars. I thought about that until we reached the airport and he went off to find some shoes.

■

Everyone's Reading Bastard

FROM *Byliner*

I.

ELAINE AND CHARLIE agreed to divorce each other sometime between 9:30 and 10 a.m. on a Monday morning, in a coffee shop near their children's school.

"Well, what on earth did you say to her? In the coffee shop? To make her want to divorce you?" Charlie's mother asked him later in the week, when he'd finally mustered the courage to tell her.

"Two points here," said Charlie. "One, I like how you automatically assume it was something *I* said. Rather than something *she* said. And two, divorces don't just come out of the blue. Like, like a sniper's bullet. You can't just be walking along, all happy, la-di-da, and then *bang!* Ow! Divorce! . . . Things have been bad for a long time."

A long, long time. *Years.* When the fatal conversation took place, he was already living out of the family home, in a rented flat that was big enough for the children to stay in at weekends, if it were ever to come to that; at the moment, they were hobbling through Saturday and Sunday together, and Charlie spent the night in the spare bedroom. (When Elaine and Charlie eventually sat the kids down and told them that the marriage was over, Emily, aged nine, said only, "Der.") Charlie and Elaine had been pretending—to themselves, to the kids—that this might not be a permanent state of affairs, that there was a way back from here if they chose to take it, but of course there wasn't, not really. Even so, there was an element of shock, despite what he'd said to his mother. The weekend had been like other weekends they'd spent over the past few months—difficult, chilly, separate, sad, but nothing out of the ordinary. Walking from the coffee shop to the tube station, he did feel as though he'd been hit by a sniper's bullet, if a sniper's bullet could also make one feel unburdened and a little merry, which, he could see, was debatable. Why that particular Monday? Exactly a week later, when Charlie discovered that he had become known—to hundred of thousands of people who still bought newspapers, and God knows how many more who didn't but who read them anyway—as somebody called Bastard, it all began to make sense. There are some who would argue that there's a point where the intolerable can no longer be tolerated, and Elaine had just snapped, fired her rifle after another two whole days of frosty misery. Charlie, however, believed that the intolerable could always be tolerated just a little longer. He was pretty sure that Elaine had seen an opportunity for professional advancement and acclaim, and therefore the time had come: he had to be vaporized.

He didn't read the Sunday newspaper that Elaine worked for, not any more. He'd had to stop. Elaine wrote profiles, features, and columns, on the face of it about current affairs and the arts, but over the years Charlie had come to feel as though her only real subject was him. No matter what she had been asked for—a love letter to an American TV star, a restaurant review, a comment piece about a suddenly famous royal bottom—she always managed to find a way to squeeze his inadequacies in somewhere. She had once launched into a tirade about his flatulence (illness-related, temporary) during an interview with Daniel Radcliffe, the star of the Harry Potter films, and reported Radcliffe's suspiciously sympathetic response. Her willingness to reveal all was what her editor loved about her, apparently. Everything was personal: the political, the cultural, the gastronomical. She had told the nation about the loss of her virginity, the current state of her pelvic floor, her sexual fantasies, her marriage, and her marriage, and her marriage. Paradoxically, the very quality that made her job at the paper secure made Elaine seem unhinged.

It was Mary at work who first alerted him to the possibility of new Elaine trouble, although she did so without saying very much. Mary was a petite, depressed single mother, and in the early days of his separation Charlie had slept with her a couple of times. There was an irony in that, if you thought about it in the right way and not in the wrong way—which was the way Elaine tended to think about things. The irony was this: he wasn't a bastard, but with Mary he had sort of behaved like one. Maybe that was what she thought, too, if she'd made the mistake of extrapolating a whole theory from the way he had brought their underwhelming, time-filling relationship to a halt. (He had never really understood the controversy surrounding text messages as a method for conveying the cessation of a sexual relationship, especially one of this duration and wattage. And he'd be as happy to receive as to give, so it wasn't that. Texts were clean and unambiguous, and required no eye contact.)

"How was your weekend?" he asked Mary as they were waiting for the lift. Her shrug indicated some bitterness, he thought, as if the disappointing nature of her weekend was his fault. He ignored it.

"Yours?" And then a little "Oh!" as if she'd remembered something, followed by what looked suspiciously like a smirk.

Oh, shit, Charlie thought. Elaine. Smirks, silences, coughs, raised eyebrows, sympathetic looks, half-finished sentences, from friends, colleagues, other parents at the school . . . They all meant the same thing, these days. It was irritating, and it made him unhappy, but he'd learned that he would live, and that in a week it would all be forgotten. But when they got out at the fifteenth floor, Charlie ran into Tim Britton from acquisitions, who was not a man for a cough or a raised eyebrow.

"Here he is," said Britton cheerfully. "Bastard!"

Tim Britton was an arse, but he'd never just walked up to Charlie and started calling him names. Charlie stared at him. Britton chuckled and shook his head.

"This is going to be great," he said.

Going to be? Charlie thought. *As in, the future?* That didn't sound good.

When he got up to his office, he went straight onto the newspaper's website and scanned the home page quickly. He couldn't immediately see anything that was going to cause him any discomfort. A three-page eyewitness report of a revolution in an Arab country, an interview with the Chancellor of the Exchequer, an appreciation of a Latin American writer on the occasion of his eightieth birthday. Even Elaine's fond editor wouldn't let her loose on any of that lot, however eccentric the results. He looked again, and then realized that the disaster was so big that he'd missed it: there was a headline right across the top of the screen, just below the masthead. "DON'T MISS ELAINE HARRIS'S BRILLIANT NEW WEEKLY COLUMN 'BASTARD!'" the headline said.

For a moment, Charlie tried to hold on to the hope that there was another bastard in Elaine's life. She didn't like her father much, for example, and there was an editor in her last job that she loathed to this day. But really, he knew. He gave himself a couple of minutes, took deep breaths to quell the panic, and clicked on the link. Just in case one or two dimwitted people still might not have been able to link him with the eponymous villain, the brilliant new weekly column called Bastard! had a helpful subheading: "LIFE WITH AN EX" it read. "HE'S GONE, BUT HE'S NOT FORGOTTEN." There was even a logo, as if the column were already a national institution: a cartoon cad, all cravat, mustache, and twinkling, lascivious eyes.

He scanned the column quickly. He recognized nearly all of the crimes she was accusing him of, all of the minor incompetencies connected with child care. The column was clearly going to be thematic. And yes, it was a sorry list, but these were the sourest plums from the last couple of years; there was no way she could keep this level of bile up weekly. There. He had found the only piece of consolation on offer: it wouldn't always be this bad. He was wrong, of course.

2.

Charlie had met Elaine at university, but they hadn't started dating then. She was, as she'd reminded him cheerfully on a regular basis throughout their marriage, out of his league then. He wasn't entirely sure what had changed in the meantime—whether he had somehow managed to elevate himself, or whether her status had become downgraded in some way, maybe by whichever agency handled God's credit rating—but when they met up again at a party, she seemed inexplicably interested in him. He was solvent and single, but she was funny, successful, and attractive, so he was still at least a division below her, by his calculations, although he wasn't going to be the one to point this out. He asked her out to dinner, and they set out on a more or less entirely conventional march toward cohabitation and parenthood.

Every now and again, he would meet someone who had known her back in the day. Sometimes that person was male; and sometimes that male would intimate that he'd had some kind of sexual relationship with Elaine; and sometimes the intimation was followed by something, a face or a gesture or a whistle, intended to indicate that Charlie was brave or foolish or naive. Charlie took no notice. He found it all thrilling. But when Elaine's career started to take off, it was mostly because of her apparently insatiable appetite for self-exposure and, unavoidably, the exposure of those who happened to be somewhere close to her. And that was what fueled her reputation—and she really was quite well known now—for eccentricity and solipsism. Some of these disclosures began to affect their marriage: they made him tense and ashamed. It is probably not fair to say that they also made him sleep with an ex-girlfriend he'd bumped into on Facebook, but that was what it felt like at the time. (His affair filled up the entire front page of the Lifestyle section.) Bastard! introduced a new and terrible idea, though, one that had never, for obvious reasons, occurred to him: what if Elaine had, despite all appearances to the contrary, actually been reining herself in? What if their marriage had been inhibiting her? Was it possible that Elaine was only just now taking the gloves off? He thought again about the timing of the request for the divorce. He was beginning to feel as though he'd been drawn against Bobby Fischer in a school chess tournament.

He called her on her mobile and got her voice mail. He left a polite message. She didn't call back. His next message was more urgent, more pained, so when his mobile rang, he thought that maybe she was feeling remorseful. But it was his mother.

"Is it true?"

"Oh, shit."

"Please don't use that language with me. It's bad enough that you use it in front of the children."

That was a reference to one of Elaine's stories in the column: the day the car had been broken into and he'd lost his iPad and a pair of stupidly expensive Prada boots, still in their box, that he'd just bought. For a moment he had been lost inside a purple fog of anger. He'd used both the F and the C words and kicked the car, and the children had burst into tears.

"Are you saying that it's worse to use it in front of you?"

"No, of course not."

"But that's how the construction goes. 'It's bad enough' is then followed by something, you know. One step on. 'It's bad enough that you forgot my birthday. But to forget Christmas as well . . . ' Do you see? The second thing's got to be worse."

He wanted to punch himself. What was he doing, banging on about grammatical constructions and Christmas? This was his mother he was talking to, a woman who was frequently confused by the rules of television quiz shows.

"I have never forgotten your birthday. And how can anyone forget Christmas? They don't let you forget Christmas. The advertisements start in October. I don't understand a single word you're saying."

"Nobody's forgotten Christmas. It doesn't matter. Who told you about the column?"

"Marjorie from the book group."

He sighed. He was tired, and it wasn't even ten o'clock.

"Thank her for me, will you?"

"I thanked her at the time. Is it all true?"

Was it all true? Yes. Yes, he had sworn in front of the children. Yes, he had forgotten to pick Em up from her after-school dance class and left her to cry in the rain. Yes, he'd had a public argument with Joe's football coach and another dad had pulled him away. Yes, he'd come home drunk at five p.m. on Christmas Eve and slept until ten the following morning. Yes to a thousand other idiocies, forgettings, mistakes, and bad decisions. And anyway, he was pretty sure that his mother had heard these stories before. Many of them had been party pieces, jokes told at his expense, sometimes by Elaine, sometimes by Charlie himself. Everybody laughed. That's what family stories were—amusing accounts of the messes and the fuckups. Take away the love and the laughter, narrate the stories as if the characters had acted with malice and self-absorption, and everybody was in a bleak independent film about alcoholism and schizophrenia and child abuse.

"No," he said to his mother, because *no* seemed closer to the spirit of the truth than yes. "Of course not."

Later, he got a call on the office line from a researcher at a radio phone-in program.

"Charlie!" she said, as if they were old friends who hadn't spoken for months. "You must be a very angry man. Why don't you come on our show and tell everyone about it?"

"Is anyone really interested?"

"You were trending on Twitter for a couple of hours this week. Everyone's reading Bastard!"

Everyone's reading Bastard! A few days ago, this sentence would have been incomprehensible. Now he not only knew what it meant, but he understood that it had a unique and depressing personal application.

"And do you think that coming on the radio would help my situation?"

"It's what I'd want to do," she said.

"I don't think so."

"Go on. We'll send a car for you." This last offer was made seductively, as if what was stopping him talking publicly about the darkest secrets of his marriage was the expense of a taxi or the discomfort of public transport.

"Oh, well, in that case . . ."

"Great."

"I was joking."

"Oh."

"Listen, I really want to keep out of trouble."

"You're just going to let her beat you up?"

"She'll win, in the end. I can't go on the radio every week."

There was a pause. He was pretty sure he could actually hear the sound of cogitation.

"Do you want me to find out about that? I'm sure we'd love it. So would our listeners."

Jesus. Was that right? He could go on the radio every single week, talking about the wrongs done to him by his ex-wife? When he was a kid, even when he was a younger man, nobody knew anyone who had been on TV or on the radio or in the national newspapers. There was still the sense then that your life had to take some extraordinary turn, for the better or the worse, to achieve that kind of fame. You had to do something remarkable, or something terrible. Now everyone could get access to something—a cable TV show, a free newspaper, a digital radio phone-in—as long as they were prepared to say something stupid and provocative, with no expectation of money. A warring couple prepared to talk about their marriage publicly: that was a gift, a two-headed goose laying golden eggs. Of course he'd be allowed on the show every week. He could probably get his own program, on radio or TV. If he pushed, they'd probably give him an entire station. Someone had to turn this tap off, before the nation drowned in all the piss and vinegar gushing from it.

"No, thanks."

He was so frightened of the weekend and the humiliation it might bring (*might!* As if there were room for doubt, or hope) that he couldn't enjoy his children as much as he'd wanted to. He left work early on Friday and picked them up from school, as agreed upon with Elaine via terse texts; they still hadn't had a conversation about the column. None of the other parents even made eye contact with him.

"Why doesn't anyone speak to you, Daddy?" Emily asked while they watched Joe kick a ball around with his friends in the playground.

"People speak to me."

"Nobody at school."

"They don't really know me. I don't pick you up often enough."

"Did Mum write something about you? Something called a bad word?"

"Oh, you mustn't worry about that."

"Why not?"

"You know Mum and her jokes."

That was one of the most desperate explanations he had ever offered a child. Elaine was known for a lot of things, both privately and publicly, but she was not known for her jokes.

"Jessica in my class says the word means your mum and dad weren't married when they had you."

He laughed. He liked the idea of his headmaster father and his church chorister mother giving birth to a child out of wedlock, somewhere on the grounds of the exclusive private school where his father had worked.

"Why are you laughing?" Emily asked.

"Well, my mum and dad, they . . ."

He was about to paint an amusing portrait of his parents' painful moral rigor before moving on to a little lecture on the history of the word, how it had become loosed from its moorings, but he stopped himself just in time. The literal meaning, he suddenly saw, was much more useful.

"They weren't married, no. So . . . so yes. I am one. I'm afraid."

"A b-a-s—?"

"Yes. Very much so. Sadly. But don't ever mention it to Granny or Grandpa. They don't like to talk about it."

"Do you mind?"

"Not any more. These days, lots of kids are born when their mummies and daddies aren't married. Nobody cares."

"Is Auntie Annie one too?"

"No. Granny and Grandpa were married by then." There was no need for his sister to deal with the same stigma he'd had to endure.

"And also, you can't be one if you're a girl."

"Really?"

"Really."

"Why?"

"I don't know. You just can't."

And it was true, he realized as he was saying it. The word had mutated, and all bastards were men. Girls could be all sorts of horrible, terrible things, but they couldn't be that. He spent Friday night and Saturday in a clammy, isolating sweat of fear.

He promised himself that he wouldn't look at the column until he'd dropped the children off on Monday morning, because he didn't want to be more distracted on Sunday than he already was; he found himself reading it as soon as it was available online, soon after midnight on Saturday night. He scanned it, looking for his new name, but it didn't seem to appear very often—a couple of times at the beginning, once at the end, nothing in the main body of the piece, as far as he could see. He read it again, properly this time, and his heartbeat started to slow. He'd been spared. She'd chosen to write about her romantic history, the long, sorry story of her sexual relationships with men, starting with her seduction by a school friend's father when she was seventeen. (That old chestnut. How many times had he heard that story? If he'd been seduced at seventeen by, say, Ian Fielding's mother, he'd have been a very happy young man.) She was placing the failure of their marriage in context. It was pretty good, the column. He'd forgotten that Elaine could actually write. It was painful, though, and raw, and angry, and self-hating. She was more or less saying that, by the time she met Charlie, she had been ruined: she'd already slept with too many men who had lied to her, disappointed her, pretended to like her and admire her but actually wanted only to turn her into something else . . .

> something that even Don Draper would have regarded as too geisha-like. We watch those women in *Mad Men* and smile, relieved that we live in different times. But that's still what men want. It's just that now they know they're not allowed to say it. When I met Bastard, I had already given up. Yes, he spent ten years trying to knead and pummel me into the shape he wanted me to be in. But actually, I didn't feel much of it. I had given up by then. My romantic soul had already left my body.

So . . . it wasn't his fault! Charlie clenched his fist in triumph. If Elaine had been sitting next to him at the computer, he would have hugged her. On Sunday he took the kids swimming, and for a pizza, and to a film, and they stayed up later than they should have done on a school night to watch the results of a singing competition on TV; he felt like a new man. Next week, she would eviscerate him again, but next week was seven days away.

3.

"Is that Charlie?"
"Speaking."
He had a mouthful of sandwich, which he was eating in a very expensive menswear shop. If he wasn't taking a client out, then he

spent most lunchtimes eating on the move—mostly because he couldn't bear the people he worked with but also because he loved the neighborhood. His office used to be in town, but he was happier here, among the brand-new high-rise office blocks and the spotless chain stores. None of this had even existed when he had begun his working life. He and the rest of his clever, unpleasant colleagues had willed it into being, somehow.

The assistants were giving him dirty looks, and he was returning fire. *You need people like me, because the whole world is turning to shit,* he wanted to say. *So if not me, then who? And if I want to eat sandwiches, even sandwiches with mayonnaise oozing out of them, then I will.*

"Hi. You don't know me. My name's Helena Wyatt. A . . . well . . . someone I know who used to work with you gave me your number."

"OK."

"I'm . . . Well, you might know me as Bitch."

"Who?"

"Bitch."

These days, he was wary of every call he got from people he didn't know. There had been others, after the radio researcher—journalists and diarists from other newspapers, a strange man from a pressure group called Angry Dads. He didn't say anything for a while—he needed to scroll through as much adult memory as he had available to him. Did he know or even think of anyone as Bitch? He did not.

"I'm afraid I don't know anyone by that name. Actually, I'm not afraid. I'm proud."

"You don't look at the paper your wife writes for?"

"I try not to. I've been reading her thing online."

"Ah. That explains it. Well, they've found someone to write a column called Bitch. My ex-husband. It's on the same page as Bastard!"

"Jesus."

"Yes. So. We're Bastard and Bitch. There's quite a fuss about it."

"How are you doing?"

"Oh, you know . . ." And then for a few moments she was unable to go on. Charlie could hear her trying to stifle sobs.

"Do you want to meet for a drink later?" she said eventually.

* * *

At work that afternoon, there was crisis after crisis, meeting after meeting. Voices were raised, and it was almost certainly all going to end with someone getting fired. It wasn't going to be Charlie, though. He was too smart to get lured into that. After New York had been up for three or four hours and it became clear that the world—their world, yes, but actually everybody's world, now—would survive yet another day, things calmed down a little, and he retreated to a conference room to investigate Bitch.

Bitch was by Anonymous, although after Charlie had finished reading, he Googled "Helena Bitch Anonymous" and found the name of the author seventeen thousand times, in 0.23 seconds. He was a well-known controversialist, someone quite happy to make his money from saying things that he knew would upset people, especially people who read liberal broadsheet newspapers, or listened to debate programs on the BBC. He was a snob, and an unrepentant drunk, too. The column was misogynistic—even Charlie the Bastard could see that. It was also unconvincing and lazy and unfocused, and for a moment Charlie was proud of Elaine. She was capable of persuading anyone that he embodied all the qualities associated with the title she'd chosen for the column. Anyone reading Anonymous, however, would see immediately that he was a nasty, inadequate little man who didn't deserve access to the children he claimed his ex-wife was keeping him from. Charlie looked at the online debate about Bitch, the blogs and Twitter and the comment pages under the column, and found only abhorrence and venom, all of it directed at Anonymous, with the odd twerp attempting to cause trouble by defending the indefensible. Bitch wasn't the soul mate Charlie had been yearning for. She was way more sinned against than sinning.

She was terribly pretty, too, if one was prepared to forgive the wan vulnerability, which Charlie presumed was temporary and related to circumstance. They met in a quiet and expensive Covent Garden hotel; she looked so young and fragile that Charlie initially discounted her when he scanned the bar looking for a likely owner of the voice he'd heard on the phone. She ended up approaching him, and he tried to joke about it.

"Clearly I look like a bastard, whereas you look nothing like a bitch," he said.

She smiled warily. Charlie gave her plenty of time and room to disagree, but she offered nothing.

"Oh, well," he said. More time, more room, more nothing.

"Friends are telling me to see a solicitor," she said. "Have you thought about that?"

"Not really."

"Why not?"

"Because . . . Well, I suppose because everything she says is true, more or less."

"Really?"

"Yep." Actually, he could see that talking to someone about what Elaine had written could be very useful. "In your opinion, what's the worst thing she's said about me?"

"I didn't like that bit about watching pornography at your mother-in-law's."

"Really? Why?"

That particular misdemeanor he didn't feel too anguished about. Not the porn part, anyway, and its inappropriateness. The isolation, the loneliness, the alienation, and the depression were another story, but neither Bitch nor Elaine was interested in that one.

"I don't know. It seemed . . . disrespectful."

"It was two o'clock in the morning. It was my laptop. I had my headphones in. Elaine just happened to wake up."

For a moment, Charlie was tempted to remind her of a few of his other offenses, argue that some of them were much more offensive, but in the nick of time he saw that this might be an unwise course of action.

"Is everything he's saying about you a lie, then?"

"Oh, I don't know," said Helena. "What's the truth? Yes, I have asked him for more money, because he's not giving us anywhere near enough. Yes, I've stopped him from taking the kids anywhere, because they're scared of him at the moment. You've probably got exactly the same stories."

Charlie thought for a moment. He really liked this woman. Or, rather, he was really attracted to her, and nothing she had said so far had weakened the attraction. He suddenly saw that Elaine's column was a sort of gift: Helena didn't have to discover his worthlessness slowly, month after disappointing month. It was being revealed to her quickly and bluntly. He didn't have to pretend that he was anything other than the person Elaine was portraying, and any subsequent evidence of sensitivity, intelligence, or parental competence would surely seem dazzling against this background.

"Well," he said. "Mine are a little different. There isn't really another side to them. Like, I don't know. I really did tell her sister to fuck off at her daughter's christening. In a church. I suppose the other side is, most days I didn't do that. It was really a one-off."

Helena laughed. This was good, he could see. It was working.

"What makes writers think they have the right to do this to us, do you think?"

"Did you know you were marrying a writer?"

"Yes. It was what he always wanted to do. Did you?"

"Yes."

"That's it, you think?"

"Yes. It's our own stupid fault."

"I won't make that mistake again," said Helena. It wasn't a come-on, exactly, but at least he didn't belong to the tiny percentage of the workforce that she'd excluded from consideration. This was as close as he'd come to a boost in confidence for a while.

Charlie suggested dinner. Her mother was visiting, so Helena called her and persuaded her to put the children to bed.

There were other dinners after that, even though Helena's status as Bitch lasted only another week. Her ex-husband's column was dropped, after much media debate and a couple of expressions of discomfort from advertisers, companies that sold women's cosmetics and tampons.

"I'm sorry," said Helena. "It's not fair."

"His column was useless," said Charlie. "And horrible."

"But you're not a bastard."

"Thank you."

"I don't understand why you're not more angry about it."

He shrugged. The truth was that Helena had no idea whether he was a bastard or not. It was easy to be nice to an attractive woman over a dinner table. The despair came later, with children and tiredness and the sheer drudgery of marriage and monogamy. The reason Charlie wasn't as outraged as he could have been was that his conscience wasn't entirely clear, what with the infidelity and the drinking and the willful lack of involvement in family life. Taking abuse in a national newspaper without attempting to hit back was actually a pretty good way of wiping the slate clean. He was hoping that when this was all over, his spiritual overdraft would have been paid off, and he'd be allowed to use the cash machine again.

It was a while before Charlie and Helena were in a position to sleep together. Charlie now had his children every weekend, and Helena's children still didn't want to stay the night with their father, even in their own home. That still left plenty of time for the sexual act, of course, and Charlie had offered to book a hotel on a working afternoon, but Helena didn't want to get dressed and go home after they had made love. Eventually she explained her dilemma to her daughter's single, childless godmother, who offered to come and stay over on a weeknight. They were, finally, all set.

And that was the week Elaine chose to write about Charlie and sex. There were many accusations, all of them damaging and none of them untrue. They could be summarized thus:

(1) Bastard didn't enjoy giving oral sex and could only rarely be persuaded to do so. He was, however, an enthusiastic and demanding recipient.

(2) He was prone to premature ejaculation.

(3) In recent years he had been able to achieve an erection only by pretending that Elaine was his school history teacher, Miss Edwards.

None of this was information that Charlie, or indeed any man, would wish to share with a potential lover forty-eight hours before their first night together. And in the unlikely event that he had chosen to do so, he certainly wouldn't have wanted to do so via the national press. He had money, and his children were well, and he wasn't in a foxhole somewhere in Afghanistan—he appreciated that. Worse things happen at sea, of course they did, but not more embarrassing things. No sailor had ever felt as humiliated as this, surely. It was hard to imagine anything more excruciating than his next conversation with Helena.

Elaine had been clever about it, because she was a clever writer. The column wasn't about how useless Charlie was in bed. It was a column about male sexuality and the modern world and the Internet and feminism and a million other important subjects. But Charlie doubted whether that was what anyone would be talking or thinking about once they'd read it.

"Which one was Miss Edwards?" his mother asked when she called on Sunday evening. "Was she the redhead?"

He was wrong about there being nothing more excruciating than his next conversation with Helena. He may even have been wrong about worse things happening at sea, or in foxholes.

"I really don't want to have this conversation with you. Why are you still reading that bloody column?"

"Because everyone tells me about it anyway. I don't see why I should be the last to know."

"If you insist on talking about what Elaine wrote today, I will have to see a psychotherapist every day for the rest of my life."

"Well, it sounds as though you need to anyway."

"Can you not just . . . be on my side? Isn't that what a parent is supposed to do?"

"Who said I wasn't? I just can't remember what your history teacher looked like. I'm not against you just because I've forgotten a teacher from thirty years ago."

Charlie suddenly realized that Miss Edwards would be in her sixties now, probably. He needed to wipe the image of an elderly lady from his mind before Tuesday, just in case the younger version was needed.

"Yes, she was the redhead."

"Oh," his mother said. "Gosh."

"What does that mean?"

"I'm just surprised, that's all."

"I don't need you being . . . surprised by redheads. What I need is for you to say, 'This must be awful for you. How are you bearing up?'"

"It's awful for all of us. Your father doesn't want to leave the house."

"Why don't you try talking to Elaine about it? Instead of me? There's nothing I can do."

"You could not make the same mistake again. How about that?"

"Which mistake? Marrying Elaine?"

"Any of it."

"I'll bear that in mind, in the unlikely event that I ever fall for someone with her own newspaper column and an insatiable desire to expose all."

But that *was* the only lesson there was to learn. All the other things Elaine had written about weren't mistakes. They were expressions of who he was and what he'd become, and he couldn't do anything about any of it, apart from retrace his steps back and back and back, until he was fifteen or ten or three years old, and start again.

Helena didn't call him after the sex column, and he couldn't bear to call her. On Tuesday he sent her a text saying, "Still on for tonight? Cxxx." He didn't hear from her for an hour, and he spent the whole of it feeling sick. He had changed his mind about the benefits of having his sins enumerated and described in advance. He was going to be the first man in the history of the world ditched for being no good at sex even before he'd had a chance to prove it one way or the other. But then his iPhone pinged. "If you are. Hxx." One less kiss than he had offered, he noticed, but two beat the dreaded one. One, in his experience, indicated downright hostility.

They met in the hotel room, early evening. There was a good deal of awkwardness. Helena sat down in the one armchair, so Charlie sat on the sofa. They weren't even facing each other.

"Do you want to talk about . . . about what Elaine said on Sunday?"

"Not really."

"No. Me neither."

Charlie poured her some champagne. The sound of the fizz drew attention to their silence. It was loud enough to make them want to smother it with whatever came into their heads. What came into Charlie's head was a cough, and then a snatch of "Rolling in the Deep," which he hummed. What came into Helena's head was an observation about the column they didn't want to discuss:

"I mean, it's different, with different people, isn't it?" she said.

"Of course it is. Shall I open a tin of nuts?"

"It might not be like that with us." And then, perhaps after having considered all the territory the "that" had to cover, she said, "I mean, you know. Some of it."

"Yes," said Charlie.

"And some of it, well, it can't be helped."

"No."

What were the kinds of things that people talked about before they had sex with each other? He tried to remember. Not work, not sport . . . Films? Were films any good? Had he seen any?

"And neither of us have to do anything we don't want to, do we?" Helena went on.

"Absolutely not."

The "absolutely" contained too much conviction, he felt, and too much relief.

"By the way. I'm not as anti some things as she made out. And I'm not as pro some of the others."

That didn't sound good, either.

"I mean, I am pro, obviously." Was it obvious? "But not . . . not to the exclusion of everything else. Whatever the everything else might or might not be."

Helena looked momentarily alarmed.

"When you say 'everything else' . . . I haven't been with anyone apart from my ex for quite a long time. I'm not sure I know . . . I don't know if I want . . ."

"No, please, I quite understand," he said. "I'm not after anything . . . I'm not interested in, in . . . I'm just normal."

"Whatever normal is," said Helena. And then, "I'm sorry."

"What are you sorry about?'

"I didn't need to add that last bit. Everyone knows what normal is. Well, maybe not everyone. But . . . in this context. Oh, God."

Charlie laughed, mostly because he was desperate to laugh, and Helena's despair provided some kind of opportunity. But then they were back to silence. Even the champagne was quiet.

It was Helena who moved things along. She drank her champagne, put the glass on the desk, sat on his lap, and kissed him. Everything was easier after that. It probably wasn't possible to be the opposite of someone in bed, but he tried: he didn't want to be the person that Elaine had written about. And he didn't need help from Miss Edwards once.

"You know that nobody deserves that, don't you?" she said afterwards.

"What?"

"That column. However angry she was with you, it was cruel. There's always something to complain about, isn't there? With sex, I mean. If you really want to. Faces and noises and . . . and demands. But it takes a very unkind person to do it. And that's what people are saying."

"Which people?"

"Her readers. They've turned. You should read the comments online. She's overstepped a mark."

Charlie had never dared to look at the comments underneath Elaine's articles, but when he got home later, he drank them in. Every now and again someone would say something cruel and mean about him, and initially he understood the sentence "This comment has been removed by the moderator," which appeared several times on each page, to be sparing him even worse abuse. But the rest of the strange, angry little paragraphs, all written by people called Slaughterhouse6 or MissMiniver or AngryBrigadier or LordOfTheFiles, were so overwhelmingly hostile to Elaine that he realized the moderated remarks almost certainly hadn't been directed at him. People hated her. Some of them hated her so much that they used the B word. There was a wrong way to be a husband, and there was a wrong way to be a parent, and there was a wrong way to read, and talk, and watch TV, and according to Elaine he had chosen the wrong way every time. But there was no wrong way to have sex, according to all the Lords and the Brigadiers, so long as nobody got hurt or bullied, and if you tried to say that there was, you got into trouble. Finally, finally, Elaine had revealed too much, and she was in trouble. He checked Twitter and he Googled her name and he found an apparently inexhaustible deluge of disgust. Her newspaper didn't need two columns to play the Bastard-versus-Bitch game, in the end: Elaine was providing a stadium where the two teams could go head to head, and even though she was playing at home, she was losing. Maybe she'd lost. Maybe this was over.

And then the following week, Charlie understood that she hadn't even been using her best players. The only comfort he could draw was that she'd had to bring them on earlier than she might have hoped—she'd misjudged the sex column, and she needed to regain the ground that she'd lost with it. But once her big hitter was stripped off and ready for action, then it was all over.

"There is something I haven't told you," the column began, "and I now realize that it's relevant."

> If you don't know what I know, you'll come to a premature conclusion about me, and how I write about my ex-husband. Some of you, I know, think that I have been too hard on him, that I have been punching below the belt, in more than one sense of the phrase.
>
> So you need to know this: Bastard is a banker. He's not some harmless golf-playing local bank manager, either, or a staid, risk-averse employee of a private bank in the City. He's a real bastard, one of the Canary Wharf bastards: a credit-swapper, a subprime lender, a quantitative easer. . . . It sounds like one of those logic exercises, that sentence: all bankers are bastards, my ex-husband is a banker, therefore Bastard is a bastard.

A quantitative easer! Who did she think he was? The chairman of the Bank of England? Charlie's first thought was that Elaine hadn't listened to a single word he'd ever said. He'd tried to explain the difference between what he did, with his lunches and his clients and his occasional trips to Berlin and Chicago, and what the quants downstairs did. He'd told her how nobody within three or four thousand miles of the office had ever even met anyone who'd granted a subprime mortgage. She'd even written it all down, back in 2008, when she wanted to understand what was going on.

But then he realized that she didn't care about accuracy, and he felt stupid. Again. She knew that he couldn't be a quantitative easer, that he wasn't a subprime mortgage lender, that his job consisted of watching screens on behalf of people with much more money than him. She was just trying to cram in as many expressions as she possibly could in a few short lines to sketch the kind of bastard he was. It wasn't about swearing in front of the children; his crimes were cosmic, and harmed everybody. He was the kind of bastard who could never be forgiven, the kind of bastard who had wrecked the economy, the country, the continent, the world, the future. He stopped reading. The worst thing was that the game wasn't over, wouldn't be over until she got bored, or her readers did; she could stand there pounding him week after week, and her readers would cheer her on.

Charlie had never spent much time wondering what he wanted for himself. It had always seemed so obvious. He had met a beautiful, smart woman and he'd married her. He had embarked on a career that seemed to want whatever talents he had, and he'd made a success of it. He'd been able to provide his family with all the money they might need. What kind of idiot would need to reflect on any of that? He wasn't even sure there had ever been any room for reflection. If there had been a fork in the road at any point in his life, then he hadn't noticed it. All he'd ever done was put one foot in front of the other and keep walking. And if he'd stopped, just for a moment, someone would have knocked him over and trodden on him.

Late on Monday afternoon, Tim Britton found him staring out of the window and down at the river below.

"Fuck her," Britton said. "Fuck her, and fuck her chippy readers, and fuck everyone else in the world who sits around scratching their balls and moaning about what we've done to them."

Charlie looked at him gratefully. Maybe Tim Britton wasn't such an arse after all.

"There's a little gang of us going out tonight. Shit day. Steaks and a few bottles of Argentinean red. Do you want to come along?"

Most of Charlie didn't, really. He wanted to go out with other people, people who'd never even been to Canary Wharf, people who despised everyone who worked here and everything they did. But he didn't seem to know anyone like that any more. He put on his jacket and took off his tie, and in the lift, surrounded by the men and women he worked with every day, men and women who had already started to flirt with each other, he found himself getting hungrier and thirstier and louder.

■

How to Slowly Kill Yourself and Others in America: A Remembrance

FROM *Cold Drank*

I'VE HAD GUNS PULLED ON ME by four people under Central Mississippi skies—once by a white undercover cop, once by a young brother trying to rob me for the leftovers of a weak work-study check, once by my mother and twice by myself. Not sure how or if I've helped many folks say yes to life but I've definitely aided in few folks dying slowly in America, all without the aid of a gun.

* * *

I'm 17, five years younger than Rekia Boyd will be when she is shot in the head by an off duty police officer in Chicago. It's the summer after I graduated high school and my teammate, Troy, is back in Jackson, Mississippi. Troy, who plays college ball in Florida, asks me if I want to go to McDonald's on I-55.

As Troy, Cleta, Leighton and I walk out of McDonald's, that Filet-o-Fish grease straight cradling my lips, I hold the door open for a tiny, scruffy-faced white man with a green John Deere hat on.

"Thanks, partner," he says.

A few minutes later, we're driving down I-55 when John Deere drives up and rolls his window down. I figure that he wants to say something funny since we'd had a cordial moment at McDonald's. As soon as I roll my window down, the man screams, "Nigger lovers!" and speeds off.

On I-55, we pull up beside John Deere and I'm throwing finger-signs, calling John Deere all kinds of clever "motherfuckers." The dude slows down and gets behind us. I turn around, hoping he pulls over.

Nope.

John Deere pulls out a police siren and places it on top of his car. Troy is cussing my ass out and frantically trying to drive his Mama's Lincoln away from John Deere. My heart is pounding out of my chest, not out of fear, but because I want a chance to choke the shit out of John Deere. I can't think of any other way of making him feel what we felt.

Troy drives into his apartment complex and parks his Mama's long Lincoln under some kind of shed. Everyone in the car is slumped down at this point. Around 20 seconds after we park, here comes the red, white and blue of the siren.

We hear a car door slam, then a loud knock on the back window. John Deere has a gun in one hand and a badge in the other. He's telling me to get out of the car. My lips still smell like Filet-o-Fish.

"Only you," he says to me. "You going to jail tonight." He's got the gun to my chest.

"Fuck you," I tell him and suck my teeth. "I ain't going nowhere." I don't know what's wrong with me.

Cleta is up front trying to reason with the man through her window when all of a sudden, in a scene straight out of *Boyz n the Hood*, a black cop approaches the car and accuses us of doing something wrong. Minutes later, a white cop tells us that John Deere has been drinking too much and he lets us go.

16 months later, I'm 18, three years older than Edward Evans will be when he is shot in the head behind an abandoned home in Jackson.

Shonda and I are walking from Subway back to Millsaps College with two of her white friends. It's nighttime. We turn off of North State Street and walk halfway past the cemetery when a red Corolla filled with brothers stops in front of us. All of the brothers have blue rags covering their noses and mouths. One of the brothers, a kid at least two years younger than me with the birdest of bird chests, gets out of the car clutching a shiny silver gun.

He comes towards Shonda and me.

"Me," I say to him. "Me. Me." I hold my hands up encouraging him to do whatever he needs to do. If he shoots me, well, I guess bullets enter and hopefully exit my chest, but if the young Nigga thinks I'm getting pistol whupped in front of a cemetery and my girlfriend off of State Street, I'm convinced I'm going to take the gun and beat him into a burnt cinnamon roll.

The boy places his gun on my chest and keeps looking back and forth to the car.

I feel a strange calm, an uncanny resolve. I don't know what's wrong with me. He's patting me down for money that I don't have since we hadn't gotten our work-study checks yet and I just spent my last little money on two veggie subs from Subway and two of those large Chocolate Chip cookies.

The young brother keeps looking back to the car, unsure what he's supposed to do. Shonda and her friends are screaming when he takes the gun off my chest and trots goofily back to the car.

I don't know what's wrong with him but a few months later, I have a gun.

A partner of mine hooks me up with a partner of his who lets me hold something. I get the gun not only to defend myself from goofy brothers in red Corollas trying to rob folks for work-study money. I guess I'm working on becoming a black writer in Mississippi and some folks around Millsaps College don't like the essays I'm writing in the school newspaper.

A few weeks earlier, George Harmon, the President of Millsaps, shuts down the campus paper in response to a satirical essay I wrote on communal masturbation and sends a letter to over 12,000 over-whelmingly white Millsaps students, friends and alumnae. The letter states that the "Key Essay in question was written by Kiese Laymon, a controversial writer who consistently editorializes on race issues."

After the President's letter goes out, my life kinda hurts.

I receive a sweet letter in the mail with the burnt up ashes of my es-says. The letter says that if I don't stop writing and give myself "over to right," my life would end up like the ashes of my writing.

The tires of my Mama's car are slashed when her car was left on cam-pus. I'm given a single room after the Dean of Students thinks it's too dangerous for me to have a roommate. Finally, Greg Miller, an English Professor, writes an essay about how and why a student in his Liberal Studies class says, "Kiese should be killed for what he's writing." I feel a lot when I read those words, but mainly I wonder what's wrong with me.

It's bid day at Millsaps.

Shonda and I are headed to our jobs at Ton-o-Fun, a fake ass Chuck E. Cheese behind Northpark Mall. We're wearing royal blue shirts with a strange smiling animal and Ton-o-Fun on the left titty. The shirts of the other boy workers at Ton-o-Fun fit them better than mine. My shirt is tight in the wrong places and slightly less royal blue. I like to add a taste of bleach so I don't stank.

As we walk out to the parking lot of my dorm, the Kappa Alpha and

Kappa Sigma fraternities are in front of our dorm receiving their new members. They've been up drinking all night. Some of them have on black face and others have on Afro wigs and Confederate capes.

We get close to Shonda's Saturn and one of the men says, "Kiese, write about this!" Then another voice calls me a "Nigger" and Shonda, a "Nigger bitch." I think and feel a lot but mostly I feel that I can't do anything to make the boys feel like they've made us feel right there, so I go back to my dorm room to get something.

On the way there, Shonda picks up a glass bottle out of the trash. I tell her to wait outside the room. I open the bottom drawer and look at the hoodies balled up on the top of my gun. I pick up my gun and think about my Grandma. I think not only about what she'd feel if I went back out there with a gun. I think about how if Grandma walked out of that room with a gun in hand, she'd use it. No question.

I am her grandson.

I throw the gun back on top of the clothes, close the drawer, go in my closet and pick up a wooden T-ball bat.

Some of the KA's and Sigs keep calling us names as we approach them. I step, throw down the bat and tell them I don't need a bat to fuck them up. I don't know what's wrong with me. My fists are balled up and the only thing I want in the world is to swing back over and over again. Shonda feels the same, I think. She's right in the mix, yelling, crying, fighting as best she can. After security and a Dean break up the mess, the frats go back to receiving their new pledges and Shonda and I go to work at Ton-o-Fun in our dirty blue shirts.

I stank.

On our first break at work, we decide that we should call a local news station so the rest of Jackson can see what's happening at Millsaps on a Saturday morning. We meet the camera crew at school. Some of the boys go after the reporter and cameraman. The camera gets a few students in Afros, blackface and Confederate capes. They also get footage of "another altercation."

A few weeks pass and George Harmon, the President of the college, doesn't like that footage of his college is now on television and in newspapers all across the country. The college decides that two individual fraternity members, Shonda and I will be put on disciplinary probation for using "racially insensitive language" and the two fraternities involved get their party privileges taken away for a semester. If there was racially insensitive language Shonda and I could have used to make those boys feel like we felt, we would have never stepped to them in the first place. Millsaps is trying to prove to the nation that it is a post-race(ist) institution and to its alums that all the Bid Day stuff is the work of an "adroit entrepreneur of racial conflict."

A few month later, Mama and I sit in President George Harmon's office. The table is an oblong mix of mahogany and ice water. All the men at the table are smiling, flipping through papers and twirling pens in their hands except for me. I am still 19, two years older than Trayvon Martin will be when he swings back.

President Harmon and his lawyers don't look me in the eye. They zero in on the eyes of Mama, as Harmon tells her that I am being suspended from Millsaps for at least a year for taking and returning *Red Badge of Courage* from the library without formally checking it out.

He ain't lying.

I took the book out of the library for Shonda's brother without checking it out and returned the book the next day. I looked right at the camera when I did it, too. I did all of this knowing I was on parole, but not believing any college in America, even one in Mississippi, would kick a student out for a year, for taking and returning a library book without properly checking it out.

I should have believed.

George Harmon tells me, while looking at my mother, that I will be allowed to come back to Millsaps College in a year only after having attended therapy sessions for racial insensitivity. We are told he has given my writing to a local psychologist and the shrink believes I need help. Even if I am admitted back as a student, I will remain formally on parole for the rest of my undergrad career, which means that I will be expelled from Millsaps College unless I'm perfect.

19-year-old black boys can not be perfect in America. Neither can 61-year-old white boys named George.

Before going on the ride home with Mama, I go to my room, put the gun in my backpack and get in her car.

On the way home, Mama stops by the zoo to talk about what just happened in George Harmon's office. She's crying and asking me over and over again why I took and returned the gotdamn book knowing they were watching me. Like a black mother of a black boy, Mama starts blaming Shonda for asking me to check the book out in the first place. I don't know what to say other than I know it wasn't Shonda's fault and I left my ID and I wanted to swing back, so I keep walking and say nothing. She says that Grandma is going to be so disappointed in me.

"Heartbroken," is the word she uses. There.

I feel this toxic miasma unlike anything I've ever felt not just in my body but in my blood. I remember the wobbly way my Grandma twitches her eyes at my Uncle Jimmy and I imagine being at the end of that twitch for the rest of my life. For the first time in almost two years, I hide my face, grit my crooked teeth and sob.

I don't stop for weeks.

The NAACP and lawyers get involved in filing a lawsuit against Millsaps on my behalf. Whenever the NAACP folks talk to me or the paper, they talk about how ironic it is that a black boy who is trying to read a book gets kicked out of college. I appreciate their work but I don't think the irony lies where they think it does. If I'd never read a book in my life, I shouldn't have been punished for taking and bringing back a library book, not when kids are smoking that good stuff, drinking themselves unconscious and doing some of everything imaginable to nonconsenting bodies.

That's what I tell all the newspapers and television reporters who ask. To my friends, I say that after stealing all those Lucky Charms, Funyons, loaves of light bread and over a hundred cold dranks out of the cafeteria in two years, how in the fuck do I get suspended for taking and returning the gotdamn *Red Badge of Courage*.

The day that I'm awarded the Benjamin Brown award, named after a 21-year-old truck driver shot in the back by police officers during a student protest near Jackson State in 1967, I take the bullets out of my gun, throw it in the Ross Barnett Reservoir and avoid my Grandma for a long, long time.

I enroll at Jackson State University in the Spring semester, where my mother teaches Political Science. Even though I'm not really living at home, everyday Mama and I fight over my job at Cutco and her staying with her boyfriend and her not letting me use the car to get to my second job at an HIV hospice since my license is suspended. Really, we're fighting because she raised me to never ever forget I was on parole, which means no black hoodies in wrong neighborhoods, no jogging at night, hands in plain sight at all times in public, no intimate relationships with white women, never driving over the speed limit or doing those rolling stops at stop signs, always speaking the king's English in the presence of white folks, never being outperformed in school or in public by white students and most importantly, always remembering that no matter what, white folks will do anything to get you.

Mama's antidote to being born a black boy on parole in Central Mississippi is not for us to seek freedom; it's to insist on excellence at all times. Mama takes it personal when she realizes that I realize she is wrong. There ain't no antidote to life, I tell her. How free can you be if you really accept that white folks are the traffic cops of your life? Mama tells me that she is not talking about freedom. She says that she is talking about survival.

One blue night my mother tells me that I need to type the rest of my application to Oberlin College after I've already hand-written the personal essay. I tell her that it doesn't matter whether I type it or not since Millsaps is sending a Dean's report attached to my transcript. I say some other truthful things I should never say to my mother. Mama goes into her room, lifts up her pillow and comes out with her gun.

It's raggedy, small, heavy and black. I always imagine the gun as an old dead crow. I'd held it a few times before with Mama hiding behind me.

Mama points the gun at me and tells me to get the fuck out of her house. I look right at the muzzle pointed at my face and smile the same way I did at the library camera at Millsaps. I don't know what's wrong with me.

"You gonna pull a gun on me over some college application?" I ask her.

"You don't listen until it's too late," she tells me. "Get out of my house and don't ever come back."

I leave the house, chuckling, shaking my head, cussing under my breath. I go sit in a shallow ditch. Outside, I wander in the topsy turvy understanding that Mama's life does not revolve around me and I'm not doing anything to make her life more joyful, spacious or happy. I'm an ungrateful burden, an obese weight on her already terrifying life. I sit there in the ditch, knowing that other things are happening in my mother's life but I also know that Mama never imagined needing to pull a gun on the child she carried on her back as a sophomore at Jackson State University. I'm playing with pine needles, wishing I had headphones—but I'm mostly regretting throwing my gun into the reservoir.

When Mama leaves for work in the morning, I break back in her house, go under her pillow and get her gun. Mama and I haven't paid the phone or the light bill so it's dark, hot and lonely in that house, even in the morning. I lie in a bathtub of cold water, still sweating and singing love songs to myself. I put the gun to my head and cock it.

I think of my Grandma and remember that old feeling of being so in love that nothing matters except seeing and being seen by her. I drop the gun to my chest. I'm so sad and I can't really see a way out of what I'm feeling but I'm leaning on memory for help. Faster. Slower. I think I want to hurt myself more than I'm already hurting. I'm not the smartest boy in the world by a long shot, but even in my funk I know that easy remedies like eating your way out of sad, or fucking your way out of sad, or lying your way out of sad, or slanging your way out of sad, or robbing your way out of sad, or gambling your way out of sad, or shooting your way out of sad, are just slower, more acceptable ways for desperate folks, and especially paroled black boys in our country, to kill ourselves and others close to us in America.

I start to spend more time at home over the next few weeks since Mama is out of town with her boyfriend. Mama and I still haven't paid the phone bill so I'm running down to the pay phone everyday, calling one of the admissions counselors at Oberlin College. He won't tell me whether they'll accept me or not, but he does say that Oberlin might want me because of, not in spite of, what happened at Millsaps.

A month passes and I haven't heard from Oberlin. I'm eating too much and dry humping a woman just as desperate as me and lying like its my first job and daring people to fuck with me more than I have in a long time. I'm writing lots of words, too, but I'm not reckoning. I'm wasting ink on bullshit political analysis and short stories and vacant poems that I never imagine being read or felt by anyone like me. I'm a waste of writing's time.

The only really joyful times in life come from playing basketball and talking shit with O.G. Raymond "Gunn" Murph, my best friend. Gunn is trying to stop himself from slowly killing himself and others, after a smoldering break up with V., his girlfriend of eight years. Some days, Gunn and I save each other's lives just by telling and listening to each other's odd-shaped truth.

One black night, Ray is destroying me in Madden and talking all that shit when we hear a woman moaning for help outside of his apartment on Capitol Street. We go downstairs and find a naked woman with open wounds, blood and bruises all over her black body. She can barely walk or talk through shivering teeth but we ask her if she wants to come upstairs while we call the ambulance. Gunn and I have taken no Sexual Assault classes and we listen to way too much *The Diary* and *Ready to Die,* but right there, we know not to get too close to the woman and just let her know we're there to do whatever she needs.

She slowly makes her way into the apartment because she's afraid the men might come back. Blood is gushing down the back of her thighs and her scalp. She tells us the three men had one gun. When she makes it up to the apartment, we give the woman a towel to sit on and something to wrap herself in. Blood seeps through both and even though she looks so scared and hurt, she also looks so embarrassed. Gunn keeps saying things like, "It's gonna be okay, sweetheart," and I just sit there weakly nodding my head, running from her eyes and getting her more glasses of water. When Gunn goes in his room to take his gun in his waistband, I look at her and know that no one man could have done this much damage to another human being. That's what I need to tell myself.

Eventually, the ambulance and police arrive. They ask her a lot of questions and keep looking at us. She tells them that we helped her after she was beaten and raped by three black men in a Monte Carlo. One of the men, she tells the police, was her boyfriend. She refuses to say his name to the police. Gunn looks at me and drops his head. Without saying anything, we know that whatever is in the boys in that car, has to also be in us. We know that whatever is encouraging them to kill themselves slowly by knowingly mangling the body and spirit of this shivering black girl, is probably the most powerful thing in our lives. We also know that whatever is in us that has been slowly encouraging us to kill ourselves and those around us slowly, is also in the heart and mind of this black girl on the couch.

A few weeks later, I get a letter saying I've been accepted to Oberlin College and they're giving me a boatload of financial aid. Gunn agrees to drive me up to Oberlin and I feel like the luckiest boy on earth, not because I got into Oberlin, but because I survived long enough to remember saying yes to life and "no" or at least "slow down" to a slow death.

My saying yes to life meant accepting the beauty of growing up black, on parole, in Mississippi. It also meant accepting that George Harmon, parts of Millsaps College, parts of my state, much of my country, my heart and mostly my own reflection, had beaten the dog shit out of me. I still don't know what all this means but I know it's true.

This isn't an essay or simply a woe-is-we narrative about how hard it is to be a black boy in America. This is a lame attempt at remembering the contours of slow death and life in America for one black American teenager under Central Mississippi skies. I wish I could get my Yoda on right now and surmise all this shit into a clean sociopolitical pull-quote that shows supreme knowledge and absolute emotional transformation, but I don't want to lie.

I want to say and mean that remembering starts not with predictable punditry, or bullshit blogs, or slick art that really ask nothing of us; I want to say that it starts with all of us willing ourselves to remember, tell and accept those complicated, muffled truths of our lives and deaths and the lives and deaths of folks all around us over and over again.

Then I want to say and mean that I am who my Grandma thinks I am.

I am not.

I'm a walking regret, a truth-teller, a liar, a survivor, a frowning ellipsis, a witness, a dreamer, a teacher, a student, a joker, a writer whose eyes stay red, and I'm a child of this nation.

I know that as I've gotten deeper into my late twenties and thirties, I have managed to continue killing myself and other folks who loved me in spite of me. I know that I've been slowly killed by folks who were as feverishly in need of life and death as I am. The really confusing part is that a few of those folk who have nudged me closer to slow death have also helped me say yes to life when I most needed it. Usually, I didn't accept it. Lots of times, we've taken turns killing ourselves slowly, before trying to bring each other back to life. Maybe that's the necessary stank of love, or maybe—like Frank Ocean says—it's all just bad religion, just tasty watered down cyanide in a Styrofoam cup.

I don't even know. For real.

I know that by the time I left Mississippi, I was 20 years old, three years older than Trayvon Martin will be when he is murdered for wearing a hoodie and swinging back in the wrong American neighborhood. Four months after I leave Mississippi, San Berry, a 20-year-old partner of mine who went to Millsaps College with Gunn and me, would be convicted for taking Pam McGill, a social worker, in the woods and shooting her in the head.

San confessed to kidnapping Ms. McGill, driving her to some woods, making her fall to her knees and pulling the trigger while a 17-year-old black boy named Azikiwe waited for him in the car. San says Azikiwe encouraged him to do it. Even today, journalists, activists and folks in Mississippi wonder what really happen with San, Azikiwe and Pam McGill that day. Was San trying to swing back? Were there mental health issues left unattended? Had Ms. McGill, San and Azikiwe talked to each other before the day? Why was Azikiwe left in the car when the murder took place?

I can't front, though. I don't wonder about any of that shit, not today. I wonder what all three of those children of our nation really remember about how to slowly kill themselves and other folks in America the day before parts of them definitely died under the blue-black sky in Central Mississippi.

ALEXANDER MAKSIK

■

Snake River Gorge

FROM *Tin House*

ARE YOU HAPPY?

Henry had been in the green easy chair, but once my parents left the room, he came around the coffee table and sat next to me on the couch.

Theo, he asked, laying his hand on my shoulder. Are you happy?

He was nothing like the skinny LDS kids my mom let in sometimes, who sat in the kitchen in their suits and black ties, drinking our lemonade. Henry wore a yellow tie around his thick, pale neck, and a stiff, blue dress shirt, and a belt with a silver tip. He reminded me of a guy I knew who worked at the Best Buy out on Bridgeview Boulevard.

Theo, man, he said like we were buddies. Brother, are you happy here? I mean, is this the way you imagined it going? Your life, I mean?

He'd taken his hand away and slunk down next to me, mirroring my posture, legs out, feet flat on the floor, like it was just the two of us at home, natural as ever, trying to work out our lives. I was thinking how incredible it was that he was there at all. That you could call a number from the *Penny Saver* and a few hours later a guy like Henry would be sitting in your living room offering you a job.

If everything's cool, you wouldn't have called us. His head was close enough that I could hear the white Life Saver clicking against his teeth. Yo, he whispered. Is he messing with you?

What do you mean?

You know what I mean, *man*. Your *dad*. Is he *fucking* with you? He said it angrily, as if he'd do something about it right then, all I needed was to say the word.

No, I said. No. No one is messing with me. Jesus *Christ*, I said, sounding just *like* my dad, who was *not* messing with me. Who, back then, was doing nothing but going out looking for work and coming home to tell us no one was building anywhere. With his hands on the edge of the bar that separated the kitchen from the little breakfast nook where we ate all our meals and where my mom kept her boxes and mailing labels, he'd tell us how he'd driven all the way to Mountain Home, or Arco, or as far as Elko once. He couldn't even find work pounding nails. We'd eat whatever my mom had spent the last hour trying to improve—chili, or corned-beef hash, or black beans and rice. Until the spring came, my mom would say. You know it'll be better in the spring.

In April she sold her car to pay the mortgage. I guess we were always quiet people, but after that, whole days would pass without a single word spoken between us. Then my sister, Caroline, fell off the earth, and we went ghostlike.

I knew we were in real trouble, but all I did those months was drink beer with Cody Thompson and fail my classes. Nobody said anything to me about that. Then I saw the ad and called.

It happens, you know? And if it's happening to you, it's not your fault. It's them. They're the ones that are sick. They're the ones with problems. It's *you* the victim, he said, as if he hadn't heard me, like he was reciting from a doctor's office pamphlet.

No one is *messing* with me, I said.

So why'd you call, Theo? If it's not that, what is it? If it's just the money, the money's good, man. But it's not *just* the money for us. For us, it's a lifestyle. You know, we're a family. But the money's good. Thousand a week if you work it hard enough. Couple hundred, easy.

Thousand a week?

If you work it hard, brother. I know guys who do fifteen, even two, in the right neighborhoods, under the right moon. He laughed. Course, you got to work up to that.

I laughed.

What does your dad do?

Contractor.

Yeah? My dad too, except no one's building shit anymore. Your mom work?

I didn't believe him about his dad being a contractor.

She sells on eBay, I said.

He nodded and we both looked out past the low table where the TV used to be and through the windows onto the street where Henry's van was parked behind my dad's truck.

So, *it's* the money.

I nodded.

It's never just the money, Theo, he said.

I heard the back screen open and smack closed and then my parents were standing in the breakfast nook looking over at us. Henry stood up right away and smoothed his pants with his thick hands.

Mr. and Mrs. Lanting, we take good care of these kids and Theo's just the kind to make some real money. I really think he'll do well.

Then he looked straight at my dad and said, At the very worst, he's bringing in two hundred. I mean, that's the honest low right there and I got to tell you, sir, I'm expecting much much more. I mean, the boy would have to *want* to fail to make so little.

So, if you or Mrs. Lanting don't have any other questions, all I need now is your permission. Henry gestured at a piece of paper that, twenty minutes before, he'd unfolded and set on the polished tabletop with a flourish, like he was proud of it. My dad bent over, and my mom smiled like something lovely had been decided. Henry smiled back at my mom like he was proud of *her*, and of all of us. My dad signed and then he walked into the backyard, where I knew he was smoking and pulling on the side fence, worrying about how much it gave and how he should have used roofing tar on the posts.

Pack a bag, brother, Henry said, folding the release form and returning it to his pocket.

How long until he comes back?

That depends on Theo, Mrs. Lanting. He can come home anytime he wants to. Anytime at all and, of course, anytime you want him home, you just call that number I gave you.

She came around the table and hugged me and whispered, It'll be good for you to get out of here for a while, kiddo. Come back in September, do those classes over. It'll be a good break.

I went into my room and packed my old Bruins duffel. I didn't sit on my bed or look out the window. It was as if I'd already gone.

At the van, it was just Henry. He opened the passenger side and waited for me to climb in. If it had been Cody holding the door with that kind of ceremony, I would have said, What—no corsage? But I didn't say anything.

The windows were rolled up and the AC was on high. Henry steered with one hand and pulled out the knot of his tie with the other.

We drove out to the Weston Inn on Blue Lakes, which took about five minutes, and I followed him through the lobby. He started taking his shirt off in the hallway and was bare-chested by the time he was knocking on a door. He wasn't quite as tall as I was, but he was built like a running back.

The motel room smelled of cigarettes and beer and hair spray and the curtains were drawn. It reminded me of parties I'd been to with Cody at the ISU dorms—guys sitting on the floor, backs against the wall, and a couple of girls at a table around a bottle of Smirnoff.

Nora had long, brown hair, too pale skin, and large breasts beneath a tight, torn-up old T-shirt. Cody would have gone crazy for her. Henry sat in the middle of the giant bed and leaned back against the headboard. It was hard to believe my parents were only five minutes away.

Give Theo your chair, Nora. Be a good host. Come sit over here. She smiled at me when she crossed the room. All of them looked exhausted and sick.

Go ahead, Theo. I sat on Nora's chair with the duffel on my knees. Give him a beer, Mattie, Henry said. A guy with wide black eyes threw me a can from the other side of the room, where he sat on a chair by the window.

This is your crew, T. Look around you. You'll be with Mattie tomorrow. He's a Mexican but you'd never know it the way he works. He'll show you what you need to know. Nobody here sells like Mattie-O except Nora and that's why they get the bed. Highest sellers always get a bed. Lowest sellers on the floor. And if you don't sell at all? He stared hard at a hangdog kid leaning against the bathroom door. You're a Bunker Baby. The kid kept his head down. But you're no Bunker Baby, Theo my man, right? We keep all your money on the books. Each day you get a twenty-buck draw for whatever. You need more than that, say the word, and if it's in there it's yours. Motel's always ten a day. A sale's a slap and you get eight a slap. Mattie'll teach you the rest, cool?

I nodded. He bit a Life Saver out of a roll, got up off the bed, and pulled a copper money clip from his pocket. You need to use that handsome face, brother. You want a first day bonus?

I nodded again.

T, you got to speak the *fuck* up. So, you want that bonus?

Okay.

Okay? He looked around the room and laughed. Some of the others smiled, but no one said a thing. Mattie-O, you've got some work to do tomorrow. Got him, Mattie-O said, looking out at the street.

Henry took a step closer to me so he was looking down and I was looking up. Give me a smile, T. Smile gets you a bill. He withdrew a hundred from the clip. Come on, T, smile for me. Smile for your crew.

I did what he asked.

With teeth, brother, let me see it with teeth, show me what I want to see.

And I showed him.

Hell yeah, that's what I'm talking about. That's the smile that sells. He returned the bill to the clip. That's a hundred on the books, plus I'll give you the room tonight. So you start tomorrow with one twenty. Cool?

Thanks, I said.

Tomorrow we jump. That means packed and gone by seven.

He nodded at me and left, saying into the hallway, Keep 'em under control, Mattie-O, and the door closed behind him with a quiet and solid click.

No one said very much that night. Mostly we sat around the table getting drunk, playing quarters, listening to that coin crashing against the glass, until midnight, when Mattie called bedtime. They all told me their names but I only remember Nora and Mattie, who slept on the bed while all the rest of us slept on the floor. One of the girls lay down next to me and wrapped a blanket around us like we'd been doing it every night the same way. That girl was so thin. I'd never been that close to another person before and when she slid in there and covered us up and pulled my arm around her and hung on to it tight like it mattered, I began to cry.

* * *

In the morning, I woke with the thin girl's sharp spine against my chest. I could see the red numbers burning inside the alarm clock on Nora's side of the bed. I liked the way they lit up her face. Whatever time it was, it wasn't too far from when we were supposed to be in the parking lot. I got brave for a second and kissed the neck in front of me and whispered *wake up wake up,* but the girl didn't move until Henry pounded on the door. Then she rolled over and looked at me and smiled and said, Thanks for keeping me warm. Everyone was awake by then, gathering their stuff together while Mattie stood by the door watching us.

Henry took us out 93 and onto the bridge. I looked down at the Snake and thought of Evel Knievel strapped into his rocket. Once, my dad snuck Caroline and me out to where the ramp had been. I sat on his shoulders and held on to his ears, terrified by the ripping wind and the depth of the vast canyon, but Caroline stood right on that fenceless edge with her arms spread, leaning forward while my dad held the hem of her T-shirt in his fist.

My dad had been there for the countdown, had shot the whole thing on Super 8. Caroline used to beg him to set up the projector and let us watch those reels—the soundless crowd, the launch, that sky cycle dangling from its parachute, blown nearly all the way back to the ramp, its long silent fall into the rocks. Sometimes, after the film ran out, my dad would lie on the floor with Caroline on his feet and fly her through the white light so she could watch her shadow sailing across the screen.

I could see her little-girl face, but not the one she had now. I tried to imagine her out there, tried to see her eyes, but all that came was the uniform and the M14 and the shadow beneath her helmet.

In Boise, Henry dropped us in around the North End. Power houses, Henry called them. Fat and white and full of money, he said. Everybody was on their own except for me and Mattie.

When they were all gone, Mattie said, Listen. You're with me all morning, but at the next pickup he'll give you your own pad case and drop you in alone. You need to sell. You understand me? You blank one or two checks, fine, but you blank the whole day, the night's ugly and I can't do anything for you. Mattie had big eyes and long lashes but his mouth at rest was down-turned and there was the same cold thing about him like with all the rest of them. You understand me, Theo?

I said I did.

He took the ring out of his lip and dropped it into his shirt pocket. Hope so, he said and started walking. I trailed him and between houses he taught me what he could. You knock at the door, you smile, you talk. You adapt to each house, each face.

Hello, ma'am, my name is Mateo. Excuse me for bothering you, but I'm at Boise State and I'm trying to win a scholarship to study in Spain next semester. I'm only ten subscriptions away from winning the prize. Ahead of everybody, he'd say. Sometimes he'd speak Spanish to make his point and he always smiled.

He sold seven that morning. All cash. In Vegas it had been UNLV. In Salt Lake, Brigham Young, in LA, USC. It didn't matter, he said. You make up your own story, but don't get behind. Make your own shit up, whatever feels natural. You get behind and they own you. Sell, don't drink too much, go easy on the weed, never go joints for points, always take cash, never touch the meth or anything else.

Henry picked us up a few hours later. Is my man T ready? Oh, I like that, he said. T-Ready. You want that name, Theo? T-Ready? T. Ready, he said, drumming hard on the steering wheel. So is he ready, Mattie-O, Mattie-O?

Mattie looked out the window, so still, a foot on the dash, and told him I was, I was.

Well, today you stick with Mattie-O. Make sure you have a *proper* education. Kid writes more business than anyone I ever seen. I was sitting behind them in the first row of seats, watching Henry's fingers drumming drumming drumming. We drove around in the foothills and then he dropped us in again, around Camel's Back Park, and tore out of there, nearly sideswiping a mailbox.

Stay away from all that shit, Mattie said first thing. He shook his head. All of it.

Mattie and I did another two hours and he sold eight more with that smile. The guy was convincing. He made *me* want to buy from him. At the last house he said I could come up on the porch with him. I was supposed to be his big brother. Rich white kid helping a Mexican from the streets, he said. The woman who answered started out serious and hard the way anyone does when there's a stranger at the door. He did a pitch about being out of a gang for a year now and almost graduated from high school. He was pointing to me saying that my family had saved him from the gutter when he stopped, looked at his feet, shook his head, and said, Ma'am, I'm sorry, but you're just making me all nervous here. I have a hard time talking to beautiful women, so I'm sorry if my voice is shaking, but no woman like you ever opened the door to me. The lady looked at me with her mouth open and she was shaking her head like she couldn't believe there was anyone so sweet in the whole world. She bought six believing she'd just secured him a full ride to BSU.

I'd never seen anything like that.

Mattie-O, man, you're smooth, I said.

Don't I know it, T-Ready. Don't I know it.

We had another hour of work before the pickup, but he cut it short and we walked down the hill and sat inside a Starbucks to get out of the heat. They had big day-old cookies for a dollar and Mattie bought me one.

What are you doing here, Theo?

Same as you, I guess.

Nah, man. You're not the same as me.

I don't know, I said. Need to make some money.

You want money, go get a job. This is no job. Nah, man, you're not the same as me and you're sure as hell not the same as Henry or *any* of the fools around here. It's all over your face and not just because you're a baby.

I'm seventeen, I said.

You're a *baby*. Man, we come from *shit*. You understand me? From shit. But you, I'll bet all the business I just wrote that your mom's like any other Jones we've been lying to all day. You ever even been in a fight, Theo?

I shook my head and looked out at some kids scrambling around in the parking lot.

You see? So what the fuck are you doing here? Is someone messing with you? Someone coming into your bedroom at night?

No.

No? Come on, man, what is it then? Your parents still alive?

I nodded.

Live in a little white house together?

Blue.

Blue. We both laughed.

Who's the most famous person in your family?

What do you mean?

I mean, who do they always talk about? Some uncle who invented the staple? Your cousin in a Pepsi commercial? Who is it? Who's the T-Ready family legend? *T-Ready*, he said again and shook his head. Fucking Henry.

My grandmother, I guess.

Your grandmother. So what'd *she* do?

She was a model.

A model. Go, grandma Theo. So, that's it?

Her older sister ended up some famous artist.

Yeah?

That's what my mom says. World famous.

That's it?

My grandpa was a boxer. Three-time heavyweight champion of the army.

Damn.

I nodded. I loved the way he looked at me like he was impressed.

We've got photos of him in a nightclub with Frank Sinatra and Joe Louis. You should have seen the building my grandparents lived in, man. Like a hotel. Doorman. The whole thing. And you think you came from shit? My grandpa came from *shit*. He came up from *nothing*, went through the army, got out, started a company that made bricks, and got rich. He belonged to country clubs and ate steak. You should see the photos. They were all style. Drove around in a convertible Mercedes.

He shook his head. You see what I'm saying? So what happened? They have money?

They used to.

Why used to?

They lost it. Gave it away. Had it stolen from them. I don't know.

They're both dead?

I nodded. On the inside of his right arm were three long burn scars the shape of fat worms.

Got a brother? You *know* all the Theos sit around a long table eating Thanksgiving dinner. Turn off the TV, pass the potatoes.

No.

No what? No potatoes?

No brother.

Sister?

Caroline.

Caroline. Caroline and Theo in the blue house on the hill and their deep, dark family secrets. Man you need to go home, Theo. Where's she in college?

She was here. At BSU.

How about you? Where you from? You have a sister? I asked, but he ignored me.

What's she do now? She's a lawyer, right?

She's in Afghanistan.

What the fuck is she doing in *Afghanistan?*

That's a damn stupid question, I said, sounding exactly like my father.

I watched one of those beautiful UPS trucks come swinging around the corner and head up the hill toward the golf course.

What? She's in the marines or some shit?

Army.

And she went over there?

ROTC. Second Lieutenant Caroline Lanting.

And *you're* out here.

She's twenty-two, I said.

Mattie stared at me with those wide black eyes, and then he said we needed to get out of there. He had his hands on the table like he was a second from standing up.

I *was* in a fight once, I said, to keep him there.

Okay, badass, go on, tell it.

Before my dad lost his job, my parents sent me down to visit my grandparents in LA.

So what, Theo?

So when I got down there my grandpa had gone all fat. The apartment smelled like piss. You've never seen so much mail. Piles all over his office and he just sat there in his big leather chair right in the middle of it. You know, that place had just gone to shit. The carpets were worn out. They had these red leather couches and they were all cracked. There was lettuce rotting in the fridge. I found yogurt under the sink.

Theo, we got to go, he said, but he was still sitting there, and I kept on talking.

There was this game room in the building, and one night I taught my grandma to play pool. Every time I made a shot, she said, Fat Man, you play a great game of pool.

Mattie laughed.

After the game, we're standing right outside the apartment and she says to me, Theo, you know how much I love you? I love you more than I love your father. And right then the door opens and there's my grandpa in his dirty old robe saying, I'm gonna break your jaw, trying to steal my woman. He squared off and threw a punch. He came out into the hall and threw another.

What happened?

Got me in the side. Knocked the wind out of me. Then he just dropped his fists and turned around and went back inside to his chair.

Then what?

I left the next day. My grandmother died a few months later. Not even a month after that, my grandpa.

Theo, man, that's a hell of a story, but, man, we've got to go, he said.

We left the coffee shop, walked into the heat, down to the corner, and waited for the pickup.

Henry drove out of there too fast, still drumming on the wheel. There was that kid at the back of the van. He had some kind of infection, his right eye covered over with hardened pus. Henry said, You see that last row of seats, Theo? That's the bunker. And you know why Jeremy is sitting on the bunker? Because the boy doesn't take his job seriously. He's *unprofessional*. That's why. That's why he's my Bunker Baby and pretty soon I'll just have to leave him by the side of the road. But you're not that kind of guy, that's why you're sitting up here in front next to Nora.

Nora reached over the seat and crossed her arms around Mattie's chest.

That night Henry bought Coors Light for everyone else and a case of Beck's for Nora and Mattie. They drank it on their bed, sitting together, backs against the headboard, green bottles in their hands. The rest of us were getting drunk playing quarters around the wide round table. As I drank, I liked watching them there, the way they were so quiet, sitting up straight, side by side, and how they held their green, silver-necked bottles like scepters.

Henry was staying in the adjoining room. For a long time the doors were closed, but later he opened them and came in dragging Bunker Baby behind him on a chair. The kid was tied up, his wrists and ankles bound to the wooden legs with T-shirts rolled into rope. Henry raised his hand, Mattie threw a Beck's into the air, Henry caught it and returned to the other room.

Later, when I was struggling to keep my balance, I went over to Bunker Boy, kneeled, and looked up into his face. He was slumped forward, head hanging, wrists pulling against his restraints. His eyelashes were gone to that crusted shell. He looked at me with his clear blue eye. I started to untie him, but Mattie called to me from his throne. Theo, he said, quick and hard. I looked back and Nora shook her head. She smiled and raised her eyebrows like I should know better and when I gave up she nodded like she was pleased with me. I fell asleep at his feet.

In the morning I woke holding the thin girl, the two of us wrapped in blankets. Someone had turned the air conditioner to high, and the room was very cold. The girl was warm against me. She smelled of sweat, cigarettes, and beer. The kid was still in the chair, head rising and falling on his chest like a buoy. We were close to him, the girl's face nearly touching his hand, which hung, swollen with blood. After a while I slipped my arm from beneath her, reached out, and untied the knot. I took his hand in mine and swung it like a piece of meat hanging from a hook. I got up and untied his other wrist and then his ankles. No one was awake. I looked over from time to time at Mattie and Nora, but they were motionless deep beneath the covers. The kid straightened and opened his good eye to look at me. He tried to stand, but his knees were too stiff, or his legs had gone numb. I bent over and he put his arms around my neck. He was shivering and smelled like he'd pissed himself. I got him to his feet and we stood there holding on to each other until he could take his own weight, and then we walked over to the bathroom, where I left him.

I returned to the girl and our blanket. I pulled our shirts up so that our skin would touch and fell asleep again like that.

We slept through the morning and it wasn't until after one that Henry woke us all up. He put a wide, flat box of Krispy Kremes on the floor, where most of us ate, wrapped up in blankets, pressed together like mice. Nora was still in bed, but Mattie was dressed and at the table with Henry, both of them sipping coffee. Bunker Baby was lying on his side under the television, which was strapped into a rack and hanging from the ceiling. He'd wrapped himself in towels and drawn his knees up to his chest.

Who knows why Jeremy was tied up last night? Henry asked like a math teacher. Who can tell me why Jeremy was tied up last night?

Someone said, Bitch can't sell, and Henry nodded.

He owes, someone else said.

He nodded again.

That's right. That's it exact. Bitch can't sell. He owes and he owes and he owes deep. So what I want to know is why he's over there on the floor wrapped up warm in our clean towels.

Who set you free, Bunker Baby? Who set you free? Henry raised his eyebrows, then his chin.

The kid didn't say anything, just closed his eye.

I was on my back with my head in the girl's lap. I could hear her stomach growling. She was moving her fingers through my hair. Even then I wasn't quite sure what she looked like. I didn't much want to know. I liked that she was warm and that she touched me without either of us having to say anything about it.

When I said, I did it, she slid back from me fast and my head dropped to the carpet.

Henry shook his head and looked at the ceiling. Ah man, T, you just got here.

I rolled my head to the side and saw the kid with his cheek against the floor, looking at me. He needed to see a doctor about that eye. I didn't want to, but I sat up and said, He'd been there all night, man. I didn't untie him until this morning.

T-Ready, Henry said, drumming his fingers fast on the tabletop, you want to stay here? He asked me slow, You want to *sell* or you want to go home?

What I wanted right then was to sleep every night with that girl, and go everywhere with Mattie and Nora.

Then Henry seemed to lose patience with his own speech. One minute he was starting out slow, the next he was standing up and moving across the room fast. He kicked me once hard in the ribs. All my breath was gone. I'd never been kicked like that before.

The pain was worse than all the pain I'd ever imagined.

He stood above me not speaking. Or maybe he was speaking. Then he kicked me again and again and I thought I would die there.

When I came to, everyone was gone, except for Mattie and Nora.

Get up, Mattie said.

He had the toe of his boot under my skull.

Nora was still on the bed, watching me.

I stood. The pain was sharp, like Henry was still there, like he was stabbing me every time I filled my lungs, and when I coughed it dropped me to my knees.

You need to go *home*, Theo, he said.

I stood in that frigid room looking at him. He'd been there all night, Mattie, I said. Tied up, *man*.

He took the ring out of his lip and dropped it into his shirt pocket. There was that cold thing on him again. That cold thing like all the rest of them had.

Mattie, Nora said. I looked over at her. When I turned back to him, he hit me hard in the face. The blow spun me around and I bent over holding my eye, but I didn't go down.

He put his mouth next to my ear and said, That hurt, Theo? You like that, Theo? Mattie, Nora called to him again. He reached beneath my chin, took me by the throat, and pulled me up. He drew his fist back. Henry doesn't want to see you walk, Theo. He'll come after you, you know. It doesn't just end with that guy.

Mateo, Nora called out, this time louder.

He hit me in the eye again—short and sharp—and let me drop.

The pain shot through my face, radiated, was in my skull, was everywhere.

I stayed on the ground and waited with my hand over my eye.

* * *

When Nora helped me up, Mattie was gone.

She'd wrapped ice in a washcloth and pressed it to my face. You're lucky, she said when I winced. You're lucky he didn't break your jaw, she whispered. You're lucky it wasn't Henry.

We were sitting together beneath the window, our backs to the wall. I held the ice to my eye. I could feel her pushed against me, warm. The air conditioner was still on high. I could hear it whir and rattle.

Henry will come back for you, Theo. He'll come back and it'll be much worse. You can't imagine how much worse. You need to leave here. You need to *leave* here.

But I didn't want to go anywhere. I wanted to sit still and pressed against Nora. That was all I wanted. I was out of fear.

Come on, she said, and slipped her hand beneath my arm. Come on, she said again and pulled. This is lucky, she said. This is lucky. She pushed my duffel into my chest. She kissed my cheek and shoved me into the hall. Go home, Theo, she said. Go home.

I walked along the carpet, past all those doors and out through the lobby and into the parking lot, where the day was hot. The sun burned my eyes. Everything hurt, but the heat, the heat was something else.

I stood on the asphalt in the sun with my eyes closed, trying to work out what to do next. I was very weak and when I opened my eyes I thought I might pass out. Then I saw the van turning into the parking lot and I slid down behind a bank of vending machines. I watched as Henry jumped out of the driver's side. He left the engine running. The windows were closed. I could see in, see those silhouettes in their seats. I squinted to see through the tint and into the far back. I knew Henry had the air conditioner on high. I drew my knees to my chest and kept myself tight against the wall. The air was hot and dry.

After a while he came back, this time with Mattie and Nora. They got in. I watched as the van returned to the street and disappeared. Then I pulled myself up and returned to the motel.

There was a heavy girl working the front desk.

Listen, I said. I stayed here last night with my family. We checked out just today. They're waiting for me outside, I said. My little sister lost her bear. She thinks she left it in the room. Do you mind if I run down there and check? It's room 220. And 222. The kids were in 220, parents were in 222. I'll be just a few minutes.

She looked at my eye. You all right? What happened to you? She had a short purple scarf tied around her throat like a stewardess might wear.

Oh, I said. Got in a fight at school. I'm fine.

She looked through the window to the parking lot. I don't see anyone out there, she said and looked back at me.

They're out there, I said. I promise they're out there. Little white sedan. Engine's running.

You don't seem okay to me, she said. You seem scared.

I'm fine, I said. I'm not *scared*. I'm just nervous. I have a hard time talking to beautiful women, I said. That's all it is.

She blushed and smiled. I see, she said, turning away to find the keys. Aren't you charming? She slid them across the counter to me. Five minutes or I call security, she said.

I found Bunker Baby on the floor of Henry's room. The chair was on its side and he was tied to it. He was in bad shape, blood all over his face, his eyes swollen.

I set him free and helped him stand. I turned off the air conditioner and cleaned him up with a washcloth soaked in very warm water. He was shivering and shivering.

Jeremy, I said, but he didn't answer me. You're all right, I said, moving the warm washcloth over his face and wringing out the blood into the sink.

When I'd done the best I could, I helped him into the hall. He kept his arm around my shoulder and we walked together into the lobby. At the desk, I gave the keys back to the woman.

What the fuck? she said, staring at us.

Thank you, I said. Thank you. And we walked out into the heat. There was a phone booth out front and I drew the glass door open and put him in there. Sit down, I said. Sit here.

It was like an oven. I got in there with him and pulled the door closed and picked up the phone.

I'm going to call my father, I said. I'm going to call my father. I put a quarter into the slot. I put my hand on Jeremy's shoulder. My father will know what to do, I said.

KYLE MINOR

∎

Seven Stories About Kenel
of Koulèv-Ville

FROM *The Iowa Review*

1. The First Day I Met Kenel

THE KIDS AT THE ORPHANAGE said Kenel is a liar.

The man at the tree place said Kenel is the best translator in Ouest Province. No French in his English.

The missionaries said Kenel is bad news. When he was a child he was always breaking things. You should see the two ladies who raised him. They're both hunched over. He wore them out.

The Canadian dentist recommended Kenel. He said one day he was up in the mountains doing field dentistry, and this husband and wife came in with vampire teeth. Triangles that came to points. They said their teeth hurt, and Kenel said, "Don't fix the vampire teeth. Just do the fillings." But the dentist didn't listen. He restored the man's teeth and the woman's teeth to happy squares. He showed them in the mirror. He thought they'd be so happy. But the woman yelled and the man cried. Kenel listened and did his translating. Kenel said, "Get out the file. They want the vampire teeth back. There's a thing they do." The man pulled the neck of his shirt to his shoulder. There were hundreds of little scars, some of them fresh.

I paid Kenel seventy dollars a day. The other translators got fifty, but he said he had a thing for sevens. He said he had seven older brothers. When he was seven days old, seven women begged his father not to give him away to the two lady missionaries. They said seven curses would befall him.

"The first curse was the curse of English," Kenel said. We were walking the village Barette, taking the census of the rabbits and the chickens. "No Creole allowed. No French. Only English."

He spoke in English, read in English, wrote in English, watched movies in English, gave tours of the missionary compound to visiting Americans and Danes in English. "They said we're your mothers now," he said. "Children speak the language of their mothers."

The day he turned seventeen, the two missionary ladies drove him up the mountain to his father's house. They said, "Now you're grown. We've done all we can." Kenel said, "Aren't you my mothers?" They cried and drove away. His father came out of the house and cried and embraced him and spoke to him in a language he couldn't understand. "The second curse was the curse of Creole," Kenel said. "It took me seven years to speak it well enough to pass for a Haitian."

Up the hill was the *houngan*'s house. His wooden roof was painted purple beneath a field of orange stars. I wanted to visit him and convince him to sell it to me to take to Florida. Kenel said, "If the houngan came to my village, we would have to kill him."

"Why?" I said.

"Because," Kenel said, "he does not have the love of Christ in his heart."

Later, I asked the elders of Kenel's village if they would kill the houngan. They laughed. "Kenel is a liar," they said. "The houngan is our friend. He goes to the church in Barette sometimes on Sundays when they need a trumpet player. The houngan is a good trumpet player."

In the village Barette, Kenel told me the third, fourth, fifth, and sixth curses. It was getting dark, and we were walking up out of the village. I asked him what was the seventh curse. "You see these people, all my neighbors? I have to live among them. You and me, we're not like them."

He headed up the hill a ways, and I followed him across the mountain to his home. From every house we passed, people called their greetings.

2. Before the Earthquake

This was before the earthquake reduced the Hotel Montana to rubble. We were sitting at the bar drinking Dominican beers, Jean-Pierre, Kenel, and me. The next morning we had to drive to Jacmel to count some rabbits and chickens. Kenel had a little cocaine, and I gave him a little money, and he gave me the cocaine, and I put it in my pocket for the morning.

We were playing a game called Who's More Heroic Than The Americans. It was a joke of a game. The first round everyone said: "Everyone who's not an American." The second round you had to tell another true story, but this one had to be specific.

"I knew a Catholic priest in Cité Soleil," Jean-Pierre said. "He was Nigerian. The people were so mean to him. This went on for years. They stole things from his house. Once, he was beaten in the street and no one came to his aid. Still, he lived seven years in a shanty house, even though he could have lived well. He could have lived anywhere. One day a little retarded boy was crossing an open sewer on a lashed-together bridge made of two halves of one tree. The sewer was five feet deep with water and every kind of human waste. People pissed in it, shit in it. The sewer was the color of disease. This little retarded boy couldn't have been more than five years old. Halfway across the bridge, some older boys came and shook both sides, just to be mean. The little retarded boy fell in. He was flailing around. There was a big crowd. People were watching him go down, but nobody wanted to jump in. Around the time the boy went over, the Nigerian priest came walking by. He didn't even hesitate. He didn't take off his clothes or his watch or take out his wallet or anything. He just jumped in, head-first, into the shitwater. He went under and came back up with that kid. That brown sludge was in his mouth, in his teeth, in his eyes."

"I can beat that," Kenel said. "I knew a man who took a blowtorch to the side of a shipping container somebody was using for a store in the village Marigot. The store owner caught him red-handed at midnight. His bag was filled up with biswuit, dry goods, Tampico juices, Coca-Colas. The store owner called for his cousins, and his

cousins called for their cousins. Soon all the men of the village surrounded this man in the shipping container. They tied him up, and
in the morning, they dragged him out into the middle of the road.
They brought out all the children to see. The store owner said, 'See
what happens when you steal.' While the man was still alive, they
hacked off his fingers and toes one by one with a machete. They
sealed the wounds with a hot iron. Then they hacked off his feet and
hands. Then they hacked off his arms at the elbows and his legs at
the knees. Then they poured gasoline over his head and set him on
fire and watched him dance around while he died."

"The store owner was a hero," Jean-Pierre said, "for protecting his
family business."

"No," Kenel said. "The thief was a hero, for risking his life to get
food for his family."

They looked at me. I shielded my part of the table with my arm. I
poured some of the powder on the table, made a line, and snorted. I
said, "I wish I had some to share."

3. After the Earthquake

We went down to the mausoleum where Kenel's dead were buried.
The earth had buckled in waves, and one of the waves split the center
of the concrete, and where it had split, the fresh corpses had fallen
out of their graves and mingled on the ground with the bones of the
longer dead, and some carrion animals were pulling at a dead woman's face. The smell is in my nostrils still.

At the graveside, I told Kenel I couldn't take this gruesome scene,
this horror movie.

Kenel lifted the bodies from the ground one by one, and held them
for awhile. "Auntie Marie," he said. "Auntie Ti-ti. Auntie Solange."

4. The Pig and the Pony

We reached a vista. All of Port-au-Prince stretched out beyond us,
the sun reflecting from the metal roofs of the bidonville shanties
like a hundred thousand daytime stars. An American Airlines jet
took off from the airport. Kenel said any child with a shoulder-fired

rocket launcher could stand on any rooftop in La Saline and blow any airplane out of the sky. Why hadn't it happened yet?

A donkey draped with yellow saddlebags came up the road from the distance. A thin man in a yellow shirt led the donkey up the hill. He waved as he got closer. His shirt and the saddlebags said DHL in red letters. We said *bonswa* and *komon ou ye* and *byen, byen*. "What do you have?" Kenel said. "Letters," the DHL courier said. "Where is your motorcycle?" Kenel said. The DHL courier said the gas tank had rusted out, so he had replaced it with a gallon milk jug, but someone had dropped a match into the milk jug while he was making a delivery at the cement store.

After the DHL courier left, six men came up the hill carrying a casket. They were dressed in fine linen suits, and white specks from the dirt in the road were soiling their shoes, which were newly shined. We made room so they could pass us, and as they passed we briefly joined in their funeral song.

We watched them disappear behind a bend where the road followed the curve of the mountain, and when they were gone, I asked Kenel who was in the casket. "That is the wife of one of the elders of the village Jean-Baptiste," he said. "She fell in love with a bourgeois man in the city. Every day she took the tap-tap to see him. He gave her so much money. When the elder found out, he fed her feet to his pony."

Later I visited the village Jean-Baptiste and played soccer with some of the men who lived there. After the game, the women made a feast of rice and stewed tomatoes and a sauce of leeks and carrots. For me, they killed their fattest rabbit, and they would not take any money for it. While we were eating, I asked about the elder who fed his wife's feet to a pony. A man stood up and said, "Come, let me show you." We walked down the orange path, past his sister's house, his brother's house, the houses of his two friends and his one sworn enemy. A bone-thin pony was tied up in the front of his own house. He petted the pony, and said, "The lies they are telling about you." Then we went to the backyard, where he kept two pigs, and he pointed to the fatter one. "It was this fellow who ate the feet," he said. "Not the pony."

We stared at the pig for a long time. I imagined the woman's feet in its mouth. Then the man laughed bitterly. "Do you think this is a village where we feed the parts of people to animals?" He said it to shame me.

When I told Kenel, he said, "Don't believe it. I don't trust that pony."

5. The Third, Fourth, Fifth, and Sixth Curses

Once, late at night, we were trying to sleep in the reclined seats of a borrowed Jeep in the middle of the treeless forest, on our way to cross the Dominican border. We both kept machetes under the seats, and I had a gun. Somewhere near enough to hear but not near enough to see, a lot of people were singing and beating drums. I kept the keys in the ignition.

Sometime before morning, Kenel said, "Tell me about your mother."

"She was a good woman," I said, "but for twenty years she refused to talk to her sister."

"Her sister slept with her husband?" Kenel said.

"No," I said. "It was a misunderstanding. Her sister forgot to pick me up from school one afternoon, and one time she left me alone in her house for a half hour while she went to the store to buy some groceries. There was an incident with somebody saying something to somebody else about what somebody else said to some other person. I'm not sure I understand it."

"After I was born, my mother ran away," Kenel said. "No one knows where. There was some kind of craziness in her family. My father said many of them had been turned into zombies. He took me to see them near Furcy. They were chained to a plow, four of them, and pulling it. My father said, 'That's voudou,' and I said, 'No, it's not. That's mental illness.' The farmer had a whip, but he wasn't driving them with it. He didn't need the whip. Their spirits were broken already. They were machines with broken brains."

He reached under his seat for his water bottle and took a sip. "Why are people so bad to each other?" he said. "There was this crazy woman. She always came into town with this mongrel dog. She only had one friend. He was a crazy person, too. A line of drool always hung from his mouth. He had gums instead of teeth. Sometimes he stole some food for her dog. I never saw her eat. She was always looking for food for the dog."

Sometimes when I think of him, now, it's this moment. He's staring out the window in the direction of the mountains of Massif de la Selle, thinking about his mother.

"Sometimes she slept on the steps of the mission school. When she did, we stepped over her. Someone might poke her with his foot, to wake her. Someone probably kicked her sometime, but I never saw anyone do it.

"One morning the dog was gone. She was walking the street, looking for the dog. All day she was looking. The next morning, she lay on the steps of the mission school. I stepped over her. We all stepped over her. Nobody poked or kicked her. We let her sleep. We felt sorry for her, because of the dog.

"She was still lying there at the end of the school day, when they opened the doors and let us free. She didn't move the whole day, and then she didn't move the whole night. One of the teachers came along and covered her body with a black sheet. Nobody wanted to take her body. Nobody wanted her to live forever with their own dead. Nobody wanted her bones with their bones.

"Nobody claimed her body until the next morning. It was the crazy man who fed her dog. He lifted her body, sheet and all. He was talking to her. He had her under the armpits, and he started spinning with her. He was dancing with her. They were turning and turning. He was making a noise like an animal soon to the slaughter.

"People were yelling. Put her down, put her down! The boys picked up rocks and threw rocks at him. He had to flee. He tried to carry her away with him, but she was too heavy. The rocks were still coming. His face was bloody from them, and his shirt was torn. Finally, he dropped her in the grass by the side of the road. She lay there for three days, and then a Dutch man paid to have her buried in another village. He sent two men to collect her body.

"For a while I didn't think about her much. But after I saw her relatives chained to the plow, I thought: Could that crazy woman have been my mother?"

6. The Tumor

The kids at the orphanage said why do you ride around with Kenel?

The missionaries said watch out. He wants things from you. He will steal things from you. Watch your guns. Watch your jewelry.

The man at the tree place told me about a cash-for-charcoal scam that ended in nobody getting any charcoal. The man at the art kiosk across the street from the mission told me about a middleman scheme. The man who built the wooden A-frame houses that were meant as temporary housing, but which the people who bought or received them meant to last a hundred years, told me about a strike-and-extortion scheme, which yielded nothing. "I have a hundred bodyguards," the man said, although he only had two. A farmer in Artiste told me of a scam where Kenel tried to sell electricity he was stealing by tying barbed wire to the new power lines the president was running up the mountainsides. "Does he think I don't have barbed wire?" the farmer said. "Everyone has barbed wire."

Almost every day, Kenel asked me for more money. He said his nephew needed money to give the school for photocopies. He said his niece needed money for needle and thread. He said the church needed money for sound equipment. He said his father needed money for a saw and a lathe and a level, so he could start a new business as a carpenter. He said he knew a man whose father had a tumor the size of a small grapefruit on his prostate. He said he needed money to take out the tumor and the prostate. "Let me see this man," I said. "Take me to see this man."

We walked down into Kenel's village. "Don't be alarmed," Kenel said, "when you see their eyes." All the members of the family had a degenerative eye disease. They all went blind by age twenty-five. "My friend is twenty-three," Kenel said. "You can see it already. The disease is eating his eyes."

There were eight small children, two teenage girls, Kenel's friend, and his father and mother, both of whom were in their seventies. Kenel's friend was a very late child. ("A miracle child," I said. "A shame and a burden," Kenel said.) The teenage girls and the children were the sons and daughters of sons and daughters and grandsons and granddaughters who had long since fled for the city. These were the unwanted children, or the too-many children, or the children taken early by the blindness. Kenel's friend was working for tips at the Hotel Kinam to bring in money, and tending the garden in the mornings. When he was gone, people stole from the garden. There was no one in the family able enough to do anything about it.

We greeted Kenel's friend. "My friend," he said, "my good friend. You will come see my father."

He led us through a maze of banana trees, past the hundred-year-old stone house, to the unfinished concrete house at the back of the property. It had holes for windows and a hole where the roof would go. The old man sat shaking in a chair at the center of the one room. Piles of construction sand filled the four corners.

The old man leaned on his cane and shook. He waved us near him and spoke. He had the breath of brown death. After he said half a sentence, he paused to catch his breath, and Kenel translated. "I saw you in a dream," he said. "Bondye sent you from America. Your journey took you over the sea. You are estranged from your mother. You are wearing glasses and you have beautiful shoes." Most of these things were true. "Bondye said this man will come," he said. "You will show him your wound. He will lay hands on your wound, and your wound will be healed."

He pushed on his cane. With some effort, he sat upright in his chair. With his shaking hand, he handed the cane to his son. With great effort, he reached both hands to his pants button and his zipper. He said, "I will show you." He unbuttoned his pants, and he unfastened his zipper. With both hands, as if presenting a bouquet of flowers, he held himself out to us. What he showed was mostly tumor. His penis and his testicles had shriveled to a flaccid tininess. Most of his hair had fallen away. Only a slight smear of peach fuzz remained, and it was slick with a yellowish-white discharge from a suppurating wound that was on the tumor but not of the tumor.

"Bondye said," the old man repeated, "this man will come. You will show him your wound. He will lay hands on your wound, and your wound will be healed."

Everyone was looking at me. Kenel, with his good eyes. The man's son, with his cataracting, failing eyes. The old man, with his blind eyes. Even the tumor seemed like a giant dying eye. The man's son was nodding, as if to say: go ahead. Kenel was watching, as if to see what kind of man I was after all our time together.

I held out my hands. I cupped them as if I were preparing to draw water from the river. I put them on either side of the tumor. My right wrist grazed the old man's tiny penis, and my left wrist grazed his testicles. The skin swollen by the tumor was hot, and the skin covering the genitals was as cold as a slab at the morgue. "You must pray," the son said. "Our Father, who art in heaven," I said. It wasn't a prayer to the sky. It was a prayer to the people in the room. If there was any belief to borrow, it was all theirs.

Then I couldn't remember the rest of the words to the prayer, even though it was the most famous prayer in the world. In my mind, it had become conflated with a less famous poem, by an American who had once been my teacher at the university. *Our Father who art in heaven, I am drunk. Again. Red wine. For which I offer thanks. I ought to start with praise, but praise comes hard to me. I stutter . . .*

I had not memorized the whole poem, but I did remember the ending, the beautiful ending. The drunk, praying, thinks of himself as an old-time cartoon character, a poor jerk who wanders out on air and then looks down. Below his feet, he sees eternity, and suddenly his shoes no longer work on nothingness, and down he goes. The drunk prays: *As I fall past, remember me.*

It seemed as fitting a prayer as the one I had forgotten. I cobbled together bits and pieces of both, and drew on the language of special pleading I remembered from all those dreary years at the Cherry Road Baptist Church. I used the words suppurating, and grapefruit, and hot and cold, and shrivel and shrink.

When I was done, nothing happened. Everyone was as blind or cataracted or tumored or lying or despicable as we had been before we prayed, and my hands were wet with white and yellow pus. I told the old man I was sorry. Nothing happened. He had not been healed. I must not be the man Bondye had sent from over the sea. He said, "We must wait. Bondye's time is not our time."

Outside, I asked Kenel, "How much is the surgery?"

Kenel said, "All surgeries are three hundred dollars."

I said, "I have four hundred dollars in my pocket. I'm going to give all of it to him."

Kenel said, "If you give him four hundred dollars for his surgery, they will use it to buy sand and Portland. Or they will use it to buy a window. Or they will use it to buy corrugated aluminum for a roof.

The old man will die soon no matter what you do."

"What can I do?" I said.

"You can give the money to me," Kenel said. "I will take it to pay the doctor, and I will pay the tap-tap to take him to the doctor."

I looked at him, and I knew. He would take the money and put it in his pocket, and I would never see him again. Or I would see him again the next time he wanted some money.

"No," I said, quietly. "No, no."

I put the money back in my pocket and vowed to return after we did the count in Mirebalais—in three weeks. Pick up the old man myself. Take him to the hospital myself. Pay for the surgery myself.

In later years, a woman told me: Who do you think you are, to play God? Who do you think you are, the savior of the world? I said: I only wanted to save this one man for a little while. I knew he was going to die soon.

Three weeks passed. We returned to the village. Another casket, a cheap one, was marching up the street. So many of the pallbearers were blind. "Don't worry," Kenel said. "You took his tumor in your hands." "But I didn't cut it out," I said. "You should have given me the money," he said.

7. At the Marché

A few days later we went to the Marché en Fer to buy fruits and vegetables. The whole market had fallen down in the earthquake, but now an Irishman had rebuilt the clock tower and the minarets, restored the masonry, and reinforced the iron columns. The Irishman said the new walls were earthquake-proof, and the roof was covered with solar panels.

These were the days when it was hard to walk into a building and not be afraid the walls and the roof might fall on you and crush your head. You looked for a space beside a sturdy piece of furniture and traced an invisible line at a forty-five degree angle, which you'd dive beneath for shelter at the first shake. Every so often, continuing to this day, another building would fall in an aftershock. All over the country we saw three-story buildings pancaked to one story, and lo these years later, the bodies still inside. They didn't even stink anymore. Almost for certain, the bacteria and the worms and the rodents had picked them to bones.

But it wasn't like the early days. People were moving. Children in uniforms walked to school in the mornings. The tap-taps were full of men carrying their work tools in canvas bags. In the city, the cell phone vendors walked the streets in their red smocks and carrying their red phones, selling *rechoj* cards, and soda and water vendors walked through the traffic jams, carrying on their heads cardboard boxes full of plastic sugar-and-caffeine concoctions and vacuum-sealed plastic bags of water.

In the Marché, I bought two bottles of Atomic Energy Drink, one for me and one for Kenel, and he bought me a Styrofoam container full of griot and fried plantains and pikliz. I bought him a pizza from a vendor billing herself as the Walt Disney Pizza Company. Famous mice and dogs and ducks decorated the sign behind her.

We took our food outside and crouched in the shade of the nearest wall. While we were eating, Kenel said, "When you leave, will you come back?"

I stopped eating for a moment. An uncharacteristic sincerity was in his eyes. I didn't trust it.

"You are my good friend," he said.

But that's what everyone said. Everyone who wanted something. I could see myself, in a few weeks, sitting on my couch in Florida, watching football. The job was over. There was no reason for me to stay. "What will you do," I asked, "after I leave?"

He patted his wallet, where he kept some of his walking-around money, and he patted his shoe, where he kept the rest. "I have met some important people," he said. He pointed at every ten degrees of the sky around us. "I'm going to buy a new suit. The future is big."

Already he had gathered ten of the best English speakers in Koulèv-Ville. He planned to drill them six days a week, in the mornings, when the mind is still fresh. He planned to lease them by the day to journalists and tourists and aid organizations of every stripe, with special rates for weekly or monthly hires. He would take twenty percent as his fee. No longer would he be the wage worker. Now he would be the collector of the real money, the wage-giver, the big boss.

"When you get home," Kenel said, "you will not remember me."

Within six months, he would be dead. The rally at the Palace. The fires. The burning tires. The gunshots, two to the head.

That day at the Marché, he said, "It's going to be the most beautiful suit. It's going to be linen. It's going to be chalk-striped, double-breasted. It's going to have a notched lapel. I'm going to get it tailored."

ALIX OHLIN

■

Casino

FROM *Guernica*

WHEN TRISHA COMES TO TOWN we have to go out. She's the bitter-
est soccer mom of all time and as part of her escape from home she
wants to get drunk and complain about her workaholic husband and
over-scheduled, ungrateful children. No one appreciates how much
she does for them. All she does is give, give, give, without getting
anything back, et cetera. I don't really mind—I enjoy a good martini, and while Trisha rants I don't have to worry about getting sloppy,
given that she's always sloppier—except that even her complaints are
part boast. She has to mention her busy husband and the two hundred thousand he rakes in a year. Her children's after-school activities *for the gifted* are just so freaking expensive and time-consuming.
There's a needle in every one of these remarks, pricking at my skin,
saying *See, Sherri? See?*

I do see. I see it perfectly clearly.

This year she shows up with new hair. Her old hair was nicer—she
inherited our mother's dark, shiny waves instead of the thin, blonde
frizz I got from our dad's side—but now she's highlighted it two
or maybe three different shades, I can't really tell. There are some
blonde stripes in there, some red, something she calls "caramel." Her
head looks like candy corn. "You like?" she asks as soon as she gets
inside my house, setting her luggage down. It's a rhetorical question,
so I don't answer. She's wearing pink Juicy sweatpants and a French
manicure and looks like she could be on one of those reality shows,
a housewife from somewhere, mascara'd and miserable. I give her a

hug and tell her I'm glad she came, which is mostly true. She is my competition, my Irish twin, the thorn in my side. Also: she is my best and oldest friend.

She takes a deep breath and looks around my house, stretching out her hands like she's feeling the air inside it. "I'm so glad to be home," she says, by which she means Easton. Because she lives off in Silver Spring, Maryland she can afford—in addition to a five-bedroom McMansion and a Lincoln Navigator—to be sentimental about the Lehigh Valley. She's always inviting me to visit her place but I don't feel comfortable. It's not her husband's fault. He's actually nice, Mike, but I sit around the table with him quizzing the kids on homework and current events and I keep a vacant smile going while I think, I'm not smart enough for this.

One time he asked me a question about Rhesus monkeys. Now I have thoughts on many aspects of the world, but on the subject of Rhesus monkeys, I will leave opinions to the experts. I just looked at him, desperately I guessed, and he dropped the subject, the kids smirking down at their plates of seared tuna and organic salad. Ever since then, I can't sit in their house without a rising panic in my mouth that I might be asked to weigh in on Rhesus monkeys. So now Trisha comes to me, usually in January after she's suffered through another Christmas that failed to live up to her Martha Stewart-generated expectations and needs to blow off some steam.

I fix her a drink.

We sit in my kitchen, sipping screwdrivers for the Vitamin C. It's snowing outside, light and dry, the kind of flakes that don't so much fall as hang in the air like dust. She asks me if I've heard from Rose.

"No," I say.

She puts her hand on mine. Her nails are so pretty. "Just had to ask," she says, and we move on.

The first night we stay up too late watching movies and drinking vodka. I wake with a headache, which I seek to repair with eggs and bacon. The house seems smaller with Trisha in it, in a good way. When Rose was little I used to make Sunday breakfasts like this, and Sid would come downstairs with his hair all mussed, what was left of it anyway, and he'd go straight from sleeping to eating. He was a

man who liked his food. I'd make a face for Rose out of a pancake
and two strips of bacon. Even when she was a teenager, even during
that gruesome year before she left, she'd still come out of her room
for Sunday breakfast.

Trisha comes in and tells me I'm cooking the eggs too long.

"You're drying them out."

"I don't like them gushy."

"Not gushy. Soft. It keeps them flavorful."

"Flavorful?" I ask. I don't know where she gets these words, probably the Food Network. "Full of salmonella is more like it."

She sighs and waves her hand dismissively. Trisha has this gourmet side. I blame it on Silver Spring. When I serve the eggs she
pokes at them, frowning sadly, like they're some poor animal that
died without dignity. She also remakes the coffee, saying mine's not
strong enough. I tell her she's being obnoxious and she says I'm
oversensitive; by the time the meal is over we're barely speaking. To
make peace, I let her dictate the plans for the day: tonight she wants
to go to the casino. And before we can do that she wants to get dolled
up—a massage, a pedicure.

When she sees the look on my face, she adds, "I'll pay for it."

I both hate and am grateful to her for this. So I say, "You mean
Mike will pay for it."

Instead of getting mad she raises an eyebrow and says, "Honey, I
pay for it *all the time*," and we both laugh.

So we doll. We sit side by side in lounge chairs at the mall while
Vietnamese girls pumice our feet. It makes me feel funny, the way
they're down there working on us, but Trisha kicks back, closes her
eyes, and moans with enjoyment. She likes to be treated like a queen.
In between the pumicing and the polish she keeps up a stream of
commentary about her life. She wants to redo the kitchen but Mike
says the current kitchen works just fine. "The current kitchen is
crap," she says. "The fridge leaks and there's mold behind it that
five different cleaning ladies haven't been able to get out. Meanwhile
the countertop, which was supposed to be scratchproof, is totally
scratched. That granite cost a fortune and it looks like a bathroom
stall in a bus station. I'm telling you, my life is a *nightmare*."

I glance at the Vietnamese girl below me, but she's half-watching music videos on a karaoke TV on the wall and doesn't seem to be paying attention.

"And then there's Kyle," my sister says. Kyle's her youngest. "Sherri, he picks his nose and wipes it on the walls of my house. He can't use a tissue why? Every time I round the corner there's another booger on the freaking wall."

I'm on her side with this one. "That's disgusting."

"Obviously," she says. "Every time I talk to him about it he just denies it. Like there are any other possible suspects. Like maybe there's some stranger that breaks into our house at night and doesn't steal anything, just leaves his boogers."

"What does Mike say?"

"What he always says. That he'll grow out of it. That I'm too negative."

We exchange a meaningful glance. Mike's always saying that Trisha's too negative. Our parents raised us to say the truth about the world, same as they did. I remember the day Trisha brought home her first boyfriend, Nick Perreira. He was no prize; he just had a car and a fake ID. "You're an idiot," our mother said. "He'll treat you like shit and you'll wind up crying on the phone to your friends on a Friday night." Six months later Trisha flung herself onto my bed sobbing because he'd gotten her pregnant and wouldn't have anything to do with her. We grew to appreciate our mother's blunt honesty. Our children don't seem to feel the same way about us. But maybe we just have to give it time.

Trisha and I agree on this much: people who look on the bright side all the time are hypocrites at least some of the time. To say that shitty things are shitty is to speak honest truth about the world.

We tip the girls and leave the salon with painted toes.

The casino opened since the last time Trisha was home and to hear her talk about it, the Lehigh Valley was a desert that just got its first oasis. Which is kind of a joke I'm making because the casino is called Sands. We go to dinner first, wearing dresses and heels, and I look OK but Trisha looks better. The older you get, the more money helps you out. When we were younger, we were both pretty, but now people's eyes skate over me and settle on her. Although this could also be because she talks real loud and keeps telling our waiter, "You're a cutie, James!" She's already a bit drunk. She gets out of James that he goes to Penn State Berks and majors in biology.

"I bet you're really smart," she says to him.

"Ask him what he thinks about Rhesus monkeys," I say.

"What?"

"Never mind." It's always around this point in her visits that I get weary of my sister. I start to crave my quiet house, the way I can talk to myself or to Sid out loud—yes, I still talk to him, even though he's been gone for three years—or shuffle around in my sweatpants eating peanut butter straight out of the jar. And that's how I feel after two days of Trisha. I can't imagine what it's like to live with her all the time.

It's still nice that she visits, though.

James brings us steak and martinis and we agree it is delicious. The casino is packed, hectic with lights and noise. It's the nicest place I've ever been around here, and as we start to gamble I'm feeling loose and happy. We play some slots, drink some cocktails, and then head over to the table games. I lose twenty bucks to an old dealer who calls me "ma'am."

We exchange a meaningful glance.

"Screw this," I say, and we hit another table where the dealer is cuter and younger. I don't mind losing money but I'd like to have a good time doing it. We order drinks and Trisha plays first. She wins fifty bucks! Like she even needs it. When she sees me glowering, she laughs and says, "The drinks are on me." Just our luck, the young dealer immediately goes on break, but the next one coming is young too. He keeps his head down as he readies the setup, muttering his dealer patter, and at first I don't recognize him. Cyril.

Trisha doesn't notice that I've stopped talking. Listening's never been her strong suit. Of course he knows it's me and he won't make eye contact. He looks better than the last time I saw him—he's put on some weight and the acne's cleared up. His hair is short now, no more braids, and in his white collared shirt he actually looks semi-respectable.

"Place your bets, place your bets," he mutters. There's one other person at the table, a middle-aged guy wearing an Eagles shirt, and he stacks his chips then looks at us expectantly.

I try to exchange a meaningful glance with Trisha, but she's not paying attention. She sips on her drink by lowering her head, without holding it in her hands. It would be cuter if she were thirty years younger.

"Hey," I say to Cyril. "I didn't know you were in town."

He mumbles unintelligibly and Trisha finally figures out something's up.

"How long have you been back?" I say.

"A while."

"Are you living at home?"

He shrugs like it's none of my business. My hands are trembling so bad that some martini sloshes on the table, and Trisha blots it with a napkin. "Sher," she says. "What's up?"

"This is Cyril," I tell her.

"Rose's Cyril?"

"The one and only."

Cyril must have pressed some button somewhere because a lady materializes beside the table, blonde, name-tagged, a supervisor. "Everything OK here?" she asks brightly.

"Fine," Trisha says, also brightly. The lady looks confused—clearly she was expecting a couple of rowdy drunks. "We're just waiting for our dealer to, you know, deal."

The lady supervisor pats Cyril on the shoulder, and he lifts his head, shooting her a plaintive, panicked look. If I didn't hate his fucking guts I'd maybe feel sorry for him.

"Go ahead and deal, Cyril," I say. "We're here to play. We're here all night."

Trisha laughs her mean laugh, the one I'm sure drives her husband and kids crazy, and I laugh too.

We play and lose, play and lose. I'm in the hole a hundred bucks, which is my budget for the night—Sid taught me that, that it's OK to lose as long as you prepare for it. He was a budget supervisor, so profit and loss sheets were his thing. But sometimes you have to throw the budget out the window. I'm playing until Cyril gets off his shift, that's my plan, then I'm going to follow him to the break room or the parking lot and beat the shit out of him until he tells me what I want to know. That's as far as I've gotten in my thinking, when

Trisha starts needling him. Are you working here full time, Cyril, shouldn't you be in school, Cyril, do you make good money, Cyril, what do young people around here do for fun, Cyril? The way she says his name is like a swear. In answer to every question he mumbles until she asks him to repeat himself. It's fun watching her torment him, like swatting mosquitoes is fun. It's satisfying to see the blood squirt out of them, even if you know it's your own. Whether because of Trisha's questions or Cyril's weird mumblings, other people are avoiding the table and for ages it's just the three of us, losing, dealing, needling, rinse, and repeat.

I'm on my fourth martini and the air in the room feels hot and thick around me, propping me up. I used to drink a lot of martinis when Sid and I first met, before Rose was born. Then I gave them up for a long while. To be a mother you have to have your wits around you. Sitting here now with Cyril across the table from me, close enough to touch his arm, the wiry black hairs above his wrist, I start thinking back to that time, and even earlier, back to when I was his age. In college I used to have these dreams—I guess they were sex guilt dreams, me being Catholic—that I'd gotten pregnant by accident and had to cover it up. In the dreams I always kept the baby but tried to hide it. I had this one recurring dream that I hid the baby by keeping it in an aquarium in my dorm room. I'd come home from class and sprinkle fish flakes over the water, my little fish baby rising to the surface to gobble them down. It looked just like a regular baby, fat-cheeked and dimpled, but it happened to live in a tank of water.

Remembering this, I get a little weepy, thinking about all the years between then and now, about the dream of a baby that you could keep in your room, suspended in a tank, safe from the world. *What happened?* I think to myself. *Where did my fish baby go?*

It's possible I say this out loud.

Cyril looks at me and says, not at all mumbling, "Oh, shit."

"Where is she?" I ask him. I mean it to sound aggressive but it comes out drunkenly morose instead. "Where's Rose?"

He shrugs. "I don't know."

"When was the last time you saw her?"

"I don't know."

"Do you know how to get in touch with her?"

He shakes his head.

The whole time we're interrogating him he never makes eye contact. This is different from before: he used to stare at me, defiant, or maybe numb, I could never tell which. His eyes were dark and featureless. He's not a particularly good-looking kid. I never heard him crack a joke or say an interesting thing. I couldn't figure out what drew Rose to him, and I used to complain about this to Trisha, on the phone, until the day she snapped at me, "She doesn't have to think he's a genius, Sherri. He's her drug dealer, for god's sake."

See what I mean? The truth.

If you could have seen her as a little girl, my Rosie, then you would know what happiness looks like. She laughed all the time. Her bed was piled so high with stuffed animals you couldn't even see the blankets, but Rose insisted on taking each of the animals into bed with her, so none of them would be lonely. I still don't know how she went from that little girl to the skinny teenager who skipped school and spiked her hair and pierced her tongue and lower lip and who just laughed at me when I told her the truth—"You're going nowhere, Rose"—and who grabbed my wrist and twisted it until my tears came and said, "*You're* nowhere, Mom, you're the definition of it," and who marched out of the house as she had a hundred times before during that long bad year, only instead of coming back at three in the morning, or the next day, she never came back at all.

She and Cyril were going to ride trains, her friends told me when I tracked them down. They said something about New York. They said they knew some people who lived in tunnels and that sounded cool.

They said they were going to California.

They said they wanted to see Spain.

They said they knew a guy who could get them work in Canada.

I thought she'd call or send a postcard, let me know she was OK. We'd been fighting for months over this and that, school, her friends, her clothes, but she knew how much I'd worry, right? She knew I'd need to know she was OK? I said this to Trisha, on the phone, but it felt like a lie, because some things I'd kept even from my sister. Like how bad the fights got. The time she spat on me in the parking lot at the mall when I wanted to buy her some nice clothes. The time I found her passed out on her bed, eyes rolled back in her head, and when I shook her awake she smiled gently at me and said, "Hi, mommy," and I was so happy to hear her talking sweet to me that for a minute I was *glad* she was on drugs.

Calls to police, calls to her friends, relatives, none of it turned up anything. Thank God Sid wasn't alive to see it, though I guess if he'd been alive, maybe it wouldn't have happened. Just the two of us together, me and Rose, was too much for that house. Sid diluted us; together, we were too strong.

"Listen, you little fucker," Trisha says to Cyril now, pointing her French manicure at him, "you tell us something about Rose or I'm going to kick your ass from here to Sunday."

She's all sparkly in her fancy dress and her jewelry and her shiny striped hair. In retrospect I can't 100 percent blame Cyril for what happens next, which is that he laughs.

"Oh my God, you little punk," she says, and hits him smack across the face.

"Trisha!" I say.

Cyril's standing there with his hand pressed to his cheek, very still, eyes blank. He looks like someone who has a lot of practice getting hit. I grab hold of Trisha's arm and pull her back. The supervisor is coming from across the room, I can see her making her way. I realize that I'm extremely drunk, like maybe going to be sick right on the table drunk.

"You're pathetic," Cyril says to Trisha.

"You're pathetic, you crystal meth-snorting piece of shit!"

Not for the first time I hear Sid's voice in my ear, calm and gentle. It's OK to lose, he used to say, as long as you prepare for it.

I look at Cyril. The room is swimming, the lights from the casino dancing unhappy steps. "She's still alive, right?" I say. "She's OK?"

He doesn't say anything. Those black eyes give nothing back. Trisha's expensive rings have cut a line along his cheek. By the time the supervisor gets to us, I am crying.

We sit in the car for a while, our breath clouding the interior.

"God, I wish I had a cigarette."

"That was pretty *COPS* back there, Trish."

"What a punk. I used to think you were exaggerating, but now I know you weren't."

"I'm too drunk to drive."

"Let's just sit here for a while."

We turn on the radio. Trisha hums along off-key and if I were more myself I'd be irritated and tell her to shut up. I think of my daughter sleeping in a tunnel beneath New York City. I think of her in Canada, huddled in a snowstorm. I think of her with a strange man in a bad house in some dark city without a name.

I don't know how much time passes before I wake up. The radio is still playing and Trisha is still staring out the window at nothing, scratching shapes into the condensation. Suddenly the back door behind me opens and Cyril gets in the car. I don't turn around, just look at him in the rearview mirror. It's so dark that I can barely make out his face.

"Last time I seen her, we was in Baltimore," he says, speaking quickly and without any mumbling. "Staying with a guy named Hank. He was all on top of Rose and she left one morning, didn't say where she was going or nothing. We didn't get along too great by that point anyway."

I nod, though I'm not sure he can see me. "Was she still using?"

In the shadows, I imagine him smirking the way kids do when adults try to talk about drugs like they know anything. *Using.* But when he answers, his voice sounds sincere.

"Sometimes. She mostly stopped though. After—"

"After what?"

He sighs, and then talks fast. "After one time in Newark when she OD'ed and I had to take her to the hospital. She was fine though," he says. "They fixed her up real good."

I'm holding my breath. Trisha seems like she's holding hers, too. Out of the corner of my eye I can sense her looking at me, and all I want is for her to shut up and keep out of it.

"Cyril," I say, and I try to pronounce it gently this time, as gently as if he were my own son, "do you think she'll ever come home?"

This time he doesn't even pause. "No way she coming back. She hated it here."

I flinch, but I know he's right.

He opens the door and gets out of the car. The last I see him he's running away across the parking lot, his white shirt ghostly in the headlights of my car. Jesus, I think, that idiot child didn't even put on a coat to go outside in January. I hope Rose has more sense than that. I don't know if she does or not.

Trisha clears her throat. I wait for her to tell me the truth: that Rose is probably involved in some terrible situation. That I might never see her again. That I'm the one who drove her away. *See, Sherri, see?*

Instead, she offers to drive home.

"I'm not sober yet but I'm close," she says.

I shake my head and say let's just wait a bit. We sit in the parking lot, watching people stream out of the casino and into the darkness, heading to their cars. They're all bundled up against the cold, young people chattering, couples leaning against each other. It's funny how they all seem thrilled and happy, their breath like flags in the dark. How you can't even tell from looking at them whether they won or lost.

MIROSLAV PENKOV

∎

East of the West

FROM *Storyville*

IT TAKES ME THIRTY YEARS, and the loss of those I love, to finally arrive in Beograd. Now I'm pacing outside my cousin's apartment, flowers in one hand and a bar of chocolate in the other, rehearsing the simple question I want to ask her. A moment ago, a Serbian cab-driver spat on me and I take time to wipe the spot on my shirt. I count to eleven.

Vera, I repeat once more in my head, *will you marry me?*

I first met Vera in the summer of 1970, when I was six. At that time my folks and I lived on the Bulgarian side of the river, in the village of Bulgarsko Selo, while she and her folks made their home on the other bank, in Srbsko. A long time ago these two villages had been one—that of Staro Selo—but after the great wars Bulgaria had lost land and that land had been given to the Serbs. The river, splitting the village in two hamlets, had served as a boundary—what lay east of the river stayed in Bulgaria and what lay west belonged to Serbia.

Because of the unusual predicament the two villages were in, our people had managed to secure permission from both countries to hold, once every five years, a major reunion, called the *sbor*. This was done officially so we wouldn't forget our roots. In reality, though, the reunion was just another excuse for everyone to eat lots of grilled meat and drink lots of *rakia*. A man had to eat until he felt sick from eating and he had to drink until he no longer cared if he felt sick from eating. The summer of 1970, the reunion was going to be in Srbsko, which meant we had to cross the river first.

This is how we cross:

Booming noise and balls of smoke above the water. Mihalaky is coming down the river on his boat. The boat is glorious. Not a boat really, but a raft with a motor. Mihalaky has taken the seat of an old Moskvich, the Russian car with the engine of a tank, and he has nailed that seat to the floor of the raft and upholstered the seat with goat skin. Hair out. Black and white spots, with brown. He sits on his throne, calm, terrible. He sucks on a pipe with an ebony mouthpiece and his long white hair flows behind him like a flag.

On the banks are our people. Waiting. My father is holding a white lamb under one arm and on his shoulder he is balancing a demijohn of grape *rakia*. His shining eyes are fixed on the boat. He licks his lips. Beside him rests a wooden cask, stuffed with white cheese. My uncle is sitting on the cask, counting Bulgarian money.

"I hope they have deutsche marks to sell," he says.

"They always do," my father tells him.

My mother is behind them, holding two sacks. One is full of *ter-litsi*—booties she has been knitting for some months, gifts for our folks on the other side. The second sack is zipped up and I can't see what's inside, but I know. Flasks of rose oil, lipstick, and mascara. She will sell them or trade them for other kinds of perfumes or lipsticks or mascara. Next to her is my sister, Elitsa, pressing to her chest a small teddy bear stuffed with money. She's been saving. She wants to buy jeans.

"Levi's," she says. "Like the rock star."

My sister knows a lot about the West.

I'm standing between Grandma and Grandpa. Grandma is wearing her most beautiful costume—a traditional dress she got from her own Grandma, which she will one day give to my sister. Motley-patterned apron, white hemp shirt, embroidery. On her ears, her most precious ornament—the silver earrings.

Grandpa is twisting his mustache.

"The little bastard," he's saying, "he better pay now. He better."

He is referring to his cousin, Uncle Radko, who owes him money on account of a football bet. Uncle Radko had taken his sheep by the cliffs, where the river narrowed, and seeing Grandpa herding his animals on the opposite bluff, shouted, "I bet your Bulgars will lose in

London," and Grandpa shouted back, "You wanna put some money on it?" And that's how the bet was made, thirty years ago.

There are nearly a hundred of us on the bank and it takes Mihalaky a day to get us all across the river. No customs—the men pay some money to the guards and all is good. When the last person sets his foot in Srbsko, the moon is bright in the sky and the air smells of grilled pork and foaming wine.

Eating, drinking, dancing. All night long. In the morning everyone has passed out in the meadow. There are only two souls not drunk or sleeping. One of them is me, and the other one, going through the pockets of my folks, is my cousin Vera.

Two things I found remarkable about my cousin: her jeans and her sneakers. Aside from that, she was a scrawny girl—a pale, round face and fragile shoulders with skin peeling from the sun. Her hair was long, I think, or was it my sister's hair that grew down to her waist? I forget. But I do recall the first thing that my cousin ever said to me:

"Let go of my hair," she said, "or I'll punch you in the mouth."

I didn't let go because I had to stop her from stealing, so, as promised, she punched me. Only she wasn't very accurate and her fist landed on my nose, crushing it like a Plain Biscuit. I spent the rest of the *sbor* with tape on my face, sneezing blood, and now I am forever marked with an ugly snoot. Which is why everyone, except my mother, calls me Nose.

Five summers slipped by. I went to school in the village and in the afternoons I helped Father with the fields. Father drove an MTZ-50, a tractor made in Minsk. He'd put me on his lap and make me hold the steering wheel and the steering wheel would shake and twitch in my hands, as the tractor plowed diagonally, leaving terribly distorted lines behind.

"My arms hurt," I'd say. "This wheel is too hard."

"Nose," Father would say, "quit whining. You're not holding a wheel. You're holding life by the throat. So get your shit together and learn how to choke the bastard, because the bastard already knows how to choke you."

Mother worked as a teacher in the school. This was awkward for me, because I could never call her "Mother" in class and because she always knew if I'd done my homework or not. But I had access to her files and could steal exams and sell them to the kids for cash.

The year of the new *sbor*, 1975, our geography teacher retired and Mother found herself teaching his classes as well. This gave me more exams to sell and I made good money. I had a goal in mind. I went to my sister, Elitsa, having first rubbed my eyes hard so they would appear filled with tears, and with my most humble and vulnerable voice I asked her, "How much for your jeans?"

"Nose," she said, "I love you, but I'll wear these jeans until the day I die."

I tried to look heartbreaking, but she didn't budge. Instead, she advised me:

"Ask cousin Vera for a pair. You'll pay her at the *sbor*." Then from a jar in her nightstand Elitsa took out a ten-lev bill and stuffed it in my pocket. "Get some nice ones," she said.

Two months before it was time for the reunion I went to the river. I yelled until a boy showed up and I asked him to call my cousin. She came an hour later.

"What do you want, Nose?"

"Levi's!" I yelled.

"You better have the money!" She yelled back.

Mihalaky came in smoke and roar. And with him came the West. My cousin Vera stepped out of the boat and everything on her screamed, *We live better than you, we have more stuff, stuff you can't have and never will.* She wore white leather shoes with a little flower on them, which she explained was called an Adidas. She had jeans. And her shirt said things in English.

"What does it say?"

"The name of a music group. They have this song that goes *'Smooook na dar voooto.'* You heard it?"

"Of course I have." But she knew better.

After lunch, the grown-ups danced around the fire, then played drunk soccer. Elitsa was absent for most of the time, and when she finally returned, her lips were burning red and her eyes shone like I'd never seen them before. She pulled me aside and whispered in my ear:

"Promise not to tell." Then she pointed at a dark-haired boy from Srbsko, skinny and with a long neck, who was just joining the soccer game. "Boban and I kissed in the forest. It was so great," she said, and her voice flickered. She nudged me in the ribs and stuck a finger at cousin Vera, who sat by the fire, yawning and raking the embers up with a stick.

"Come on, Nose, be a man. Take her to the woods."

And she laughed so loud even the deaf old grandmas turned to look at us.

I scurried away, disgusted and ashamed, but finally I had to approach Vera. I asked her if she had my jeans, then took out the money and began to count it.

"Not here, you fool," she said, and slapped me on the hand with the smoldering stick.

We walked through the village until we reached the old bridge, which stood solitary in the middle of the road. Yellow grass grew between each stone, and the riverbed was dry and fissured.

We hid under the bridge and completed the swap. Thirty levs for a pair of jeans. Best deal I'd ever made.

"You wanna go for a walk?" Vera said after she had counted the bills twice. She rubbed them on her face, the way our fathers did, and stuffed them in her pocket.

We picked mushrooms in the woods while she told me things about her school and complained about a Serbian boy who always pestered her.

"I can teach him a lesson," I said. "Next time I come there you just show him to me."

"Yeah, Nose, like you know how to fight."

And then, just like that, she hit me in the nose. Crushed it, once more, like a biscuit.

"Why did you do that?"

She shrugged. I made a fist to smack her back, but how do you hit a girl? Or how, for that matter, will hitting another person in the face stop the blood gushing from your own nose? I tried to suck it up and act like the pain was easy to ignore.

She took me by the hand and dragged me toward the river.

"I like you, Nose," she said. "Let's go wash your face."

We lay on the bank and chewed thyme leaves.

"Nose," my cousin said, "you know what they told us in school?"

She rolled over and I did the same to look her in the eyes. They were very dark, shaped like apricot kernels. Her face was all speckled and she had a tiny spot on her upper lip, delicate, hard to notice, that got redder when she was nervous or angry. The spot was red now.

"You look like a mouse," I told her.

She rolled her eyes.

"Our history teacher," she said, "told us we were all Serbs. You know. Like, a hundred percent."

"Well, you talk funny," I said. "I mean you talk Serbianish."

"So you think I'm a Serb?"

"Where do you live?" I asked her.

"You know where I live."

"But do you live in Serbia or in Bulgaria?"

Her eyes darkened and she held them shut for a long time. I knew she was sad. And I liked it. She had nice shoes, and jeans, and could listen to bands from the West, but I owned something that had been taken away from her forever.

"The only Bulgarian here is me," I told her.

She got up and stared at the river. "Let's swim to the drowned church," she said.

"I don't want to get shot."

"Get shot? Who cares for churches in no-man's-water? Besides, I've swum there before." She stood up, took her shirt off and jumped in. The murky current rippled around her shoulders and they glistened, smooth, round pebbles the river had polished for ages. Yet her skin was soft, I could imagine. I almost reached out to touch it.

We swam the river slowly, staying along the bank. I caught a small chub under a rock, but Vera made me let it go. Finally we saw the cross sticking up above the water, massive, with rusty feet and arms that caught the evening sun.

We all knew well the story of the drowned church. Back in the day, before the Balkan Wars, a rich man lived east of the river. He had no offspring and no wife, so when he lay down dying he called his servant with a final wish: to build, with his money, a village church. The church was built, west of the river, and the peasants hired from afar a young *zograf*, a master of icons. The master painted for two years and there he met a girl and fell in love with her and married her and they, too, lived west of the river, near the church.

Then came the Balkan Wars and after that the First World War. All these wars Bulgaria lost, and much Bulgarian land was given to the Serbs. Three officials arrived in the village; one was a Russian, one was French, and one was British. East of the river, they said, stays in Bulgaria. West of the river from now on belongs to Serbia. Soldiers guarded the banks and planned to take the bridge down, and when the young master, who had gone away to work on another church, came back, the soldiers refused to let him cross the border and return to his wife.

In his desperation he gathered people and convinced them to divert the river, to push it west until it went around the village. Because according to the orders, what lay east of the river stayed in Bulgaria.

How they carried all those stones, all those logs, how they piled them up, I cannot imagine. Why the soldiers did not stop them, I don't know. The river moved west and it looked like she would serpent around the village. But then she twisted, wiggled, and tasted with her tongue a route of lesser resistance; through the lower hamlet she swept, devouring people and houses. Even the church, in which the master had left two years of his life, was lost in her belly.

We stared at the cross for some time, then I got out on the bank and sat in the sun.

"It's pretty deep," I said. "You sure you've been down there?"

She put a hand on my back. "It's okay if you're scared."

But it was not okay. I closed my eyes, took a deep breath, and dove off the bank.

"Swim to the cross!" She yelled after me. I swam like I wore shoes of iron. I held the cross tightly and stepped on the slimy dome underneath. Soon Vera stood by me, in turn gripping the cross so she wouldn't slip and drift away.

"Let's look at the walls," she said.

"What if we get stuck?"

"Then we'll drown."

She laughed and nudged me in the chest.

"Come on, Nose, do it for me."

It was difficult to keep my eyes open at first. The current pushed us away so we had to work hard to reach the small window below the dome. We grabbed the bars on the window and looked inside. And despite the murky water, my eyes fell on a painting of a bearded man kneeling by a rock, his hands entwined. The man was looking down, and in the distance, approaching, was a little bird. Below the bird, I saw a cup.

"It's a nice church," Vera said after we surfaced.

"Do you want to dive again?"

"No." She moved closer and quickly she kissed me on the lips.

"Why did you do that?" I said, and felt the hairs on my arms and neck stand up, though they were wet.

She shrugged, then pushed herself off the dome, and laughing, swam splashing up the river.

The jeans Vera sold me that summer were about two sizes too large, and it seemed like they'd been worn before, but that didn't bother me. I even slept in them. I liked how loose they were around my waist, how much space, how much Western freedom they provided around my legs.

But for my sister, Elitsa, life worsened. The West gave her ideas. She would often go to the river and sit on the bank and stare, quietly, for hours on end. She would sigh and her bony shoulders would drop, like the earth below her was pulling on her arms.

As the weeks went by, her face lost its plumpness. Her skin got grayer, her eyes muddier. At dinner she kept her head down and played with her food. She never spoke, not to Mother, not to me. She was as quiet as a painting on a wall.

A doctor came and left puzzled. "I leave puzzled," he said, "she's healthy. I just don't know what's wrong with her."

But I knew. That longing in my sister's eyes, that disappointment, I'd seen them in Vera's eyes before, on the day she had wished to be Bulgarian. It was the same look of defeat, scary and contagious, and because of that look, I kept my distance.

I didn't see Vera for a year. Then, one summer day in 1976 as I was washing my jeans in the river, she yelled from the other side.

"Nose, you're buck naked."

That was supposed to embarrass me, but I didn't even twitch.

"I like to rub my ass in the face of the West," I yelled back, and raised the jeans, dripping with soap.

"What?" she yelled.

"I like to . . ." I waved. "What do you want?"

"Nose, I got something for you. Wait for—and—to—church. All right?"

"What?"

"Wait for the dark. And swim. You hear me?"

"Yeah, I hear you. Are you gonna be there?"

"What?"

I didn't bother. I waved, bent over, and went on washing my jeans.

I waited for my folks to go to sleep and then I snuck out the window. The lights in my sister's room were still on and I imagined her in bed, eyes tragically fixed on the ceiling.

I hid my clothes under a bush and stepped into the cool water. On the other side I could see the flashlight of the guard, and the tip of his cigarette, red in the dark. I swam slowly, making as little noise as possible. In places the river flowed so narrow people could stand on both sides and talk and almost hear each other, but around the drowned church the river was broad, a quarter mile between the banks.

I stepped on the algae-slick dome and ran my fingers along a string tied to the base of the cross. A nylon bag was fixed to the other end. I freed the bag and was ready to glide away when someone said, "This is for you."

"Vera?"

"I hope you like them."

She swam closer, and was suddenly locked in a circle of light.

"Who's there?" the guard shouted, and his dog barked.

"Go, go, you stupid," Vera said, and splashed away. The circle of light followed.

I held the cross tight, not making a sound. I knew this was no joke. The guards would shoot trespassers if they had to. But Vera swam unhurriedly.

"Faster!" The guard shouted. "Get out here."

The beam of light etched her naked body in the night. She had the breasts of a woman.

He asked her something and she spoke back. Then he slapped her. He held her very close and felt her body. She kneed him in the groin. He laughed on the ground long after she'd run away naked.

All through, of course, I watched in silence. I could have yelled something to stop him, but then, he had a gun. And so I held the cross and so the river flowed black with night around me and even out on the bank I felt sticky with dirty water.

Inside the bag were Vera's old Adidas shoes. The laces were in bad shape, and the left shoe was a bit torn at the front, but they were still excellent. And suddenly all shame was gone and my heart pounded so hard with new excitement, I was afraid the guards might hear it. On the banks I put the shoes on and they fit perfectly. Well, they were a bit too small for my feet—actually, they were really quite tight—but they were worth the pain. I didn't walk. I swam across the air.

I was striding back home, when someone giggled in the bush. Grass rustled. I hesitated, but snuck through the dark, and I saw two people rolling on the ground, and would have watched them in secret if it weren't for the squelching shoes.

"Nose, is that you?" a girl asked. She flinched, and tried to cover herself with a shirt, but this was the night I saw my second pair of breasts. These belonged to my sister.

I lay in my room, head under the blanket, trying to make sense of what I'd seen, when someone walked in.

"Nose? Are you sleeping?"

My sister sat on the bed and put her hand on my chest.

"Come on. I know you're awake."

"What do you want?" I said, and threw the blanket off. I could not see her face for the dark, but I could feel that piercing gaze of hers. The house was quiet. Only Father snored in the other room.

"Are you going to tell them?" she said.

"No. What you do is your own business."

She leaned forward and kissed me on the forehead.

"You smell like cigarettes," I said.

"Good night, Nose."

She got up to leave, but I pulled her down.

"Elitsa, what are you ashamed of? Why don't you tell them?"

"They won't understand. Boban's from Srbsko."

"So what?"

I sat up in my bed and took her cold hand.

"What are you gonna do?" I asked her. She shrugged.

"I want to run away with him," she said, and her voice suddenly became softer, calmer, though what she spoke of scared me deeply. "We're going to go West. Get married, have kids. I want to work as a hairstylist in Munich. Boban has a cousin there. She is a hairstylist, or she washes dogs or something." She ran her fingers through my hair. "Oh, Nose," she said. "Tell me what to do."

I couldn't tell her. And so she kept living unhappy, wanting to be with that boy day and night but seeing him rarely and in secret. "I am alive," she told me, "only when I'm with him." And then she spoke of their plans; hitchhiking to Munich, staying with Boban's cousin and helping her cut hair. "It's a sure thing, Nose," she'd say, and I believed her.

It was the spring of 1980 when Josip Tito died and even I knew things were about to change in Yugoslavia. The old men in our village whispered that now, with the Yugoslav president finally planted in a mausoleum, our western neighbor would fall apart. I pictured in my mind the aberration I'd seen in a film, a monster sewn together from the legs and arms and torso of different people. I pictured someone pulling on the thread that held these body parts, the thread unraveling, until the legs and arms and torso came undone. We could snatch a finger then, the land across the river, and patch it up back to our land. That's what the old folks spoke about, drinking their *rakia* in the tavern. Meanwhile, the young folks escaped to the city, following new jobs. There weren't enough children in the village anymore to justify our own school, and so we had to go to another village and study with other kids. Mother lost her job. Grandpa got sick with pneumonia, but Grandma gave him herbs for a month, and he got better. Mostly. Father worked two jobs, plus he stacked hay on the weekends. He no longer had the time to take me plowing.

But Vera and I saw each other often, sometimes twice a month. I never found the courage to speak of the soldier. At night, we swam to the drowned church and played around the cross, very quiet, like river rats. And there, by the cross, we kissed our first real kiss. Was it joy I felt? Or was it sadness? To hold her so close and taste her breath, her lips, to slide a finger down her neck, her shoulder, down her back. To lay my palm upon her breasts and know that someone else had done this, with force, while I had watched, tongue swallowed. Her face was silver with moonlight, her hair dripped dark with dark water.

"Do you love me?" she said.

"Yes. Very much," I said. I said, "I wish we never had to leave the water."

"You fool," she said, and kissed me again. "People can't live in rivers."

That June, two months before the new *sbor*, our parents found out about Boban. One evening, when I came home for supper, I discovered the whole family quiet in the yard, under the trellis. The village priest was there. The village doctor. Elitsa was weeping, her face flaming red. The priest made her kiss an iron cross and sprinkled her with holy water from an enormous copper. The doctor buckled his bag and glass rattled inside when he picked it up. He winked at me and made for the gate. On his way out, the priest gave my forehead a thrashing with the boxwood foliage.

"What's the matter?" I said, dripping holy water.

Grandpa shook his head. Mother put her hand on my sister's. "You've had your cry," she said.

"Father," I said, "why was the doctor winking? And why did the priest bring such a large copper?"

Father looked at me, furious. "Because your sister, Nose," he said, "requires an Olympic pool to cleanse her."

"Meaning?" I said.

"Meaning," he said, "your sister is pregnant. Meaning," he said, "we'll have to get her married."

My family, all dressed up, went to the river. On the other bank Boban's family already waited for us. Mother had washed the collar of my shirt with sugar water so it would stay stiff, and now I felt like that sugar was running down my back in a sweaty, syrupy stream. It itched and I tried to scratch it, but Grandpa told me to quit fidgeting and act like a man. My back got itchier.

From the other side, Boban's father shouted at us, "We want your daughter's hand!"

Father took out a flask and drank *rakia,* then passed it around. The drink tasted bad and set my throat on fire. I coughed and Grandpa smacked my back and shook his head. Father took the flask from me and spilled some liquor on the ground for the departed. The family on the other side did the same.

"I give you my daughter's hand!" Father yelled. "We'll wed them at the *sbor.*"

Elitsa's wedding was going to be the culmination of the *sbor,* so everyone prepared. Vera told me that with special permission Mihalaky had transported seven calves across the river, and two had already been slain for jerky. The two of us met often, secretly, by the drowned church.

One evening, after dinner, my family gathered under the vines of the trellis. The grown-ups smoked and talked of the wedding. My sister and I listened and smiled at each other every time our eyes met.

"Elitsa," Grandma said, and lay a thick bundle on the table. "This is yours now."

My sister untied the bundle and her eyes teared up when she recognized Grandma's best costume readied for the wedding. They lay each part of the dress on its own: the white hemp shirt, the motley apron, the linen gown, festoons of coins, the intricately worked silver earrings. Elitsa lifted the gown, and felt the linen between her fingers, and then began to put it on.

"My God, child," Mother said, "take your jeans off."

Without shame, for we are all blood, Elitsa folded her jeans aside and carefully slipped inside the glowing gown. Mother helped her with the shirt. Grandpa strapped on the apron, and Father, with his fingers shaking, gently put on her ears the silver earrings.

I woke up in the middle of the night, because I'd heard a dog howl in my sleep. I turned the lights on and sat up, sweaty in the silence. I went to the kitchen to get a drink of water and I saw Elitsa, ready to sneak out.

"What are you doing?" I said.

"Quiet, *dechko*. I'll be back in no time."

"Are you going out to see him?"

"I want to show him these." She dangled the earrings in her hand.

"And if they catch you?"

She put a finger to her lips, then spun on her heel. Her jeans rasped softly and she sank into the dark. I was this close to waking up Father, but how can you judge others when love is involved? I trusted she knew what she was doing.

For a very long time I could not fall asleep, remembering the howling dog in my dream. And then from the river, a machine gun rattled. The guard dogs started barking and the village dogs answered. I lay in bed petrified, and did not move even when someone banged on the gates.

My sister never used to swim to the Serbian side. Boban always came to meet her on our bank. But that night, strangely, they had decided to meet in Srbsko one last time before the wedding. A soldier in training had seen her climb out of the river. He'd told them both to stop. Two bullets had gone through Elitsa's back as she tried to run.

This moment in my life I do not want to remember again:

Mihalaky in smoke and roar is coming up the river, and on his boat lies my sister.

There was no *sbor* that year. There were, instead, two funerals. We dressed Elitsa in her wedding costume and laid her beautiful body in a terrible coffin. The silver earrings were not beside her.

The village gathered on our side of the river. On the other side was the other village, burying their boy. I could see the grave they had dug, and the earth was the same, and the depth was the same.

There were three priests on our side, because Grandma would not accept any Communist godlessness. Each of us held a candle, and the people across from us also held candles, and the banks came alive with fire, two hands of fire that could not come together. Between those hands was the river.

The first priest began to sing, and both sides listened. My eyes were on Elitsa. I couldn't let her go and things misted in my head.

"One generation passes away," I thought the priest was singing, "and another comes; but the earth remains forever. The sun rises and the sun goes down, and hastens to the place where it rises. The wind goes toward the West, toward Serbia, and all the rivers run away, East of the West. What has been is what will be, and what has been done is what will be done. Nothing is new under the sun."

The voice of the priest died down, and then a priest on the other side sang. The words piled on my heart like stones and I thought how much I wanted to be like the river, which had no memory, and how little like the earth, which could never forget.

Mother quit the factory and locked herself home. She said her hands burned with her daughter's blood. Father began to frequent the co-operative distillery at the end of the village. At first he claimed that assisting people with loading their plums, peaches, grapes into the cauldrons kept his mind blank; then that he was simply sampling the first *rakia* which trickled out the spout, so he could advise the folk how to boil better drink.

He lost both his jobs soon, and so it was up to me to feed the family. I started working in the coal mine, because the money was good, and because I wanted, with my pick, to gut the land we walked on.

The control across the borders tightened. Both countries put nets along the banks and blocked buffer zones at the narrow waist of the river where the villagers used to call to one another. The *sbors* were canceled. Vera and I no longer met, though we found two small hills we could sort of see each other from, like dots in the distance. But these hills were too far away and we did not go there often.

Almost every night, I dreamed of Elitsa.

"I saw her just before she left," I would tell my mother. "I could have stopped her."

"Then why didn't you?" Mother would ask.

Sometimes I went to the river and threw stones over the fence, into the water, and imagined those two silver earrings, settling into the silty bottom.

"Give back the earrings," I'd scream, "you spineless, muddy thief!" I worked double shifts in the mine and was able to put something aside. I took care of Mother who never left her bed, and occasionally brought bread and cheese to Father at the distillers. "Mother is sick," I'd tell him, but he pretended not to hear. "More heat," he'd call, and kneel by the trickle to sample some *parvak*.

Vera and I wrote letters for a while, but after each letter there was a longer period of silence before the new one arrived. One day, in the summer of 1990, I received a brief note:

Dear Nose. I'm getting married. I want you at my wedding. I live in Beograd now. I'm sending you money. Please come.

There was, of course, no money in the envelope. Someone had stolen it on the way.

Each day I reread the letter, and thought of the way Vera had written those words, in her elegant, thin writing, and I thought of this man she had fallen in love with, and I wondered if she loved him as much as she had loved me, by the cross, in the river. I made plans to get a passport.

Two weeks before the wedding, Mother died. The doctor couldn't tell us of what. Of grief, the wailers said, and threw their black kerchiefs over their heads like ash. Father brought his drinking guiltily to the empty house. One day he poured me a glass of *rakia* and made me gulp it down. We killed the bottle. Then he looked me in the eye and grabbed my hand. Poor soul, he thought he was squeezing it hard.

"My son," he said, "I want to see the fields."

We staggered out of the village, finishing a second bottle. When we reached the fields we sat down and watched in silence. After the fall of communism, organized agriculture had died in many areas, and now everything was overgrown with thornbush and nettles.

"What happened, Nose?" Father said. "I thought we held him good, this bastard, in both hands. Remember what I taught you? Hold tight, choke the bastard, and things will be all right? Well, shit, Nose. I was wrong."

And he spat against the wind, in his own face.

Three years passed before Vera wrote again. *Nose, I have a son. I'm sending you a picture. His name is Vladislav. Guess who we named him after? Come and visit us. We have money now, so don't worry. Goran just got back from a mission in Kosovo. Can you come?*

My father wanted to see the picture. He stared at it for a long time, and his eyes watered.

"My God, Nose," he said. "I can't see anything. I think I've finally gone blind."

"You want me to call the doctor?"

"Yes," he said, "but for yourself. Quit the mine, or that cough will take you."

"And what do we do for money?"

"You'll find some for my funeral. Then you'll go away."

I sat by his side and lay a hand on his forehead. "You're burning. I'll call the doctor."

"Nose," he said, "I've finally figured it out. Here is my paternal advice: Go away. You can't have a life here. You must forget about your sister, about your mother, about me. Go west. Get a job in Spain, or in Germany, or anywhere; start from scratch. Break each chain. This land is a bitch and you can't expect anything good from a bitch."

He took my hand and he kissed it.

"Go get the priest," he said.

I worked the mine until, in the spring of 1995, my boss, who'd come from some big, important city to the east, asked me, three times in a row, to repeat my request for an extra shift. Three times I repeated it before he threw his arms up in despair. "I can't understand your dialect, *mayna*," he said. "Too Serbian for me." So I beat him up and was fired.

After that, I spent my days in the village tavern, every now and then lifting my hand before my eyes to check if I hadn't finally gone blind. It's a tough lot to be last in your bloodline. I thought of my father's advice, which seemed foolish, of my sister making plans to go west, and of how I had done nothing to stop her from swimming to her death.

Almost every night I had the same dream. I was diving at the drowned church, looking through its window, at walls no longer covered with the murals of saints and martyrs. Instead, I could see my sister and my mother, my father, Grandpa, Grandma, Vera, people from our village, and from the village across the border, painted motionless on the walls, with their eyes on my face. And every time, as

I tried to push up to the surface, I discovered that my hands were locked together on the other side of the bars.

I would wake up with a yell, the voice of my sister echoing in the room.

I have some doubts, she would say, *some suspicions, that these earrings aren't really silver.*

In the spring of 1999 the United States attacked Serbia. Kosovo, the field where the Serb had once, many centuries ago, surrendered to the Turk, had once again become the ground of battle. Three or four times I saw American planes swoop over our village with a boom. Serbia, it seemed, was land not large enough for their maneuvers at ultrasonic speed. They cut corners from our sky and went back to drop their bombs on our neighbors. The news that Vera's husband was killed came as no surprise. Her letter ended like this: *Nose, I have my son and you. Please come. There is no one else.*

The day I received the letter I swam to the drowned church, without taking my shoes or my clothes off. I held the cross and shivered for a long time, and finally I dove down and down to the rocky bottom. I gripped the bars on the church gates tightly and listened to the screaming of my lungs while they squeezed out every molecule of oxygen. I wish I could say that I saw my life unwinding thread by thread before my eyes: happy moments alternating with sad, or that my sister, bathed in glorious light, came out of the church to take my drowning hand. But there was only darkness, booming of water, of blood.

Yes, I am a coward. I have an ugly nose, and the heart of a mouse, and the only drowning I can do is in a bottle of *rakia.* I swam out and lay on the bank. And as I breathed with new thirst, a boom shook the air, and I saw a silver plane storm out of Serbia. The plane thundered over my head and, chasing it, I saw a missile, quickly losing height. Hissing, the missile stabbed the river, the rusty cross, the drowned church underneath. A large, muddy finger shook at the sky.

I wrote Vera right away. *When Sister died,* I wrote, *I thought half of my world ended. With my parents, the other half. I thought these deaths were meant to punish me for something. I was chained to this village, and the pull of all the bones below me was impossible to escape. But now I see that these deaths were meant to set me free, to get me moving. Like links in*

a chain snapping, one after the other. If the church can sever its brick roots
so can I. I'm free at last, so wait for me. I'm coming as soon as I save up
some cash.

Not long after, a Greek company opened a chicken factory in the village. My job was to make sure no bad eggs made it into the cartons.
I saved some money, tried to drink less. I even cleaned the house. In
the basement, in a dusty chestnut box, I found the leather shoes, the
old forgotten flowers. I cut off the toe caps and put them on, and felt
so good, so quick and light. Unlucky, wretched brothers. No laces,
worn-out soles from walking in circles. Where will you take me?

I dug up the two jars of money I kept hidden in the yard and
caught a bus to town. It wasn't hard to buy American dollars. I returned to the village and lay carnations on the graves and asked
the dead for forgiveness. Then I went to the river. I put most of the
money and Vladislav's picture in a plastic bag, tucked the bag in my
pocket along with some cash for bribes, and with my eyes closed
swam toward Srbsko.

Cool water, the pull of current, brown old leaves whirlpooling in
clumps. A thick branch flows by, bark gone, smooth and rotten. What
binds a man to land or water?

When I stepped on the Serbian bank two guards already held me
in the aim of their guns.

"Two hundred," I said, and took out the soaking wad.

"We could kill you instead."

"Or give me a kiss. A pat on the ass?"

They started laughing. The good thing about our countries, the
reassuring thing that keeps us falling harder, is that if you can't buy
something with money, you can buy it with a lot of money. I counted
off two hundred more.

They escorted me up the road, to a frontier post where I paid the last
hundred I'd prepared. A Turkish truck driver agreed to take me to Beograd. There I caught a cab and showed an envelope Vera had sent me.

"I need to get there," I said.

"You Bulgarian?" the cabdriver asked.

"Does it matter?"

"Well, shit, it matters. If you're Serbian, that's fine. But if you're a *Bugar,* it isn't. It's also not fine if you are Albanian, or if you are a Croat. And if you are Muslim, well, shit, then it also isn't fine."

"Just take me to this address."

The cabdriver turned around and fixed me with his blue eyes.

"I'm only gonna ask you once," he said. "Are you Bulgarian or are you a Serb?"

"I don't know."

"Oh, well, then," he said, "get the fuck out of my cab and think it over. You ugly-nosed Bulgarian bastard. Letting Americans bomb us, handing over your bases. Slavic brothers!"

Then, as I was getting out, he spat on me.

And now, we are back at the beginning. I'm standing outside Vera's apartment, with flowers in one hand and a bar of Milka chocolate in the other. I'm rehearsing the question. I think of how I'm going to greet her, of what I'm going to say. Will the little boy like me? Will she? Will she let me help her raise him? Can we get married, have children of our own? Because I'm finally ready.

An iron safety grid protects the door. I ring the bell and little feet run on the other side.

"Who's there?" a thin voice asks.

"It's Nose," I say.

"Step closer to the spy hole."

I lean forward.

"No, to the lower one." I kneel down so the boy can peep through the hole drilled at his height.

"Put your face closer," he says. He's quiet for a moment. "Did Mama do that?"

"It's no big deal."

He unlocks the door, but keeps the iron grid between us.

"Sorry to say it, but it looks like a big deal," he says in all seriousness.

"Can I come in?"

"I'm alone. But you can sit outside and wait until they return. I'll keep you company."

We sit on both sides of the grid. He is a tiny boy and looks like Vera. Her eyes, her chin, her bright, white face. All that will change with time.

"I haven't had Milka in forever," he says as I pass him the chocolate through the grid. "Thanks, Uncle."

"Don't eat things a stranger gives you."

"You are no stranger. You're Nose."

He tells me about kindergarten. About a boy who beats him up. His face is grave. Oh, little friend, those troubles now seem big.

"But I'm a soldier," he says, "like Daddy. I won't give up. I'll fight."

Then he is quiet. He munches on the chocolate. He offers me a block that I refuse.

"You miss your dad?" I say.

He nods. "But now we have Dadan and Mama is happy."

"Who's Dadan?" My throat gets dry.

"Dadan," the boy says. "My second father."

"Your second father," I say, and rest my head against the cold iron.

"He's very nice to me," the boy says. "Yes, very nice."

He talks, sweet voice, and I struggle to resist the venom of my thoughts.

The elevator arrives with a rattle. Its door slides open, bright light out of the cell. Dadan, tall, handsome in his face, walks out with a string bag of groceries—potatoes, yogurt, green onions, white bread. He looks at me and nods, confused.

Then out comes Vera. Bright speckled face, firm sappy lips.

"My God," she says. The old spot grows red above her lip and she hangs on my neck.

I lose my grip, the earth below my feet. It feels then like everything is over. She's found someone else to care for her, she's built a new life in which there is no room for me. In a moment, I'll smile politely and follow them inside their place, I'll eat the dinner they feed me—*musaka* with *tarator*. I'll listen to Vladislav sing songs and recite poems. Then afterward, while Vera tucks him in, I'll talk to Dadan, or rather he'll talk to me, about how much he loves her, about *their* plans, and I will listen and agree. At last he'll go to bed, and under the dim kitchen light Vera and I will wade deep into the night. She'll finish the wine Dadan shared with her for dinner, she'll put her hand on mine. "My dear Nose," she'll say, or something to that effect. But even then I won't find courage to speak. Broken, not having slept all night, I'll rise up early, and, cowardly again, I'll slip out and hitchhike home.

"My dear Nose," Vera says now, and really leads me inside the apartment, "you look beaten from the road." *Beaten* is the word she uses. And then it hits me, the way a hoe hits a snake over the skull. This is the last link of the chain falling. Vera and Dadan will set me free. With them, the last connection to the past is gone.

Who binds a man to land or water, I wonder, if not that man himself?

"I've never felt so good before," I say, and mean it, and watch her lead the way through the dark hallway. I am no river, but I'm not made of clay.

KIM PHILLEY

■

Two Deaths

FROM *Epiphany*

WE HAD BEEN DATING FOR THREE MONTHS when I spotted the passport on the small rattan table, lying on top of the visa application he had brought back with him from the Australian Embassy. I sprawled across his lap, twisting the passport sideways to inspect the photo. The photo was of a very young version of Jonathan—I'm guessing nineteen, twenty—with his head shaved smooth as a brazil nut. High, haughty cheekbones. A handsome but unformed face at odds with everything I saw when he stripped off his clothes in my bedroom: mysterious sutures laid like railroad tracks across his arm; a mark from a bullet that had once entered, and cleanly exited, his left thigh; a massive keloid scar over his heart where he may or may not have been doused with scalding water.

The night we had met he wore long sleeves. He told me he was twenty-eight and I suspected he was low-balling even then.

I had not thought very hard about the ramifications of dating him. Despite being almost thirty. Despite wanting a serious relationship, a reciprocal relationship after years of dating selfish, embattled men. Men who revisited old correspondences and emailed me—now that I was working in Cambodia and had finally left Portland—to atone for their previous inability to confront the heart they had broken. I say "men," but I don't want to make out like there were a lot of them. There were two in particular, both adrift in the dead calm of their first marriages. One needed to remind himself that he had once had power over someone; the other rushed toward confrontation now that it was 8,000 miles away.

Jonathan did not remind me of either of these men. Our first dance was to Akon's "Beautiful." *I see you in the club and I want to get with you.* He walked over to me and the group of girls I was dancing with swung open like a blonde curtain. I remember looking up at him and thinking *tall, fit.* He wore his dreadlocks gathered in a red cord at the top of his head. He was a good dancer, but unlike the other men in the bar he kept a respectful distance—a buffer between our two bodies that he never once breached. I danced with him for a few songs and then he grabbed my left hand and held it up to the blue light.

"Good—no ring," he said. "If I'd seen you with a ring it would have been like a little dog was barking from your finger—*woof woof!*"

"A dog barking, really?"

He leaned in, crushing his nose against my cheek as he whispered in my ear: "I'm afraid of animals."

"Afraid of animals?" I laughed. "A big man like you?"

"Don't you know," he answered quickly. "We have very big animals in Nigeria (he pronounces it "beeg"). Crocodile. Anaconda. Beeg cat!"

"Lions?"

"Not lions—beeg housecat! They are easily inhabited by spirits. Where I come from we are very scared of cat."

Scared of housecat, I thought. There was something about this that charmed me in the way women are sometimes charmed by sweet idiocy.

I was now scrutinizing the type beside the passport photo.

"Jonathan, this says you were born in 1990!"

"Don't you know—that's my football age. All the players do it."

Jonathan was the season's top-scoring striker for one of the Cambodian club teams. Professional soccer, like so much else, was new to the country—the league only a couple years old—and Jonathan had been among the first wave of Africans recruited to help build the capacity of the Cambodian players.

"How did you get this passport?"

"From the passport office in Warri," he deadpanned.

"You know that's not what I mean—didn't you have to show them I.D.? Your birth certificate?"

"In those days, you would just tell them what year you were

born . . . listen, baby, this is a very good thing. I'm twenty-eight, right? I have maybe ten more years to play if I'm lucky. This pass-port buys me time."

"But they're going to take one look at you and know that's a lie! And I'm going to feel like a pervert writing an embassy to vouch for my teenage boyfriend."

"It doesn't matter what I look like now. You think an immigration police looks up your nose? We all look the same to them."

"What about white people? How do you even *begin* to tell us apart?"

"Can't tell one white face from another," he said, smiling broadly.

"Except for you, of course—my Beyoncé, my Lady Gaga." At this he grabbed my decidedly un-Beyoncé-like hips and shook the meager flesh from side to side.

It was like having a conversation with a cartoon: no matter what came out of Jonathan's mouth in those first love-drunk months, the result was laughter. I felt like I hadn't laughed in a long time and here was this helium balloon, this nitrous oxide. I thought of the tan-dem pop stars writhing side by side in the music video for "Video Phone": leotards, blown-out hair, both pulsing their hips from the seats of identical chairs. Never had two bodies, juxtaposed, looked more incredulous: Beyoncé like an African fertility goddess and Gaga with the hips of Joey Ramone.

Jonathan said nothing ironically. I often had the urge to look over my shoulder when I was alone with him to see if anyone was lis-tening. Sometimes I thought I heard a laugh track in my own head, but it was always a few seconds behind the beat, behind the punch line—as if the laughter had been laid down on a separate track long before we started talking.

It had been two weeks since Jonathan returned from the embassy with his barely legal passport. He was now running around col-lecting letters and forms from a variety of sources, many of whom seemed available for negotiation only through the instant messaging service on his Nokia phone. The small favors Jonathan asked me for were clerical: a color scan here, a photocopy there, and all of the legal odds and ends like the letter stating his salary (shockingly low) and other contract particulars from the manager of his club team. For everything else he had his friends—Nigerian men I kept a conscious distance from, as I did my ex-boyfriends. Jonathan had his friends and I had mine. During the rare moments our social Venn diagrams overlapped, they formed an elliptical of heavy drinking. I realize it's not unusual for couples to have their separate orbits, but our social worlds were not separate in the sense of "your friend Rob could bring dessert wine to our dinner party." Our realms were fundamentally distant. Jonathan's friends brought nothing to the party, in my eyes, except trouble.

The week slipped by. Finishing up at my office, I filed my second story of the week for *Bloomberg* and then began in earnest uploading party photos to my Facebook. I was about to call it a day. It was Friday afternoon and I was restless—Jonathan and I had only gone out once since Monday, since the day that Austin died.

When I rang him up I was distracted, fiddling around with cropping an ugliness out of one of my photos, and there was a great commotion in the background when he answered:

"My Sexy. Can you call me back in thirty minutes time, please? We are trying to bury my friend. His coff is beautiful baby—we all gave money. Please call me back, okay?"

Austin. I knew Jonathan was one of the pallbearers, but I had forgotten the funeral was today. Not because Austin's death hadn't entered my world through my boyfriend, his close friend—all week Jonathan had been subject to peculiar cross-currents in which he amped back and forth between histrionic mourning and declarations of future vengeance toward individuals I did not know or care to know. And not because Austin's death wasn't a frequent topic of conversation around Phnom Penh; there had been three newspaper articles thus far, including an investigation into the Cambodian League's treatment of its African recruits.

The real reason the funeral had crept up on me was that no one could seem to settle on who should pay for it.

I was with Jonathan on Monday, eating a late lunch in the restaurant with the pink halogen lights on Mao Tse Tung Boulevard. There was a crowd glommed around the corner TV set. The monitor was dim, but in the murk we could make out a tiny telescoped figure lying on a pitch, on his back with his knees bent, surrounded by other players. The soccer ball lay untouched, in perfect equipoise outside the circle the crowd made. From between the calves of one of the men I could make out a face: eyes closed, whiskey-colored skin, an unusually long, thin nose for a Nigerian; thick lips, slightly parted: Austin.

The game was being broadcast live from Phnom Penh's Olympic Stadium. The lunchtime crowd, Cambodian and Chinese men in their office clothes who had wandered over from steaming bowls of duck's blood soup, tilted their heads philosophically toward the screen, cigarettes held out stiffly at their sides as the smoke curled and eddied around them. Our waiter, having finally located the remote, punched up the brightness on the monitor.

A medic was sprinting out onto the field—a Cambodian boy who looked all of sixteen. He was wearing a white polo shirt with a blue cross monogrammed on the back, and the footballers parted to let him by. The medic dropped to his knees beside Austin's head and cocked his ear between the boy's nose and mouth, listening.

And then it happened: the medic began massaging Austin's limbs in the direction of his heart. Long, slow, stylized strokes like a Balinese massage. He massaged the body limb-by-limb, as if he had all the time in the world, as if everything that was going to happen had already happened and the critical thing was this charade, this languorous reenactment.

As I watched I felt a *whoosh!* in my chest as if a decade of encrusted emotional matter was about to pour forth from a spillway in my ribcage. I rummaged in my purse. I always tried to take what was in the Altoids tin discretely, but when I tipped the pills into my mouth I saw that our waiter, from across the room, was once again studying me. He had been shooting me glances ever since Jonathan—his back against the restaurant's far concrete wall—had sunk down to the floor and began rocking back and forth, muttering to himself. Slipping the tin back in my purse, I met the waiter's eyes and shrugged. It was inconceivable to me that I looked to him like someone who could do something. I knew how I looked to myself: I was standing in a duck's blood soup restaurant in which there happened to be

Chinese, Cambodians, and a huge, collapsed Nigerian, head in his hands, intoning *O God O God O God*. I walked over to Jonathan and placed my hand on his shoulder. Under the lights my arm glowed lurid pink.

Monday night, after we had watched it all on TV, Jonathan had run off to join the group assembling at the morgue:

"He was still in his soccer kit," he told me afterward. "The exact same clothes he collapsed in! Baby, they did not even wipe the grass from his face. And so many dead Cambodians! Motorbike accidents. They were all hit by beeg car—a field of them!"

A 70,000 square mile emergency room, Cambodia is not a country for getting emotionally involved in dramatic situations. Once I was walking in the shoulder of a wide boulevard with Jonathan when I noticed the pavement below us was now a patchwork of spent condoms. I squealed, hopping in an impossible attempt to sidestep the rubbers. Jonathan laughed at me, pointing to a utility worker a few yards ahead of us. Only the man's head was visible; his body was swallowed by a manhole and submerged under the street. My eyes took in the three pyramidal piles surrounding the manhole: they were the color of dirty snow and made up of thousands of used condoms. I looked up in horror to the shops lining the street: the worker was clearing the sewage main in front of a love hotel.

Seconds later came a loud WHACK and shouts from up the street. A Lexus had turned into oncoming traffic, hitting two boys zipping down the boulevard on a motorcycle. Their convulsing bodies lay in the street ahead. This was about as much as I could take. *I've got to get out of here*, I said through gritted teeth, but Jonathan was too interested in the surrounding drama—*note: not traumatized; not disgusted*—to hear me. The utility worker looked up from his task for a moment and then quickly resumed his shoveling. The whole abject scene contained a small epiphany for me: I was not as aloof as I thought I was. I needed to work at being aloofer.

When Jonathan told me about the motorbike dead I did not grimace like a girl at his description.

They had carried Austin off the field—after his massage—and loaded him into an ambulance that was nothing more than a white van with heavy curtains, an open interior, and "ambulance" decaled on its sides. The van had taken him to the hospital, where he was rolled into the ER under ancient oscillating fans and exactly nothing more was done for him.

He was pronounced dead. In short order the body had been dispatched to the hospital morgue where it created a little stir among the Cambodian motorbike dead. Austin had been at the hospital for practically no time at all, so when Africans began showing up on the hospital steps an orderly was assigned to stand outside—there were that many of them—to shepherd the men to the morgue where they soon became the problem of the sour, liver-spotted coroner who had the aggressive, blood-shot stare of a former Khmer Rouge.

They stood in a group of upward of twenty men, praying around the body. Towering over the group, massive as an old baobob tree of the variety round which West African witches have long held their covens—Agbeze.

"Look around you," Agbeze was saying to the assembled. "Do you see any Cambodians here who are not DEAD? Where is the owner of the team? Where is Austin's coach? Where is your coach?" he said, looking pointedly at two hollow-eyed boys, also still wearing their white kits, their hands clasped pensively in front of them.

The coroner and his two staff were eyeing the crowd warily, from the doorway of their corner office.

"Do you see any of them here? Do you know why? Because they are too scared to show their faces! Because they know they did this to him! Because they brought him to their country like chattel and did not pay him even the money that would keep an old dog alive!"

When Jonathan related this part of Agbeze's speech, I said I didn't know what slavery had to do with it.

"Agbeze is a very powerful man," Jonathan quietly replied.

This was the first time I had heard my boyfriend refer to Agbeze as anything other than the "Nigerian President." Agbeze was president of the Nigerian Community Association—a position I understood to be two parts conflict resolution, one part something else that couldn't be discussed—and also held a professorship at one of the city universities. Doing interviews for the news wire, I had set foot in enough Cambodian institutions to picture his desk: a dark mahogany slab off a choked corridor, students in identical white shirts with gelled hair streaming past in the *en plein air* hallways, geckos with oversized vocals croaking from every corner and perhaps a chunk or two of wall missing. Nothing about this picture aroused my awe or respect. And yet Jonathan held Agbeze in high esteem. But what did I know? After all, it seemed the man wore many hats.

At six o'clock I went home to my apartment. My roommate was out for the evening, and Jonathan had called me back at work (I had forgotten about the agreed upon thirty minutes) to tell me he was going out with Austin's teammates, post-funeral, for a night of drinking. After dragging up five sets of stairs I walked out onto my balcony and slumped into the lavender-cushioned papasan chair. On my way home from work I had stopped by a pharmacy for two blisters of pills and a bottle of water. The pills were green and yellow and I popped four quickly through the foil before raising the water bottle to my lips.

The previous weekend, Jonathan and I had attended a party on a colonial-era train recommissioned by a Belgian party promoter. Departing from the city's rail yard an hour before sunset, the train had all the structural integrity of a Dorito chip: its boxcars crumbled and ricketed along the tracks, swaying under the weight of their twenty-first century revelers. A local DJ claimed an outpost for his MacBook between two of the cars and swing music percolated from small white speakers tethered to the same ceiling mounts as the train's ancient fans, squealing within fan guards of loose and rusted wire.

A tuxedoed man sweated up and down the aisles, replenishing the partygoers' plastic cups from a seemingly endless bottle of champagne. Lurching in the aisle as the train picked up speed, Jonathan grabbed an empty seat and pulled me down onto his lap. Directly in front of us a group of detached-looking girls smoked Alain Delon cigarettes. Balancing me on his knee, Jonathan took back the cup he had handed to me during the lurch. The passenger seats had obviously been measured to the scale of a long-gone world: Jonathan's thighs interlocked with the legs of the women opposite us like teeth on a zipper. "All my party people!" he said to our impromptu company, raising his plastic cup.

The girls looked us up and down. I felt the gaze of a tall brunette flick between my face and Jonathan's as if trying to assess if we were her joke or she was ours.

The brunette raised her cup and locked eyes with Jonathan: *"Santé!* You are visiting Cambodia, no?"

"No, no—I live here, in Phnom Penh." Jonathan tipped back his entire cup of champagne like it was a whiskey shot. "My name's Jonathan"—he licked his lips and extended his hand—"and this is my girl."

"Bonsoir," I said, giving the ladies a noncommittal wave from Jonathan's lap. All inquiries were directed toward Jonathan; he was obviously the experimental subject.

"So, Jonathan," the brunette continued, "and exactly where do you come from?"

"I'm Nigerian," he said with pride. "From Delta State. You're French, right?"

"Oui."

"What state?"

"Pardon?"

"I mean, what state are you from in France?"

The brunette shot a glance to the companion to her right, arching her eyebrow. "Alsace," she said, looking back at the two of us. "In France we call them *provinces.*"

"Oh yeah," Jonathan said. "Pardon me, okay?" I felt a prick of embarrassment run up my spine for him, but Jonathan appeared nonplussed. His eyes were wandering over the heads of the girls to the man in the tuxedo, now making another pass with the bottle down the aisle. I jumped up and grabbed my boyfriend's hand.

"Excuse us," I said. "I need to get some air." Down the aisle I pressed with Jonathan, gripping his hands like a trapeze bar. A man I knew—an Australian reporter—had a private bottle of champagne and was dancing on his seat, two unlit cigarettes dangling out of the corner of his mouth, around him, a flock of micro-skirted Vietnamese. A girl in four-inch Plexiglas heels wobbled atop her upholstered seat. *Ay!* She squealed as we pushed our way by, tugging at a strand of her long black hair that had caught in one of the wire fans.

A trapdoor in my heart gave way and I felt like I was sinking deep into the floor: suddenly, Jonathan seemed very tall and far away. Walking behind him, I grabbed his shoulder and hoisted myself on my tippy-toes to whisper in his ear: "You're so much better than these people, okay? I don't want you to ever forget it."

"What's that you say, baby?" His lips brushed against my ear but I shook my head, sphinx-like. The moment had passed. He turned again to face the back of the train, and, with his hands gripping mine behind his back, pulled me toward the caboose where a windy doorframe without its door gave way to a small viewing platform.

When we stepped out, Jonathan turned his sights to the garbage slipping by under the platform's metal latticework.

"Those girls were mocking me."

"Just a little bit," I said, reaching for his hand. I held it lightly, worrying my thumb along the valley of his palm. "Thank you for escaping with me."

"You know I'll always stand by you anytime and anywhere. You mean a lot to me." His voice was soft. "You know some people ask if love is worth fighting for—" Jonathan paused and looked up at me; I could see the red capillaries forked against the whites of his eyes. "Then I remember your face and baby, I'm ready for war."

Not even a week had passed since the train party but I could no longer recall what I said to Jonathan in reply. What I do remember is Jonathan framed against the sunset in his cheap white suit and the filthy children running after the slow-going train waving and shouting their *Hello hello hello hello!* I looked beyond the children and noticed the lean-tos extended to within kissing distance of the tracks. This was their living room and we were riding a train through the center of it. Never before had I stood on such a threshold: behind me was a glowing golden gyrating train full of cocktail dresses and assholes. Before me, the shantytown chased after us like a motley serpent, into the flooded rice fields.

It was the street noise that finally jarred me back to the present. From my perch in the papasan chair I could hear children shouting in the street below and the man hawking his cart of pickled eggs. The density of Asian life, each apartment level like a cross-section of stone in which can be found sedimentary deposits of grandfathers, aunties, shopkeepers, kids, made my loneliness flare brightly for a second like a gas flame the moment the pilot is lit.

It was then that I spied yesterday's paper—it was under the rattan side table and I decided to revisit the piece on Austin's death. As I re-read the article, I realized that Agbeze was being quoted:

They are engaged in human trafficking. A Cambodian Club Team pays for the boy to come here. They pay for his passage. They make all the necessary arrangements and pay for his business visa. Thereafter, they pay him 200 U.S. a month to play 1:00 P.M. games five days a week in the tropical heat. This is all in the player's contract. What is not in his contract is medical insurance. Or visa renewal. If a boy is sick or injured and cannot play, his salary stops. The team cuts him loose with no way to pay for his medical care and perhaps a visa that's about to expire, and no ticket home. And where does this leave the African recruits? Very, very vulnerable. That's where it leaves them.

The article continued on the back page. I flipped the paper over and kept on reading, scanning the text for another quote by Agbeze:

But the Cambodian Football Association is not entirely to blame, you see—they have just hit upon a strange fact about the African footballer: They will play for free if they have to. They love the game too much. And some of them will die for it.

The green and yellow pills were sloppy (manufactured in Malaysia and full of God knows what), but necessary to my getaway. In case you think of me as a stoic or insensitive, let me tell you this: without narcotics I am soft as a Monchhichi. I have vast migratory pains that swoop and settle across my whole body. When I was fifteen, the doctors labeled them "fibromyalgia," which is a medical term for pain anywhere and everywhere of unknown origin. It has something to do with my nerves, the nerve-endings as well as my emotions, both of which are often over-stimulated.

Childhood: rarely the largest cross-section of a life, but the period that forms the duplicating pattern in the grain. I was beaten—badly—as a child. Once she yanked me up with such force my arm popped clear of its socket. I have been to a few shrinks since then and I have learned to be wary of peoples' motives. *Motive* is just a gussied-up word for reason, and with some people it doesn't take much. *It was ungodly hot and the kids wouldn't stop shooting those rubber bands,* my mother, during one of her hearings, told the appellate.

I saw a medical intuitive once. He said he saw dark brown fetid knots in the parts of my body that needed to move the most: my knee and elbow joints, my ankles, the shoulder socket that was briefly relieved of its arm. He said the question I should be asking myself wasn't, *Why was I abused?*, but *What kind of person would choose to be an abused child?* I was appalled. I had told him nothing, aside from my name and date of birth, before I entered the room. It took me days to sufficiently calm down enough to give his question serious thought. *What kind of person?* A person who believed—as my uncle was fond of saying—*Life's a bitch and then you die?* No, that wasn't it. Perhaps a person who was easily distracted, who thought life moved too fast to accomplish much? From my pain I had fashioned myself a tidy little Bastille with a full library and Moroccan rug. As much as I railed against it I was snug here. The pills made me feel detached and floating. They did nothing for the pain, but they made me not care so much that it was there. My dysfunction—and I know it is clearly just that: *my* dysfunction—afforded me the constraints I believed I needed to create.

Jonathan fit neatly into this program. My culture was so outside his purview—as was his, mine—that he was unaware that I was using. I could have told him that Americans must swallow twenty pills a day and he would have taken it as a citizenship requirement. Such was the permissive ignorant oasis of Cambodia: this is where people who knew better came to get away with things.

The Nigerian "President"'s language was becoming increasingly baroque with each passing day. When Jonathan and I went to him on Thursday to discuss Jonathan's passport issue, Austin's want of a burial was all Agbeze could speak of.

"It has been almost one week. Is our friend to be unhoused? Is he to lack a sepulcher? Is his crypt a metal tray at the Cambodian hospital? No! He deserves eternal rest next to his mother and father. When their time comes," he added hastily. Agbeze had just spoken to the bereaved, or so he told us, over a Skype connection at the nearby Internet cafe. "But who is to pay for this?"

The owner of Austin's club team—despite it being known that he was also a partner in the new riverside casino—claimed the football team had no money to pay for a funeral, let alone repatriating the body. The family in Lagos was notified, and when it became apparent that they had no money either and would not consent to a cremation (as they were Muslim), Agbeze raised a further stink.

Who is to pay? This sounded like a question of a different sort. We had come to Agbeze tentatively—Jonathan with an unpleasant taste in his mouth—but he had said this was the only way. The three of us were now sitting at a table in the No Name, the restaurant at the African bar, soaking up our Egusi soup with white, doughy balls of fufu. A Khmer waitress in a *No Money, No Honey* baby-T shuttled pitchers of Angkor between rattan tables as a Lil Wayne video played overloud in the backdrop.

In the African bar there had been an attempt over the past few days to raise enough money for Austin's burial at a local cemetery. When the Crown Royal bag finally reached our table I stuffed a ten-dollar bill deep within its velvet folds. I watched Jonathan quickly stuff a wadded up dollar into the collection bag and then pass the bag along. He looked embarrassed, but I knew he was holding onto every cent right now in light of his sudden issue.

After seeing a YouTube clip of him playing in a Thai match, an Australian soccer team had emailed a letter of invitation to Jonathan. The team, as of a couple months ago, was newly minted Premiere League and all they needed was for him to obtain a tourist visa to Australia for the audition. Once he got to Australia the team said they could arrange for the rest. So Jonathan had made an appointment at the embassy in Phnom Penh, where the interviewer flipped through his visa pages past the Thai visas, the Vietnamese visas, the Singapore visa, to the passport's last remaining pages.

"This passport looks good," the man said. "Your visa history is strong, but you can't fly to Australia with only two pages left in this passport. You're going to need to get a new one. After you've taken care of that, you can make another appointment and we'll discuss the matter of the visa."

The man had then tapped Jonathan's papers together sharply and handed them back to him.

I think Jonathan must have felt a headache wincing on: the nearest Nigerian Embassy was in Kuala Lumpur. Unless he could get a Malaysian visa and fly to KL—and that would surely eat all of his money—everything would need to be arranged through a go-between. As for me, I was beginning to understand that Jonathan's future pointed toward Australia. Late at night I tried to convince myself that this might be my destiny too, but all I had to go on was a birthmark, roughly the shape of the Australian continent, on my inner right thigh. Never mind Australian accents made me cringe or that when I tried to recall any Australian literature what came to mind were the dirty passages from *The Thorn Birds*. Still, it was more comforting to think of myself as having a mismatched destiny in a mismatched country with Jonathan than to think of myself as having no destiny at all.

"I'm sorry I only have small money to give to Austin," Jonathan was saying to Agbeze—as if Austin was right now squatting outside the African bar with a plastic cup, begging for his dinner. "But I am having BEEG passport problem. I tell you, I just gave the police 600 dollars for my visa extension and now they are telling me I need a new passport. Time is pressing on me, Agbeze, and I cannot lose this opportunity. You say you look on me like a son, and I believe you, but I need you to think of me as your son now because I must ask for—"

"Where is the passport?" Agbeze interrupted. I thought he wouldn't want to discuss it with him, not this week of all weeks, but the older man was right on the point, asking him to give it here. Jonathan began rummaging through his messenger bag and removing various articles, which he placed precisely on the table: a huge padded set of headphones swaddled in their own cord; rolled-up Adidas gym shorts; a navy blue Gideon's Bible spotted in flecks of white paint; at last, the passport.

Agbeze took it from him and immediately began flipping through the visa pages, holding the passport up to the bar light to scrutinize each visa. When he turned to the I.D. page, he lingered on the photo. Sitting between the two men, I rocked my stool a few inches closer to Agbeze and lowered my head to peer at the photo beside him. There were the wide nose, long indulgent eyelashes and big lips curved up at the corners in a natural bow even though he wasn't smiling—*you have Buddha lips*, I would often say to Jonathan.

I had never had a chance to grow accustomed to my boyfriend's face. And if I was honest with myself, I think my initial attraction to Jonathan was because of this face. When I looked into it I saw great pain. And there was something I recognized in his pain that cleared my head with its sharpness, like jumping into a cold lake on a sweltering day.

When I looked up from the photo it was as if I was seeing clearly for the first time: at least a dozen African boys were congregated around three pitchers of beer; some were staring vacantly at the flat screen TV; others, text messaging. And this is when it hit me. The boy in the photo, this much younger version of Jonathan, could be any of them.

"I can make all the arrangements," Agbeze said. His voice was measured, business-like: "but you must know this is not an inexpensive process. I will need to pass on the appropriate amounts to facilitate this, and we will have to mail your photo and paperwork to Malaysia as well as courier the new passport back." Agbeze paused. "The cost of all of this is usually $1,400, but I can give you a special price—a consideration. Perhaps we can take care of this for $950?"

This is when Jonathan lifted one last item out of his bag—a dog-eared envelope, from which he took out eight bills all with the improbable face of Ulysses S. Grant.

"This is the best I can do for now. Please Agbeze. I am praying to my God that he will see me out of this situation." (I had never detected this note before in Jonathan's voice, this beseeching.) "I will do everything in my power to get you the rest of the money. But I need my passport now. The police are on my back and they could deport me like that"—Jonathan snapped his fingers and looked over at me—"and then what would happen to my girl? We have a life together—not in Delta State, not in Sydney—we have a life together, *here*, in Phnom Penh. It's not just my own life I'm asking you for."

Agbeze tapped the 400 dollars into his wallet; then looked hard at me and smiled. "You are lucky you have a woman who sees you through the hard times, no?"

I thought I detected a note of condescension in this—some cold draft of insincerity in the older man's tone.

Well. The money in the envelope was mine. In fact, I had just withdrawn my maximum daily limit from the ATM, but this much was none of Agbeze's business. I sat there with my lips pursed, trying to think of something to say. In the meantime, Agbeze palmed Jonathan's passport.

"I'll see what I can do." We both watched as he slipped the passport into a long manila folder and then rose from the table. "Excuse me, Jonathan—*Miss,*" he said to me. The word hissed off his tongue. "I need to visit the washroom."

Rumors spread about Austin's death. That at the time of the match, he had not eaten in three days. That he wasn't even signed to the team and had been playing for free. That the skinny Khmer girlfriend who keened shamelessly at his funeral was pregnant by him. That he had been forced, by a cruel kind of economy, to pedal a bicycle the forty-five minutes to Olympic Stadium to and from practice each day, returning in rush hour traffic with a gauze surgical mask over his mouth and one arm held out to shield his eyes from the glare and the carbon monoxide.

That he had been poisoned.

The last theory was the most disturbing, but I had overheard all of them being bandied about at the bar at one point or another by the legions of African boys who said they were footballers, but as far as I could tell had no profession besides chain-smoking.

I was waiting for Jonathan to meet me at the African bar on Thursday, before our business with Agbeze, when a long-limbed boy approached me at the bar and immediately began fumbling with a crumpled pack of cigarettes.

"Do you smoke?" he asked me.

"Sure," I said, thinking he meant marijuana. But he offered me a cigarette. "Oh no, no thank you," I said, shooing it away and crossing my legs. "I quit."

"I thought you said you smoke?" He looked at me reproachfully.

"Not cigarettes." There was something unsettling about him. I was constantly being hit on by men who were ridiculous; some energy in me must have leapt out and met the aggrieved, the thespians, the men who lingered on their own reflections in store windows and tripped over obstacles in the street. He said his name was Freedom, and helped himself to the stool next to me.

"Me, I love to smoke. Cigarettes. Hookah. Blow smoke. Take a slow drag. After sex." As he confessed he looked up at me, from lazy lowered cat's eyes. "Where are you from?"

"The U.S.," I said, craning my neck to look past his shoulder to the tables crowding the bar. I felt eyes on me while we were talking, but none of them belonged to anyone I knew.

"Ah, an American." He leaned back, shook his head. "You are very, very lucky. I would like to visit your country someday."

I needed to grab control of the conversation and move on. "So where are you from?"

"Hah! Don't you know?" he snorted. "Are you not living in this country?"

"Well, I assume you're from Nigeria, yeah. But you never know. You could be Cameroonian and then I've offended you." I took a sip from the straw bobbing up and down in my bottle of soda water. "Do you like it here?"

"It's okay." He shifted his body weight. "I'm stuck here until I can play again." At this he motioned toward the floor—he was wearing baggy shorts to his knee—and I noticed, for the first time, a white bandage swaddled around his leg, mid-calf. "A Cambodian did this to me. A stupid ass," he added darkly.

"Is it a football injury?"

"Yeah." I peered down at it, into the gloom of the scuffed tile floor. It didn't look like any sports injury I'd ever seen.

"What happened?" I asked.

"You see this player, he put his leg out"—Freedom flexed his good leg and held it out from the bar stool—"and he tripped me. It was—how do you say?—purposeful. The Cambodian ref he didn't do nothing." The boy snorted. "What can you do with these kind of people? They have no rules, no education. My brother warned me this could happen. He said, these people you're playing with, they're uncivilized. They can do anything to you and nothing will happen to them—you'll see." He paused a second, as if contemplating whether or not to continue. "This never would have happened to me in any other league."

"What did you sprain?" I pressed him.

"That muzzle, uh"—he pronounced "muscle" *muzzle*—"that muzzle that runs down the back of your leg. I think it's called hamstring."

"Your hamstring is above your knee," I pointed out. Jonathan was late, Agbeze hadn't shown his face yet, and I was not feeling generous.

"You know what I'm saying," Freedom rejoined. He was looking at me strangely. "He injured me, okay? Now that I can't play my team stopped my paychecks. What else am I supposed to do here?" He leaned in conspiratorially and spoke his next words softly, transferring his left hand to my thigh: "Just look around this room and tell me"—he squeezed my leg—"*what else am I supposed to do?*"

The passport had been with the President for ten days and there had been no new developments aside from Jonathan having to fast talk his way out of two new police raids on his all-male, all-Nigerian living situation with only a color copy of his passport and visa page, which I had scanned and printed out at my office, to present to the immigration police. On Saturday morning I awoke to Jonathan's ringtone: harsh, tinny notes of Lady Gaga. I felt him searching under his pillow for the phone. When I opened my eyes he was folded mantis-like with his knees tucked under his chin at the edge of the bed, pinching his phone to his ear with his shoulder and pulling on his shoes.

"I told you that's all the documents I have, man—I gave you everything I had last week!"

Agbeze, I thought and rolled over, groaning as I twisted the pillow around to cover my head.

"I'm with my girl right now, okay? Why can't you tell me over the phone?"

There was a barrage of rapid-fire pidgin from Jonathan's end: "Okay, okay. Five minutes, okay?" He cut the phone and turned to me, tugging the sheets down over my ass and grabbing a handful of my flesh. "My Sexy," he said, "my Mary J. Blige. Pardon me, okay? I've got to meet Agbeze—I'll be a few minutes, just a few minutes okay?"

"Where're you going?"

"The Laos Embassy—it's just up the street."

"Why the Laos Embassy?" I was vaguely annoyed; why did everything with Jonathan have to be a non sequitur?

"I'm meeting him in front, okay baby? I think he needs to hand me some forms. I'll come right back, okay?"

He didn't appear worried and so I settled back on my side, gathering the sheets around me. He dropped down on bended knee beside the bed, kissed the tip of his own index and middle finger with a loud, juicy smack and then touched it to my lips. He then kissed his fingers again and reached for my face, using his fingertips like a brush to paint an imaginary diagonal across each of my cheekbones. It was a silly ritual between us. At last he planted a final finger kiss on my forehead and, leaning his head back theatrically with the flat palm of his hand tapping against his pursed lips, let out an Indian war whoop: *WAH WA WA WAH WA WA WA WAH!*

Jonathan, when he was a teenager, had lived through a tribal war in which he saw many people beheaded—"heads rolled—literally," he was fond of saying; the war whoop was another of his favorite jokes. As he closed the door, he poked his head into the bedroom one last time and batted his eyelashes: "Red Indian kisses, baby, Red Indian kisses."

When I woke up I had no idea what time it was. A flat white light was leaking in at the edge of the curtains. It could have been 10 A.M.; it could be two in the afternoon. I staggered to the bathroom to pee and my legs stung with the usual nerve pain from the Fibro—it took a little while to get them going. As I walked through the kitchen I noticed that the metal security door was ajar.

"Jonathan?"

Nothing. I swung open the door and stepped out onto the balcony.

He was sitting on the steps of the fire escape with his giant headphones on and when he looked up at me I could see that his eyes were wet.

"Baby, what's wrong?"

"Agbeze lost my passport."

"Excuse me?" I had and hadn't heard him: I was thinking about my pills, which I had left in my bedroom, on the nightstand. There would be no going back for them now.

"He lost it. MY LIFE ABROAD. He leaves MY LIFE on his desk! Wait—I take that back. He doesn't even know where he left MY LIFE."

"Oh baby . . ." I clambered down the steps to sit beside him. "How could that be? What did he do with it?"

"That's why he had to meet in person. To tell me. I was so ANGRY, baby—I could have ripped up the roots of trees! I said to him, *I give you MY LIFE and you leave it on your desk for anyone to pick through?*"

With this he gathered the fingers of one hand into a point and made a twisting motion at his temple: "I say to him, *Are you PSYCH?*"

"That's terrible—just terrible. Jesus." I sucked in my breath and pondered what else I should say. "Don't you think he could have just misplaced it?" I finally offered. "Has he checked his car?"

"Don't you know—we turned that car UPSIDE DOWN!" Jonathan made a chinking motion with both hands held up to the air like an imaginary gear belt turning over. "He was waving his folder at me in front of the Laos Embassy. He was carrying around MY LIFE in that rat-ass folder! He's not even sure he left the passport on his desk."

"Do you think someone could have taken it?"

His eyes narrowed. "You know, that's what I've been sitting out here thinking. That's exactly what I've been thinking. He's told all the staff in the office that there's a reward. If a Cambodian took it, they will hand it over for the money."

"What makes you think a Cambodian took it?"

"Because they are thieves. Don't you know? Cambodians are beeg thieves! Tssst."

He was disgusted by my questions and I couldn't blame him. He was now document-less; illegal in a country that suspected everything about him anyway. *Unhouseled. Sepulchered.* But I couldn't think of a single Cambodian who would want anything to do with a Nigerian passport. I could, however, picture a bar full of idle, indolent African boys who had overstayed their visas—some by as long as two years.

None of it made any sense and yet it was so.

Suddenly my head felt very clear. There was one thing I understood: that passport with Jonathan's visa history would be very valuable to someone. Someone young. Someone who needed to leave the country fast. Someone who could pay.

"You white people don't believe in anything."

We were walking down Street 63 and his comment felt splashed out of nowhere, like an acid attack. I stopped walking and turned to face him.

"And how did you arrive at this deduction? From everything you've learned about white people watching StarWorld TV? Or perhaps from that German girl you dated? Either way, I'm impressed. So just because I tell you to take something a so-called voodoo priest is text messaging you from 10,000 miles away with a grain of salt, I'm godless, right? I'm completely lacking in faith because I don't follow a VOODOO PRIEST—is that it?"

My heart was scampering up my ribcage.

Jonathan had told me how the priest worked for the African bar on consultancy. Every time a violent fight broke out or a cell phone so much as disappeared, the proprietor of the bar text messaged this man a list of the names of all of the men who had set foot in his establishment on the evening in question. This is where the voodoo came in: Jonathan claimed that the priest would then text back a single name to the proprietor—the culprit's—a task he had carried out for years with 98 percent accuracy. Regarding his missing passport, the list of names he had sent to the priest was relatively short: a few employees with whom the President shared his office space, including the cleaning lady; two African boys rumored to be involved in drug deals gone sour; last but not least, Agbeze.

The priest had advised Jonathan to fast and pray for five days, but mid-afternoon on the third day he must have texted him a name. I recall the little chirp of the Nokia when the message hit his inbox. Jonathan refused to show me the text, but it was obvious to me the priest had told him to go after Agbeze. This was two days ago, and despite having already received what he believed to be ironclad information about the culprit, Jonathan had insisted on completing his fast.

I did everything within my power to keep him in my bedroom for those last two days. A fasting Jonathan could hurt only himself, but I was beginning to wonder what a non-fasting Jonathan might do. During his fast an expression crept into my boyfriend's face that spooked me: Jonathan would be hunched over contemplating his problems, staring into space; I would glance over at him and for a second his face would appear like an object made of wood. His features would become crude as if carved with a hatchet and the crevices in the wood burned until their contours were defined by charcoal. Then the body underneath the mask would materialize muscular and seething, vibrating with supernatural force. This body had the same scars as Jonathan; the same tattoos. But if I looked too long in this peculiar state I became terrified: his face was obviously a mask; underneath it could be anyone.

If I shook my head and quickly looked away it would release the spell. I knew it was a sick game but—alone with him in my room—I kept playing it.

Jonathan passed the time sipping water and SMS-ing threats to Agbeze, which the older man treated with the utmost composure and concern. He had shown me one of Agbeze's responses, tilting the screen of his phone toward me so I could read it myself:

MY GOD KNOWS I HAVE NOT TOUCHED YOUR PASSPORT. I HAVE DONE EVERYTHING TO LOCATE IT FOR YOU. ASK MY WIFE AND MY CHILDREN I HAVE NOT SLEPT A NIGHT SINCE IT WENT MISSING. PLACE YOUR FAITH IN GOD, JONATHAN. PLEASE KEEP FAITH.

"And he says he hasn't slept?" Jonathan snorted as he showed me the SMS. "What kind of man is this? If I had lost his passport I would not be sleeping or eating ONE DAY; I would be running around like chicken." At this he pointed both of his index fingers and wagged them side-by-side in imitation of a runner. "And what is he doing? Going to classes? Preaching at the African bar? I am beginning to think this is a very bad man, Agbeze. I am believing this priest that he sold my passport to someone and I will not rest until he tells me what he knows."

By the time night fell Jonathan was senseless with hunger and an old paranoia was rumbling up inside me that the pills could not put down. The noise carried over from a wedding party in the street below seemed loud and too much and yet the sounds muffled together with Jonathan's speech in a way that made me feel like I was groping to understand anything. My bedroom was stifling, full of hot dead air. When Jonathan moved his arm suddenly to swat a fly I drew my knees into my chest and screamed.

"What the fuck is wrong with you!" he yelled. He jumped up and left the bedroom, slamming the door behind him. When he finally returned more than an hour had past. He had showered and reeked of my sweet lime and cedar Jo Malone.

"Are you wearing my perfume?"

"It's called cologne. Jo Malone makes cologne."

"Did you go through my things?" I hadn't moved from my fetal position, but was looking up at him with my one eye that wasn't buried by the pillow.

"I borrowed a bit of your *cologne,* okay? I need to get the hell out of this apartment."

Hm. So he was ready to break his fast? "I could scramble you up some eggs." I said it weakly, but it was still a peace offering.

I was standing in the kitchen and had already begun cracking the eggs over a bowl when I felt his eyes on me. I turned around. Jonathan was studying me from a folding chair in the hallway from which he had displaced a pile of laundry. My silk, hand-wash blouses were now occupying the tile floor alongside the dust and dead bugs.

"What? What is it this time?"

"I don't want to eat any eggs, okay? I've changed my mind—all I want is fufu."

Jonathan had insisted on walking and that is how we landed on Street 63, amid the food stalls of the night vendors on our way to the No Name. Each vendor had a long halogen light illuminating a Plexiglas box of food—fried cricket, candied meat, mystery noodles. The lights hung above the stalls at fractured, warring angles like sparring light sabers. There were dozens of these vendors crowded up and down the street and the combined effect of all that akimbo halogen was that even the sky appeared to be fighting.

When we reached the corner I noticed a motorbike driver, a "motodop," as they call the hired drivers in Cambodia, leaning against the seat of his parked bike, smoking.

"*Lok kmoa,*" I thought I heard the man say as we passed by.

At first we kept on arguing. Every time Jonathan accused me of lacking faith I took a broader interpretation: he was calling me an infidel. I was hell-bent on explaining to Jonathan what I, a white person, believed in, when I heard the driver say it again, much louder this time and to our backs for we had passed by him and were now walking away: "*Lok kmoa.*"

Black man.

I grabbed Jonathan's hand to guide him around the corner, into the African bar, but it was too late.

"Say it again, man, say it again." He had spun around to face the motodop.

The man leaned his head over the handlebars of his bike and by the sound of things was working up a full mouth of spit. Then he hocked it out, letting the loogie dangle from his lips and then slowly detach. When it hit the ground he looked straight at Jonathan with bloodshot eyes. Only then did it occur to me that the driver was high. "*Lok kmoa,*" he repeated, adding in English, "Why you come to my country? Why you don't go back your country?"

This is when Jonathan snapped. And by snapping I mean he took something out of his messenger bag; something I didn't know he had.

Jonathan was a crack shot. The motodop stumbled backwards and fell against his Honda. His slight body was enough to rock the bike against the gate behind it but not to knock it from its stand. He slumped down against it, his back in its tattered cotton shirt coming to rest against the bike's metal exhaust pipe.

"He's going to burn himself!" I screamed. There were still aspects of my mind that were working logically but the logic belonged to a different situation all together than the one I was in. Two fruit sellers conferring on the opposite corner had scooped up their baskets. The women—one with the primatal loping gait of a clubfoot—were now scuttling toward the alleyway.

"Move!" Jonathan shouted. He pointed the pistol towards the ground and with his free hand made a grab for me. The motodop had not stirred since collapsing against his bike. One of the man's arms rested lightly across his chest and blood bloomed from underneath his hand. I clocked all of this before looking aghast at Jonathan, or whatever entity said it was Jonathan and was wearing his heavy mask.

"You're coming with me to the bar," Jonathan ordered. "You and Agbeze—I want to see you put your heads together." He yanked me hard by my arm and I stumbled along behind him.

From here on out everything I remember comes in tunnel vision: the wide-eyed face of the Cambodian passer-by who would no sooner call for the police than pay the bribe for summoning them; the cheap electronic readout that flashed "PUB," and, incongruously, "BISTRO"; Jonathan's leopard tattoo; the way the cat's paw leapt across the tendons of his forearm as he flexed his hand and pushed aside the blackout curtain.

There were two men seated together at the bar and a bar girl, alone in the corner, dancing with her own reflection in the floor-to-ceiling mirror. Chike, the bartender, his hands braced against the bar, was leaning in convivially chatting with the two customers. The fat red jalapeño lights strung up around the bottles of whiskey and gin conspired to make the whole scene somehow homey. Jonathan had kept the gun behind my back as we entered through the curtain. It must have looked to the people in the room like he had his arm around me.

"*Haffa!*" Chike turned his head and winked at us. I hung back when Jonathan stepped forward. He held his right hand at his side with his left hand clasped over it; when the men looked down he quickly lifted his hand to flash the pistol.

"Ibuzor! What is this?" Agbeze had called him by his tribal name. The President's eyes flicked over the two of us and then settled back on Jonathan. "There's no need to bring her into this."

Jonathan snorted: "You think I don't know she's been talking to Freedom? You think everyone who passes through this bar"—he made a pinching motion in the air as if plucking the hairs off invisible heads—"hasn't told me about the two of them?" Heat flushed across my thighs. "The three of you?"

I didn't understand. Agbeze shot a glance at his companion and the man moved one of his legs off the rung of the bar stool, touching the tip of his shoe to the floor like a runner. When Jonathan turned around to grab me the man rushed for the door at the back of the room. I noticed the bar girl had vanished but Chike had barely deviated from his original position: he had moved one hand behind the counter but the other hand was still steadily gripping the wood grain of the bar, same as it had been when he was deep in conversation.

"Freedom?" Agbeze countered, "What does this have to do with Freedom?" The President was obviously trying to attach a face to the name.

"Don't you know!" Jonathan shouted. He shoved me down onto the empty stool next to Agbeze. "Why don't you ask her? Freedom is gone and so is my passport and she has a very *beeg* stack of money in her apartment!"

I racked my brain. I did, in fact, have a very big stack of money in my apartment: three thousand dollars squirreled away in a bronze Estée Lauder case. I had been running up my credit card with cash advances—so Jonathan could fly to Australia as soon as he had his passport back.

On some level I had wanted to be rid of him.

"Listen, my friend, you are not thinking clearly." Spreading his palm wide, Agbeze held one arm out at his side in deference but I already knew he was taking the wrong tack: betrayal, real or imagined, has a life of its own. Like a pill, it begins its work of changing who we are from the moment it is swallowed.

Jonathan could not afford his troubles. I had stepped in to rescue him, forever changing the dimensions of the game. Pride was now on the table. Fealty was on the table. With each play Austin had sunk deeper out of sight until no one could say plainly how it started: with unavenged death and with rumor. With pain, without the civilizing force of sympathy. I had watched, poker-faced, as Jonathan withered and distorted. I had exoticized his world because his world—if not Jonathan himself—was outside the boundaries of my compassion. Part of the seduction of being an ex-pat was getting to skip along the surface of a chasm as deep as culture. We were swimmers who had not allowed for the possibility of drowning and it made us heedless—with our own bodies as well as the strange bodies we flailed against.

Chike never took his eyes off the pistol. When Jonathan laid his hand on Agbeze it was Chike who put an end to it.

When I was a little girl I stepped on a bee in our backyard. My mother had warned me not to go barefoot, but I had disobeyed. The sensation of being stung was at first so foreign that I leapt onto my other foot but did not cry out. It wasn't until I looked down and saw the crumpled bee, stiff in his signature jacket, that my shock mutated into tears.

I remember my mother scooping me up in her arms and taking me inside. Great hiccupping sobs rose from the sofa where she had laid me down to operate. All the while she worked out the stinger with a pair of tweezers I was crying. As she swabbed my heel with alcohol, I was crying. Finally, exasperated, my mother turned on me: "I know it doesn't hurt that much!" she snapped.

That shut me up; I swallowed my own sobs. The pain was still there but I let it slide down to all the strange places, to wet backlit caverns where it would later crystallize and hang from my very bones.

Jonathan is in Cambodian jail now and the nearest Nigerian Embassy is still in KL. I still file two stories a week for *Bloomberg*—Uighurs deported to China; new hydropower dams choking off the Mekong—but these are other peoples' stories. When I think of Jonathan, I try to remember him as he was before he suspected me.

On one of our first dates he asked if he could "crest" me. I asked him what it meant, *crest*? He said, "To crest is to draw, baby. I'm going to draw you all right? Hold still." I was sitting across from him in a Vietnamese restaurant and I remember vamping—holding my chopsticks to my lips as he scribbled with his pen across the paper placemat that came under our bowls of pho.

When he was done he turned the placemat around to show me. It was a good likeness: he'd captured my long face, my almond eyes. But he had also drawn a riot of decorative ferns, devouring my head like a mane. The plant's leaves drooped over my ears and forehead and made me look telescoped and jungley.

"What's all this?" I asked, pointing to the ferns.

"It's a plant that grows in Nigeria. It's kind of like—how do you say it—a Touch-me-not? But instead of closing to touch it closes to sound. But there's only one thing you can say that will make it close. You have to say, *Your husband is coming, your husband is coming* . . . When you say those words"—he snapped his fingers together like a clam shell—"the plant will hide."

For a long time I thought this was just another of Jonathan's stories, but a few weeks ago it occurred to me to look it up: the plant, of the species *M. Pudica,* is also known as "Sensitive Plant" and when "touched" by these words does, in fact, fold its leaflets neatly inward like a row of collapsing dominoes or a venetian blind being drawn up smoothly by its cord. I do not cry anymore when I think of Jonathan, but I cried when he told me the story about the plant in Nigeria and I am crying now, as I think of it again, but for different reasons. This is where my story is located: on the shy tips of that shadowy fern. This is where my story is filed away.

DAVY ROTHBART

■

Human Snowball

FROM *The Paris Review*

ON FEBRUARY 14, 2000, I took the Greyhound bus from Detroit to Buffalo to visit a girl named Lauren Hill. Not Lauryn Hill, the singer who did that song "Killing Me Softly," but another Lauren Hill, who'd gone to my high school, and now, almost ten years later, was about to become my girlfriend, I hoped. I'd seen her at a party when she was home in Michigan over the holidays, and we'd spent the night talking and dancing. Around four in the morning, when the party closed down, we'd kissed for about twelve minutes out on the street, as thick, heavy snowflakes swept around us, melting on our eyebrows and eyelashes. She'd left town the next morning, and in the six weeks since, we'd traded a few soulful letters and had two very brief, awkward phone conversations. As Valentine's Day came near, I didn't know if I should send her flowers, call her, not call her, or what. I thought it might be romantic to just show up at her door and surprise her.

I switched buses in Cleveland and took a seat next to an ancient-looking black guy who was in a deep sleep. Twenty minutes from Buffalo, when darkness fell, he woke up, offered me a sip of Jim Beam from his coat pocket, and we started talking. His name was Vernon. He told me that when midnight rolled around, it was going to be his hundred-and-tenth birthday.

"A hundred and ten?" I squealed, unabashedly skeptical.

Happy to prove it, he showed me a public housing ID card from Little Rock, Arkansas, that listed his birth date as 2/15/90.

"Who was president when—"

"Benjamin Harrison," he said quickly, cutting me off before I was even done with my question, as though he'd heard it many times before. I had no clue if this was true, but he winked and popped a set of false teeth from his mouth, and in the short moment they glistened in his hand, it seemed suddenly believable that he was a hundred and ten, and not just, like, eighty-nine. His bottom gums, jutting tall, were shaped like the Prudential rock and were the color of raw fish, pink and red with dark gray speckles. The skin on his face was pulled taut around his cheekbones and eye sockets, as leathery and soft looking as some antique baseball mitt in its display case at Cooperstown.

I found myself telling Vernon all about Lauren Hill and explained how nervous I was to see her—surely he'd have some experience he could draw on to help me out. I told him I thought I was taking a pretty risky gamble by popping up in Buffalo unannounced. Things were either going to be really fucking awesome or really fucking weird, and I figured I'd probably know which within the first couple of minutes I saw her. Vernon, it turned out, was in a vaguely similar situation. After a century plus of astonishingly robust health, he'd been ailing the past eighteen months, and before he kicked off he wanted to make amends with his great-granddaughter, whom he was the closest to out of all of his relatives. But, he admitted, he'd let her down so many times—with the drinking, the drugs, and even stealing her money and kitchen appliances—that she might not be willing to let him past the front door. Twice he used my cell phone to try calling her, but nobody answered. So much for sage advice.

We both got quiet and brooded to ourselves as the bus rolled off the freeway ramp and wound its way through empty downtown streets lined with soot-sprayed mounds of snow and ice. Buffalo in winter is a bleak Hoth-like wasteland, and the only sign of life I saw was a pair of drunks who'd faced off in front of an adult bookstore and begun to fight, staggering like zombies. One of them had a pink stuffed animal and was clubbing the other in the face with it. A steady snow began to fall, and I felt a wave of desperate sorrow crash over me. Whatever blind optimism I'd had about the night and how Lauren Hill might receive me had been lost somewhere along the way (maybe at the rest stop in Erie, Pennsylvania, in the bathroom stall with shit smeared on the walls). The trip, I realized now, was a mistake, but at the same time I knew that the only thing to do was to go ahead with my fucked up plan anyway and go surprise Lauren, because once you're sitting there and you've got a needle in your hands, what else is there to do but poke your finger and see the blood?

At the Greyhound Station, a sort-of friend of mine named Chris Hendershot was there to pick me up in a shiny black Ford Explorer with only four hundred miles on the odometer but its front end and passenger side bashed to shit. "You get in a rollover?" I asked him, after hopping in up front.

"Naw, I just boosted this bitch yesterday in Rochester, it was already like this. Who's your friend?"

"This is Vernon. He's gonna ride with us, if that's cool. In a few hours it's gonna be his hundred-and-tenth birthday."

"No shit?" Chris glanced in the rearview and nodded to Vernon, in the backseat. "Fuck if I make it to twenty-five," he said, gunning it out of the lot.

Chris was the kind of guy who always made these sorts of claims, hoping, perhaps, to sound tougher, but really he was a sweetheart with a swashbuckler's twinkle who was rarely in serious danger and probably had decades of fun times ahead of him, if he could stay out of prison. He had pale white skin, a rash of acne on his neck, and his own initials carved into his buzz-cut hair in several places. He looked Canadian and sounded Canadian and was indeed Canadian—he'd grown up on the meanest street of Hamilton, Ontario, and, as he'd told me more than a few times, he and his older brother had stolen seventy-six cars before getting finally caught when Chris was nineteen. Chris did the time—three years—while his brother skated. Then Chris moved in with an uncle in Cincinnati and got a job as an airline reservationist, which was how I'd met him a couple of years before. He had a gregarious nature, and after we'd found ourselves in deep conversation while I was buying tickets over the phone, he'd come to Chicago a few weekends in a row and stayed on my couch while pursuing his dream of becoming a stand-up comic. The problem was that he was absolutely sorry as a stand-up comic, just woefully bad. I saw him perform once, at the ImprovOlympic at Clark and Addison, and it was one of the hardest, saddest things I've ever had to watch—someone's dream unraveling and being chopped dead with each blast of silence that followed his punch lines. But where I would've been destroyed by this, Chris was over it by the next morning, and freshly chipper. He told me the lesson he'd learned was that he needed to focus on his strengths, and he knew himself to be an ace car thief. Before long, he'd moved to Buffalo and was working at his older brother's "mechanic" shop. When I called and told him I was coming to town and explained why, he told me he actually knew Lauren Hill, because for a while he'd been a regular at Freighter's, the bar where she worked, though he doubted she knew him by name, and anyway, he said, he wasn't allowed in there anymore because he'd left twice without paying when he'd realized at the end of the night that he'd left his cash at home. "I'll tell you one thing," he said. "That girl's beautiful. Every guy who wanders into that damn bar, they leave in love with her."

Vernon had asked if he could roll with us for a bit while he kept trying to reach his great-granddaughter. If nothing else, he suggested, we could drop him off later at the YMCA and he'd track her down the next morning. He sat quietly in the backseat, looking out the window while we cruised toward the east side of town, running every sixth light, Chris catching me up on some of his recent escapades, half-shouting to make himself heard over the blare of a modern rock station out of Niagara Falls, Ontario, that slipped in and out of range. "Hey, check this out," he said. He reached beneath the driver's seat and passed me a fat roll of New York Lottery scratch tickets. "You can win like ten grand!" he cried. "Scratch some off if you want."

"Where'd you get these, man?"

"Get this—they were in the car when I got it! Just sitting in the backseat! I already scratched off some winners, like forty bucks' worth." He passed me a tin Buffalo Sabres lighter from his coat pocket, its sharp bottom edge gummed with shavings from the tickets he'd scratched. "Go on," he said, "make us some money."

I tore off a long band of tickets and handed them back to Vernon, along with a quarter from the center console, and Chris cranked up the volume until the windows shook and piloted us through his frozen, desolate town toward Lauren Hill's apartment, singing along to the radio, while me and Vernon scratched away: *"You make me come. / You make me complete. / You make me completely miserable."* I looked up and saw him grinning at me and nodding his head, as if to ask, Doesn't this song fucking rock? I grinned and nodded back, because yes, in a crazy way it kind of did. A barely perceptible but definitely perceptible drip of hopefulness had started to seep back into the night.

No one was home at Lauren's place; in fact, the lights were out in all six apartments in her building even though it was only seven-thirty.

Chris cracked his window and flicked a pile of my losing scratch tickets through like cigarette butts. "She's probably at the bar," he said. "She works every night, and she's there hanging out even when she ain't working. We'll go find her." He whipped the Explorer around the corner and we fishtailed a bit in the gathering snow.

A mile down, five tiny side streets spilled together at a jagged-shaped intersection, and from its farthest corners, two squat and battered bars glared across at each other like warring crabs, panels of wood nailed over the windows and painted to match the outside walls and one neon beer sign hanging over each door—Yuengling and Budweiser—as though they were the names of the bars.

Chris pulled over and pointed to the bar with the Yuengling sign. "That's Freighter's," he said. "See if she's in there. And if she is, see if you can call off the dogs so I can get in there, too."

I jumped out and took a few steps, then had a thought and went back to the truck and asked Vernon if he wanted to come in with me. I was nervous to see Lauren and afraid she would find something creepy and stalker-like about me taking a Greyhound bus a few hundred miles to make an uninvited appearance on Valentine's Day. If I rolled in there with Vernon, it seemed to me, any initial awkwardness might be diffused.

Vernon was a little unsteady on his feet, either from the whiskey or the quilt of fresh snow lining the street paired with his ludicrously advanced age, so I held him by the arm as we crossed the intersection. A plume of merriment rose in my chest that was six parts the gentle glow of heading into any bar on a cold, snowy night, and four parts the wonderful, unpredictable madness of having a hundred-and-ten-year-old man I'd just met on the Greyhound bus as my wingman. I heaved open the heavy door to Freighter's, letting out a blast of noise and hot, smoky air, and once Vernon shuffled past, I followed him in.

Inside, it was so dark and hot and loud it took me a few seconds to get my bearings. People shouted over the thump of a jukebox and the rattle of empty bottles being tossed into a metal drum. Directly overhead, two hockey games roared from a pair of giant TVs. It smelled like someone had puked on a campfire. All of which is to say, just the way I liked it and just like the 8 Ball Saloon back in Michigan where Lauren had worked before moving to Buffalo for school.

A hulking, tattooed guy on a stool was asking me and Vernon for our IDs. I flashed him mine, while Vernon pulled out the same fraying ID card he'd showed me earlier. The doorman plucked it from his hand, inspected it, and passed it back, shaking his head. "Nope," he shouted over the din. "I need a driver's license or state ID." At first I laughed, thinking he was just fucking with us, but then I saw he was serious.

I leaned to his ear and protested, "But he's a hundred and ten years old! Look at the guy!"

The doorman shook his head and pointed at the exit. It was useless to try to reason with him over the din, and I figured once I found Lauren, she'd help me get Vernon and Chris in.

"Wait in the truck," I shouted in Vernon's ear. "I'll come get you guys in a few minutes."

He nodded and slipped out into the cold. I took a few steps further in. The place was packed, mostly older, rugged-looking dudes—factory workers, construction workers, bikers, and their equally rugged-looking girlfriends—with a sprinkling of younger indie kids and punk rockers mixed in. All of a sudden I caught sight of Lauren Hill behind the bar and my heart twisted like a wet rag—she had her back turned to me and was getting her shoulders thoroughly massaged by a tall, skinny, dark-haired guy in a sleeveless shirt, dozens of tattoos slathered on his arms. My first thought was to immediately leave, but I also knew that would be silly—this was surely just some guy who worked with her, not a true threat. The guy finished his little rubdown and they both turned back to the bar. Lauren's beauty made my stomach lurch. She had long, straight hair, dyed black; big, expressive eyes; and her usual enormous, bright smile. I made my way over, feeling stupid for having spent the last eight hours on buses without the foresight to dream up a single witty or romantic thing to say when I greeted her.

I edged between a few guys at the bar and pulled a ten-dollar bill from my back pocket. When Lauren came close, I called out, "Can I get a Bell's Amber?"—a local Michigan brew that wasn't served in Buffalo—my spontaneous, wilted stab at a joke. Even Chris Hendershot could've conjured up something funnier.

She looked at me and the smile drained off her face. "Davy? Oh my God, what the hell are you doing here?" There was no way to hug across the bar; instead, Lauren offered what seemed to me a slightly awkward and tepid two-handed high five.

I slapped her hands and said, "I came here to surprise you," feeling suddenly lost in space.

"Oh, that's so awesome," she said, sounding possibly genuine. "But what are you doing in Buffalo?"

"No, I came to Buffalo because I wanted to see you." I shrugged and heard the next words tumble out of my mouth, even as I instantly regretted them. "Happy Valentine's Day!"

Just then, a bar-back rushing past with a tub full of empty glasses crashed into her, knocking her a couple of feet to the side. Now she was within shouting range of a few guys further along the bar, and they started barking out their drink orders. She leaned back toward me and hollered, "I'm sorry, Monday nights are always like this, and we're short a guy. Can you come back later? It'll be less insane."

"Sure, no problem," I said, putting both hands up idiotically for another slap of hands, but she'd already turned and was cranking the caps off a row of Yuenglings. I slowly lowered my hands, waited another fifteen seconds or so until she happened to glance my way, and gave her a little wave. She flashed a polite smile in return, and I whirled and slunk out the door, utterly defeated, making a promise to myself not to come back later in the night unless she called my phone in the next few hours and begged me to. It was just past eight o'clock. I'd give her till midnight.

"Should we come inside?" Chris asked as I climbed in the backseat; Vernon had made it back to the car and was up riding shotgun.

"It's kind of busy in there. Let's get some grub and come back later."

"Well, how'd it go?" asked Vernon, once we were moving again.

"Not too bad. I don't know. Not too good, either." I told them what had gone down. They both tried to reassure me that Lauren was probably really excited I was in town, but that it's always hard when someone pops in to see you and you're busy at work. I granted them that, but it still seemed like she could've maybe flipped me the keys to her apartment, in case I wanted to take a nap or chill out and watch a movie until she got home. Or really had done anything to give me the sense that she was happy I'd rolled in.

"Don't worry, man," Vernon said. "Trust me, it'll be cool." This from the guy who was now using Chris's cell phone—and had been the whole time I was in the bar—to try to reach his great-grand-daughter, to no avail. He was hoping we could stop by her house, which was on the west side of town, about a twenty-minute drive.

"I'm down," I said. "Chris?"

"Rock 'n' roll." He pumped up the Green Day song on the radio, zoomed through side streets to the on-ramp for an expressway, and looped the Explorer back toward the lights of downtown, slapping the steering wheel along to the music. Vernon tore off a few scratch tickets for himself, passed me the rest of the roll, and we both went to work.

Each losing ticket I scratched out socked me a little blow to the heart. Why didn't scratch cards just have a single box that told you if you'd won or not? Why the slow build, all the teasing hoopla of tic-tac-toe game boards and wheels of fortune? You kept thinking you were getting close and then, once again: loser. All of the unanswered questions made my head hurt: Had I blown things by coming to Buffalo and putting unfair pressure on Lauren Hill? Should I simply have come on any day other than Valentine's Day? Had she meant all the things she'd said in her letters? Some of it? None of it? And what would be the best way to salvage the night when I went back to the bar? (Because, face it, I was headed back there later whether she called me or not.) A small heap of losing tickets gathered at my feet.

"Holy shit!" cried Vernon from up front. "I think we got a win-ner!"

"How much?" said Chris, suddenly alert, punching the radio off.

"Wait a second. Did I win? Yeah, I did. Ten bucks!"

"Not bad." Chris nodded enthusiastically. "That's yours to keep," he told Vernon. "You guys just keep on scratching."

"You bet your goddamn ass," said Vernon, still believing a bigger payday was near.

His minor stroke of glory made me glad, but to me, winning ten bucks instead of ten grand was like getting a drunken kiss on the corner of the mouth from a stranger at the bar that you'll never see again. What I really wanted was to spend the night in Lauren Hill's arms, kissing her and holding her tight; to wake up with her at dawn, make love once or twice, and walk hand in hand through the woodsy park I'd glimpsed by her apartment, which by morning, I imagined—if it kept snowing the way it was now—would be transformed into a place of quiet and exquisite majesty. That was my wish. Anything less I'd just as soon chuck out the window.

From the outside, Vernon's great-granddaughter's house looked like a haunted mansion out of *Scooby-Doo*. It sat on a wide section of an abandoned half-acre lot overgrown with weeds, brambles, and the remaining debris from houses that had been leveled on either side. Across the street, TVs flickered dimly from the windows of a low-rise housing project, and at the end of the block a closed-down liquor store with both doors missing gaped like a sea cave, open to the elements. As we pulled up in front, Vernon looked back at me and said, "Hey, would you come inside with me?" It was my turn to be wingman.

I followed him up the front walk and up three stairs to the porch, and he lifted the enormous, rusted horseshoe knocker on the front door and let it land with a heavy thud. We waited. I watched snowflakes touch down on the Explorer's windshield and instantly melt. The knocker squeaked as he lifted it again, but then, from somewhere deep in the house, came a woman's voice, "I hear you, I'm coming."

Her footsteps padded near and Vernon edged back until he was practically hiding behind me. "Who's there?" the woman called.

I looked over to Vernon, waiting for him to respond. He had the look of a dog who'd strewn trash through the kitchen. "It's your granddaddy," he said at last, weakly.

"Who?"

"Vernon Wallace." He kicked the porch concrete. "Your great-granddaddy."

The door opened a couple of inches and a woman's face appeared, eyebrows raised, hair wrapped in a towel above her head. She was in maybe her early fifties. Through a pair of oversize glasses, she took a long look at Vernon, sighed, shook her head, and said, "Granddaddy, what're you doing up here in the wintertime?" As he cleared his throat and began to respond, she said, "Hold on, let me get my coat." The door closed, and for a half-minute Vernon painted hieroglyphics with the toe of his old shoe in a pyramid of drifting snow, looking suddenly frail and ancient. Exhaust panted from the Explorer's tailpipe out on the street, and I could make out the hard-rock bass line rattling its windows but didn't recognize the song.

After a moment, the door opened again and the woman stepped out and joined us on the front porch, hair still tucked up in a towel. Over a matching pink sweat suit she wore a puffy, oversize, black winter coat, and her feet, sockless, were stuffed into a pair of unlaced low-top Nikes. She gave Vernon a big, friendly hug, and said, "I love you, Granddaddy, it's good to see you," and then turned to me and said, "Hi there, I'm Darla Kenney," and once I'd introduced myself she said, "Well, it's good to meet you, I appreciate you bringing Vernon by." She turned back to face him and crossed her arms. "What you been drinking tonight, Granddaddy?"

He flinched slightly but didn't respond.

"Listen," she said, "I love you, but I ain't got no money. You know my whole situation. You're gonna have to stay with your friend here, 'cause I can't just invite you in."

Vernon nodded deeply, unable to meet her gaze. "I was just hoping we could spend time together."

"We can!" she said. "But not tonight. I got all kinds of shit to deal with tonight. I can't even get the damn car started. You got to learn to call people ahead of time so they know you coming." She softened. "How long you gonna stay in town for?"

Vernon shrugged. "A week or two?"

"Okay, then. Look, you give me a call tomorrow, or the next day, and we'll go for a drive, we'll play cards at Calvin's. He know you're in town?"

Vernon shook his head.

Darla looked past us, to the Explorer out on the street, its motor revving, Chris Hendershot behind the wheel, slapping his hands on the dash and crooning to himself. "That your friend?" she asked me.

"Yeah. That's Chris."

Darla tugged her coat closed and fought with the zipper. "Hey, listen," she said. "I got cables. Think I can get a jump?"

Ten minutes later, Chris was shouting instructions to me, banging under the hood of Darla Kenney's '84 Lincoln Continental with a wrench while I pounded the gas and jammed the ignition. Is there any sound more full of frustration and futility than a car that won't start when you turn the key? Click-click-click-click-click. All I could think of was Lauren Hill's dismayed expression in the bar when she'd first seen me.

"Okay, cut it!" Chris shouted. I felt his weight on the engine block as he bobbed deep within. A ping and a clatter. "Now try."

Click-click-click-click.

"Cut it!"

I heard Chris disconnecting the jumper cables, and then he dropped the hood with a magnificent crash. "I'll tell you what's happening, ma'am," he said to Darla, who stood in the street, looking on, still in her unlaced sneakers and coat with a towel on her head. "Your battery cable's a little frizzy, down by the starter relay. We get this in the shop, it's nothing—ten minutes, you're on your way. Tonight, though, no tools? Ain't gonna be easy." He passed her the jumper cables and put a consoling hand on her shoulder. "I'm really sorry. Usually I can get anything moving." I was touched by his level of kindness—if this was how sweetly he treated a woman he'd just met, it was hard to imagine there was anything he wouldn't do for his friends.

I climbed from the car and joined Chris and Darla. Vernon was sitting in the Explorer, keeping warm up front, scratching off lotto tickets.

"Well, it was nice of you to try," said Darla. She looked back and forth between us. "How do you guys know my granddaddy, anyhow?"

I wasn't sure how to answer. "Well, we met on a Greyhound bus once; we were seatmates." The word "once" tossed in there made it seem like this was years ago.

But Darla saw through it. "Oh, okay, when was that?"

"Well. Tonight."

She weighed this for a second. "Is he staying with you guys?"

"I don't know," I said. "I think he was saying something about the Y." The way my awesome surprise had gone over with Lauren Hill, I'd probably end up in the next bunk.

"I stay with my brother," Chris piped up. "But we got a cot at the garage, right around the corner. It's heated. I mean, that's where we work. Shit, he can stay in my room and I'll stay on the cot."

"We're not gonna leave him on the street," I said. I meant to be re-assuring, but realized a second later that my words could be taken as an accusation.

Darla toyed with the clamps of the jumper cables in her hands; the metal jaws, squeaking open and shut, looked like angry, puppet-size gators shit-talking back and forth. As little as she seemed to want to deal with Vernon, she also seemed aware that he was her responsibility as much as anyone else's, and she wasn't ready to ditch him with two white kids he'd met an hour before. "Here's the thing," she said. "He can't stay at my house, and I got no money to give him right now. But I've got a tenant that owes me four hundred fifty dollars—I was gonna stop there tonight anyhow. We get some of that money together, I'll give my granddaddy half and put him up a week at the Front Park Inn."

Me and Chris nodded. "That'll work," I said. Fuck the Y—maybe at the Front Park Inn there'd be an extra bed for me.

Darla went to the Lincoln, heaved open the back door, and tossed the jumper cables on the floor behind the driver's seat. She turned back toward us. "Can I get a ride over to this house with you guys? It's really close, like ten, fifteen blocks from here. Larchmont, just the other side of Lake Avenue."

"Ain't no thing," said Chris.

I asked Darla if she wanted to get dressed first, at least pull on some socks, but she was already climbing into the backseat of Chris's Explorer and sliding over to make room for me. "We're just going and coming right back," she said. "Come on, hop in."

The snow kept falling. On the way to her tenant's house, Darla filled me in on a few things while Chris blasted music up front. It both irritated and charmed me that he kept the radio going max force no matter who was in the car with him. Even when he'd stayed with me in Chicago all those weekends, every time we were in my truck he'd reach over and crank the volume. Vernon rode shotgun, dozing, the dwindling spool of lotto tickets in his lap.

Darla had four children, she told me. She'd had the same job—quality control at a metal-stamping plant—for almost thirty years, and as she was careful with her money, she'd been able to buy homes for each of her children in nearby West Buffalo neighborhoods. "Nothing fancy," she said, "but a roof over their heads." One daughter had split up with her husband two years before and moved to Tampa, Florida. Darla rented out one half of their house to a friend from work, and the ex had stayed on in the other half, though Darla had begun to charge him three hundred bucks a month in rent, which was more than fair, she said, and less than what she could get from somebody else. But her daughter's ex, whose name was Anthony, and who was, overall, a decent, hardworking man, had fallen behind—he still owed her for January, and now half of February. It was time for her to pay a visit, Darla said.

She coached Chris through a few turns. We crossed a big four-lane road and the neighborhood deteriorated, making Darla's street look regal by comparison. Every third house was shuttered or burned out. On a side street I glimpsed four guys loading furniture out of a squat apartment building into a U-Haul trailer. "Okay," said Darla, "take this right and it's the first one on the right."

We pulled up in front of a tiny, ramshackle house with cardboard taped over a missing window and its gutters hanging off, dangling to the ground. Still, the dusting of snow softened its features, and there were hopeful signs of upkeep—Christmas lights draped over a hedge by the side door and a pair of well-stocked bird feeders, swinging from low branches in the front yard, which had attracted a gang of sickly but grateful-looking squirrels.

"I'll be back in a couple minutes," said Darla, stepping gingerly down to the snow-filled street. She closed her door, picked her way across the lawn to the side of the house, knocked a few times, and disappeared inside.

Chris's cell phone rang and he answered it and had a quick, angry spat with his older brother. He'd explained to me that he'd been in hot water with his brother all month. His brother had a rule that anytime Chris boosted a car he was supposed to get it immediately to their shop to be dismantled (or at least stripped of its VIN) and resold. Chris admitted that he had a habit of keeping stolen cars for a while and driving around in them to impress girls. A couple of weeks before, another guy who worked with them had landed a cherry-red PT Cruiser in Pittsburgh, and Chris had whipped it around Buffalo over Super Bowl weekend while his brother was out of town. His brother found out, of course, and had been hounding him about it ever since. Now he seemed to be giving Chris grief for driving the Explorer; I could hear his brother on the other end of the phone, shouting at him to bring it back to base. "Fuck that motherfucker!" Chris shouted, hanging up and slamming his phone on the dash. "Who the fuck does he think he is?" To me, there was something ecstatically rich and appealing in someone who acted so gangsta but sounded so Canadian; at the same time, I could see in the rearview mirror that Chris's eyes had gone teary, and I felt a guilty and despairing tug of responsibility for dragging him around town and sticking him deeper into his brother's doghouse.

The shouting roused Vernon from his mini-nap, and without missing a beat he resumed work scratching off the squares of each lotto ticket. A heaviness had settled over him. He inspected a ticket after scratching it off, sighed greatly, and let it slip from his fingers.

In the front yard of the house next door, a band of ragtag little kids wrestled in the snow and hurled snowballs at parked cars and each other, shouting, "I'ma blast you, nigga!" The oldest of them, a boy around ten, was trying to rally the rest of them through the early stages of building a snowman. I powered my window down a few inches so I could hear his pitch. "Start with a giant snowball," he said breathlessly, as he worked on packing one together, then placed it on the ground. "Then we keep rolling this thing, and rolling it, and rolling it, until it's as big as a house, and then we'll have the biggest snowman in all of Buffalo!" The other kids dove in to help him, and they slid around the yard, accumulating more snow, then breaking off chunks accidentally as they pushed in opposite directions. Everyone shouted instructions at everyone else: "Roll it that way!" "Get those Doritos off it!" "You're fucking it up!"

Lauren Hill had been about the same age—nine or ten—when her dad was killed by a drunk driver. She'd told me the story in the most recent letter she'd sent me; her mom had appeared at the park where Lauren was playing with her friends and pulled her away and told her the news. Even though that had happened in summertime, I couldn't help but picture a fifth-grade Lauren Hill building a snowman with her neighborhood pals, her mom galloping up, crazed and wild-eyed, and dragging her away to a sucky, dadless future in a grim apartment complex near the Detroit airport, populated by creepy neighbors and a steady stream of her mom's low-life live-in boyfriends. When you first got involved with any girl who'd been punctured by that kind of sadness, I'd learned, you had to be extra cautious about flooding them with goodness and light. A gentle and steady kindness appealed to them, but too much love straight out of the gate was uncomfortable, even painful, and impossible to handle. I felt like an idiot for coming to Buffalo and freaking Lauren out.

"Hey, Vernon," I said, leaning between the front seats. "Did you ever get married?"

"Yes I did. Wanda May. Fifty years we were married." He paused, passing a scratch-off to Chris. "I think this one wins a free ticket." Then, to me, with a sudden touch of melancholy, "She died in 1964."

"Damn. That's way before I was born."

Vernon slipped his whiskey bottle out, touched it to his lips, and gave me a look. "You want some advice?" he said.

"Definitely."

"You should marry this girl you came to see. Marry her right away. Tomorrow, if you want. You don't know how much time you get with someone, so you might as well start right away."

"The problem is, it's not up to me. She gets a say."

"It's more up to you than you think."

I let that sink in, watching the kids in the neighbor's yard. Their snowman's round trunk had quickly swelled from the size of a soccer ball to the size of a dorm fridge. It took all of them, pushing and shouldering it together, to keep it rolling across the lawn. Finally they ran out of juice and came to a stop, slumping against their massive boulder of snow, tall as the oldest boy. There seemed to be two opinions about what to do next. The boy in charge wanted to go down the street and recruit his older cousin and some of his cousin's friends to keep pushing. But one tiny girl pointed out that the snowman had already gotten too big for them to add a middle and a top. Also, she suspected that if the boy's cousin and his friends glimpsed the half-built snowman, all they'd want to do is destroy it. "We made it, we should get to knock it down," she said.

Vernon passed his bottle to Chris, who took a long gulp and passed it back to me. I drained the last of the whiskey down and watched as the kids gave their big, round heap of snow a pair of stick arms, then collaborated on the face—two deep holes for eyes, a Dorito for a nose, and, strangely, no mouth.

By now, Chris and Vernon were watching them, too. "You want some more advice?" Vernon asked.

"Yes, I do."

"Okay. Don't outlive your wife."

The oldest kid pulled off his red knit cap and plopped it on top of the snowman's head, and at last the whole crew of munchkins stood back to silently admire their handiwork. It was surely the saddest, fattest, strangest, and most beautiful snowman I'd ever seen.

After a few long moments, there was the sound of voices, as Vernon's great-granddaughter Darla banged her way through the side door of the house she owned. The towel on her head had been replaced by a black baseball cap, and she was trailed by two others in heavy coats with their hoods pulled up. Her appearance seemed to somehow release the kids in the neighbors' yard from their spell. The oldest boy let out a mighty cry and charged the snowman—he plowed into its shoulder, driving loose its left arm and a wedge of its face, before crashing to the ground. The other kids followed, flailing with arms and feet, and even using the snowman's own arms to beat its torso quickly to powdery rubble.

Darla and her two companions crossed the yard toward us.

Vernon turned to me and Chris. "That's how long I was married, feels like," he said, eyes blazing. "As long as that snowman was alive."

We took on two new passengers—Anthony, the ex-husband of Darla's daughter who owed Darla all the back rent, and his shy, pregnant girlfriend, Kandy. They squeezed in back with me and Darla, and we circled around the block and headed back the way we'd come. Our next destination was a Chinese restaurant where Anthony worked as a dishwasher, on the east end of town, not far from Lauren Hill's bar. Anthony told us that his car was dead, too; apparently, one of the few operational vehicles in all of Buffalo was Chris's Explorer, which he'd driven off the lot of a body shop in Rochester the night before.

Anthony and Darla continued a conversation they must have started in the house. Anthony—dark skinned, small and compact, with a thin mustache, roughly forty years old—spoke softly, but had a thoughtful, commanding presence. He was explaining why he hadn't quit his job, even though he hadn't been paid in a month. "Here's the thing about Mr. Liu," he said. "Last winter, business got so slow, sometimes there was no customers in there, he could've sent me home. But he knows I got bills, and I'm scheduled to work, so he gave me the hours and found shit for me to do. You know, shovel the parking lot, clean out the walk-in cooler. Sometimes he paid me just to sit on a stool in back and watch basketball. Now his wallet thin for a minute, how'm I just gonna walk out on him?"

"What if he goes out of business?" Darla asked. "He gonna pay you those paychecks?"

"That's what *I'm* saying," said Kandy. She sat on the far side of the backseat, deeply ensconced in the hood of her jacket; it was hard for me to get a good look at her, but she seemed no older than me or Chris, and was maybe seven months pregnant.

"We talked about that," said Anthony. "First of all, we ain't goin' out of business. It's slow every winter, Mr. Liu just had some extra costs this winter. Second of all, he do go out of business? Mr. Liu told me he's gonna sell the building and all the equipment an' shit, and he'll have plenty enough to pay me what he owe."

The general plan, it seemed, was for Anthony to ask his boss for at least a portion of his paycheck so he could turn the money over to Darla, who might then have enough to support Vernon during his visit and buy him a ticket home to Little Rock. My own plan was to get some shrimp lo mein and ask Chris for a ride back to Freighter's. I wondered if bringing Lauren a carton of Chinese food would be a sweet gesture or just seem demented.

Chris had been quiet since the phone call with his brother, but now he dropped the music a few notches, glanced back at Kandy, and said, "You having a girl or a boy?"

"A boy," she peeped.

"What you gonna name it?"

"Floyd."

"That was her granddaddy's name," Anthony offered.

Chris nodded. "I like that name. Question is, he gonna take after his mom or his dad?"

"Not his dad, I hope," Anthony said cryptically.

"Well, I'll tell you what," said Vernon. "I'm sick of these scratch tickets."

Over the seat, he handed back what remained of the roll. "Here ya go. I'm too old for this shit." His night, like mine, was not going the way he'd hoped. He reached for the radio, turned the volume back up, and sank into his seat, eyes out the window.

This was a song I knew: "What It's Like" by Everlast. Chris slid us back onto the Kensington Expressway, and the swirling snow gusted this way and that, rocking the SUV like a baby plane in turbulence. I closed my eyes and let myself sway.

Then you really might know what it's like.
Yeah, then you really might know what it's like . . . to have to lose.

Mr. Liu's Chinese Restaurant anchored a shambling commercial strip between a Popeyes and a defunct video store. It was called the Golden Panda, though just the right letters had burned out on the neon sign in its front window to leave THE GOLDEN AN. "Look!" I cried, rallying from the darkness, "it's the Golden AN!" Everyone stared at me flatly. "You know, from *Sesame Street*?"

"Wait a second," said Chris. "I know this fucking place. My brother loves this place. He always gets takeout here. It's so fucking *nasty* but he loves it." He looked at Anthony in the rearview mirror. "I mean, no offense."

Vernon and Kandy hung back in the Explorer while me, Chris, and Darla followed Anthony inside. The place had an odd, foul, but unidentifiable smell. It had just closed for the night, and a pretty Chinese girl in her late teens was blowing out red candles on each table that I supposed had been set out for Valentine's Day, and loading an enormous tray with dirty dishes. "Hey, Anthony," she said, tired but friendly. "If you came for dinner, you better let my mom know, she's shutting down the kitchen right now." She flipped a switch for the overhead fluorescents, and as they flickered on, the restaurant's interior grew more drab and dingy.

Anthony asked the girl if her dad was still around, and the girl told him he was. "Hey, Mary, these are my friends," he said, and told us he'd be back in a minute.

"Hi, Anthony's friends," she said. "You can have a seat if you want."

"Oh," said Anthony. "Did you hear back yet?"

"Not yet," said the girl. "The admissions office, they were supposed to call or e-mail everybody last week, but they never called me. So that's not a good sign. That reminds me, I need to check my e-mail."

"Well, look, if it don't work out, you just keep on trying." Anthony pushed his way through a blue silk curtain at the back of the dining area and disappeared down a hallway.

The three of us found a table that the girl had already cleared and sat down. Darla lowered her voice and said, "That's a fine young man right there. You know, that baby, Floyd, that's not even his baby. But he's gonna raise it and take care of that baby like it is." She shook her head. "I still call him my son. And that baby will be my grandson." Then, in a near whisper, "I hate putting the squeeze on him, but that ain't right he ain't getting paid." She eyed Mary, the owner's daughter, and said, under her breath, "This ain't the plantation. This is Buffalo!"

"I'm sure the guy'll give him some cash," I said.

As if on cue, a sudden, jarring eruption of shouting rose from deep in back. It was Anthony's voice, but the only word I could make out was "motherfucker." Soon a second voice joined the fray—Mr. Liu, no doubt, shouting back. And then a woman's voice jumped in, yelling in Chinese, followed by the sound of pots and pans clattering to the floor. Mary set down her tray and rushed through the blue curtains, and Darla said, "Oh no," and leapt up and dashed after her.

Chris gave me a dismal look and sank his head to the table. "Today's retarded," he said, sounding truly pained, his voice cracking a bit. "You know what sucks?"

"Yeah," I said, as the shouting in back increased. "That old man out there, Vernon, he thinks I should marry Lauren Hill tomorrow, but I don't think she wants anything to do with me, and you know, she's probably fucking this dude at her work."

"Yeah, that does suck," said Chris. "And I'll tell you what else sucks. I am really, really, incredibly fucking hungry."

"Maybe it'll all boil over back there and mellow out," I suggested, and again, Anthony's timing was splendid—he came ripping through the curtain just then, shouting and cursing, Darla at his heels, tugging at his sleeve and begging him to chill out.

"Get your fucking hands off me!" he said. "Fuck that motherfucker. I'll kill that slant-eyed faggot." He stopped in his tracks, turned, and screamed full force, "Fuck you, Mr. Liu! Suck my fucking dick, you little bitch!" From in back somewhere, Mr. Liu was shouting in return. Anthony kicked over a chair, and said, "Come get some of this! You want some? Come out here and get some!" Darla grabbed his shoulders and steered him toward the front door. "Fuck this place," Anthony said, deeply aggrieved, shoving her arm away. He fought his way outside.

"Come on," said Darla to me and Chris, holding the door open. "Time to go."

Back in the Explorer, Anthony was still shouting. We sat in the lot, trying to calm him down. Kandy seemed inappropriately entertained, a strange smile on her face as she pleaded with him to explain what had happened.

"That fucker," he said, jaw clenched, breathing hard through flared nostrils. "I told him he better pay me, not the whole month he owes me, just like two weeks, and he's, like"—here Anthony mocked Mr. Liu's Chinese accent—"'I no have your money. Give me more time.' And I said, 'Fuck that. Pay me.' So then he's, like, 'I can't afford you no more. I hafta let you go.'" Anthony rubbed his face. With great anger, sadness, and shame, he said, "I didn't come all the way down here tonight to get my ass fired." He had tears in his eyes.

I saw that Darla, beside him, had tears in her eyes, too. She put her arm around Anthony and soothed him. "Okay, it'll be all right. It'll all be all right." I caught Chris's gaze in the rearview mirror. Even his eyes were wet. Strangely enough, I realized, mine were, too. I thought of the kids we'd seen building the snowman—how blissfully carefree they'd seemed—and felt a mournful gulf open up inside me. Whatever lumps those kids were taking as they sprouted in their bleak, tundra-like ghetto had nothing on the disappointments and humiliations of adulthood.

Kandy took Anthony's hand and said, "Listen, baby. You need to take a few deep breaths. I got to show you something."

"Five fucking years," said Anthony. "You know how many times I coulda gone somewhere else? My cousin in Syracuse, he's roofing now, twenty bucks an hour. That job coulda been mine." He blasted the back of the front passenger seat with his fist and Vernon bolted upright. "Sorry, Vernon," said Anthony. He looked at the empty front room of the Golden Panda. "Five years. Chinese people don't know shit about loyalty."

"It'll be all right," said Kandy. Her odd smile broadened. "Vernon, come on, will you just tell 'em?"

Vernon turned the radio off and looked around, gathering our attention, wide-eyed and mysterious. Then he melted into a smile, held up a scratched-out lotto ticket, and said, "We just won two thousand dollars."

Darla immediately screamed and slapped her hands to her cheeks in astonishment. Chris's eyes bugged out of his head. Anthony turned to his girlfriend, Kandy: "Say what?"

Kandy laughed. "It's true! I scratched it off!"

Vernon handed the ticket to Chris. "Really, how it is, *you* won two thousand dollars. We were just the first ones to find out."

Everyone grew suddenly quiet, watching Chris as he brought the ticket close to check it out. He nodded slowly, gave a low whistle, and flipped it over to read the fine print on back. "Looks like . . . redeem anywhere," he said softly, to himself. "They just print you a check right there. Damn. Two grand." He twisted around, looked back at all of us, and laughed. "Shit, this ain't a funeral," he said. "If I won, we all won. What the fuck, we're splittin' this fucker!"

Wild, joyous whoops of celebration filled the SUV, and all at the same time Vernon, Darla, Anthony, and Kandy hugged Chris and rubbed his shaved head. Everyone began shaking back and forth and the whole Explorer rocked side to side.

"Chris," I said. "You are a great American."

He was giggling, giddy at this sudden turn of events and all of the combined adulation. "Fuck you, dude. I'm Canadian!" Then he sobered up. "Okay, when I say we're splitting it, what I mean is, I get half, and the rest of you split the other half."

Everyone settled down a little, doing the math in their hands, and then murmured agreeably—this seemed like a more-than-fair arrangement, without asking Chris to be unreasonably generous.

Chris went on, peering back toward the restaurant, where Mr. Liu's daughter, Mary, had emerged to gather the last of the dishes. "Look, Anthony," he said, "I know the last thing you wanna do right now is go back in there. But yo, I got an idea. And I *need* some fried wontons."

A minute later, there were nine people clustered in the cramped, pungent kitchen of the Golden Panda—me, Chris, Old Man Vernon, Darla, Anthony, and Kandy, along with Mr. Liu, his wife, and their daughter, Mary, who sat on a milk crate, pecking away at a laptop. Mr. Liu had small, round glasses and graying hair and wore an apron over a dirty white T-shirt and baggy, brightly patterned swim trunks. He was bent over an industrial-size sink, wiping it out with a blue sponge, still tense, it seemed, from his confrontation with Anthony, who stood behind Vernon, glowering at the floor.

I could guess that Chris was aiming to broker a truce between the two of them, but didn't see the tack he planned on taking even as he dove right in. "Mr. Liu," he said. "I have been a customer of your fine establishment here for a couple of years. My brother, Shawn, he's been coming here for longer than that. I love the food you have here. It's kind of nasty sometimes, but it's good nasty. It's filling. I especially like the pork fried rice. And I like how you give fortune cookies even on to-go orders."

"Thank you," said Mr. Liu, with a heavy accent, standing straight. "I see you in here before. I think I know your brother." His wife, tiny and anxious, wearing a Buffalo Bills hoodie and a hairnet, said a few rapid words in Chinese to Mary, and Mary gave a one-word response without looking up.

"I recently came into some money," Chris went on. "And knowing me, I'll spend it, it'll be gone, and that'll be that." He took a breath. "I've got an idea, though. It'll be a good thing for me, and maybe it'll help you, too. Here's what I'm thinking—I want to come here tomorrow and give you . . . let's say . . . eight hundred bucks, cash money."

Mr. Liu crossed his arms, not quite sure where Chris was going with this.

"I'm thinking I give you eight hundred up front," said Chris, "and me and my brother eat here free for the rest of the year." He explained that they wouldn't take advantage of the arrangement—they'd only come by once or twice a week. Basically, Chris said, he was offering to pay in advance for a year's worth of meals. But he had a few conditions. "I want you to hire Anthony back. He's been loyal to you, you gotta be loyal to him. And you gotta pay him at least half of what you owe him right now in back wages."

Mr. Liu and Anthony glanced up toward each other without actually letting their eyes meet. Mr. Liu said to Chris, "I want Anthony to work. But not enough customers."

"Well, for one thing," Chris said, "you guys need to have delivery. A Chinese place without delivery, that's like a dog with no dick. That's why my brother always sends me down here to pick up. In snowstorms and shit. I hate that shit. You have delivery, you'll double your sales. Anthony can wash dishes and go on runs, both. You need a delivery car, I can even help you find one, for a good price."

Mr. Liu spoke to his wife in Chinese, translating Chris's appeal. She responded at great length, gesturing at Anthony, Mary, and at

Chris. I couldn't help but marvel at Chris's command of the situation. My image of him as a failed comic and petty criminal could barely accommodate the ease and confidence he now seemed to possess. At last Mrs. Liu fell silent, and Mr. Liu turned and said to Anthony, "Okay. You want to work here?"

Without unclenching his jaw, still staring down, burning holes in the tile, Anthony nodded.

"Good," said Chris. "Now hug it out, you two. Seriously. Go on. It's part of the deal."

Shyly, like two bludgeoned boxers embracing at the end of twelve rounds, Anthony and Mr. Liu edged near each other and slumped close in a kind of half hug, patting each other quickly on the back, but not without an evident bit of emotion.

Darla started clapping, and I found myself joining in, unexpectedly stirred; soon Kandy, Vernon, and even Mrs. Liu were clapping, too. Chris was beaming. "That's good," he said. "That's perfect." I had goose bumps. My only sorrow was that Lauren wasn't there to witness the moment.

Chris laughed, growing comfortable in his role as peacemaker. "Now, before we hit the bar to celebrate—and drinks are on me tonight—there's just one more part of the deal."

Mr. Liu eyed him nervously.

"If it's not too inconvenient," Chris said, "I was hoping we could all dig into some grub. Golden Panda leftovers, I don't care. I could eat a horse, this guy's been on a bus the last twenty-four hours"—he pointed at Vernon—"and this girl's eating for two," with a sideways nod toward Kandy. "What do you say?"

"No problem," said Mr. Liu.

All of a sudden, his daughter Mary shrieked and leapt to her feet like she'd been stung on the butt by a bee. She let out some rapid birdsong to her parents in Chinese, and Mr. Liu took the laptop from her hands and inspected the screen while Mrs. Liu threw her arms around Mary and began to sob into her shoulder. Mary looked at Anthony, tearing up herself, and cried, "I got in! I got in! Medaille College e-mailed me! Anthony, I got in!"

A half hour later, well fed, all nine of us were crammed into Chris's

Explorer, speeding toward Freighter's. I sat up front in the passenger seat; behind me sat old Vernon Wallace, his great-granddaughter Darla, and Anthony and Kandy. Squashed way in back, and squealing like kindergarteners with every pothole we bounced over, were Mr. Liu and his wife and daughter. Chris was driving, phone clamped between his ear and his shoulder, talking to his older brother. "Shawn, just meet us there. It's good news, I'm saying, though."

I could hear Chris's brother chewing him out on the other end, calling him a moron, a loser, and a punk. All of the merriment and gladness quickly drained from Chris's face. "Yes, Shawn. Okay. Okay, Shawn. Yes, I understand." He closed his phone and tossed it up on the dash, shaking his head and biting at a thumbnail. In the back, full of jolly banter, no one else had caught the exchange.

"Fuck that, dude," I said to Chris. "Shake it off."

"It's not that easy," he said, hurt and sinking. He mashed on the gas pedal and we veered right, back tires sliding out a little, and bolted through a light that had just turned red. A few blocks down, the five-way intersection with Lauren's bar came into sight. I felt supremely nervous, but fortified by the size of my brand-new posse.

Chris clouded over with a look of fierce intensity. He reached for his phone again, dialed his brother, and propped the phone to his ear, battleready. Then, without warning, a siren whooped in the night, and a blinding strobe of red and blue lights filled the SUV. "Yo, man," said Anthony, "you just blew right past that stop sign." I twisted around and saw, through the back window, a cop car right on our tail, flashers twirling giddily, high beams punching the air, one-two, one-two.

"No fucking way!" Chris cried, as the phone slipped from his shoulder to the center console and tumbled to the floor at my feet. "What the fuck do we do?" He kept rolling forward, while everyone in back began shouting instructions. I was pretty sure that only Vernon and me knew the truck was stolen. A forlorn tide rose in my chest.

I could hear Shawn's voice on the phone, saying Chris's name. I plucked it up and said, "He's gotta call you back," and folded the phone closed.

"Okay," said Chris frantically. "Here's what we're gonna do. I'm gonna pull over up here, and then all of us, we're just gonna scatter in every direction. Just fuckin' haul ass into the alleyways, all these side streets, into the bushes. They can't get more than one or two of us."

"Are you crazy, boy?" said Darla. "You think my granddaddy's gonna take off running? You think *I* am? I ain't got nothing to hide from. Cops can't fuck with me."

From the way back, Mary said, "You know, there's always policemen at the restaurant. I know a ton of 'em. I got my friend out of a speeding ticket once."

"I'm not worried about a damn ticket," Chris said.

Anthony sat forward and got close to Chris's ear. "Nobody's running," he said. "Chris—listen to me—you got warrants?"

"No."

"Is this shit hot?"

Chris nodded. "Burning."

"Okay. Listen, just pull over and talk to the guy. Just act like it's nothing. Play it cool, like everything's cool. I'm telling you, I've seen dudes talk their way outta way worse."

"I'm not going down tonight," said Chris. He was so deeply spooked, it made me remember the time I'd suggested he incorporate his time in prison into his stand-up routines and he'd told me with a grave, distant stare that there was nothing funny about being in prison.

"That's right," said Anthony. "You're not going down. Now pull over and talk to this man."

Chris pulled to the curb and turned off the radio. He reached slowly for his shoulder belt and clanked it into its buckle.

"The guy's coming!" Mary called from in back.

I watched the cop's cautious approach. He wielded a powerful flashlight and shined it at each of our windows, but they were so fogged up from all the bodies in the car, I doubted he could see much. He took position just behind Chris's window and tapped on the glass with gloved fingers.

Chris lowered the window. "Hello there, sir, good evening," he said, laying on a healthy dose of Canadian politeness.

"License and registration." I couldn't see the cop's face, but he sounded young, which to me seemed like a bad thing. Seasoned cops, I'd found, were more likely to play things fast and loose; rookies went by the book.

"Here's my license," said Chris, passing over his New York State ID. "As far as the registration, I don't have any. I just bought this thing yesterday at an auction in Rochester. I know I shouldn't be driving it around till I get over to the DMV, that's my bad." Fat snowflakes spiraled in through his window and tumbled along the dash.

"You know you ran a light back there?"

"Yes, sir. I believe I ran a stop sign just now, too. I was talking to my brother on the phone and I got distracted. That's my bad. I'm really sorry about that."

Chris was handling things as well as he possibly could, I thought. But once the cop checked the plates, we'd be doomed. If I bailed and ran, it occurred to me, maybe the cop would chase after me and Chris could peel away. My heart jangled, and my fingers crawled to the door handle, ready to make a move.

"You been doing any drinking tonight?" asked the cop.

"Not really, sir," said Chris. He ejected a bark-like laugh. "Planning to, though. We're just going up there to Freighter's." He hitched his thumb toward me. "Even got a designated driver."

The cop bent his head down and poked his flashlight at me. He had dark, close-cropped hair, and was maybe in his mid-thirties. I dropped my hand from the door handle. Then he leaned through Chris's window a shade more and played his light over our bizarre array of passengers—four generations of black folk in the backseat, and a Chinese family in the trunk. His face crinkled up in utter bafflement. Either we were human traffickers with a payload of Asians or a tour bus covering the last leg of the Underground Railroad.

I heard Mr. Liu's daughter call out from the back, "Officer Ralston?"

He ducked his head further into the Explorer. "Who's that?"

"Mary. From the Golden Panda."

"Oh!" said the cop. "Mary! Hey, is that your dad?"

"Yeah. Guess what? I got into Medaille College! We're all going out to celebrate. These are our employees and some of our regulars. You might know some of them."

"But you're not old enough to drink."

"Don't tell the bouncer!" Mary giggled, playfully—even masterfully—redirecting the conversation. "I'm just gonna have a glass of wine."

The cop said, "All right, then," and withdrew his head from inside the truck. He handed Chris back his license. "I'll tell you what," he told Chris. "No more driving with your head up your—you know. Especially when the roads are this bad. You all take care." He doused his flashlight and headed back to his cruiser.

Chris zipped his window up. "Wait for it," he said tersely. "Wait for it."

The cop's flashers went dark, and a moment later his squad car swished past, hung a left at the next side street, and disappeared. Chris turned to look at all of us and broke out into relieved, maniacal laughter. "Holy shit!" he said. "What just happened? This is a magical night!"

Even as everyone began cheering and dancing around in their seats, slapping each other on the back, a cold ball pitted itself in my stomach. It was time to go see Lauren Hill.

"Fuck no, you can't bring all these people in here," the massive bouncer at Freighter's told me, shouting over the music. He eased from his perch and barged forward, using his bulk to crowd us back toward the door. He pointed at Vernon. "That dude didn't have an ID earlier. And this little fucker right here"—he jabbed Chris in the chest—"he's eighty-sixed for life." He took a look at Mary. "She's underage, I'll put money on that. Get these clowns out of my face. Try Cole's, across the street. They'll serve anybody."

I said in his ear, "I'm Lauren Hill's boyfriend. And these are my friends."

"Darrell is Lauren Hill's boyfriend," said the bouncer. "Get your Rainbow Coalition the fuck outta here."

Darrell? Who the *fuck* was Darrell? "Just let me go find Lauren," I pleaded.

"Knock yourself out," said the bouncer. "But these people got to wait outside."

I hustled everyone back through the door, into the freezing night. "Just give me two minutes," I said. "I'll be right back."

I rushed in, my neck hot, blood crashing through my veins. In the three or four hours I'd been away, the Freighter's crowd had gone from tipsy to riotously drunk. Two old bikers had their shirts off and were holding a tough-man contest, affectionately slugging each other in the gut. A pair of young punk rockers dry-humped in a booth. People were screaming along to a song on the jukebox and hooting at hockey highlights on the TVs. At a table in the middle of the room, a man in a winter coat dumped a humongous boot-shaped glass of beer over his own head. I was desperate to be that drunk.

The crowd tossed and turned me like a piece of driftwood, until finally I reached the bar and stood a few feet from Lauren Hill, staring at the back of her neck and her bare shoulders as she mixed a row of drinks at the rear counter. I felt like a vampire, dying to taste her skin. Lauren turned toward me, and the whole scene seemed to grind into slow motion and go mute. I waited for the moment of truth—the expression on her face when she saw that I was back. She set the drinks down in front of the guys next to me, and as she looked up she saw me and smiled—a jolting, radiant, zillion-watt smile. The room's roar slammed back in and the world returned to normal speed. "There you are," she shouted. "What do you want to drink?"

"I made some friends," I shouted back. "Can you help me get 'em in?"

"Just tell Greg I said it was cool."

"I think you better come with me."

She looked around. The other bartender had left and she was now the only person serving drinks, but there seemed to be a momentary lull. "Okay," she said. "Really quick." She ducked under the bar and followed me through the raucous crowd to the front door.

"Come outside for a second," I said. I blasted the door open and we spilled out onto the sidewalk, where a stocky, young white guy in a powder-blue FUBU sweatshirt and Timberland boots was talking to Chris and Mr. Liu while the rest of the crew looked on.

"All the food we want, all year long?" the guy said.

"My guests," said Mr. Liu.

"Rock on!" The guy wrapped his arm over Chris's shoulders, pulled him close, and rubbed his head with his knuckles. "I love you, ya little fuckhead," he said, laughing. "You are just full of surprises." This,

I realized, had to be Chris's older brother, Shawn. Chris scrapped his way loose and looked up at me with a magnificent gleam.

"Davy! Let's get our drink on," Chris hollered. "They gonna let us in or what?"

"Yes, sir," I said. "But wait, you guys, everyone come here, I want you meet someone. This is Lauren Hill." The whole group gathered close, joining us in a tight little huddle. "Lauren," I said, "these are my new friends." I went around the circle, introducing her to each of them, and as I introduced them, they each gave her a friendly hello. "This is Mr. and Mrs. Liu, they own the Golden Panda on Fillmore Avenue. And Mary, their daughter, she just found out she got into college tonight! This is Anthony, and this is Kandy—they're having a baby soon." I pointed to Kandy's stomach. "That's little Floyd in there. And this is my Canadian friend Chris I was telling you about, a man of many talents. And, Shawn, right?"

He nodded. "That's right. You're Davy?"

"Yup." I explained to Lauren that Shawn was Chris's older brother.

"And evil boss," said Shawn with a grin.

"But how'd you meet all these people?" Lauren said, a bit dazzled.

"Hold on." I continued around the circle. "This is Darla Kenney. She lives over on the West Side, in Front Park. And here's her grandfather, actually her great-grandfather, Vernon Wallace. Hey, wait a second, what time is it?"

Shawn glanced at his cell phone. "Ten to midnight."

"In ten minutes," I told Lauren, "it's gonna be Vernon's hundred-and-tenth birthday!"

"No way!" she said.

"It's true!" said Darla.

Lauren looked at me with wide, whirling eyes, really taking me in, as beautiful a girl as I'd ever seen in my life. "You were only gone a couple hours," she said. "This is crazy. This is awesome." She shivered.

"Let's go inside and have a drink," I said.

"Let's drink!" Chris echoed.

Lauren reached for the door, glowing. "Okay, all of you come on in, I'll pour a round of birthday shots. Let me tell Greg what's up."

Then she paused, giving Chris an odd look. She seemed to recall his status on the Freighter's blacklist. "Except you," she said, pointing at him. "I'm sorry, but . . . you just can't skip out on a tab. Not three or four times. Not here. Not in Buffalo."

"I just, sometimes I leave my wallet at home," Chris sputtered.

"I'm sorry," said Lauren.

"Wait," said Anthony. "What if we pay off everything he owes? Can he be forgiven then?"

Lauren thought about this. "Not forgiven. But if he pays every dollar he owes, plus a twenty-*five* percent tip, then he's allowed back in."

"Done," said Shawn.

"All right, then," Lauren said. She hauled open the door and grasped my hand and led me through. My heart thrummed.

For a moment she leaned close to Greg the bouncer and explained the situation. At last he nodded and Lauren waved everyone past, into the mad melee inside. She squeezed my hand as we swept across the room to the bar and whispered in my ear, so close I could feel her hot breath, "Thank you for being here." The universe had finally, improbably—almost unbelievably—become perfectly aligned.

Our whole crew stood in a crushed knot against the bar. Lauren ducked under and popped up on the far side. "What'll it be?" she shouted, spreading out a constellation of shot glasses.

"It's Vernon's night," said Chris.

Vernon peered around, the tallest of us, soaking it all in like an ancient willow admiring an orchard of saplings. "Knob Creek!" he declared.

Lauren found the bottle and poured nine Knob Creeks, plus a shot of Dr. Pepper for Mrs. Liu, who asked for root beer instead, and, at Kandy's request, a shot of Molson Ice. As Lauren passed them out, I saw Greg, the bouncer, waddling quickly in our direction. I had the gut-shot feeling that everything was about to go from wildly festive to ferociously violent in the next several seconds. But instead, Greg howled, "Let me get in on that!"

Lauren saw the confusion in my face. "Greg loves to be a badass," she said, "but he's just a big softie. He goes to those Renaissance fairs. He swings swords around and wears dresses!"

"They're called kilts!" Greg bellowed, grumpy and happy at the same time. Lauren handed him a shot of whiskey; in his massive paw it looked the size of a thimble.

Lauren slipped under the bar again and pressed herself against me. We all raised our glasses, mashed tightly together, and looked around at one another, everyone's face filled with a golden glow. Darla and Vernon had their arms around each other, as did Anthony and Kandy, and Chris and Shawn Hendershot, and Mr. Liu, Mrs. Liu, and Mary. I put my arm around Lauren's waist and pulled her close.

Later in the night, much later, I ended up telling Lauren that I loved her, and she told me she loved me, too. And the next afternoon, when we woke up, hung over but in fine spirits, we went for the walk I'd fantasized about, through a city transformed by almost two feet of snow. Every tree, every bush, every fire hydrant, and every garbage can was laced with soft, gentle beauty, like we'd crossed through a portal into some distant, magic land. In a few weeks, of course, Lauren Hill was no longer with me, she was with that dude named Darrell, the other bartender at Freighter's, and Mr. Liu's restaurant, I learned, went out of business just a few months after that. Vernon made it to late summer, Darla told me later, then simply lay down on a park bench in Little Rock and died. But don't you see, none of that mattered, none of that mattered, none of that mattered. Because you can take away Lauren Hill, you can take away the love we had for each other, but you can't take away the feeling I had that night at midnight, as I squeezed her hand and looked around at my new, glorious tangle of friends, letting my eyes briefly catch their eyes and linger on each of their faces, the whiskey in each shot glass sparkling like a supernova. If there's ever been a happier moment in my life, I can't remember it.

"To Vernon!" someone cried out.

"To Vernon!" we shouted in chorus.

The Knob Creek went down like a furious, molten potion. I turned and looked at Lauren. She was smiling at me, sweet, soulful, and open.

"Happy Valentine's Day," I said.

"Happy Valentine's Day," she said.

And we kissed.

KAREN RUSSELL

∎

The Blind Faith
of the One-Eyed Matador

FROM *GQ*

I. Zaragoza, Spain—October 7, 2011

WHAT DOES THE BULL SEE as it charges the matador? What does the bull feel? This is an ancient mystery, but it seems like a safe bet that to *this* bull, Marques—ashy black, 5 years old, 1,100 pounds—the bullfighter is just a moving target, a shadow to catch and penetrate and rip apart. Not a man with a history, not Juan Jose Padilla, the Cyclone of Jerez, 38 years old, father of two, one of Spain's top matadors, taking on his last bull of the afternoon here at the Feria del Pilar, a hugely anticipated date on the bullfighting calendar.

When Marques comes galloping across the sand at Padilla, the bullfighter also begins to run—not away from the animal but toward its horns. Padilla is luminously scaled in fuchsia and gold, his "suit of lights." He lifts his arms high above his head, like a viper preparing to strike. For fangs, he has two wooden sticks with harpoonlike barbs, two banderillas, old technologies for turning a bull's confusion into rage. Padilla and Marques are alone in the sandy pit, but a carousel of faces swirls around them. A thousand eyes beat down on Padilla, causing sweat to bead on his neck. Just before Marques can gore him, he jumps up and jabs the sticks into the bull's furry shoulder. He brings down both sticks at once, an outrageous risk. Then he spins around so that he is *facing* Marques, running backward on the sand, toe to heel.

A glancing blow from Marques unsteadies Padilla; his feet get tangled. At the apex of his fall, he still has time to right himself, escape the bull. His chin tilts up: There is the wheeling sky, all blue. His last-ever binocular view. This milestone whistles past him, the whole sky flooding through the bracket of the bull's horns, and now he's lost it. The sun flickers on and off. *My balance—*

Padilla has the bad luck, the terrible luck, of landing on his side. And now his luck gets worse.

Marques scoops his head toward Padilla's face on the sandy floor, a move that resembles canine tenderness, as if he's leaning down to lick him, but instead the bull drives his sharp left horn through the bullfighter's jaw. When Marques tusks up, the horn crunches through Padilla's skin and bone, exiting through his left eye socket. Cameras clock the instant that a glistening orb pops loose onto the matador's cheek. A frightening silence descends on the crowd. Nobody knows the depth of the wound.

Marques gallops on, and Padilla gets towed for a few feet, pulled by his cheek. He loses a shoe. Skin stretches away from his jawbone with the fragile elasticity of taffy.

Then Padilla's prone body is left in the bull's dust. He springs up like a jack-in-the-box and hops around. His face is completely red. As the blood gushes down his cheek, he holds his dislodged eye in place with his pinkie. He thinks he must be dying. *I can't breathe. I can't see.*

Marques, meanwhile, has trotted a little ways down the sand. He stands there panting softly. His four legs are perfectly still. What unfolds is a scene that Beckett and Hemingway and Stephen King might have collaborated to produce, because this is real horror, the blackest gallows humor: the contrast between the bullfighter crying out *"Oh, my eye! I can't see! I can't see!"* and the cud-chewing obliviousness of the animal.

In the bullring, other bullfighters spill onto the sand and rush to Padilla's aid. They lift him, hustle him toward the infirmary. Meanwhile, the bullfight must go on. Miguel Abellan, another matador on the bill, steps in for Padilla. He kills Marques in a trance-like state that he later swears he can't remember. Tears run down his cheeks. He's survived twenty-seven gorings himself, but what he sees in Zaragoza makes him consider quitting the profession.

Cornadas—gorings—are so common that every plaza is legally required to have a surgeon on site. Bullfighters now routinely survive injuries that would have killed their fathers and grandfathers. Good luck, now, excellent luck: Carlos Val-Carreres is the Zaragoza surgeon, one of the best in Spain.

"I'm asphyxiating," Padilla gasps as they bring him in. Many hands guide him into the shadowy infirmary. Someone scissors off his clothing. Someone inserts a breathing tube into his windpipe. Val-Carreres understands instantly that this is a potentially fatal *cornada*, one of the worst he's seen in thirty years, and one they are ill-equipped to handle in the infirmary. Padilla, now tracheally intubated, is loaded into an ambulance.

Pronóstico muy grave, Val-Carreres tells reporters.

At 7:52 p.m., half an hour after the goring, Padilla arrives at the emergency room. He presents with multiple fractures to the left side of his face, a detached ear, a protruding eyeball, and hemorrhage at the base of his skull. A five-hour operation saves his life. The surgeons rebuild his cheekbone and eyelid and nose, with mesh and titanium plates. But they are unable to repair his split facial nerve, which has been divided by the bull's horn, because they cannot locate the base of the nerve. Padilla wakes up from the anesthesia to discover that he can no longer move the left side of his face. It is paralyzed.

When he comes to, his first words to his manager, Diego Robles, are: "Don't cancel any of my contracts in South America." Padilla has November bullfights in Venezuela, Peru, and Ecuador.

His first words to his youngest brother, Jaime, who is also a bullfighter, a banderillero, and scheduled to perform in two days' time: "Don't cancel your fight. You have to do it for us. You can't let this get the best of you."

His first words to his wife, Lidia: "Where is my eye?"

The eye is back in its proper place, but sightless—the optic nerve has been elongated and lesioned by the horn. He's also deaf in his left ear, and the entire left side of his face is purple and bloated, like something viewed underwater. His eyelid is sealed shut. His mouth curls inward like a wilted leaf.

"I was there when he saw himself for the first time after the accident," recalls Diego. "He saw the reality in front of him. He said, '*Es que no soy yo—*'"

No. That's not me. Here is a vertigo a thousand times more destabilizing than his slip in the plaza: He does not recognize himself.

There is the physical pain, which the doctors reduce with morphine, and then there is the terror. They're telling him he might never again wear his "suit of lights." Never stand before another bull. If he can't return to a plaza, he'll be exiled from his life. Evicted from his own skin.

In his hospital room, as soon as he can move again, he begins to rehearse bullfighting moves with the sheets. And on October 19, less than two weeks after the accident, he gives a press conference in a wheelchair with his face uncovered.

"I have no rancor toward this bull or toward my profession," he slurs into the mike. He makes the following pledge: "I will return to dress as a torero."

II. The Wild Feast and the Matador's Famine

A millennium and a half after Moorish cavaliers rode into Spain and began to cultivate the bullfighting tradition, a few hundred years after trendy nobles staged bullfights to celebrate weddings and Catholic festivals, nearly a century since the golden age of the matador, when Juan Belmonte and Joselito "the Little Rooster" pioneered the mad modern style of "artistic" caping (working within inches of the enraged animal), bullfighting remains the national fiesta or the *fiesta brava*—"the wild feast."

In a standard *corrida de toros*, the common term for the spectacle, there are three matadors on the bill and six matches total. The fame and fees of twenty-first-century matadors range wildly, depending on official ranking and also "cachet"—a torero's reputation. Group A matadors such as Padilla must perform in at least forty-three corridas per season. These guys are the *figuras*, and the industry can support only a dozen or so of them. To maintain their status, Group A's need to be frequent fliers and serial killers, traveling fiendishly from February to October, sometimes performing in plazas on opposite coasts in the same week. For Group B matadors, the minimum is thirteen corridas. Group C? No minimums. It's the ladder rung where rookies get classed with semiretired stars. Padilla spent years in Group C before finally breaking through.

Today it's harder than it's ever been to earn a living in the bullring. Unemployment in Spain is nearing 25 percent, and the country's flailing economy is taking its toll on the *mundo taurino*. ("We will *torear la crisis*," said Prime Minister Mariano Rajoy in a press conference, invoking the figure of the bullfighter to salve Eurozone panic.) Nearly a hundred corridas have been cut from the season, and still plazas are often only half full.

Is bullfighting an art, a sport, torture? Dying out, or more popular than ever? You can find evidence in every direction. Spanish newspapers cover bullfighting in the culture pages, alongside theater reviews. In 2010, Catalonia outlawed *corridas de toros;* in Madrid they are legally protected as a "cultural good" and publicly subsidized, like the National Ballet. Telemadrid's latest reality show is *Quiero Ser Torero*—"I Want to Be a Bullfighter."

"We Spaniards don't understand ourselves, the majority of Spaniards, we don't understand our country without our fiesta," says Juan Jose Padilla. "The fiesta unites the nation."

Bullshit, say Spain's anti-*taurinos*. "The majority of Spaniards are against the bullfight," says Silvia Barquero, spokeswoman for Spain's animal-rights party, PACMA, who believes the Catalonian ban augurs a new and enlightened era in Spain. "We should not cause suffering to an animal that has the same right to life as our species." (You certainly don't have to be a member of PACMA or PETA to find a corrida alienating, cruel, and atavistic.)

Then there is the controversy over televised corridas. In 2006, when the socialist party was in charge, Spain's national TV network, TVE, stopped showing them. Now, with Rajoy and his conservative Popular Party back in power, the bulls have returned to the public airwaves. On August 24, TVE said that it would again air live bullfights after the six-year hiatus. Previously the network had pulled them from its schedule to protect minors from violence, but superfans could still get the afternoon corridas on premium cable channels. This is how Pepe and Ana Padilla were able to watch their son's goring in the instant it occurred.

Not only could they watch it—thanks to a freakish coincidence, you can now watch them watching it: On October 7, a Canal Sur production crew happened to be taping in the home of Ana and Pepe, filming them seated in front of their son's televised image for a newsmagazine segment titled "The Courage of a Bullfighter." When Marques gored Juan Jose, the glass eye of the camera was trained on Ana Padilla's face.

Should I stop taping? asked the cameraman.

"*Siga! Siga!*" said Pepe. Keep rolling. If these were Juan's *pasos ultimos,* his final moments, he wanted a record of them.

The cameraman obliged, and the result is an uncanny hall of mirrors. The nested footage of Ana and Pepe reacting in real time to the goring makes the scene exponentially more horrifying. Suddenly the tiny bullfighter is no remote cartoon of pain but a fully dimensioned human: their son. After Marques spears Padilla, his mother's face erupts in sobs. Pepe doesn't think he will ever recover from his son's accident.

"I thought that I had killed him," he says in a raw voice. "I thought that I had murdered my son. I was the one who encouraged him in this profession . . ."

Pepe Padilla has raised three toreros. (Oscar, the middle son, retired as a banderillero the day after Juan Jose's goring and now runs a chain of pet-supply stores.) Pepe coached his sons after school, caping cows with them in the green hills around Jerez. He once dreamed of being a matador himself. As a teenager, he was a *novillero,* a matador in training. "But I was a coward," he says, smiling. "Not like my Juan."

Today, Pepe is a charmer in his sixties with uncorrected teeth, gold jewelry wreathed by silver chest hair, and one droopy eyelid. For decades he worked as a baker in Jerez, sleeping three or four hours, heading back out before dawn to support his seven children. (Seven children! Franco years, he grins, shaking his head. Everything scarce and hard-won, including condoms.) Juan Jose appeared on May 23, 1973; Pepe says he was born to *torear.* When he was 8, he was written up in a bullfighting journal for having "the courage of a 30-year-old matador." When he was 12, he killed his first bull. At 21, he became the first and only man in his family to achieve the rank of professional matador.

"All of my sons were good," Pepe says. "But Juan had something special." He stares into space for a long time, as if seeking the precise descriptor for this ineffable quality.

"Huevos!" He grins. "Cojones!"

Later, as Juan Jose made his bones as a young matador, he earned a reputation for fighting the world's most difficult and aggressive bulls: Victorinos, Pablo Romeros, and especially Miuras, a strain of fighting bull notorious for maiming and killing many toreros. Padilla's style was defined by his incredible—and lunatic—valor. He did moves nobody else would dare. He was one of the few matadors to put in his own banderillas, to cape bulls on his knees. One consequence of this bravura is that Padilla might well be the record holder when it comes to bullring injuries: Before the Zaragoza goring, he had already been seriously wounded by the *toros* thirty-eight times. He nearly died in Pamplona in 2001, when a Miura bull gored him in the neck.

Overnight, Padilla's story flies around the globe: He's a hero in Spain, elsewhere a grotesque footnote to the "real" daily news. A Twitter sensation: #Fuerzapadilla. His shattered face becomes the public face of bullfighting.

Once the media storm dies down and his condition is stabilized, Juan travels home to the seaside pueblo of Sanlucar, where he lives with Lidia and their two children, Paloma, 8, and Martin, 6. At home, he is left to relearn kindergarten skills in private, miles from any bullring. How to chew and swallow. How to ride his bicycle and grocery shop, cycloptically. The ringing in his left ear never stops. It hurts to talk. Unable to train for a corrida, some days he can't stop crying. Prior to the accident, he was a joyful, open, easygoing guy. Which is not to say that he was necessarily an even-keeler. He has always had a strong character, just like the noble bulls he fights, Pepe explains, "because of his *raza*," his fiery lineage. Juan Jose can be tempestuous, irritable, "and then there's nothing to be done, you have to leave him alone!"

But the mood that sucks him under in October is something new. Like the eye he can't open, it's black and unchanging.

"I fell into a great depression," says Padilla.

"*Estaba fatal,*" says Diego, his manager. "*Estaba hundido hundido hundido.*"

He was sunk, sunk, sunk.

Lidia is not used to seeing her husband ashamed, in pain. "We were so afraid for him—the children, too, it affected them . . ."

Lidia Padilla is a sedately beautiful woman, dark-haired, with a doll's porcelain face, and she's been Juan Jose's girl since *antes antes,* cradle-robbed when she was 14 and he was a high school senior, the handsome bread-delivery boy. Their first date was during Semana Santa, an Easter festival. Juan Jose believed it was his destiny to have a wife like Lidia, a woman both "passionate" and devoutly Catholic. "I found the balance I needed in her," he says.

Lidia has been with Juan his whole career, but she has never once watched her husband perform. Not in a plaza and not on TV, and during the eleven-hour drive to Zaragoza, after the accident, she imagined begging him to retire. But when she saw him in the hospital, the speech she'd prepared dissolved. "I couldn't take that dream from him," she says. "To ask him not to be a torero. It would be like killing him while he was still alive."

Padilla realizes he needs to get back into the bullring as soon as humanly possible. So many people had suffered as a result of his accident, he says, that he wanted to give them "tranquillity, normalcy." He has a habit of describing his "return to normalcy" as something he has to do for other people, as if the Zaragoza fall upset some cosmic equilibrium, knocked the whole world (and not just his world) off its axis.

But what's the rush to resume a career that nearly killed him? Why the sprint back to such a chronically risky kind of normal?

"I couldn't conceive of my life without *el toreo,*" he says. "If I couldn't have returned to my profession, it's clear that I would have been really affected. I could have dedicated myself to other things, business. I had some good offers, but none of that was going to fill me . . . Oh, it was affecting my head, I felt such a heaviness, at the beginning I was anguished, it was a tremendous anguish."

In the bullfighting world, there is this saying, *Torear la suerte:* an aphorism that contains an entire philosophy. Brutishly translated: "Bullfight your fate." Whatever bull God drums up for you, you face off against, you dance with, you dominate, and it's up to you to put on a splendid show, to use every bull as an opportunity to demonstrate all of your *arte.* Your valor and skill. *Torear la suerte,* in other words, combines religious fatalism with Nietzschean will.

Padilla's years as a torero, then, have prepared him to view his recovery as a special kind of corrida—a chance to use his faith and courage outside the bullring.

In late October, Padilla travels north to Oviedo to consult with an internationally renowned ophthalmic surgeon, who warns him that his comeback plan seems "unrealistic"—his optic nerve is still not responding to light. The next specialist to evaluate Padilla is Alberto Garcia-Perla, a maxillofacial surgeon. As Padilla recalls their first meeting, his voice grows rough with gratitude: "There was never a moment when Dr. Garcia-Perla responded negatively to my dream of returning to *torear.* He's always said that I would be the one to decide."

Garcia-Perla, the chief surgeon at Seville's Virgen del Rocio Hospital, will direct a team of eighteen doctors, including plastic surgeons, ear-nose-and-throat surgeons, and an anesthesiologist, in an attempt to repair Padilla's facial nerve. The plan is to reconnect the two ends of the nerve using an implant from the sural nerve in Padilla's leg. If the operation succeeds, Juan might regain the ability to blink and chew, lift both brows in surprise. Garcia-Perla is no stranger to this kind of high-stakes reconstructive surgery; his team successfully performed the second face-transplant surgery in Spain, the eleventh in the world. But they've never had a case quite like Padilla's.

"We've seen facial trauma like Juan's before. What's unique here is the method: the horn of a bull. Ordinarily a goring of that depth to the face . . . it could have killed him." Think how narrowly he avoided brain damage, says Garcia-Perla. "It was a question of millimeters. He's lucky to be alive, and he's conscious of that."

The surgery gets under way at 9 a.m. on November 22. It lasts fourteen hours. Moonrise, and Juan Padilla has a new face. And within weeks, the repaired facial nerve begins to "awaken." Little by little, Padilla regains limited motor control of his left eyebrow and lips. Over the next six months, Garcia-Perla believes, Padilla might recover as much as 80 percent of his facial mobility. But nerve regeneration is a slow process. One millimeter, more or less, per day.

On December 30, five weeks after his epic operation, Padilla stands in front of a *vaca brava,* a 2-year-old cow, at Fuente Ymbro, a ranch in Cadiz that breeds fighting bulls. He's here to *torear* with a live animal for the first time since the accident. The day is cold and cloudless. Scallion green hills descend to an azure lake, and bulls that look camel-humped with muscle tissue percolate slowly around the low buildings. A dozen close friends and family members are standing around the miniature bullring, waiting to see what Juan Jose is capable of in his reconstructed body. It's a "closed-doors corrida"—a test and a performance.

With his eye patch in place, he shakes out the muleta, his red cape, and shouts: *"Toro!"* Everybody's eyes are full. Only the young cow, with her velvety, bumblebee-like ruff, seems distracted, unaware of the import of this moment. She charges Juan's blind side, and he expertly sidesteps her.

Padilla insisted on this date because he refused to let the year end without "the sensation of dressing as a bullfighter" and standing before an animal. He describes his desire to "grab the cape" in supple, tactile terms, with the longing of a ghost recalling its body. "And above all I wanted to share it, to offer it as a gift to my family and those close to me who suffered through this, to the doctors. Afterward I realized that I hadn't been wrong, to have this hope of returning."

In January the surgeon in Oviedo, the skeptic, examines Padilla and is so impressed by the adaptation of his right eye that he revises his initial prognosis: Padilla is able to measure distances and spaces with only one eye, and so it's "perfectly fine" for him to return to the bullring. Garcia-Perla, who attended the private corrida on the thirtieth, agrees.

So on March 4, in the southwestern town of Olivenza, the Cyclone reappeared, looking like a glittering apparition of his former self, haunting the afternoon, wearing a black eye patch and a laurel green suit of lights. Olivenza is not a major venue on the calendar *taurino,* but Juan Jose's one-eyed return magnetized the world's gaze. In the moments before his first bull came rampaging onto the sand, nobody knew what to expect: Were they about to watch a man's suicide, a second goring? How much could he really see? Wasn't it just yesterday, practically, that his face was torn apart in Zaragoza? Journalists flinched preemptively, prepared for a literal collision between the man's blind ambition and the sprinting animal. But Padilla swept his cape over the bulls' horns a dozen times, as if he were intent on violently, defiantly erasing every doubt.

III. Homecoming

At eight thirty every weekday morning, Juan Jose Padilla drives from his home in Sanlucar to meet with a physical therapist. For thirty minutes, he endures an electroshock treatment that causes his face to convulse and contort. This is exercise for his paralyzed facial muscles, a daily attempt to coax that nerve to regenerate. He also meets with his speech therapist and his ear doctor. Mornings are for doctors' visits, afternoons for the bulls.

At noon, Padilla drives his white Mercedes to the Sanlucar Plaza de Toros, a small, intimate bullring. "My office," he jokes. Walking through the archway feels like entering a seashell, scrubbed clean by years of sand and salt and light. Today, a Thursday in early May, the audience is me, my translator, and Diego's strawberry blond dog, Geto.

What does training look like for a bullfighter?

Padilla strides into the ring, skeletally gaunt in a T-shirt and black bike leggings. An athlete, no question, but with a mauled look. Wild and fragile at once. He's dropped forty pounds since Zaragoza. He's average height, but his extreme weight loss makes him look like a gangly giant; his large hands dangle from his wrists, and his Adam's apple tents his long throat. If Goya were to paint a *taurino* trading card, it would look like Juan Jose.

"*Toro!*" Padilla screams at Diego, furiously wagging his red cape.

Diego lowers his head and runs at him.

Diego Robles is 60-plus and leather-skinned, so super-*marrón* he seems to be getting tan from within, as if at any moment he might hiccup a tiny sun. He's an ex-torero with startlingly blue eyes, and he'll grab his jerky-lean stomach muscles to show you he has no "Michelins"—nary a spare tire.

Diego adjusts his backward powder blue baseball cap, paws the sand with a sneaker toe, and charges again. He runs with his head down, holding a pair of real bull's horns that look like yellowed saber teeth. He circles Padilla, huffing in an unconvincing imitation of a deranged bull. Padilla holds his body erect, drawing the cape over Diego's head with animatronic evenness.

Next, Diego disappears from the plaza and returns with what appears to be a Tim Burton movie prop—a wheelbarrow with a bull's skull affixed to its front end. The skull's a little crooked, which makes its grin look somehow bashful. A hay bale is lashed to the cart behind it, frizzing golden straw.

"What do bullfighters call that wheelbarrow?" I ask, preparing for a whimsical yet terrifying new vocabulary word.

"The wheelbarrow," says Diego, looking flustered. Geto greets the skull in cosmopolitan fashion, licking first one bony cheek and then the other.

The skull-barrow rolls my way.

"Grip the horns," says Diego. They're a foot long at least, thicker around than my wrist. It's a sickening exercise to imagine this bovine stalagmite tunneling through Padilla's eye socket.

Now Padilla practices the *volapié*—a death blow delivered to the bull by an airborne matador. He runs at the wheelbarrow, leaps over the skull's horns, and sinks his *estoque*, the needle-like sword, into the center of the hay bale. *"Bien!"* claps Diego. The hay bale looks like a cheese cube at the end of a gigantic toothpick. The skull grins vacantly into the stands; Geto, bored, has wandered off to lick his own foot.

To a foreigner, it's an almost comically surreal scene. *"Toro!"* Padilla screams into the empty ring.

Every May for nineteen years, Padilla has returned to his hometown of Jerez de la Frontera, a thirty-minute drive from Sanlucar, to *torear* at Jerez's annual fair.

My twentieth Feria.

In Spain, every locality from Madrid to the most rinky-dink *pueblecito* celebrates its annual fair: a big weeklong street party, usually tied to a religious holiday. Portable tents go up like luminous mushrooms; inside these temporary pavilions, everybody boozes and shimmies. Jerez de la Frontera, the fifth-largest city in Andalucía, is located in Cadiz province. Halfway between the sea and the blue burrs of the mountains, it's the true cradle of what Americans consider to be stereotypically *Español*: sherry, stallions, flamenco, fighting bulls. The Jerez Feria is one of the major events on the bullfighting calendar, this year even more than usual. Padilla's canted face is on posters everywhere in town; he's wearing the laurel green jacket, extending his *montera*. On the posters his snarl looks stagy and flirtatious, deliberate; in person, you can see that this grimace is frozen onto him, a half smile he can't straighten.

It's Saturday, May 12, and I've been invited to Padilla's house about an hour before he'll leave for the corrida in Jerez. The Padilla homestead turns out to be a Sanlucar monument. Kids on bikes don't know the street address, but when I say "Padilla" their eyes go wide—"Ah! The house of the torero." Sanlucar and Jerez are not wealthy towns—Sanlucar has one of the lowest per capita incomes in Spain—so bullfighting can be something analogous to Hoop Dreams for the poor kids of Andalucía.

The house is a modest mansion surrounded by an eight-foot magenta wall, with a massive backyard that hosts a lemon tree and a bluish tile of Christ's face. There's a play area for Paloma and Martin, and a sandy junior bullring where their dad trains. The interior of the two-story house is set up like a self-curated museum: Every room contains displays of bullfighting memorabilia. Swords, hats, and so many sequined jackets that you wonder if there's not a naked army of Prince's backup dancers wandering around Sanlucar.

The accident, in career terms, has been a remarkable boon. Padilla has contracts everywhere—this season, he is planning to perform in sixty to seventy corridas. Diego can negotiate for fees that are double or in some cases triple what he was making before. He's also getting better bulls: "The people have always associated me with Miuras," Padilla says. "Now there's been a complete change in my professional life. They're giving me new opportunities." For the first time, he's facing off against the best-bred bulls in Spain. Stylistically, he explains, a different choreography is possible with a *toro* that charges rhythmically and follows the cape.

Half a dozen close family friends, including Dr. Garcia-Perla, are gathered around the coffee table, waiting for their audience with the Cyclone. (The title of the Padillas' lone coffee-table book: *The Cyclone*.) A papal hush drapes the house. Somehow, thanks to the mysterious intervention of Diego, I am admitted to Juan Jose's dressing room. In the inner chamber, Padilla is putting on a short, rigid jacket, the matador's exoskeleton. It's snowflake white with gold embroidery. He's wearing the matador's *coleta,* a clip-on bun made of his own hair. He's already got on the cropped breeches, the flamingo pink socks. After his weight loss last fall, he needed a whole new wardrobe.

He says he has around fifty suits, but only eight in rotation for any given season. The sword boy cleans them after each corrida. Padilla's sword "boy" is a kind, bespectacled man in his fifties named Juan Muñoz. He dresses and undresses Juan Jose and hands him his sword at the "hour of truth" and is perhaps the most feudal-manservant-seeming member of Team Padilla. Muñoz doesn't use OxiClean or Shout—no, nothing like that. He says he gets the blood off his boss's sequins with soap and water.

Padilla adjusts his skinny tie in the mirror. He smiles nervously at Lidia, who smiles back. Strides out to greet his fan base.

"How do I look?"

Spotlit by the risk that he's about to undertake in the plaza, Juan looks frailer than he has all week. Mummy-like in white. His legs are matchsticks. His eye patch is a blindfold he can't lift. Suddenly I feel very scared, truly scared, for this corrida.

"Very handsome!" everyone responds. People hug Padilla one by one and file out to their cars. We leave Lidia behind in the foyer.

The next time Juan Jose Padilla appears, he is a completely different person.

The plaza is crammed solid with Jerezanos. It's 7 p.m., but the enormous, cheerfully brutal *sol* of Andalucía is still shining above the bullring. Every matador on today's lineup is a star—Cayetano, in fact, is the scion of the Ordoñez bullfighting dynasty, and Morante de la Puebla is a legendary artist with the cape. But Padilla is the major attraction, hero and homeboy to all.

"Jerez, it's his *tierra,*" says Diego. "It's going to be an incredibly emotional moment. You have to be strong so that so much emotion doesn't overwhelm you. It can make you tender, weak . . . "

Acute excitement pulses in the stands. Two nights ago, at the Thursday corrida, this same plaza was nearly empty. Everybody blamed the economy: Even the cheap seats cost twenty-eight euros.

But tonight there is no evidence that money is weighing on anybody's mind. FUERZAPADILLA! read banners unscrolling throughout the stadium.

When Padilla, Cayetano, and Morante parade onto the sand, a roar erupts from the open mouth of the stadium into the blue sky of Jerez, loud enough to ripple a flock of low-flying birds. In the foyer of his home, Padilla looked so thin, like something prematurely sprung from its cocoon. But now he is fast, strong; the eye patch looks menacing. His hoarse cry of "Jerez!" brings down the house.

Padilla's first bull comes charging out and silences the rowdy crowd. In a *corrida de toros*, the matador will have roughly twenty minutes to dominate and kill the bull. This block of time is subdivided into three *tercios*: "the act of the lances," "the act of the banderillas," and "the act of death." If the matador performs well, the crowd will petition the president of the bullfight to award him trophies: the dead bull's ears or, for an exceptional corrida, the gristly gray ribbon of the bull's tail. Death is always the outcome for the bull, except in rare cases when an unusually "valiant" animal is pardoned.

Many have pointed out that the bullfight is not really a fight at all—a contest between equals—but "a tragedy in three acts." The rite's brutality can make bullfighting feel incomprehensible to a foreigner and indefensible to an animal lover; and yet every bullfighter I spoke to professed to feel what struck me as a genuine love for the *toros*. What kind of love is this? How is it possible to publicly kill the animal to which you have dedicated all your waking hours? "I give the *toro* everything, and he gives me everything," Padilla told me. His profession, he says proudly, is "the most dignified in the world" because of "its truth, its reality"—its blood red engagement with the fate shared by all species. Every corrida, the matador greets his future death cloaked in fur, and today is no exception.

Act I: Juan Jose and his banderilleros swing their pink capotes around wildly, each man caping the bull in turn. Out trot the picadors, looking like dapper Lego men on horseback in their wide-brimmed hats and squarish leg armor. Their horses are swaddled in *petos*, mattress-like cloaks to protect them from the bulls' horns. The picadors insert their lances into the hump of muscle tissue at the base of the neck, the *morillo*, to get the bull to lower its head; otherwise Padilla won't be able to get over its horns to make the final kill. There is something scarily perfunctory about the way the picadors jab the bull with their long lances—they're like a cavalry of gas jockeys, only instead of filling up the tank, they are draining the bull's life.

Act II: Padilla dismisses his assistants, signals to the crowd that he will put in his own banderillas. Goddamnit, Padilla, *qué fuerte*. Everyone is aware that this is exactly how he lost his eye. And now, one-eyed, Padilla is flying onto the wooden running boards behind the bull. How does he get so high? He takes a running leap as if the sand were a trampoline and sinks another wooden flag into the bull. He places the final pair of banderillas *al violín,* a one-handed maneuver that recalls the dramatic acrobatics that caused his fall in Zaragoza.

Act III: *Tercio de la muerte.* Now Padilla is stalking the bull, with an unexpected sultriness and mock haughtiness. Via a sort of feline strut across the sand toward the animal, he slinks up to the bull and goads it into charging. It lowers its horns, tosses its head in a dozen vain attempts to catch the cape. When it comes up on Padilla's blind left side, we recoil, but we don't have to worry; he seems to have no trouble gauging distance or responding to the unhinged shadows in the bullring.

Padilla's body language changes tone continually over the next seven minutes, as his *pasos* transmit contempt and urgency, comedy and reverence. Sometimes the bullfight looks a lot like a game of freeze tag, and his pranks get juvenile; he does everything short of blowing a raspberry at the bull. Sometimes it's more like an awkward cocktail party: the bull refusing to charge, Padilla doing the *torero* catcall that is like emphatic forced laughter: "*Eh, toro!* He-he-HEH!"

Soon everyone can tell from the bull's ragged breathing that the end is near. Padilla and the bull are staring into each other's faces with an opaque intimacy. Something visible to everyone in the stands, but as ultimately impenetrable as any couple's love-or-hate affair. It's almost sunset now; the planks of blood down the bull's back look violet. As if on the conductor's cue, two seagulls choose this moment to swoop through the invisible membrane between bull and man. Padilla's dark hair is sticking to his head. The matador, underweight, with his twisted face and his eye patch, appears unmistakably mortal. His face fossilizes his brush with death, the way that fire gets incarnated by cold, tender welts. His return to the ring, one could argue, gives the crowd a sense that death will come for all of us, sooner or later, that death is certainly imminent, but *it ain't here yet.*

Inside the plaza's walls, the concrete parentheses that enclose Padilla and the bull, everybody straightens; *erguirse* is the Spanish verb for this, electric shivers racing up spines. Juan Jose directs the creature's horns around his waist, as if he is carving his own hips out of black space. Drawing beautiful shapes with the cape and the bull. Drawing breaths.

Padilla squares his feet, positions himself for the kill. The bull is four feet away from him. Here it comes: the "hour of truth." It's a crazy, horrible, ugly, enraging, senseless, sublime, endless moment to witness—a moment that swallows every adjective you want to hurl at it.

In the balcony, the orchestra has stopped playing. The conductor is craning over his shoulder, watching Padilla for his cue. His baton trembles in midair at the exact angle as Padilla's sword.

Padilla draws the sword back at eye level, as if the *estoque* is an arrow in an invisible quiver.

He runs. He flies, just as he did during his training with the wheelbarrow. *Volapié.* He leaps and leans his torso over the bull's lowered horns and plunges the sword into the vulnerable *morillo.*

The crowd lets out one single, tidal exhalation.

Did he "win"? Bullfighting is less straightforward than American spectacles like pro football; in this regard, it's a little more like *American Idol.* But thanks to the thunderous petition of the crowd, tonight the president awards him two ears from his first bull and two ears from his second. Before he exits the arena, Padilla drops onto his knees and kisses the sand of Jerez. Then he is carried through the great doors of his home plaza, *de hombros,* twinkling like a living torch on his brother Jaime's shoulders. Escorted by the longest ovation you have ever heard.

Forty minutes after his triumphant exit through the Puerta Grande, Padilla is back home in Sanlucar, changing out of his work clothes. Outside, a few guys are loading up the shuttle bus; at 4:30 a.m. tomorrow, Padilla and his entourage will leave for their next fight in Talavera. Some freckly taurine roadie carries swords and a bleached skull to the trunk.

Where is the wild torero afterparty? Lidia and the family friends are having a quiet dinner. Paloma is bouncing around, getting ready for bed. The Cyclone of Jerez emerges from his dressing room as Juan Jose, wearing a suit jacket and spiffy loafers.

"Four ears, Paloma!" he crows to his daughter, sinking into his armchair. ("The kids are always begging him, 'Papi, bring me two ears!'—you know the typical things," Lidia explains.) He smooches her to make her giggle.

How does he feel about tonight's corrida?

"This was one of the afternoons of maximum responsibility in my life," he says. "To be able to dress in my suit of lights in this new phase of my life, in front of my countrymen, my doctors, my family—" He smiles. For the past week, he explains, he's been terrified that it would be "an empty afternoon, a sad afternoon, that the bulls wouldn't help me . . ." That he would fail to achieve his dream of leaving *de hombros*, piggybacking on his brother's shoulders through the great gates.

"Well, I think it was a triumphant afternoon. I dedicate it to *toda mi tierra*."

Is it uncomfortable to get sedimented into legend while you are still alive? Is it like another sort of paralysis?

"I feel supremely content, proud, for all that the bull has given me, all that it's added to my life, personal as well as professional. I can't complain or feel victimized by my injury; this is the profession I chose. And this accident of mine, my recovery, I think it's touched the whole world . . ." He leans forward, his enormous hands cupping his bony knees, shaping his words carefully. "There was a time when I couldn't show my face, when my head was a little screwed up. But now I've entered a period of great pride, great happiness."

His working eye follows his daughter, who is babbling some song under the taxidermied heads of six Miura bulls that Padilla killed in a single afternoon in Bilbao.

"And there is always a new goal tomorrow." It's the *"amor por los toros,"* he says—his love of the bulls—that drives him.

If some of these phrases sound like Hallmark propaganda, you have to imagine them spoken by a man who is teaching himself to speak again. It's a legitimate medical miracle that Juan Jose Padilla can even vocalize his "love for the *toros*" today. Tomorrow he'll fight three horned beasts in Talavera; on Monday it's back to the ABCs in speech therapy. Somehow he's managed to surrender without bitterness to his new situation while simultaneously working without pause to reclaim his life. His feats in the bullring are as impressive as they've ever been, but for my money it's Padilla's daily diligence, his unglorious microsteps back from paralysis, that distinguish him as a true *figura*.

For all the talk of rewards and triumphs and miracles, the life of a bullfighter seems incredibly grueling, dangerous, uncertain.

Vale la pena? Is it worth it?

No, says Padilla's mother without a second's hesitation.

No, says Pepe Padilla, who during the Franco years used to ride trains and sleep under the stars to stand before a fighting bull. For the parents of a torero, "there is more *pena* than *gloria*."

Sí, says Lidia, *because you see his happiness!*

Sí, says Juan Jose Padilla, smiling as wide as his new face permits him, because God is giving me my *recompensa*. Now I see better with one eye than two.

ALEXIS SCHAITKIN

■

Bones

FROM *The Southwest Review*

KAYLA AND LUZ WERE DESPERATE FOR BROKEN BONES. Splints, slings, casts, and layer upon layer of snowy gauze danced in their eyes each afternoon as they formulated their plans. They took the Bible from Mrs. Lopez's shrine to the Virgin Mary and dropped it on each other's fingers. They ran into the punching bag in Luz's basement, which her brother Manuel used for training. They roller-skated down the big hill in the road, aiming for the patch of sand and gravel at the bottom.

But they chickened out every time: they pulled their fingers out from under the Bible, slowed before they hit the bag, swerved clear at the last possible second. Kayla tried to float up like a dead girl and watch herself from a place of tranquil indifference to her own pain, but at the critical moment she always darted back into herself.

"It's like our bodies force us to protect them," Kayla said.

"Like how you can't hold your breath until you die because once you faint your body starts breathing for you," Luz said.

Kayla imagined her skinny arm weighed down with stiff plaster and her classmates asking if it hurt. "It's not so bad," she would say, wincing just enough to let them know how much her snapped bones pained her.

Two of her classmates had already been touched by the kind of pain she was after. A boy blown off his bike by a passing truck had broken his femur. A girl thrown from her pony had cracked a rib. They seemed to know things she didn't. They had been to the bottom, and they carried with them the things they had seen there. She was ready to be anointed and ennobled by suffering, to inhabit the world as a person who knew how bad bad could be.

Kayla and Luz had been inseparable for eight months, since the Lopez family arrived in town in September, a few weeks after the school year began. It was a wealthy town in the northernmost reaches of the New York suburbs. The school district was one of the very best in the nation. The houses, not Kayla's or Luz's, but most of them, were either architecturally jangly new luxury homes on dusty treeless plots (this was 1994, a few years before terms like Hummer House, Starter Castle, and McMansion caught on) or old-money country estates that burst out of their wooded surroundings like bright white teeth.

Kayla's family—her mother Tammy, her grandfather, and she—lived in an apartment with tiny windows above a sushi restaurant on the street that led from the quaint downtown to the highway. The apartment stank of fish. The smell was so deeply ingrained it was as if the cotton in the curtains had come from a field fertilized with fish carcasses, as if the bumpy plaster walls were made of ground fish bones. Tammy covered the smell with vanilla air freshener, apple cinnamon candles, and spritzes of Angel, a perfume that came in a glass star.

The Lopezes rented a house at the edge of the school district that bordered a fifty-acre wetland. The basement was constantly flooding and the backyard was a slick of goose droppings. It was a shabby '6os ranch house, the sort that went on the market in this town with the tagline "Tear down and build DREAM HOUSE" in the real estate listings.

Luz was the youngest of four children. Her brother Manuel was twenty and worked as a dancer for a DJ company. He could do a standing back flip and had a stomach like a case of gold bars. Pilar was sixteen and her body spilled over in all the right places (not at her stomach, like Kayla's mother; even when Tammy was naked it looked like her stomach was pouring over the top of an invisible pair of too-tight jeans). Estela was thirteen and already fatter than Mrs. Lopez. Mrs. Lopez cleaned houses. Mr. Lopez did something for which he wore an olive green uniform. They had emigrated from Guatemala when Luz was four, and Luz had lived all kinds of places: Los Angeles, Phoenix, California's Central Valley, and what seemed to Kayla like dozens of cities in Texas with Spanish names.

To the other children in their class, Kayla and Luz's friendship was a natural thing that didn't require explanation—outcast with outcast, that was all. Before Luz, Kayla had mostly kept to herself. There had been a time, a few years ago in kindergarten and first grade, when she had gone to other girls' houses and eaten from their walk-in pantries and played with them in the gauzy pink enclaves of their canopy beds. But the few times she had girls over to the apartment, they were squeamish about the snacks Kayla offered. When their mothers picked them up the women spoke to her grandfather with strained politeness—who was this old man in a stained shirt, watching their daughters play?—as they scanned the dim apartment, smelled its salmony stink.

Now Kayla slept at Luz's house on Friday and Saturday nights. Luz shared a bedroom with her sisters. Estela was always around.

"No plans tonight, Stelbell?" Luz would say very sweetly.

"Yeah, I have plans. Staying away from you two losers."

Pilar usually went out. The high school pulled in students from several neighboring towns that were poorer and less white, and Pilar led a clique of Guatemalan girls, some of them born in the United States, some more recent arrivals than herself. She kept a stash of clothes from Charlotte Russe and Wet Seal under her bed, and the younger girls would watch as she tried on various combinations: a pleather miniskirt with a silver tank, a sparkly black halter top with red pants, a strapless pink dress so tight and thin you could see the floral print on her thong. Between outfits she hung out in her underwear and bra, sorting indecisively through her clothes and slinking around the room (stealing glimpses of herself in the mirror as she passed it).

Once, Pilar said "You're staring," and Kayla burned with shame. Now she stole glances only when the others weren't looking. Looking at Pilar's body filled her with a feeling of being left behind. Not because she would never look like that; she *knew* she would never look like that. But Luz probably would in a few years, and in Pilar's body Kayla sensed the unlikelihood of their friendship surviving such a transformation.

If Manuel was out at a dancing gig, Pilar would throw a coat over her skimpy clothes and kiss her mama and papa goodbye on the cheek before her girlfriends picked her up. If Manuel was at home, she would fold her party clothes up as tiny as she could and stuff them into her purse, then put on a pair of loose jeans and a T-shirt. One time, before she learned, he'd made her unbutton her coat and sent her back up to change when he saw what she had on underneath.

"Be good," he would say to her.

"Yes, *Dad*."

"Remember—"

"You only have one reputation," she would say.

After Pilar left, Kayla and Luz would retreat to the bedroom. Sometimes they tried to close the closet doors on their fingers, or to prick themselves with pins. For a full hour one night they took turns rolling off Pilar's bed, which was raised high on cinderblocks.

"Keep your arm stiff when you fall," Kayla said.

"I want my cast to be periwinkle," Luz said.

"You're so dumb," said Estela, who had stopped in the doorway to watch.

"Where are your friends tonight? I don't see them anywhere," Luz said.

When Pilar returned home, she would tell the younger girls about her night as she washed the makeup from her face and brushed out her long hair. She strung along this white boy and that one, the captain of the lacrosse team, and a stoner who played guitar for her, and a nerd who was a little afraid of her. She told the girls that the older brothers of kids who ignored them had testicles like old grapes and penises that looked like little baby mice. The girls laughed until their stomachs hurt.

"It's always the same," Pilar said one night. "I'm bored of it all." She flung her body onto her bed and looked up at the ceiling. "I met a boy tonight who said he can make the seven in my birth year into a five on my ID. He does it with chalk and red pencil. There are clubs in White Plains where you only have to be eighteen."

"Mamá and Papá will never let you," Estela said.

"I'll tell them I'm sleeping at a friend's."

"They'll call her parents to check."

"Not if they'd have to speak English to them. Have I told you about my new friend Caitlin?" Pilar said with a smirk.

"No, make her Ashley!" Luz said.

"Jenna!" Estela said.

"Amber," Kayla offered.

"Yes! Amber!" Pilar said, laughing. "You know your white girls, girl."

Kayla was always the last one awake. Alone in the darkness, she would replay the night's scenes in her head: Pilar appraising herself in her lingerie, Luz's ritual meanness to Estela, and Pilar as Kayla loved her best—storytelling with her heavy black hair let down. For the rest of them this was normal, this was home; but for Kayla, even after several months, these nights were shot through with a frantic excitement. In the night's dark, solitary phase, she enjoyed it all a second time, calmly. She had fallen in love with the operation of the Lopez sisters.

On Sunday mornings, Kayla piled into the minivan with the rest of them for church. The sisters waited in line for communion with pious expressions, clutched at the delicate gold crosses around their necks, and crossed themselves with great feeling. Kayla would wave her hand across her shoulders and up and down her face in what she hoped was a convincing imitation, and Mrs. Lopez would look at her with a kind, amused smile.

Tammy always pulled into the Lopezes' driveway a little after lunchtime on Sunday to bring Kayla home. She never got out of the car. She exchanged a mutually disinterested wave with Mrs. Lopez, who stood in the doorway as Kayla gathered her things. The two women had never spoken.

"What are we?" Kayla asker her mother after the first service she attended.

"Protestant mutts. Why, what did you think you were, High Anglican?"

The rest of Sunday was spent in the apartment with her mother and grandfather. It was her mother's one day off from the Crane House, a restaurant where the mothers of Kayla's classmates lunched on turkey wraps and Niçoise salads. On Sundays, Tammy kept her feet up and caught up on the soaps she had taped during the week.

"Go out and play," Tammy would say to Kayla. But "out" was just the gravel parking lot behind the building and the scrubby sliver of trees between the lot and a gas station. A few minutes after leaving the apartment she would slip back in and hope her mother wouldn't decide to have a problem with it.

"Could we get a little news?" her grandfather might venture between episodes of the soaps.

"Get a little news on your other six days off," Tammy would say.

Tammy liked to keep the lights off, like she was watching a movie. Through the tiny windows, the very bright sun outside seemed hostile and malevolent to Kayla. She could be bored to tears and still not want to leave the apartment and go out into the light. There was something about these afternoons that she at once hated and required, something about them that steeled her for the week ahead.

Tammy was twenty-seven years old. Her hair was dyed yellow and her skin had an orange tone from her weekly tan. When Kayla thought of her mother, she saw her dressed to go out: faded hip huggers, silver eye shadow, and gold hoop earrings with crystal hearts dangling in the centers.

The man Tammy thought was Kayla's father was a casting agent who had come to her high school in central Pennsylvania looking for fresh-faced extras for a horror film when Tammy was sixteen. For the rest of her life she would see the other life she might have lived if he had spirited her away to Hollywood instead of leaving her, pregnant, in Juniata County. It ran alongside this life like the beautiful and untouchable scenery falling away at the sides of a train.

Tammy's mother, Pearl, had left when Tammy was thirteen. Tammy took over the management of the household immediately: cooking, paying bills, doing her father's wash, buying him new corduroys when his old ones had worn smooth. Often dinner was just soup from a can, but even then it was Tammy who dumped the soup into a saucepan on the stove. He let her do these things for him. He did not tell her to remain a child.

"You're too young to be sitting around waiting to die," she told him for the first time when she was fourteen. It was what her mother used to say to him. Then Tammy had thought her mother was cruel for saying it, and had hugged her father's neck and kissed his cheek and told him she loved him.

Tammy remembered her mother as a distant, blunt woman who

clung to rules of personal hygiene with evangelical intensity but was altogether unable to maintain a clean and tidy household. By the time she left, Tammy knew her temper—its cycles and rhythms and the things that were like fire-starter to it—as intimately as she knew her own body.

Pearl had worked on the line at Empire Kosher Poultry as a salter. She coated the opalescent skins of chickens (and, once every eight days, of turkeys) with coarse salt. Perhaps because her hands were so accustomed to handling things that didn't care how they were handled, she handled Tammy with the same rough and unceremonious physicality: every night she twisted cotton rags into Tammy's wet hair so tightly her scalp throbbed; she didn't work knots out of Tammy's fine hair so much as drag the brush through until the hairs broke apart.

Tammy's father was known in the town as a sad case, a meandering soul who could never hold down a job. Friends dug up temporary work for him. He loaded vending machines, folded clothing, polished cars, and harvested for Amish farmers around the county. When he took Pearl out for their first date, he arrived on her doorstep carrying a paper bag full of blackberries. The bottom of the bag had already softened from the juices. Purple ran down his hands.

Pearl felt her heart crack like a cube of ice submerged suddenly in warm water. It was the sweetest gesture that had ever been directed at her. She was twenty-three and this was the first date of her life. Everyone knew her mother, Vera, was in an institution in Harrisburg, and it was gospel among the men in town that the cunt of an Empire girl smelled like raw chicken flesh. She couldn't blame men for staying away, especially when she knew the part of her mother that rattled inside of her. She felt it like gritty iron filings, which at odd moments of attraction would stand on end. "It's the only place for me," her mother had told her, stroking Pearl's hair with a rigid hand, on the day Pearl's father drove her to Harrisburg. As Pearl watched them drive away, the filings stood at attention along the front of her body, pulled in the direction of her mother, who disappeared down the road.

Pearl pulled him inside and washed the juice from his hands. Despite what she knew about him, she put her hopes in him. For a while, it seemed she was a good influence. When they married, he'd been working at the Army Navy Surplus store for four months. But it didn't last.

When a light bulb burnt out in the house it would stay that way for days, sometimes weeks, until Pearl stood over him in his chair, pointed to it and said, "What's that?"

"A burnt out bulb," he would say.

"And what are you?" she would say.

"The man of the house."

And then he would finally get up and change it.

Kayla's eyes were locked on the sky. Vines tangled through the sparse crowns of thin trees. At the top of her stride the trees slipped from view and she saw only the sky, which was colorless today, and alternated between looking flat like a sheet of paper and infinitely deep, depending on how she thought about it as she looked at it. Mud sucked at her sneakers. She was walking with Luz through the swamp behind the Lopezes' house to the pond at its center, and hoping to trip on a root or a rock and cut herself. But of course she couldn't help stealing glances at the ground and lifting her feet when she knew a rock was coming.

Luz carried her father's fishing pole and a pink plastic bucket. Kayla held a dish of leftover cooked meat for bait. If they caught a fish, Mrs. Lopez would gut and filet it and set a dish with morsels of fried fish on the table between Luz and Kayla at dinner, alongside whatever else she had cooked.

"You going fishing?" Estela had asked before they set out.

"Would you like to be invited, Stelbell?" Luz said.

"Go slip in the shit," Estela said.

Rotting stumps rose through bright green sludge at the edges of the pond. The air was thick with the sweetness of goose droppings.

Today they only caught three bitty brown fish no bigger than sardines. Back at the house, Luz handed the bucket to her mother. Kayla could hear the fish spasming in the inch of swamp water at the bottom of the bucket. Mrs. Lopez smacked Luz gently upside the head. "Too small," she said. "How I cut?" Luz looked up at her with a syrupy smile. Mrs. Lopez sighed and took the bucket into the kitchen. A few minutes later, Luz led Kayla back to the kitchen to peek in at her mother bent over the little fish, a knife in her fat hands, muttering to herself in Spanish as she did her best to filet them. Luz laughed and Mrs. Lopez spun around. Kayla felt her face redden with shame as they fled up the stairs.

Upstairs, Luz changed out of her muddy shorts into track pants.

"You forgot new underwear," Kayla said.

"You don't need underwear. It doesn't do anything," Luz said, like this was obvious.

Immediately it seemed to Kayla that it was true, and she was embarrassed it hadn't occurred to her before. They decided that the next day they wouldn't wear any to school.

After dinner, the girls retreated to the bedroom. Pilar lay on her bed listening to the radio. Estela sat on the floor with her homework in her lap. Luz and Kayla drew tattoos on their hands with marker.

"You want to see something?" Pilar said to the younger girls. She took her wallet from her purse and removed her driver's license. "He gave it back to me today."

They crowded their heads over the license.

"It looks so fake," Estela said. "The five is a different color."

"It's good enough," Pilar said. "They want to let girls in. I just need something to flash at them. We're going tomorrow night."

"You mean you're sleeping at Amber's Friday night," Luz said.

"Isn't that what I just said?" Pilar said, smiling.

The next morning, Kayla felt a small illicit thrill as she pulled her shorts on without any underwear beneath. The roughness of denim on her naked skin and the cool early morning air coming directly against her crotch were unfamiliar and pleasant. But when she arrived at school, Luz was wearing long pants. This possibility had not occurred to her, but as soon as she saw Luz she felt herself go weak and she knew she had done a stupid thing.

They were in gym class, the whole class sitting in a circle doing the butterfly stretch, flapping their legs like wings, when the boy next to her said, "Kayla's not wearing any underwear!" and scooted away from her.

She straightened her legs but it was too late. The class went wild. The gym teacher, a balding man with teeth stained so badly they seemed to have rusted, shouted at them to settle down. He put a boy in charge of leading the rest of the stretching and walked Kayla to the nurse's office.

Her mother was called at work. The nurse suggested that she bring Kayla home for the rest of the day so the sting of embarrassment could wear off. Tammy arrived breathless. "I don't know where she could have gotten the idea from," she said with exaggerated cheeriness to the nurse.

She squeezed Kayla's hand harder and harder as they walked across the school parking lot to the car. As soon as the doors were closed Kayla burst into tears. "Don't you dare," Tammy said. "Nobody is in the mood to feel sorry for you right now."

Tammy looked straight ahead, eyes focused on the road.

"What were you thinking?" she said.

"I forgot," Kayla said.

"The hell you forgot. Nobody forgets to wear underwear."

"It's true," Kayla said quietly.

"Your whole class is going to go home and tell their moms about it. Is that what you wanted?"

She looked at her mother helplessly. All she could see was Luz looking right at her with a peaceful, bored expression as the gym teacher led her away, as if none of this had anything to do with her.

Tammy had called her father to let him know she would be dropping Kayla at home, and he was waiting with a cup of milk and a plate of glazed donut holes when they walked in the door.

"You *would* think this called for a reward," Tammy said to him. She walked to her bedroom and shut the door behind her. Kayla fell into her grandfather's arms.

She curled up on the couch with her head in his lap and he stroked her hair. "Someday you'll barely even remember," he said.

Tammy came back into the room, her car keys jingling in her hand.

"Are you a baby? Get your head out of that lap," she said. "Have you even put on underpants?"

Kayla shook her head.

"Are you waiting for some sort of further humiliation? Have you not had enough fun yet?"

Her daughter looked at her with small scared features. The resemblance was uncanny: If you could go back in time and switch Kayla for Tammy during one of her own mother's rages, Pearl might not have even noticed the change. And she supposed her daughter thought of her in this moment as she had so often thought of Pearl: a monster. She wanted to tell Kayla she was lucky. This was nothing. This was just the soft gray ashes of her own mother's combustible temper.

Her mother looked at her with eyes that dazzled with anger. She will never do this. When she has a daughter, she will never.

The summer before Kayla was to start kindergarten, Tammy went to the Juniata County public library and photocopied the rankings of America's Best Public Schools in *US News and World Report*. She circled all the schools in Pennsylvania and states that touched it. She left her father at home with a refrigerator full of labeled meals and took Kayla with her all over the breadbasket states. When they arrived in the town that would become their home, Tammy felt it at once. Downtown, red roofs shone in the gold sun. Food shops sold jewel-toned salads of baby vegetables. The stone elementary school had been built at the turn of the century. Kayla was so young—after a few years, she might not even remember that anywhere else had ever been home.

After they moved to the town later that summer, Tammy took Kayla to the school to register her. Tammy wore pinstriped pants and a white collared shirt. In the cafeteria where the registration was being held, the other mothers wore sundresses or shorts. Children raced around; a game of tag was in progress. Kayla leaned against Tammy's leg.

"You don't want to go play? You want to stand in line instead?"

Kayla nodded.

"But it will be fun," Tammy said.

"It will," said the woman in front of them. The woman smiled warmly at Tammy and then at Kayla. Kayla turned her face into Tammy's hip.

"I hope you have them paying you overtime for waiting in this," the woman said, rolling her eyes at the length of the line.

Tammy looked at her quizzically. Then she understood: the woman had mistaken her for a babysitter.

"I'm Tammy," she said, holding out her hand. "And this is Kayla. My daughter."

The woman shook Tammy's hand and introduced herself, looking at Tammy vaguely. Then she turned around to face the front of the line.

At the school's annual parent nights, the way the husbands looked at her made her sick.

"Which one is yours?" a man said to her once, as she surveyed collages hung by clothespins on a wire. He wore a suit. They all did—they had all rushed home from jobs in the city.

"That one," Tammy said, pointing to a sheet on which squares of pink and orange tissue paper had been glued. Kayla's name was written in the corner.

"I didn't know we had a Kayla in this class," he said.

"We do," she said.

Then a woman, rail thin and with a neck full of tendons, came over, her eyes twinkling with displeasure: "Oh *there* you are," she said, putting a hand on the man's shoulder. "And you've made a friend."

What did these women think she was here for? To land a rich daddy for Kayla? To seduce their husbands with her young breasts and the dark circles under her eyes?

For Kayla's sixth birthday Tammy threw a party at the town park. The day was cloudless and warm. She had sent out invitations to all of the children in Kayla's kindergarten class and reserved two picnic tables shaded by big oaks at the edge of a grassy field. She moored bouquets of balloons with rocks at the ends of the tables and set her father up in a folding chair with a disposable camera. The pastry chef at the Crane House had even baked a cake, the top of it sprinkled with the shake leftover from the gold leaf ornaments he made for dessert garnishes. When the mothers came with their children, she told them they could return in two hours. Instead they lingered. It was a nice day, they said. Besides, couldn't she use an extra hand? It was the benevolence with which they said it that indicated to her they had discussed their intention to stay amongst themselves. They didn't trust her with their children. As soon as the last child arrived, one of the mothers clapped her hands. "All right kids, into the sun, time for a game." And just like that the party was lifted out of her hands.

* * *

The next night, Kayla was at Luz's as usual, running into the concrete walls in the basement. They did not talk about what had happened yesterday. A part of Kayla knew she had been betrayed by Luz, that a truer friend would have specified that they should both wear long pants if they were going without underwear. But starting a fight with Luz would mean the loss of the entire Lopez family and the universe of their home. The power dynamic between them was clear: Luz had her sisters to fall back on and Kayla had no one. Luz could afford to push and Kayla could not afford to push back.

Besides, she did not want to miss tonight. Pilar and her girl-friends were driving down to the eighteen and over clubs in White Plains. Pilar had already cleared a sleepover at her new friend Am-ber's house with her parents. The plan was to stay out until the clubs closed at two, then crash at her friend Maria's because Maria's parents both worked night shifts and wouldn't be home to notice how late the girls came in.

"Who's Amber?" Manuel said as Pilar waited for her ride.

"I've told you about her," Pilar said.

"She does gymnastics," Luz said.

"Her boyfriend's on the soccer team," Kayla said, pleased with the lie.

Pilar returned home at nine the next morning, just in time to put on fresh makeup, throw on a lavender dress and cardigan and pile into the minivan with the rest of them for the drive to church.

By the time the priest started in on the sermon, Luz had run out of patience.

"How was Amber's house?" she whispered.

"Like a night is supposed to be," Pilar said. "Like I'm done doing anything else."

After church, the girls took cold tamales up to the bedroom. Pilar pulled off her dress, revealing a lacy yellow bra and panties. "Get me out of this!" she said, unclipping the bra and flinging it across the room. "*¡Mira!*" she said, pulling up her breasts. Beneath them, where the underwire had been, were two tender red arcs. "I danced myself raw," she said. She lay down on her bed, settled into it as if into a meadow in a dream.

"Tell us about the boys," Luz said.

"What boys? These were men."

"They're all under twenty-one, or they'd go to a real club that doesn't let high school girls in," Estela said.

Pilar shook her head in frustration. "The girls are all under twenty-one. A lot of the men are older."

"That's messed up," Estela said.

"Don't worry, Stelbell. I'm sure when you're in high school you'll never go to such a messed up club," Luz said.

"I won't need to. I'll have a boyfriend."

"You'll have a boyfriend like she's got a best friend named Amber."

"Shut up, you two," Pilar said. "Some of us need our rest."

From then on, every Saturday night Pilar told her parents she was sleeping at Amber's house, and every Sunday she threw a dress over her lingerie and came to church. She danced so long her legs continued to feel like they were moving all through church. If she'd kissed a man for a long time, her tongue kept feeling like it was moving, too, the whole of her body rocking and quivering like coming off of a boat onto dry land.

She met DeMarcus Moore on her fourth trip to the clubs. He was from Yonkers and was working at his cousin's garage while taking classes towards his real estate license. At the end of the night he wrote his phone number on the underside of her wrist. He kissed her neck and told her he would need to see her again.

"It's all smudged. You can't even read it," Estela said when Pilar showed the girls her wrist the next morning.

"Nine one four one nine three nine," Pilar said, dreamily.

"They'll kill you," Estela said. She meant their parents and Manuel. A Hispanic boy, good, fine. A white boy, so long as he was Catholic, even better. But a black boy could be Jesus's own altar boy and Pilar wouldn't be allowed to date him.

"Only if they know," Pilar said. "Swear."

They swore.

After that Pilar wasn't going to the clubs to tease as many men as possible. She was going to be with DeMarcus. She told the girls he moved slow, like a gentleman. He didn't even slip his tongue into her mouth until the third time they saw each other. When DeMarcus's friends found them locked together on a chair in a dark corner, they asked him what had taken him so long. "In case you didn't notice, this is a lady," he said.

On weekday afternoons, she called him from the payphone at school to tell him how much she missed him. Two months after they first met, he pulled her out of the line on the sidewalk in front of the club. "I'm tired of dancing," he said. "And my ma's not home."

He spread a blanket on the roof of his apartment building.

"The view was so romantic," she told the girls.

"You were in Yonkers," Estela pointed out.

A week later, Pilar pulled a little red box from her purse. Inside was a crystal charm of an angel wing on a silver chain. She put the necklace on. The tiny crystals threw bursts of rainbows onto the white bedroom walls, and Pilar tilted her chest back and forth so the rainbows danced. "I think I'm in love," she said. She looked at the rainbows as if this feeling of love were located there, in the radiance cast by his gift.

Kayla could no longer pretend not to stare. Pilar had been blinding just lazing around after a boring party in town. Pilar enshrined in the light of forbidden love was something else altogether. Kayla got his strange name stuck in her head like a song. DeMarcus DeMarcus DeMarcus.

"Where did you get that?" Manuel asked Pilar one day, pointing at the necklace.

"I bought it," she said. "Amber and I got matching ones."

"You're getting tight with this gringa."

"Luz has a white best friend. Why can't I?"

Kayla felt warm with pride. Her position as steward of Pilar's secret injected an energized quality into her days. At night she imagined she'd been injured in some brave act to protect the secret from Manuel. Pilar and DeMarcus nursed her to health in a cabin surrounded by tall pines. Pilar brushed her hair. DeMarcus spooned broth between her lips. He put his smooth dark palm against her cheek.

On the drive home from the Lopez's one Sunday, Kayla asked Tammy what she would think if Kayla fell in love with a black man.

"Why? You haven't actually found one in this town, have you?" Tammy said, laughing. She had just come from her weekly visit to Miami Tan and she was feeling good. The twelve minutes she spent surrounded by the hot white lights of a tanning bed, in the dry warmth that reminded her of how a desert might feel, maybe in Southern California, were her favorite part of the week. She didn't even like the color it turned her anymore. She knew the orange cast of her skin looked harsh and artificial. It was the peace of those minutes she returned for, and would return for every Sunday of her life until she was forty-one and a dentist, of all people, told her she had better get the mole on her shoulder checked.

It was a Saturday night in mid-June. Kayla lay awake. She heard Estela's soft snores, Luz's dream-fueled murmurings, and a chorus of frogsong floating in from the swamp. A car came up the driveway, and then she heard doors slam and voices growing louder as they approached the house. She recognized them immediately as belonging to Pilar and Manuel. "What's happening?" said Luz, who had been roused by the noise. "What's she doing back?" Estela whispered.

The front door was thrown open and they heard Pilar yell. The girls raced down the stairs. Pilar struggled against Manuel but he held her tightly against him. On his white T-shirt, starbursts of red shone brightly. Against Pilar's skin were stains of darker red.

Mr. and Mrs. Lopez came down the hall from their bedroom. When Mrs. Lopez saw the blood she bent over and emitted a low, lowing sound.

"Estela. Luz. *Ven arriba,*" Mr. Lopez said quietly.

The girls didn't move.

"*¡Ya!*" Mrs. Lopez said.

From the bedroom they listened to the shouting below. It was like being inside of a dream: the vividness obscured things rather than clarified them. Kayla heard a slap and a little cry from Pilar, then another slap and a grunt from Manuel, and knew it must be Mr. Lopez delivering them.

"What happened? Is it his blood or hers?" Kayla whispered to Luz.

"It's DeMarcus's. Manuel followed her and found her with him."

Mrs. Lopez's heavy steps came up the stairs. She stood in the doorway of the bedroom with the telephone in her hand. "Kayla, you call mama," she said. "She come take you home."

* * *

Luz and Estela were not in school on Monday. That afternoon Kayla called Luz's house over and over. Nobody answered. When Luz wasn't in school again the day after that, their teacher asked Kayla if she was sick. Kayla shook her head. When four days passed and neither Luz nor Estela had shown up at school, Kayla was called to the school counselor's office. The woman explained that she wanted to talk to her to see if she knew anything that might help her friends.

What did she know? Who could she help? She knew that Pilar had been in love with a black man she met at a club and that four days ago Manuel had come home covered in his blood. She knew the man was DeMarcus Moore from Yonkers. She knew he had given Pilar a crystal necklace, and that it was her dream to be given such a gift by a man someday.

She was sent back to class, but later that afternoon a woman from the front office knocked on the classroom door and asked for her. The woman led her back down the hall to the counselor's office. Her mother was there, waiting for her. "I thought I'd take you home a little early today," Tammy said. "There are some things I want to tell you about."

On the drive home, Tammy was quiet for the first few minutes. Kayla pressed her face to the window and watched the lush foliage of early summer flutter by.

"Your friend's family left town," Tammy said. "They were illegal."

"Illegal?"

"It means they're not supposed to be here. They snuck into the country without permission. Your counselor got in touch with the kid your friend's sister was seeing. He said he thought his friends drove up and threatened your friend's family after what her brother did."

"Where did they go?" she said.

"Who knows? Another town. Somewhere they can get work."

Kayla nodded. Tammy reached over and tousled her hair roughly.

"Oh, they'll be fine," Tammy said. "They probably do this every few years. Your friend and her sisters are probably used to it by now."

Luz had told Kayla the names of places they had lived, yet somehow these names had made Kayla think only of things Luz had seen that she hadn't: cacti, the City of Angels, the Pacific. She had not connected these names with the frequent departures they implied. She had not made the connection and Luz had never summoned it. But Luz had known. And when she waited with Kayla on the front steps for Tammy to pick her up on that final night, she must have suspected that they were seeing each other for the last time. She had said nothing. She had issued no warning and no declaration of enduring friendship or of love.

"Maybe she'll write you a letter," her grandfather said when they got home.

"That's a help, Dad, get her hoping for that," Tammy said.

Kayla knew her mother was right. There would be no letter.

"You know, I always thought they were illegal," Tammy said.

Kayla felt everything she had lost with the departure of the Lopez family converge upon her mother's words as upon the blade of a knife. The months of summer stretched before her, endless and humid and lonely. It was her mother's fault. She could not explain why, or how, but it had something to do with these words, as if when she spoke them she had retroactively set everything in motion, and taken everything away.

Right after Tammy's mother left, her father had sent Tammy away to the country for a week to stay with the family of an Amish man who had given him seasonal work as a picker a few times. It was the height of summer. The family's five children brought Tammy around on their daily chores. She pulled a warm egg out from under a chicken, squeezed the rough teat of a cow, and ran out before supper to the dooryard garden for green beans. In the mornings, the eldest daughter worked Tammy's hair gently into twin French braids, and every night Tammy awaited the moment when the sisters took off their white caps and unpinned their hair, revealing the hidden wonder of its length. They had no television; at night they sat together and sang songs Tammy didn't know. One in particular she loved, a German hymn she sang to herself for years after out of fear of forgetting it, until she finally did.

It was a capsule of time existing apart from the rest of her life: the kitchen table that was a thick velvety slab of wood, the sweet flutter of Amens after grace, and the mysterious wild flavor of deer meat. It was all so wonderful, and how badly she wished she had been born into a family like this. Yet all week she was rocked by feelings of lone-liness, discomfort, and yearning she could not explain.

When her father brought her home, she entered the dark house and saw that he had neither washed a dish nor put a single thing away all week. The disorder landed on her with the soothing relief of a familiar hand, and she realized that what she had felt at the Amish family's house was nothing more than simple homesickness. There it was, then, the intractable problem of her life: No matter what she did, all of her best efforts to remake her life would always be a little bit spoiled, because the best things would never feel like home.

The tree was an oak behind the blue dumpster at the far edge of the sushi restaurant's gravel lot. It had a disorganized crown of branches—the limbs twisted as if engaged in a dull struggle against each other.

Kayla climbed to a branch six feet off the ground. The smell of rot-ting fish rose from the dumpster. Below her was a patch of packed dirt just large enough for a girl. It was the first day of summer va-cation. The sky was glacial blue but the sun was hot, and seemed to bear down from just above her shoulder.

Through the tiny window that looked out onto the lot, Tammy watched her daughter. Kayla's legs were so skinny they glinted in and out of view—sometimes you just had to believe they were there be-cause of her big white sneakers and her bright yellow shorts. Tammy was pleased when Kayla hoisted herself up into the tree. She so rarely saw her daughter evince signs of a spirited, courageous self. Tammy worried she had failed her in this way: She had managed to raise a good daughter, but had been too tired, stretched too thin, to culti-vate an animating spark. Sometimes when Tammy came home from work and found Kayla and her grandfather asleep against each other on the couch with the television on low, she worried Kayla secretly wished to be her grandfather's little old wife, the bulk of life gotten over with already, the quiet glide to the finish all that remained.

She watched Kayla stand up on the branch, her left arm anchored to the trunk. Kayla leaned forward and peered down at the ground below her. She began to lift her hand away from the trunk.

"Kayla!" Tammy shouted through the window.

Kayla, who in her head had already been falling like a dream, her bent arm gunning for the packed dirt, looked across the lot and saw her mother's face in the window. She put her hand back on the trunk.

Tammy was beneath the tree before Kayla even reached the ground. She scooped her daughter into her arms and held her so firmly against her body that it was painful for them both, parts of each of them poking and jabbing at the other.

"What were you thinking?" she said, squeezing Kayla tighter. "For fuck's sake why did you want to do a thing like that?"

Kayla didn't know what she could say.

"Why?"

It was many years later, and Kayla was the age Tammy had been then, before she thought of what she should have said to her mother. With Luz, she had longed for the accessories of injury—casts, slings, the envy of classmates—but had been too afraid of the pain to let anything happen. Up in the tree it was the pain itself she wanted. She wanted to feel the loss of the Lopez family in her bones, to alchemize all that had happened into a suffering whose parameters were com- pletely knowable. She wanted her mother to carry her in her arms to the emergency room feeling guilty and neglectful. Most of all, though, she wanted to show her mother that she, too, could bravely endure whatever was thrown at her. She, too, could carry on.

But by then Tammy had been dead for two years. Kayla would never get to tell her why, or to say that she was sorry—all that time she had thought Tammy was nothing but her mother. She would never get to ask her how she kept her head up in that town, where everybody discounted her and nobody admired or even acknowledged all she had sacrificed, the miracles she had worked to give her daughter a chance at something better.

Vera. Pearl. Tammy. Kayla. They were a string of missed connections. Wisdom was slipping through the cracks between the generations. Essential things were not being passed on. What things? The kinds you couldn't learn from anybody else. The kind you just had to make do without.

ANDREW TONKOVICH

■

Falling

FROM *Ecotone*

THE SIR JAMES TEMPLEMAN I KNOW liked nothing better than to
instruct the groundskeepers to dig another foxhole and install into
it another atheist. We had at the plantation at the time of the "accident" 145 full-time nonbelievers enrolled in the campus's subterra-
nean residency program: skeptics, freethinkers, atheists, agnostics,
some of them scientists and some academics, and some just sad,
angry, bitter individuals who took Sir James up on his offer of free
room and board, as it were, and a generous stipend upon comple-
tion of the program, one of many grants, fellowships, and endowed
chair positions sponsored by the International Templeman Prize for
Faith in Science.

There had been only five vacancies that summer, though we at
TempleLand held every confidence that they'd soon be filled too. The
holes had since the program's inception become quite elaborate, cozy
even, each with carpeting and satellite, Wi-Fi, and hot meals delivered by our on-site service staff, island locals who live in the small
fishing village at the far end of the bay. Among the professional and
academic anti-god crowd the place had become, I was told, something of an easy prize, low-hanging fruit on the foundation and conference and grants circuit. Most of them didn't take the challenge at
all seriously, and TempleLand's complex of palm-circled foxholes was
considered by them, cynically if you ask me, a de facto artist's colony
or even a kind of writer's retreat. It was a free tropical vacation away
from the lab, classroom, or lecture hall, a respite from what must
be for these cynics the exhausting if otherwise unrewarding work of

setting good people against the divine, the miraculous, the unknow-able. And, after all, as Sir James liked to point out privately, nobody listened to or compensated them adequately for their atheism, hu-manism, or rationalism, not the secular foundations or the govern-ment—not at the rates he did anyway—nobody except a sincere old man who loved and feared his Jesus.

Still, considering we had graduated only three scholars in five years of the program, it must be conceded that this was never what you'd call a particularly successful experiment. Lacking what they called a con-trol model, the secular critics asked, how would results be measured? Faith, answered Sir James, is not of the quotidian or the calculable.

This was a problem, of course, or would have been except that the problem of calculating the unknowable, the unseeable had as far as I could tell most always worked *for* us, not against us, had worked to our advantage as believers and to the disadvantage, it seemed, of the nonbelievers, who demanded more.

Sir James liked to speculate further that, although the results of the program would be, like the divine itself, indeed difficult to quantify on the skeptics' terms, these results would nonetheless ex-ist, publicly documented or not. There would be, he was confident, deathbed conversions and secret confessions, children of our alumni baptized in private. There would be doubt and prayer, and submis-sion and redemption, that no one would ever, ever know about ex-cept, yes, our Lord and Savior. Hard hearts would be softened. For that possibility Sir James Templeman, philanthropist, was willing to spend a few million dollars of a fortune one hundred times that size, built on faith, and yes, on prudent investing in commercial real es-tate and mutual funds.

We were located on a private island in the West Indies, with guest houses, a dining room, library, landing field, swimming pool, golf course and lawn bowling, a small chapel and on-site medical support, in addition to the magnificently restored colonial mansion in which Sir James, a widower, resided. I had my own comfortable apartment in the carriage house, with a view of the sea on one side and the hills from the other. Sir James took his tea each morning in the solarium of the main residence, among his beloved prizewinning orchids, of-ten with a personal guest who was staying with us just then, a congressman, member of Parliament, college dean or chancellor, writer, minister, rabbi, lama, or mullah.

After breakfast they often toured the grounds together, Sir James and the visiting senator or journalist or clergyman, stopping occasionally to chat briefly with a subterranean-dwelling nonbeliever-in-residence working in his or her quarters. Walking with the aid of a cane, Sir James would point out a foxhole, sitting inside it a well-known prizewinner, esteemed scholar, PBS host, investigative journalist, or somebody else unable to resist what must have seemed the jackpot of free time to conduct research, read, collect no-strings-attached fellowship money—round-trip airfare from anywhere in the world included—just to show up the famous philanthropist even while, yes, the scholar humbled himself before God if also perhaps humiliating himself in the eyes of his colleagues back home. So, yes, the conversations were brief, if mostly cordial.

A residency lasted forty days, the same period Christ wrestled Satan in the desert. If the participants left early, they naturally forfeited the money. But if they completed their underground tenure, when they stepped out of their foxholes each received generous compensation and could take the opportunity to elaborate on the mystical or, as more likely occurred, exercise their God-given (as Sir James liked to remind them) right to brag that they still rejected the spirit, had found no evidence of it, and so had cheated the foundation after enduring five weeks in a luxurious burrow.

We were proud of our successes, however few. The three men who'd indeed come to embrace the divine, to find faith, were a Danish chemist, an American MBA, and an Indian hydrologist. They used their time in the foxhole to study Scripture, search their souls, and write scientific papers that affirmed a spiritual dimension in, respectively, the areas of chemistry, the free market, and the study of water movement, distribution, and quality. The title of the hydrologist's report, "Living Waters," delighted Sir James.

The three scholars had looked for and found scientific proof of the hand of the divine, and were eager to share it. Their subsequent proposals to fund research in this important work were accepted by the Templeman Science Institute in Colorado Springs, Colorado. They eventually left their home institutions and were given permanent positions, fully endowed research chairs, at the institute, and they and their work were featured on our website.

You might have heard that Sir James had plans beyond the foxholes and the universities. Yes, there were other big ideas in the works: a privately funded manned space launch, a faith-based interplanetary satellite exploration program, an all-Christian professional baseball league. Mystery may be found and experienced everywhere, Sir James always said, and the Templeman Fund helped to sponsor the search for it. I looked forward to helping him realize this dream as his secretary, his trusted confidante. But this was not to be, not after the disappearance of the atheist Dr. Simon Killacky, age forty-eight, a part-time geology instructor, speech team faculty advisor, and women's softball coach from a small community college in Orange County, California. He had been at the estate fewer than three days. An unattractive if gentle man, Killacky had been welcomed at the landing field on a Friday, provided a lei and a Bible, been driven in a golf cart to his assigned hole, and clocked in by noon, thus beginning his first day. I myself did not speak to him beyond reviewing the rules. I observed him sign our standard legal agreements, answered a few routine questions, and had no interactions with him on Saturday at all. He seemed tired, perhaps anxious, when I met him, which is what I later told the investigating authorities, who reconstructed events based on evidence found in his foxhole, which is to say very little evidence at all.

It seems Dr. Killacky ate his early evening dinner on both Friday and Saturday nights, read portions of Scripture and sections from textbooks and scientific journals (passages still marked with Post-its), made some notes, sent a handful of e-mails, called his lawyer on his cell phone, used the small bathroom facility, and then pulled the fiberglass roof over his hole and, it seems, went to sleep. Thus he passed his first two days, giving no indication of any behavior other than we anticipated.

Indeed, on the second night, the authorities concluded, he retired at about the same time, though, of course, there were no witnesses. Individual foxholes are purposely distant from one another, perhaps fifty meters apart, and neither of the two nearest residents, a black lady Marxist historian from Oakland or a botanist from Winnipeg, noticed or heard anything. In retrospect, we might have installed sensors or even surveillance cameras, but, even now, these seem an intrusion and a violation of the spirit of the wager, the contract, the premise of what was, to Sir James's mind, both a scientific laboratory and hallowed ground.

On Sunday morning at 8 a.m., the staff delivered Dr. Killacky's breakfast tray at the edge of his as-yet unopened residence. An hour later, observing the breakfast untouched, and concerned that he had not yet awakened, the server summoned the security chief, who pulled back the opaque roof to discover Dr. Killacky missing and in his place a new hole, situated in the center of the foxhole, about a meter wide. This second hole, clearly much deeper, was very dark. The circumference of this perfect circle—there is no other way to say this—was of a human torso.

All items in Killacky's accommodations remained, untouched, the laptop and Bible and his personal notebooks, the scene suggesting that the atheist had dug down a few feet for some reason and was perhaps trapped down there, or even hiding.

Alas, investigation of the hole quickly established that this was not at all the situation. Security summoned me almost immediately and, skeptical, I soon had to concede what was obvious if unbelievable: that this was a very, very deep hole, perhaps indeed bottomless, as our security chief, a local man, would insist over and over. And which would later seem to be proven.

And, yes, certain facts could not be denied even early on: absent footprints or other evidence, it seemed Killacky had to still be down there, deep down inside of the hole, however shallow or deep. Feeling foolish, if desperate, I directed the staff to secure first one ladder, then a longer ladder, then a length of stout rope. Then they tied that rope to a longer rope, weighted with a hammer of all things, the handiest object available, lowering and lowering the whole contraption until we soon ran out of line, forty, fifty, one hundred meters, neither locating Killacky nor reaching bottom, and hearing and seeing not a thing.

News of Killacky's disappearance leaked before I could notify his wife or the embassy, and soon the media arrived, the print reporters and TV people with cameras. I apologized to Sir James, who personally supervised the rescue attempt from his wheelchair, parked at the edge of the site, but he understood and agreed that we should cooperate and provide the press complete access. "We have nothing to hide," he said.

The scene soon became a familiar one, day and night, quickly developing into the "Atheist Lost in a Hole" story and the "Earth Swallows up Nonbeliever," with the twenty-four-hour cable stations sending their celebrity anchors and investigative reporters, these familiar on-camera personalities standing on the lawn wearing khakis and guayaberas, attempting to answer for their viewers the question of how this was possible and who Killacky was and, of course, where we were and what the Institute's work was. They reminded viewers and listeners and readers of Sir James's remarkable biography, the life story of a southern-born gentleman, Rhodes scholar, lifetime Presbyterian knighted by the Queen of England, who had renounced his US citizenship and moved to the island for tax reasons and to promote the investigation of the universal and divine, to advance the consideration of the holy as part of a new model of scientific inquiry.

Soon we at the compound were working with the national police and the Red Cross, and had contracted an outfit to assemble heavy equipment toward facilitating Killacky's rescue: a crane—an industrial block and tackle pulley really—generator, lights, and seismic listening devices. Ten hours went by, then nightfall. Soon it had been twenty-four hours, when arrived the second tragedy.

An over-eager rescue dog put to work sniffing for Killacky's scent jumped into the hole, or fell, and soon Jo-Jo, a German shepherd from Wyoming, became the second subject of the search and rescue operation, her photograph appearing below Killacky's on the television screen and in the newspapers.

This continued for some days, all of it of course profoundly disrupting life and study in TempleLand, not to mention the nearby village, so that we were soon forced to send the other resident scholars home. I chartered a small jet and handed them envelopes as they departed, a check for each, thanking them for their good faith effort and inviting them to visit again. Yes, I assured them, they would receive credit for days in their hole so far and could pick up at a time convenient to them. Each expressed their various concerns for Killacky, some angrily, insisting that he had been kidnapped, even murdered, most likely by us, by me or by Sir John, speculating, as these scientists will, that what now appeared to be a seemingly perfect, symmetrically-bored vertical chasm, a tunnel really, must certainly have been there before Killacky had been installed in foxhole number 139.

As for Killacky, facts soon emerged painting an alternately gratifying and unflattering portrait, and pointing to motives that led to jokes about his handiness with a shovel or his need to disappear, and fast. Yet the notes and diagrams, scribblings and mathematical equations left in his hole suggested that his reason for being at TempleLand went well beyond the grant. There were calculations and a timeline, and rough sketches, all of which seemed to point to serious scholarship regarding the actual age of the planet and examining the record of a pre-scientific history which likely corresponded to that story outlined in, yes, holy texts.

But, disappointingly, it also emerged that Dr. Killacky had needed cash to pay off a student blackmailing him after he had done things to her in his office, nasty and wrong things that she'd memorialized on her cell phone's camera feature, and that she'd threatened to share with his wife and then with the world, to spin on her website, like straw into gold. In my immediate post-disappearance discussions with Sir James, we agreed that Dr. Killacky perhaps had not been the very best choice among applicants and that the staff and I might have vetted him more thoroughly. Sir James was, naturally, disappointed, but he was never angry, and I value even now that moment when he took me aside one afternoon and explained that God worked in mysterious ways and that we might be witnesses to a phenomenon right here on the grounds that was well beyond the reckoning of mere man, and that Killacky himself was perhaps playing a role important to the moment, which might be a kind of revelation—about what he could only speculate, but would not—a revelation that would no doubt point further to the connectedness of spirit and science.

"And so," he promised, "ultimately contribute to the success of our endeavors here."

Killacky's wife, Mrs. Judith Killacky of Rancho Santa Margarita in Orange County, felt otherwise. She arrived on a special flight we chartered. Mrs. Killacky resembled a well-known blonde movie actress who'd once been young and sexy but who now, middle-aged and fat, appeared on late-night television commercials pleading on behalf of starving and dying African children.

She'd recently filed for divorce and had not even known her missing soon-to-be ex-husband was staying with us at TempleLand. Mrs. Killacky—"Jude" she called herself—was of little use to the authorities, had long suspected her husband's infidelity, and so was the subject of plenty of media attention. There were the couple's small children at home, four of them, and a suspiciously large life insurance policy, all of these reliably tawdry details assembled to provoke curiosity and inspire contempt. Even more attention was paid, most of it speculation, to those available details of Dr. Killacky's work in the area of the geological record of the earth and, surprisingly, the New Testament stories of the birth of Jesus of Nazareth. This was an unexpected development, at least to me, but Sir James seemed unsurprised, and was encouraged. "The direction of Dr. Killacky's scientific work," he said, "will redeem him, and will vindicate our own."

Meanwhile, after just two weeks, the young woman student in possession of the sex video shared it with a British tabloid, which printed stills, for which she was compensated, it was widely believed, quite generously. Then she herself disappeared, on the same day the whole thing appeared on a porn site online.

After four full weeks of searching and waiting, after using sonar and radar, after taking X-rays and employing a psychic and bringing in medical forensics experts from around the world, after lowering a camera and losing not one but two mini robotic units, we still had not found the actual bottom of the hole, or established the existence of a bottom, or located either Killacky or the dog. Neither had any evidence at all been discovered of either, not in the hole or on the steep walls of the chasm or anywhere else. There was no shovel, no disturbed earth. There were no footprints.

Bit by bit the press corps abandoned the story and left the island. Embarrassed, frustrated, the authorities seemed to give up too, the local police and military, Interpol, the FBI, the army of private investigators we'd hired, all of them packing up, defeated, and likely convinced that, in the absence of evidence to the contrary, TempleLand, Sir James and I, somebody on the plantation, Killacky himself, had somehow contrived to make him disappear, perhaps for the insurance money, or arranged a hoax.

With the departure of the media and the police, the area around the hole was cordoned off, a round-the-clock pair of guards posted, and a single klieg light left to illuminate the site at night.

We at TempleLand held a small commemorative service in the chapel, where Sir James himself paid tribute to the lost man, offering generously that he believed in his own true heart that Dr. Simon Killacky might indeed have become number four on our roster of scholar converts, and might yet. Our Lazarus, Sir James called Killacky, someday to be revived, resurrected, and reborn.

He further lamented the cruel attacks on poor Dr. Killacky, who had been revealed not only, it seemed, as a philanderer and sexual predator, but as a poor scholar too, having done little research or writing, it turned out, in his field prior to his brief stay with us. The newspapers reported that he'd actually published only one paper, not in a juried scientific journal, and had in fact never completed his doctoral work, so that he was not a PhD after all. None of this mattered to us, said Sir James, or to an island, a nation, a world that cared so deeply for his journey, ongoing, or to those who loved him, and certainly not to the Creator who directed the lives of us all.

The miraculous had occurred, Sir James insisted, although we had at first not seen it, not recognized it, this marvel, not at all an "accident," he assured us, no, not in the mechanistic way of our secular world. The mystery would still teach the world somehow. God had chosen His servant Simon, as he'd chosen Saul and Simon Peter, on whose name and shoulders He had once built his own church, the rock on whom was anchored the faith of millions. That Killacky was, he pointed out, a teacher whose subject was the history of rocks, was further promise and assurance of His plan.

Geologists and seismologists, geophysicists and earth scientists of all stripe responded predictably to Sir James's remarks and to his interview on 60 Minutes with anger, skepticism, speculation, with theories and more questions, suggesting the unlikelihood of an anomalous fissure. They pointed to what they called the "obviously sculpted" shape of the hole, its perfect, precise route straight down, the centerline of a cylindrical crevasse, the smoothness of the walls.

They mocked us, and others, suggesting that maybe, yes, something or someone had reached up from the earth's center, maybe a giant or demon with a machine or device as yet unbuilt had drilled up to the surface. This image appeared in an editorial cartoon, as did many others, ridiculous and yet tapping into something exciting and appealing, which Sir James chose to celebrate.

Indeed, there was always an artist's rendering, a sketch or a digitally assembled cutaway of the earth, on television or printed alongside the newspaper articles. There was an illustration of the shaft with Killacky and Jo-Jo falling, and mathematical equations of velocity, speculating how long it would have taken them to fall, minutes or hours or days. There was the color-coded journey, always with a tiny cartoon dog and cartoon man, through the crust to the upper mantle, then the outer core, and finally to the inner core where the man and the dog would reach the impossible heat and be melted, as if to engage the problem and the premise, and the impossibility of each at the same time.

There were interviews and commentaries by oil-drilling experts and spelunkers, hydrologists—including our own born-again prizewinner—survivors of underground and underwater falls and cave-ins. The constant printing and airing of that image, of the tiny man in free fall and the faithful dog above him, must have caused many, as it did me, to see them as eternally falling, and to understand falling as a journey and not an end, and to begin to appreciate that journey as somehow infinite despite, of course, being reminded, over and over, that science was working hard to find an ending—in their deaths.

But not Sir James, who insisted on the infinite. He offered that this was all God's plan, for He has a plan for us all. For He is not done with us here, and neither is His work complete. He is in control, He has used His servant Dr. Killacky, and He will reveal in His time the meaning and purpose of this phenomenon, this miraculous moment, this scientific experiment, this bringing together of the nations, of his disciples, to witness the power, glory, love, and caring of a Creator who can do whatever pleases Him. Remember, said Sir James, that He has counted the sparrows and numbered the hairs on our heads and created this very world, seen and unseen, so that our job, our duty, is to marvel and to wait for Him to further make real a revelation.

"Dr. Killacky is with God, and with us, somewhere," offered Sir James. "As is Jo-Jo. Because God is everywhere, on the earth and inside it as well." And that place, he insisted, is forever, is infinite.

Yet soon Sir James was forced to direct me to terminate the foxhole program altogether, in part on orders from the authorities, and to have the remaining holes filled in. I sent letters to those scholars whose research we'd been forced to interrupt, apologizing again and including a second check and the requisite legal paperwork removing from TempleLand any further liability or responsibility.

The two security guards remained, even as the holes were filled in, every landscaped berm razed and squares of new grass laid in. Life as we'd known it resumed, if tentatively, with Sir James steadfast and confident, even happy. This is the Sir James I knew, who again greeted with smiles and a wave those remaining on the grounds. The disciples, we called them, those faithful hundreds who'd arrived at the site almost immediately and who still camped on the perimeter. They cooked meals on small camp stoves and built jolly fires at night, sang and prayed and held vigil. Most seemed to have chosen to wear white, often with a skein of gauze wrapped around their heads. They decorated the great lawn with crosses, candles, cans of dog food.

The earth had swallowed up a sinner, some said. He was testing a man, and mankind. Like Jonah in the belly of the whale, or Daniel in the lion's den. Some argued that a prophet, heretofore unknown, unrecognized, had been taken from us. Either way, it was a test. God had expressed His will and would not be mocked or questioned, would only be worshipped. The disciples were there to witness the awesome power when Dr. Killacky, God's servant, reappeared or that awesome if immeasurable authority revealed.

It was a surprise then even to me, a challenge to my own understanding of His power and requirement of faith, when the first disciple leapt into the hole and the others quickly followed her. Apparently nobody else had expected this either, stupid in retrospect, a failing, a misunderstanding for which I blame myself.

The woman who jumped did not even bother to distract the two guards, who sat eating their suppers at sunset just a few meters from the edge of the short wall around the hole and the yellow warning tape. Eating plates of red beans and white rice, yams, roast pork, and plantains, they observed her approaching from the darkness, walking into the splay of the artificial white light, thinking perhaps that she might be heading to the portable facilities we'd organized or adding another candle to the hundreds of votive lights that flickered and waned, the smell of their wax and the heat of their flames suggesting an outdoor cathedral under the palms.

They continued eating as she approached and, as they later reported, heard only the gentlest ruffle of air in between forkfuls of dinner. They looked up, surprised to see the tape broken. A note lay on the ground, its message written in bold, elegant, and clearly female handwriting on a sheet of blue-lined notebook paper: "Follow me." And the small space that had briefly been occupied—by a young woman, was all they could say, veiled, slight—was left a vacuum now somehow larger than anything that surrounded it, the lawn, the palms, and the night itself.

These were local men, island men, untrained, unarmed. They called out for help, then screamed into their walkie-talkies. One ran to the main house to summon Sir James and me, leaving the other guard alone at the hole. The man could offer little resistance when the rest of them, the dozen other devotees who'd hid at the perimeter of the light until they'd seen Sister Alpha, as she'd called herself, leap into the hole, then rushed forward themselves, running together past the lone guard and disappearing one after the other, one onto another, down the redemptive oblivion of faith and mystery, a narrow, deep hole in the ground wherein, it was assumed, they meant to find not only evidence of their faith but perhaps, in their action, faith itself.

And so the police and the news crews returned. A handwriting expert quickly confirmed the woman's identity not as an island local but as Sarah Melissa Jean Hoolihan, age twenty, Killacky's former community college student who'd gone missing after selling the dirty photographs and the video taken on her cell phone.

Her parents were flown to the island and spent some days with us, living in a guest cottage adjacent to the house in which Mrs. Killacky stayed. They were longtime practitioners of Transcendental Meditation and each morning and evening sat cross-legged near the hole for fifteen minutes, humming and being still. They otherwise cooperated with the authorities, showed little anger toward us or toward

Killacky, and were concerned that their daughter, a "good girl," a "shy girl," had somehow inspired or convinced others to jump.

The Hoolihans were still there a week later when the authorities, confounded again after renewing and then abandoning the exploration of the hole, accepted Sir James's proposal to construct a viewing platform and a small amphitheater, with a thick Plexiglas barrier around the hole. Men in hard hats poured cement pilings and trimmed lumber, built steps and a turnstile.

It was important, Sir James insisted, that the hole itself be left open. "They might be anywhere. They might be here, with us even now."

We sat together in the rose garden, he in his wheelchair. I had been taking Paxil for a week, prescribed by Sir James's own personal physician, and yet I was still not sleeping well. I was not myself. My own faith, in the divine, in the unknowable, in Sir James, had been shaken, I don't mind telling you, and there was also the matter of a civil suit filed against us by Judith Killacky and her four orphaned children, who appeared every morning at breakfast but otherwise stayed in her quarters.

Sir James tried to comfort, to reassure me. "These children of God," he reminded me, "they also are scientists in their way. They are astronauts, explorers. Of another realm perhaps, but on an adventure we can only dream of, and envy." Sir James, aged eighty, did not hesitate. His hands did not tremble. He spoke softly but firmly: "I only wish that I could join them."

"Do you really, sir?" I asked. "Do you?"

He looked at me, this man of faith, his pale blue eyes searching my face. And where I had always imagined he'd found something deep, had encouraged and affirmed it in me, his mouthpiece, his servant, his friend and fellow worshipper, I saw that now he looked quickly away. I was, I felt, no longer the receptive pool, the reflection, the loving gaze. And, not finding in me the reciprocity of understanding and faith and wisdom, the pool into which this great man-prophet might drop a pebble of his knowledge, I saw that he glanced away, out the window, and I knew then that I risked losing him.

And so I got up from the roses and left him there in the garden and walked slowly but deliberately in the direction of whatever he might have been seeing, summoning, that element no one had proven, the dimension unseen, the realm into which I had invited myself to dwell, had been invited by Sir James, a place that for me had been as real as the plantation, the sea, the orchids in the solarium, the roses in the garden, the palms, the very stars above. Needing to know myself whether I might be reclaimed, whether I could live there again and always, I walked across the lawn, greeted the two guards and a dozen workers in boots and hard hats, passed under the frame of the platform under construction, considered not one moment further that I would do this, removed the plastic tarpaulin that covered the hole, and leapt.

I fell and fell and fell, and must also, in my falling, have fallen asleep. I had no sense of time, which was to me a relief, and I found it easy enough to hold my arms tightly at my sides so as not to limit my progress or hurt myself. I had time to think, to remember. As a child I was taken to Disneyland, not far from Professor Killacky's former home, and to a ride sponsored by the Monsanto Corporation in which visitors to the Magic Kingdom entered what appeared to be a giant microscope, ostensibly to be shrunken to microscopic size in order to visit the internal workings of the human body, the molecules and cells, or to explore the atom, the universe, I could not recall exactly now. Such, however, was my vision of myself descending, as of a grown man reduced to the size of a small one or a child, even as it seemed to me the diameter of the hole itself also narrowed, gradually.

This could have taken days, this journey, yet my vision, in direct opposite proportion to my shrinking size, only broadened as I shrank and the tunnel shrank. And so I saw all around me a giant tableau of history, time, faith, layers and layers of geological strata corresponding, yes, directly and precisely to the story of our Creator's handiwork, the destruction, the birth, just as the missing scientist had explained in his paper and no doubt further detailed in his notes for those who knew how to read them.

I was Jonah, and then Daniel. I was Jacob, climbing down a ladder. As I fell I knew it was also on top of, above, and behind Dr. Killacky and the dog Jo-Jo, that I was borne on the tailwind of Sister Alpha and the twelve other disciples, even, lo, on the bodies and spirits of multitudes. I seemed not to be falling faster. My body would, I knew, reach something called free fall, a point where I would not drop any faster, but I was not sure if this was true for falling down holes, or of how gravity worked miles and miles under TempleLand and the island. I had entered the portal to another world, if not yet entered that world itself, by looking into Sir James's wise, ancient eyes and finding nothing of myself left. I needed to be here, for him as much as for myself.

I woke after some time to darkness and coolness, reached out gingerly to touch the slick, wet walls of the tunnel, brushing them barely with my fingertips, at a speed of what felt sometimes fast, but sometimes so slow I might not be falling at all. Proximity to what must have been the earth's core began to warm the tunnel. It was dark there, but not as dark as you might imagine.

And who, I wondered as I fell, is anyone to judge me, or science, or Sir James? I heard his voice as I fell, and felt relief, peace. I wondered now what everyone, except Sir James, had been so scared of. I felt more alive than I had ever been, or felt, in my life up above. Still, I expected only more, and I looked forward to reaching the end.

I heard my own voice. There was no echo here. There was no beginning after awhile, not that I could recall, not to me and not to my journey. There was no end, not to believing, not to faith, not yet anyway, and I fell, fell, fell confidently, which is a feeling unwelcome to those on the surface, frightening, but which I assure you was the anticipation and excitement of arrival. "Remember this always," was all I thought, spoke, heard, all three of them the same expression.

And when I woke, here I was in, yes, this small chamber in the very center of the planet. I had indeed become smaller, and so fit perfectly with the others, and I took my place standing in the crèche. The scene was arranged as it should have been, with Dr. Simon Killacky standing on one side, wearing a beard and robe and carrying a staff, Sister Alpha sitting in her blue gown, and Jo-Jo guarding the manger.

She smiled at me, this young and beautiful Sarah Hoolihan, and then beckoned, and the humiliating scenes of her on the video and in the photographs were no more. I approached, welcoming her invitation, and peered inside the humble cradle to adore the infant and to feel, at last, the complete joy and assurance of the sight of him, here, in the world at last, that world rediscovered by a man of science and a man of faith and, lo, there he was, Sir James, a tiny baby at rest in swaddling clothes, laid in the warm, dry straw. Around us knelt and prayed the rest of the disciples wearing their purest white, with candles burning eternally around us, the grotto illuminated by the tiny flames as well as by the bright blue eyes of the child.

And after I had adored him, and been found again in those strong and gentle eyes, I returned to my own station, where I am now, kneeling forever and eternally, together with the others here in the enduring and real world where science and hydrology will never, ever find us and cannot deny us, no, not hidden deep in the earth's core.

MADHURI VIJAY

■

Lorry Raja

FROM *Narrative Magazine*

WHAT HAPPENED was that my older brother, Siju, got a job as a lorry driver at the mine and started acting like a big shot. He stopped playing with Munna the way he used to, tossing him into the air like a sack of sand, making him sputter with laughter. When Amma asked him anything, he would give her a pitying look and not answer. He stopped speaking to his girlfriend, Manju, altogether. He taunted me about playing in the mud, as he called it, breaking chunks of iron ore with my hammer. With Appa especially he was reckless, not bothering to conceal his disdain, until he said something about *failed drivers who are only good for digging and drinking,* and Appa wrestled him to the ground and forced him to eat a handful of the red, iron-rich earth, shouting that this was our living now and he should bloody learn to respect it. Siju complained to the mine's labor officer, Mr. Subbu, but Mr. Subbu dismissed it as a domestic matter and refused to interfere. After that, Siju maintained a glowering silence in Appa's presence. When Appa wasn't around, Siju sneered at our tent, a swatch of blue plastic stretched over a bamboo skeleton. Never mind that he was being paid half a regular driver's salary by the owner of the lorry, a *paan*-chewing Andhra fellow called Rajappa, because Siju was only fourteen and could not bargain for more.

Never mind that Rajappa's lorry permit was fake, a flimsy transparent chit of paper with no expiry date and half the words illegible, which meant that Siju was allowed to transport the ore only to the railway station in Hospet and not, like the other drivers, all the way to port cities like Mangalore and Chennai, where he'd run the risk of arrest by border authorities. Never mind that the mine's lorry cleaners, most of whom were boys my age, called him Lorry Raja behind his back and imitated his high-stepping walk. None of it seemed to matter to him. And, as little as I wanted to admit it, he *was* a raja in the cab of that lorry, and moreover he looked it. His hair was thick and black, and a long tuft descended at the back of his neck, like a crow's glossy tail feathers. His nose was straight, and his eyeballs were untouched by yellow. His teeth remained white in spite of breathing the iron-laden air. He seemed, when he was in the cab of that lorry, like someone impossible and important, someone I didn't know at all.

The ore went to the port cities, and then it went onto ships the size of buildings. I hadn't seen them, but the labor officer, Mr. Subbu, had told us about them. He said the ships crossed the ocean, and the journey took weeks. The ships went to Australia and Japan, but mostly they went to China. They were building a stadium in China for something called the Lympic Games. Mr. Subbu explained that the Lympic Games were like the World Cup, except for all sports instead of just cricket. Swimming, tennis, shooting, running. If you won you got a gold medal, Mr. Subbu said. India had won a gold medal in boxing the last time the games were held.

The stadium in China would be round like a cricket stadium, except ten times bigger. Mr. Subbu spread his arms out wide when he said this, and we could see patches of sweat under the arms of his nice ironed shirt.

The whole world worked in the mines. At least that is what it seemed like then. There was a drought in Karnataka and neighboring Andhra Pradesh, and things were so bad people were starting to eye the mangy street dogs. Our neighbor poured kerosene on himself and three daughters and lit them ablaze; his wife burned her face but escaped. Then came the news of the mines, hundreds of them opening in Bellary, needing workers. And people went. It seemed to happen overnight. They asked their brothers-in-law or their uncles to look after their plots and their houses, or simply sold them. They pulled their children out of school. Whole villages were suddenly abandoned, cropless fields left to wither. Families waited near bus depots plastered with faded film signs, carrying big bundles stuffed with steel pots and plastic shoes and flimsy clothes. The buses were so full they tilted to one side. There wasn't enough space for everyone. The people who were left behind tried running alongside the buses, and some of the more foolish ones tried to jump in as the bus was moving. They would invariably fall, lie in the dust for a while, staring up at the rainless sky. Then they would get up, brush off their clothes, and go back to wait for the next bus. For months my family watched this happen. We didn't worry, not at first. Appa had a job as a driver for a subinspector of the Raichur Thermal Power Plant, and we thought we were fine. Then there was the accident, and Appa lost the job. He spent the next few weeks at the rum shop, coming home long enough to belt me or my brother Siju or Amma. After that was over he cried for a long time. Then he announced that we were going to work in the mines. All of us. Siju, who was in the seventh standard at the time, tried to protest, but Appa twisted a bruise into his arm and Siju stopped complaining. I was in the fifth standard, and to me it seemed like a grand adventure. Amma said nothing. She was pregnant with Munna then, and her feet had swollen to the size of papayas. She hobbled into the hut to pack our things.

Within a week, we squeezed onto a bus that was leaking black droplets of oil from its heavy bottom, and Appa bought us each a newspaper cone of hot peanuts for the journey. I flicked the burnt peanuts into my mouth and watched as the land slowly got dryer and redder, until the buildings in the huddled villages we passed were red too, and so was the bark of the trees, and so were the fingers of the ticket collector who checked the stub in Appa's hand and said, "Next stop." We lurched into a teeming bus station with a cracked floor, and I asked Appa why the ground was red, and he told me this was because of the iron in it. While Appa was busy asking directions to the nearest mine that was hiring, and Amma was searching in her blouse for money to buy a packet of Tiger biscuits and a bottle of 7Up for our lunch, Siju came up to me and whispered that, really, the ground was red because there was blood in it, seeping up to the surface from the miners' bodies buried underneath. For months I believed him, and every step I took was in fear, bracing for the sticky wetness of blood, the crunch of bone, the squelch of an organ. When

I realized the truth I tried to hit him, but he held my wrists so hard they hurt, and he bared his teeth close to my face, laughing.

That afternoon, just about a year after we had come to the mine, I was working an open pit beside the highway, along with a few other children and a handful of women. I squatted by the edge of the road, close enough that the warm exhaust from the vehicles billowed my faded T-shirt and seeped under my shorts. The pinch of tobacco Amma had given me that morning to stave off my hunger had long since lost its flavor. It was now a bland, warm glob tucked in my cheek. Heat pressed down on my skin, and there was a sharp, metallic tinge to the air that made me uneasy. The women, who usually laughed and teased each other, curved their backs into shells and hammered in silence. The children seemed more careless than usual because I kept hearing small cries whenever one of them brought a hammer down on a thumb by accident. The horizon to the west was congested with a dark breast of clouds, but above me the sun blazed white through a gauze sky. The monsoons were late, too late for crops, but I knew they would hit anytime now. Over the past week, furious little rainstorms had begun to tear up the red earth, flooding various pits, making them almost impossible to mine. I remembered that during the last monsoon, a drunk man had wandered away one night and fallen into a flooded pit. His body, by the time it was discovered, was bloated and black.

Lorries crawled in sluggish streams in both directions on the highway. The ones heading away from Bellary were weighed down with ore, great mounds wrapped in gray and green tarpaulin and lashed with lengths of rope as thick as my ankle. The empty ones returning from the port cities rattled with stray pebbles jumping in the back. The faces of the lorry drivers were glistening with sweat, and they blared their horns as if it might make the nearly immobile line of traffic speed up. Now and then a foreign car, belonging to one of the mine owners, slipped noiselessly through the stalled traffic. I recited the names of the cars, tonguing the tobacco in my mouth: Mascrati. Jaguar. Mercedes. Jaguar. Their shimmering bodies caught the sun and played with it, light sliding across their hoods, winking in their taillights. The mine owners lived in huge pink and white houses on the highway, houses with fountains and the grim heads of stone lions staring from the balconies. I looked up as a sleek black Maserati went by, and in its tinted window I saw myself, a boy in shorts and a baggy T-shirt, crouching close to the dirt. And standing behind me, the distorted shape of a girl. I stood up quickly, hammer in hand, and whirled around.

Manju flinched, as if I might attack her with it. A few days before, I had seen two kids get into a hammer fight over a Titan watch they had found together. One of them smashed the other's hand. Later I found a small square fingernail stamped into the ground where they fought.

"I'm not going to hit you," I said.

Her slow smile pulled her cheeks into small brown hills sunk with shadowy dimples. She smoothed down the front of her dress, which was actually a school uniform. It had once been white but was now tinged with red iron dust. It wrapped around her thin body, ending below her knees and buttoning high at her throat. Her hair spilled in knotted waves down her back. She and her mother had arrived at the mine around the same time as we had. Her mother was sick and never came out of their tent. I didn't know what was wrong with her. For a while Manju had been Siju's girlfriend, saving up her extra tobacco for him, nodding seriously when he spoke, following him everywhere. Then he had stopped speaking to her. The one time I asked him about it, Siju leaned to one side, curled his lip, and spat delicately into the mud.

"Hi, Manju," I said. We were the same height, though she was a few years older, maybe fifteen.

"Hi, Guna," she said, and squatted at my feet. I squatted too and waited for her to do something. She picked up the piece of ore I had been working on and gave it two halfhearted taps with her hammer. Then she seemed to lose interest. She let it fall and said, "He came by already?"

"No," I said.

I liked Manju. Whenever journalists or NGO workers came to tour the mines, Manju and I would drop our hammers and prance in circles, shouting, "No child-y labor here!" According to the mine owners, it was our parents who were supposed to be working. We simply lived with them and played around the mine. The hammers and basins were our toys. The journalists would scribble in their notepads, and the NGO workers would whisper to one another, and Manju would grin widely at me. Then, after we found out about the Lympic Games, we had contests of our own. Running contests, stone-throwing contests, rock-piling contests. The winner got the gold medal, the runner-up clapped and stomped the dirt in applause. I liked playing with Manju because I almost always won, and she never got angry when she lost, like the boys sometimes did.

"Manju," I said now. "Want to race? Bet I'll get the gold medal."

But she just shook her head. She stared up at the lorries. She was thin, and the bones at the top of her spine pushed like pebbles against her uniform. I wanted to reach out and tap them gently with my hammer. One of the lorry drivers, a man with a thick mustache, saw her watching and made a wet kissing sound with his lips, like he was sucking an invisible straw. His tongue came out, fleshy and purple. He shouted, "Hi, sexy girl! Sexy-fun girl!" My cheeks burned for her, and I could feel the weight of the women's gazes, but Manju looked at him as if he had told her that rain was on the way. I busied myself with filling my *puttu* with lumps of ore. Each full basin I took to the weighing station would earn me five and a half rupees. On a good day I could fill seven or eight *puttus,* if I ignored the blisters at the base of my thumb.

I felt the other workers looking at us, the frank stares of the children. I carefully shifted the glob of tobacco from my right cheek to my left.

"You shouldn't be playing those dumb-stupid games anyway," Manju said.

"No?" I said cautiously. "Why not?"

Manju said, "You should be in school."

I didn't know what to say. It had been two years since I sat in a classroom. I had only vague recollections of it. The cold mud floor. Sitting next to a boy called Dheeraj, who smelled of castor oil. Slates with cracked plastic frames. The maths teacher who called us human head lice when we couldn't solve the sum on the board. All of us chanting in unison an English poem we didn't understand. *The boy stood on the burning deck.* The antiseptic smell of the girls' toilet covering another, mustier, smell. Dheeraj giggling outside. Then three, four, five whacks on the fleshy part of my palm with a wooden ruler, and trying not to show that it hurt. *The boy stood on the burning deck whence all but he had fled.*

"You used to come first in class, no?" Manju said. A gray gust of exhaust blew a wisp of hair between her teeth. She chewed on it. Her face was whiskered with red dust.

"How do you know?"

"Siju told me," she said, which surprised me. "Siju said you got a hundred in every subject, even the difficult ones like maths. He said you shouldn't be wasting your potential here."

I had never heard him say anything like that. It sounded like something an NGO worker might say. I wondered where he had heard the phrase.

"But, Manju," I said, "I like it here."

"Why?"

I was about to tell her why—because I could play with her every day and because the mine was vast and open and I was free to go where I liked, and, yes, the work was hard but there was an excitement to the way the lorries rumbled past, straining under their heavy cargo—but right then Manju dropped her hammer.

In a strained voice she said, "He's coming."

Siju's lorry looked no different than any of the others, except that it had been freshly cleaned. It had an orange cab, and the outer sides of the long bed were painted brown. The bed bulged with ore, like the belly of a fat man. Siju was clearly on his way to the Hospet railway station. The back panel of the lorry was decorated with painted animals—a lion and two deer. The lion, its thick mane rippling, stood in a lush forest, and the two deer flanked it, their delicate orange heads raised and looking off to the sides. Siju was especially proud of the painting, and I knew he stood over his lorry cleaner each morning, breathing down the boy's neck to make sure that all the red dust was properly wiped off the faces of the animals. His insistence on keeping the lorry spick-and-span was part of why the lorry cleaners made fun of him.

He must have seen us squatting there by the highway, but he kept his eyes on the road. I raised my hand and waved. When he didn't respond, I said, "Oy, Siju! Look this way!"

He swiveled his head toward us briefly.

Manju's big eyes followed him.

Then one of the women working nearby, a woman with a missing eye whose eyelid drooped over the empty socket, spat out her tobacco with a harsh smack and said to Manju, "Enough of your nonsense. Go sit somewhere else. Leave those boys to do their work."

Manju didn't answer, so the woman said more loudly, "You! Heard me? Go sit—"

Manju picked up a pebble and flung it at her. It hit the woman on the shoulder, and she yelped.

"*Soole!*" the woman hissed.

Manju turned her thin face to the woman. "*Soole?*" Manju's voice trembled. "You're calling me a *soole*? You old dirty one-eyed monkey."

I looked at Manju, afraid to speak. She picked up my ore and began hammering at it.

"Manju—" I began. I thought she was going to cry, but then she looked up. "I wish you had a lorry," she said. "Then you and me could drive to China."

Later I took my full *puttu* to the weighing station. On my way I passed Amma working with a group of women at the base of a slope. I stopped to watch her. She was shaking a sieve, holding it away from her body, a red cloud billowing around her. Dark pebbles of ore danced and shivered in the wide shallow basin. A few feet away Munna, naked except for an old shirt of mine, crawled in aimless circles. If he got too far or tried to stuff a fistful of dirt into his mouth, Amma or one of the women would reach out an arm or a leg and hook him back in. When Munna saw me, he stretched out his short arms, ridiculous in their baggy sleeves, and screamed with delight. Amma looked up. She put down the sieve and straightened her back. She was as small as a child, her hands barely bigger than mine. The other women glanced at me and continued working. The muscles in their forearms were laid like train tracks.

"How many?" Amma called up.

"Three," I said. I held up the *puttu*. "This is the fourth one." There were still a few hours of daylight left. A few hours before the red hills of Bellary turned black and the day's totals were tallied and announced by the sweating labor officer, Mr. Subbu, and no matter the numbers, how high or how low, the workers would be expected to cheer.

With her eyes on me, she put a hand inside her blouse to touch the small velvet jewelry pouch she kept there. Whatever jewelry had been in there was pawned long ago. I knew that now it contained a few hundred rupees, two or maybe three. This was what she had saved, in secrecy, for months, money that Appa overlooked or was too drunk to account for. It was for me, my school fees, and she liked to remind me it was there. She eyed me, her lower lip hanging open. I knew she was debating whether to speak.

"Guna," she said finally. "Tonight, when Appa comes—"

"Have to go," I said. "Lots of work. It's going to rain later."

She sighed. "You don't want to go back to school?" she asked. "You don't want to study hard and get a proper job?" She lowered her voice. "Such a clever boy you are, Guna. Such good marks you used to get. You want to waste your brains, fill your head with iron like a *puttu?*"

I made no reply. I remembered what Manju had said about my potential, and I saw myself flinging the entire contents of the *puttu* in Amma's face, iron flying everywhere, scattershot.

Amma was keeping half an eye on Munna, who was trying to climb into the sieve. "Did Siju get a trip today?" she asked.

"You're asking about Lorry Raja?" I said.

"Don't act like those lorry-cleaner boys. He drives well."

I hopped from one foot to the other, balancing the *puttu* like a tray. "Lorry Raja tries to turn on his indicators and turns on the windshield wipers instead."

"Guna!" Amma said.

"Lorry Raja is always combing his hair in the rearview mirror."

One of the women working next to Amma laughed. She had large yellow teeth and a gold stud in her flared nostril. Amma glanced at her, then at the ground.

Encouraged by the woman's laugh, I added, "Lorry Raja's lorry doesn't even go in a straight line." I waggled my palm to show the route Siju's lorry took.

Amma scooped up Munna before he overturned the sieve. She sucked the edge of her sari's *pallu* and scrubbed his cheek, which was, like her own, like mine, red with iron dust. The dust mixed with our sweat and formed a gummy red paste, which stuck to our skin and was almost impossible to get off without soap and water, of which we had little, except for whatever dank rain gathered in stray pits and puddles. It was easy to tell who the mine workers were. We all looked like we were bleeding.

Amma put Munna down, and he began to try to crawl up the slope to me. She held her small body very straight and looked at the other women. "Siju is the youngest driver on-site," she announced loudly. The other women, even the one who laughed earlier, took no notice.

"Only fourteen and already driving a lorry." Amma was breathing heavily, and under her red mask she was flushed.

Munna slid back down the slope and landed on his bottom. He began to wail, his toothless mouth open in protest and outrage.

"He's your brother," Amma said.

We looked at Munna. Neither of us moved to pick him up.

"I know," I said.

I registered my fourth load at the weighing station and emptied my *puttu* into the first of a line of lorries waiting there. The weighing station was marked off from the neighboring permit yard by a low wall of scrap metal: short iron pipes and rusted carburetors and hubcaps that sometimes dislodged and rolled of their own accord across the yard, stopping with a clang when they hit Mr. Subbu's aluminum-walled shed. This shed, a square, burnished structure three times as big as the tent we lived in, was the labor office. Complaints were lodged there, and labor records were written down in a big book. How many laborers worked per day; how many *puttus* they filled; how many laborers were residents at the mine camp; how many were floaters, men and women who arrived by the busload in the mornings and stood in a ragged line, waiting to be given work. Mr. Subbu would come out of his office and point at random, and those who were not chosen would shuffle back to the bus depot on the highway, where they would take a bus to the next mine to try their luck. Those who stayed were given a hammer and *puttu*. Most of them, used to this routine, brought their own. During the day Mr. Subbu's shed could be seen from anywhere at the mine. All you had to do was look up from your hammering, and there it was, a sparkle on the rust-colored hillside. His maroon Esteem was parked outside, a green, tree-shaped air freshener twirling slowly from the rearview mirror. I noticed the greenness of the air freshener because there was not a single green tree near the mine; they all bore red leaves.

Mr. Subbu stood in the shade thrown by a backhoe loader, drinking a bottle of Pepsi. He was wearing a full-sleeved shirt with the top button undone, and I could see the triangle of a white undershirt and a few black tangles of hair peeping from the top. He sweated profusely, and there were large damp patches on his chest and lower back, and two damp crescents in his armpits, which swelled to full moons when he raised his arms.

I stood there, watching him. One of the workers, a young woman with two long braids, came up to him to say something. Mr. Subbu listened with his head bent. Then he put his hand on the girl's shoulder and replied. The girl stood so still that her braids did not even swish. When he finished speaking, he let his hand fall, then she turned and walked away. There had been a rumor in the mine camp about one of the new babies, and how it had Mr. Subbu's nose, and the mother, a rail-thin woman called Savithri, had been forced to sneak away from the camp at night before her husband came for her with the metal end of a belt. I had heard Appa call Mr. Subbu shameless and a *soole magane*, but something about the way he stood all alone in his nice clothes seemed lonely and promising. And as I stood there watching him, it occurred to me suddenly that he might be able to help me. My heart beat faster, and I pictured myself standing in the shade with him, talking, him smiling and nodding.

I went over to stand by him, my empty *puttu* thudding against my thighs. He finished the Pepsi and threw the bottle under the backhoe loader, all without paying attention to me. Then he wiped his mouth with a handkerchief.

"Taking rest?" he said. He had seen me around the mine, but he didn't know my name, of course. There were hundreds of children running everywhere, and under that coat of red we must have all looked the same to him.

"Yes, sir," I said. "Only five minutes," I added, lest he think I was shirking.

"Very good," said Mr. Subbu.

His eyelids drooped, and he nodded his head slowly. I waited for him to offer me a Pepsi, and when he didn't, I kept standing there. I wondered what a man like that thought about. I looked out over the mine, the land cut open in wide red swatches. Compared to the mine, the plain beyond seemed colorless, the trees sitting low to the ground, hardly different from the bushes, whose woody stems bore patches of dry leaves. In the distance there were hills that had not yet been mined, and they looked impossibly lush, rising and falling in deep, green waves against the sky. And the sun, the sun was a white ball that tore into everything, into the blistered skin on the backs of my hands, into the body of the backhoe loader, into the yawning red mouth of the mine.

I cleared my throat. Mr. Subbu's mouth parted and closed, parted and closed. Long strings of spit stretched and contracted between his lips.

"Sir," I said.

Mr. Subbu's eyes snapped open. "Hm?"

"Sir, I want to ask something."

He looked at me. I took a deep breath and held his eyes. They were not unkind eyes, only a little distant, a little distracted.

"I want to become a driver, sir. Lorry driver," I said, speaking quickly.

Mr. Subbu seemed to be waiting for more, so I continued, "I know driving, sir. My father taught me. He was the driver for the subinspector of the Raichur Thermal Station, sir. He drove an Esteem, sir, just like yours." And I pointed to the maroon car that was parked outside his shed.

I didn't think of it as a lie. When Appa had driven for the subinspector, I had sat in his lap whenever the subinspector was in a meeting or on an inspection tour or at the flat of a woman who was not his wife. I would hold the Esteem's steering wheel, dizzy from the musky odor of the leather upholstery, while Appa drove us slowly around the streets of Raichur, his foot barely touching the accelerator, whispering in my ear, "Left, now. Get ready. Turn the wheel slowly." And his hands would close over mine, swallowing them, and I would feel the pressure of his fingers and respond to them, pulling as he pulled, inhaling the spice of the cheap home-brewed *daru* that was always on his breath, waiting for those moments when his lips brushed the back of my head, and we would guide the car together, the big maroon bird making a graceful swoop and coming straight again. "Expert," Appa would whisper warm and rich into my hair as I frowned at the road to hide my pleasure. "So young and already driving like an expert."

I said nothing about the accident, about how Appa had been drunker than usual, how he had shattered the knee of the woman, how he had cried later because of the noise the woman made—a resigned sigh, *oh*—before she fell.

Mr. Subbu's fingers kneaded one another.

"Please, sir," I said.

"How old are you?" he asked.

I paused. "Thirteen," I said, rounding up.

"Thirteen," Mr. Subbu said. He squinted out into the sun, and then he pointed to the one of the workers moving over the surface of the red, undulating plain. The sun shrank him into a black dot, no bigger than one of the pebbles I filled my *puttu* with. "See him?" he asked.

"Yes, sir," I said. And together we watched him for a while.

Then Mr. Subbu said, as if posing a maths problem, "What is he doing?"

"Working," I said.

"Exactly," said Mr. Subbu. "Smart boy. He's working."

I watched a lorry wind its way to the bottom of a hill, heading to the highway, on an uneven road sawn into the hillside. Behind it trailed a hazy red cloud.

"Work hard, and you will get whatever you want," Mr. Subbu said, his voice louder than necessary, as if many people had gathered to hear to him. "That's the best advice I can give you, my boy. Your father would tell you the same thing." And he touched me on the shoulder, a fatherly touch, at the same time pushing me lightly so that I found myself back in the sun again.

Instead of going back to the site beside the highway, I went to find Appa. Half-hidden behind a mound of earth, I watched him being lowered into a pit, a rope tied under his arms and passing across his bare chest. He had taken off his pants and wore only a pair of frayed striped boxer shorts. He carried a long-handled hammer like an extension of his arm. The loose end of the rope was held by three men, who braced their feet to hold the weight of Appa's body. And then earth swallowed him, feet first.

I often came to watch him work like this, when he didn't know I was there. I would count the seconds he was down in the pit, listening for the steady crash of his hammer, muffled thunder. I would wait, alert to the slightest sound of panic, the faintest jerking of the rope. I knew that no matter how many times one did a job, the worst could happen the next time. And just as the waiting became unbearable, and I was about to run into the open, to give myself away, he emerged, red-faced, dangling, gasping like a man being pulled from water.

They untied him, and he began rubbing his skin where the rope had cut into him. One of the men said, "Nice weather down there?" and Appa said, "Sunny like your wife's *thullu.*" The man laughed. Appa said, "One day I want to tie up that bastard Subbu and send him down there." The other man said, "He'd get stuck, first of all. Second thing is he's too busy putting his fat hands all over girls. What else you think he does in that office all day?"

"Fat bastard," Appa said. He raised his hammer and brought it down once, hard. Then he lifted it again and let it crash down, and then he did it again, the rise and fall of the hammer all part of the same smooth motion. I could feel the impact of each blow travel through the ground between our bodies, from the muscles in his arms to the muscles in my legs, connecting us.

"Thank god I have only sons," Appa said, and the man laughed again.

When I returned to the site beside the highway, Manju had disappeared. The ground where she had been squatting was scuffed. I crouched over it and tried to make out the marks of her bare feet. A few women were still hunched over, their hammers clinking in rhythm. The woman with the missing eye pulled a pinch of tobacco from a large gray wad and handed it to me. I took it and chewed on it slowly. The bitter tobacco juice flooded my mouth.

The woman watched me chew. "Want to know where that girl went?" she asked.

I tried to imagine what could have happened to her eye. I wanted to apologize for Manju throwing a stone at her, but I was angry at the woman for calling Manju a *soole*.

"She probably went back to her tent," I said.

"Take another guess," the woman said. "Shall I tell you?"

"No," I said.

"Smart boy," she said.

Then she leaned forward and lowered her voice. "Listen to me. That girl is not nice. Okay? Not nice. You should stay away from her."

"Excuse me," I said. "I have to work."

For the next few hours I worked without stopping. I pounded the ore with my hammer, the blows precise, never faltering, the ring of metal against metal filling my head. Sweat poured down my wrists, and I had to keep wiping my hands on my shorts. Lorries ticked by on the highway, marking time. Siju's lorry did not drive past again. After a while the women stood up and stretched their backs. They flexed their fingers and curled their toes in the dirt. The one who had given me the tobacco smiled, but with just one eye her smile looked insincere. They took up their full *puttus* and their hammers and walked off in the direction of the weighing station. As they walked, I noted their square backs, their strong thigh muscles showing through their saris, their strange bowlegged gait, their gnarled feet caked with dirt. None of them owned shoes except for the odd pair of rubber or plastic sandals. Manju had been right, I thought. They looked less like women and more like monkeys, the muscular brown monkeys that would swarm our village outside Raichur. They were fearless and feral, those monkeys, grabbing peanuts from children's hands, attacking people with their small, sharp teeth. A pack of them would sit on top of a low, crumbling wall, chattering and picking lice from each other's fur, in the way that these women scratched their armpits and laughed in low, coarse voices.

The day ripened into purple and then rotted into black, the air sagging with the smells I never noticed when the sun was there to burn it all away, the stench from pools filled with stagnant water and buzzing with mosquitoes, the sweet whiff of shit drifting from the field we all used, furtively or defiantly, even the women and girls. I registered my last load of iron and returned to our tent, where Amma was preparing the coals for dinner. Clouds pressed down on the camp, our city of plastic tents, and we could hear the voices of the men coming down from the top of the rise where they gathered to drink after work every evening. I could hear Appa's voice above the others, his laugh the loudest. Amma glanced up every now and again, her face a shining red circle of worry in the light of the coals. I held Munna on my lap, and he blinked sleepily into the coals. When we heard Appa's singing, the notes warbling as he came down the rise toward us, Amma glanced quickly at me and began blowing at the coals. I pressed my nose into Munna's neck and smelled his sour baby smell. The coals pulsed brightly every time Amma blew, her cheeks puffed with the effort.

"Guna, the *paan*," Amma hissed, and I rummaged in a plastic bag for the battered shoe-polish tin in which we kept a stock of crumbled areca nut and a small stack of betel leaves.

"Wipe Munna's nose," she ordered, and I used Munna's sleeve to wipe away the shining thread of mucus that trickled out of one nostril.

"Guna—" and that was all she had time to say before Appa ducked his head under the tent and collapsed among us, creating a confused tangle of arms and legs. Amma smoothly moved out of his way and began pressing balls of dough between her palms and pinching the edges until the dough became round and flat, and she laid them over the coals to bake. She stared at them intently, as if they might fly away. Appa leaned on his elbow. He was no longer stripped down but was wearing his torn T-shirt that said *Calvin Kline* and his faded pants rolled up to his knees. In January he had smashed his hammer into the large toe of his left foot, and it had healed crooked, like a bird's beak.

"Supriya," Appa said, drawing her name out. *Shoopreeya.*

Amma said nothing.

"So serious you look," Appa said. His face seemed to contract and expand, and his *daru*-scented breath filled the tent. "Not happy to see me? Not even one smile for your husband? Your poor husband who has been working like a dog all day?"

Amma bit her lip so hard the bottom of her face twisted. She picked a baked roti off the coals with her bare fingers and laid it on a sheet of newspaper. Appa hiccupped.

I held out the shoe-polish tin. Appa took it, popped it open, and sprinkled some areca nut on a betel leaf. He folded the leaf into a neat square and began chewing it. Red juice came out of the side of his mouth. I watched it trickle down his chin.

"Guna," he said then, his mouth red and wet. "How many *puttus* today, Guna?"

I was about to say eight when I caught sight of Amma's face, looking engorged and pleading in the light from the coals. Without taking her eyes off the rotis, she slipped a hand into her blouse and touched her breast where the velvet pouch was.

I said, "Six."

"Six," Appa repeated. "That's all?"

"Yes," I said. "Sorry, Appa." I waited for the sting of the slap.

But instead he reached out and slowly caressed the side of my face. He ran his hand from the top of my head down my cheek, over my chin, and to the soft spot on my neck, where my pulse had begun to race. His hand was like sandpaper, covered in scabs and blisters, some that had burst and scarred, some that were still ripe. I felt every bump and welt against my skin, every dip and hollow. It was as if he were leaving the living imprint of his hand on my face.

"No, no," he said in a rich voice, his singing voice. "Don't say sorry. I should be sorry. I should be the one saying sorry. It's because of me you are here. All of you. It is all my fault." His voice trembled on the edge of a cliff, and his eyes were so dark.

I felt a pricking behind my eyes. My face was humming. There was a heaviness to my limbs. I wondered if this was what he felt like when he was drunk.

"My fault," Appa said. "I'm a bad father."

Appa held out his hand, and I dropped my wages into it. All of it, even the eleven rupees I had just lied to him about. Appa's palm closed around the money, and he dropped it into his pocket. I tightened my arms around Munna. I didn't dare look at Amma.

I heard her body shift. She let out a breath she'd been holding.

"That is his school money," she said.

Appa didn't turn to look at her.

"That is his school money," she said again. "We said this year he would go back. You have to keep some of that for tuition fees."

He said, "You're telling me what to do? In my own house you're telling me?"

Black spots appeared on the rotis, each accompanied by a small hiss.

"You're just one man," Amma said, staring at the spots. "How much *daru* will you drink?" She paused. "I should have had a daughter."

"What bloody daughter?" said Appa. "Why you want a daughter? You want for me to pay dowry? Some snot-nosed fellow comes and says, I want to marry her, and I have to go into my own pocket and lick his bum? No, thank you."

"Daughters help their mothers. And you'd drink all of her dowry anyway," muttered Amma.

I thought he was going to caress her too, the way his hand went out, but then I saw he was pinching her, clamping down on the fleshiest part of her waist, right above her hipbone, the strip of bare skin between the top of her petticoat and the bottom of her blouse. She flailed, her mouth open without screaming. One of her hands caught Munna on the side of the head, and she kicked a stray coal so close to my foot that I could feel it scorch my toe. I drew my foot back and waited for Munna to cry, but he didn't.

When Appa let go, there were two semicircles of bright red on Amma's hip, the skin slightly puckered. She was moaning softly but did not let the rotis burn. She picked them off and put them on the newspaper. She was breathing hard through her teeth.

"Supriya, you know what problem you have? You don't smile enough," Appa told her. "You should smile more. A woman who doesn't smile is ugly."

Then Amma's gaze traveled beyond the coals, beyond Appa's prone form, and I turned to see Siju standing at the entrance of the tent. He looked fresh. His hair was combed, of all things. He stood there, watching us, and suddenly I could see us through his eyes, the picture we presented, me with my toes curled in, Munna swaying with sleep in my arms, Appa reclining on his elbow, Amma hunched over the coals. I saw what he saw, and then I wished I hadn't seen it.

"What you think you're staring at?" Appa said. "Sit down."

Siju picked his way to an empty spot between Appa and me. As soon as he sat down, the tent felt full, too full. We were too close together, fear and anger flying around like rockets.

"Where did you go today?" Amma asked Siju. To my surprise, he didn't turn away like he usually did but looked at her with a distant sort of sympathy, as if she were a stranger he had made up his mind to be kind to.

"Hospet," he said.

"Hospet," Amma repeated gratefully. "Is it a nice place?"

With the same careful kindness he said, "Actually, I've never seen a dirtier place."

"What the hell you were expecting?" Appa said, trying to provoke him. "All cities are dirty. You want to eat your food off the street, or what?"

Siju ignored him, and I could sense Appa stiffening.

"How many trips did you get?" Amma asked.

"Trips!" Appa snorted. "He drives that bloody lorry ten kilometers to the railway station. Ten kilometers! How do you call that a trip?"

Siju began to massage his feet. Amma put another roti on the coals. Appa glared at them both, their exclusion of him causing the pressure inside to build and build.

"So? How many?" Appa said. His head swiveled slowly in Siju's direction. "How many *trips*? Your mother asked a question, can't you hear? You're deaf or something?"

"Three," said Siju curtly.

"Don't talk like I'm some peon who cleans your shit. Say it properly."

"Three," repeated Siju.

"You're listening, Supriya?" drawled Appa with exaggerated awe. "You want something to smile about? Your son got three trips to the bloody railway station in a bloody lorry. *Three trips!* What you want a daughter for? With a son like this?"

His glassy gaze never left Siju's face. Amma laid the last roti over the coals.

"Bloody lorry driver thinks he's a bloody raja," muttered Appa.

I pinched Munna under the arm, hoping to make him cry, hoping to create a distraction, but he wouldn't. I pinched again harder, but he sat still, a soft, surprisingly heavy weight on my lap. One of the coals popped, and my heart jumped. I remembered the way the manager of the thermal station had come to our house after Appa's accident. Spit flew from the manager's mouth as he screamed, landing lightly on Appa's face, and I remembered how Appa didn't wipe it off. I remembered the way Appa had said, "No, sir. Sorry, sir. No, sir. Sorry, sir," like he didn't understand the words. Like they were a poem he had memorized. That night he went and lay down on the road, and when Amma went to bring him back in, he said, "Supriya, leave me alone! I deserve this." And I remembered the way she held his head, speaking to him softly until he dragged himself up and followed her back inside.

Now he waited to see what Siju would do.

For a second I thought he would hit Appa. Then he shrugged. "Being a bloody lorry driver is better than hammering bloody pieces of iron all day." He looked at me as he said this, and I looked away.

Amma used her finger to smear the rotis with lime pickle, rolled them into tubes, and handed them to us. She held her arms out for Munna, slipping her blouse down her shoulder, baring her slack breast with its wine-colored nipple. Munna latched on, his black eyes shining in the semidarkness, unblinking, gazing at us. The roti was warm and tasted of smoke, and the pickle was tart, the lime stringy and tough. I thought only about the food, about how it was filling my mouth, sliding tight down my throat, unlocking something. It was always this way. The food loosened something in all of us, a tightly wound spring uncoiling. I felt myself starting to relax. Food could do this, and warmth, and the approach of sleep. There were these moments of calm, when no one spoke, and there were only the coals and the insistent flapping of the plastic tent and the mumble of other families and the sky hanging low.

Then Siju, leaning toward me, spoiled it all by saying, "I have something to say to you."

I swallowed quickly. "I don't want to hear anything," I said. We kept our voices down because Appa seemed to have fallen asleep. He was snoring lightly.

"Listen just one second."

"Oh-ho, Lorry Raja wants to say something," I said.

"Don't—"

I put my fingers in my ears and chanted, "Lorry Raja! Lorry Raja!" I knew it was silly, but I wanted to keep this fragile peace, to clutch it tightly in my fist like a precious stone.

"Guna, listen!" Siju said, louder than he had intended.

"What's the racket?" said Appa, coming out of his doze.

"Nothing," said Siju.

"Nothing," I repeated.

Appa closed his eyes again. Amma was still breast-feeding Munna, her head bent in contemplation of his placid sucking.

"That monkey woman called Manju a *soole*," I said quietly.

Siju picked at a scab on his knee.

"What are you two talking about?" Amma asked.

Before Siju could reply, I said, "Manju. *His* girlfriend."

"The girl whose mother is sick?"

I nodded.

"Poor thing," Amma said. "Maybe I should go see if I can do something."

But then Munna fell asleep, still making halfhearted sucks at her nipple, and her eyes went soft. She brushed her hand against the tuft of hair sticking up from his red-stained forehead.

"Don't bother," Siju spat. "*She* knows how to get what she wants."

"I'm going to see if she's okay," I said, standing up. To my surprise, Siju stood up too.

"I'll come with you," he said.

"No!" I shouted.

"Yes," said Amma. "Both of you go."

"Siju," Appa said. He was still in that reclining position. His calves under the rolled-up pants were like polished cannonballs. I remembered the way I had seen him earlier that day, bare chested, bent at the waist, his long-handled hammer making smooth strokes, crashing against the ground. He was not a big man or a tall one, but he was a man who broke iron for ten hours every day.

Siju looked at him for a long moment, then nodded and reached into his pocket. He brought out a set of folded notes and pressed it into Appa's outstretched palm. Appa tucked it into his pocket, where my own wages nestled. He hummed something tuneless and closed his eyes.

Amma was watching us both. "Here," she said. "Take something for them." She made me wrap two rotis in newspaper. "Come back before it rains."

"You don't have to come if you don't want to," I told Siju as we picked our way through the maze of tents. "I won't tell."

Instead of answering he was quiet, which made me nervous. A rat the size of my foot ran across our path and disappeared into the blackness to our right. The rats were a problem in the camp. They got into our food, chewed holes in our blankets, bit babies as they slept. Last year a baby had died from a rat bite. I thought of Munna asleep, of the whole camp silent, a ship of blue plastic afloat on these hairy black bodies that moved and rustled under it, restless and hungry as the ocean.

Manju wasn't in her tent. From inside came the loud, ragged breathing of her mother. Siju raised his eyebrows at me and jerked his chin in the direction of the tent's opening. I shook my head; I could just make out the shadowy figure wrapped in a blanket, smaller than a person should be. Then Manju's mother coughed, a colorless wheezing cough, like wind passing through a narrow, lonely corridor. I took an unconscious step backward.

"She's not there," I whispered.

"Smart fellow," Siju whispered back.

"So now what?"

"We go back to our tent."

"*You* go back," I said. "I'll wait for her here. She must have gone to the toilet."

Siju gave me a long, searching look. "Guna," he said. "Just forget her."

"No!" I almost shouted. I felt the start of tears, burning in the ridge of my nose. Before I could stop myself, I said, "She wants me to take her to China."

"What?" His voice was flat.

"In my lorry," I said. I knew I was babbling. I squeezed the rotis and felt the warmth seep through the newspaper. "She said if I could drive a lorry, I could take her to China. To see the Lympic Games. I asked Mr. Subbu, but he said no. He said if I work hard I'll get what I want."

Siju let out a long breath. "You asked Subbu?" he said. "That fat bastard? You asked him?"

"Yes," I said.

"My god." My brother shook his head. "Come with me," he said.

Mr. Subbu's Esteem was still parked outside his aluminum-walled shed. The shed was directly under a single lamppost, whose light cast it in a liquid, silver glow. The lamppost was connected to a generator, which growled like a sleeping dog. We crept up to the backhoe loader, which was just outside the shoreline of light.

Siju put his hand on my shoulder. "Not too close," he said.

"Why are we here?" I asked. He put a finger on his lips.

We waited, partly hidden by the massive machine. I leaned against it, and the cold of its metal body was a shock. Siju was standing behind me, very close. There was a strange calmness to the whole scene, the glowing shed, the purring of the generator, the still air.

And then, with a movement so smooth and natural that I forgot to be surprised, Manju stepped from Mr. Subbu's shed. She stood there for a moment, her uniform and thin legs perfectly outlined in the light of the lamp, her face lifted like one of the deer on the back panel of Siju's lorry. Then she turned and looked straight at us. I jumped, but Siju's hand was on my shoulder again.

"Be still," he whispered.

But Manju had seen us. Her uniform seemed even bigger on her frame than it had earlier in the day. She was floating in it as she came over to us. Her feet were soundless in the dirt. As soon as she was level with the backhoe loader, Siju stepped out and pulled her behind it. She put her hands on her hips and looked at us for a long time without speaking. Behind her, the lamppost snapped off, plunging everything into darkness. Then the headlights of Mr. Subbu's Esteem came on, and the car floated away, as if borne on an invisible river.

"So," Manju said. As my eyes adjusted slowly, I noticed that her eyes were swollen. She had been crying. I thought of the shed, of Mr. Subbu's hands kneading each other, of the cold bottle of Pepsi, of the way he'd put his hand on the shoulder of the girl with the braids. I thought of the woman with one eye saying, *That girl is not nice.*

"How long have you been standing here?" Manju asked.

"Relax," said Siju coolly. "Guna felt like taking a walk."

"A walk," Manju repeated. She looked at me quickly, accusingly, and I felt a spike of guilt. "And you just walked this way," she said.

Siju shrugged. "That's how it happened."

I said, "We came to give you these rotis." I pressed the newspaper-wrapped rotis into her hand. She looked at them as if I had done something meaningless.

"Let's go back to the tent," I told Siju. I wanted to get away from Manju's raw, swollen face. Her tears had made clear channels in the red paste on her cheeks.

"Just one minute," Siju said. He leaned in close to Manju so that his face was barely inches from hers. He smiled. It was not a nice smile.

"Guna told me you want to go to China," he said.

Manju looked at me, puzzled. I closed my eyes. "What?" She said uncertainly.

"Still want to go?"

He had made a copy of the lorry key. In Hospet. He had waited in the lorry while a shopkeeper fashioned a new one, which was raw and shining and silver. It made me uncomfortable to look at it.

In the lorry yard, the smell of grease and diesel strong in my nose, I whispered, "Mr. Subbu will throw you out if he finds out. Appa will kill you."

"Shut up," Siju said in a normal voice. "Mr. Subbu! Appa! You think I care? Come with us or stay here and shut up. Your decision."

He climbed into the high cab of the lorry. He reached over and held a hand out for Manju, who held it indifferently, as if she were being asked to hold a piece of wood. He let me struggle in by myself. When I had shut the door, he inserted the shining key into the ignition.

"They're going to hear us," I said.

"No, they're not," he said grimly. He turned the key and started the engine.

It sounded like thunder rolling across the plain. I closed my eyes and waited for a shout, a light shining in our faces, the relief of discovery. But no one came. The city of tents stayed dark, except for the glimmer of burning coals. The sky answered with thunder of its own.

Siju did not turn on the headlights, and the lorry drifted out of the yard, past the weighing station, past the permit yard, rounding the perimeter, the camp turning silently on its axis like a black globe, the dirt road invisible.

"On your marks," I heard Siju say. He sounded calm. "Get set. Go."

And then I felt the pressure release, the lorry pick up speed, and we were driving downhill, and there was wind rushing in through the windows, filling my lungs. I could feel Manju's shoulder against mine, and there were Siju's hands curled on the wheel, and the floorboard thrummed under my feet, and I was suddenly awake, wide awake, filled with the cold night air.

Siju flipped on the headlights, and I saw that we were no longer within the boundaries of the mine, we had left it behind, and trees flashed by, their lowest branches scraping the sides of the lorry. There was no time to feel anything. All I could do was keep my balance, keep my shoulder from slamming against the door. We hurtled past rocks that were big enough to jump off. Siju drove leaning forward, without slowing for anything, and the lorry bounced and jostled, and its springs screeched, and in the yellow beam of the headlights I saw the ground jump sharply into focus for an instant before we swallowed it. The hills in the distance were getting closer, and I wondered if Siju intended to drive to the top of them, or even beyond. I wanted him to. I wanted him to drive forever. As long as he kept driving, we would be safe.

But then he stopped, let the engine idle fall into silence. We were in the middle of the plains, far enough away from the mine to seem like a different country. The ground stretched away on every side. The trees provided no orientation. They simply carved out darker shapes in the darkness. Siju took his hands off the wheel and ran them through his hair. Manju's chest rose and fell under the uniform. She stared straight ahead, through the grimy windshield, even after we had been sitting there in silence for minutes.

"Gold medal," I heard Siju whisper.

I opened and closed my mouth, each time to say something that crumbled and became a confused tangle of words.

"You shouldn't have brought Guna," Manju said. The sound of my name made me shiver, as if by naming me she had made me responsible. For this, for the three of us, here. As if whatever happened here would be because of me.

"Why not?" Siju said. "He deserves to come, no? You know, he even went to Subbu today and asked if he could be a lorry driver. All because of you. Sweet, no? Bastard said no, of course. I could have told him not to waste his time; Subbu has his fat hands filled with your—"

"You think I like this?" she said. She spoke to the windshield, to the open plain. "Begging for money? Sir, please give money for medicine. Sir, please give money for surgery. Sir, Mummy's coughing again. Doctor says her lungs are weak. Sir, please give money for doctor's fees. You think it's nice to stand still and let him do whatever he wants? And he gives too little money, so every time I have to go back. You think it's a big game?"

I could tell that Siju was taken aback. "You could work—"

"Fifty rupees per day!" Manju said. "Even if I work all day and night, it would not even be enough for food. Sometimes you're so stupid. Even Guna is smarter than you." After she said this, she seemed to collapse. I could feel her shoulder sag against mine.

"Manju," I said. For no reason other than to say her name.

Siju sat in silence for a while. Then he made a strangled sound in his throat, like he was coming to a decision he already hated himself for. He opened his door and jumped out.

"Come on," he said to Manju.

I made a move to get out.

"No, you stay here," Siju said.

"But—" I started to say.

"Guna, just stay here," Manju said. She sounded tired.

I bit down on my lip. Manju put her arm around my shoulders and pulled me close. I could smell metal in her hair. It was the most vivid thing I had ever smelled. It was a smell that had a shape, edges as solid as a building. And then for no reason I thought of our neighbor's wife, the one who survived after her husband tried to burn them all. She lived in the temple courtyard after that, and the priests fed her. Sometime she would take dried pats of cow dung and put them on her head like a hat and stare at passersby, the skin of her cheek rippled pink. I don't know why I thought of that woman just then, but I did. And while I was remembering her, Manju was sliding away from me, into the driver's seat, her legs stretching to the ground. She dropped with a little grunt.

I heard them walk around the lorry, heard the clink of the chain and the rusted creak as the back panel was lowered. I felt the vibrations of their movements come to me through the empty lorry bed. A scraping noise, and I knew Siju was spreading a tarpaulin sheet across the back. Through the metal, through the fake leather of the seat, through the cogs and gears and machinery, I could feel their movements, the positioning of one body over another. I heard Siju say something in a low voice. I don't remember hearing Manju reply.

And then I didn't want to hear any more, so I listened instead to the whirring of insects in the bushes, the nighttime howls of dogs from the villages whose fires hung suspended in the distance, the wind that traveled close to the ground, scraping dry leaves into piles. The darkness made it vast, vaster than the mine, which in the daytime seemed so large to me. It was different in every way from the camp, where the sounds were either machine sounds, lifting and loading and dumping and digging, or people sounds, eating or snoring or crying or swearing at someone to shut up so they could sleep.

A light wind brushed my face, carried the smell of rain. Tomorrow the work would be impossible, the ground too wet to dig, the ore slippery and slick, the puddles swollen to ponds. The men would slide around, knee-deep, and curse. The children would push each other, making it into a rough game. The lorries would get stuck, their wheels spinning, flinging mud in all directions, and we would have to spend an extra hour digging them out. There would be red mud in the crooks of our elbows, in our fingernails, in our ears. The coals, in the evening, would refuse to light.

For a second I couldn't move, as if the coming days and weeks and months and years were piling on top of me like a load of ore, pinning me against the darkness, and then I found myself slipping into the driver's seat and taking hold of the shining key, which stuck out of the ignition like a small cold hand asking to be grasped. I tried to remember what to do, what I had seen others do. I carefully pressed the clutch. I needed to slide forward to the edge of the seat to do it. I turned the key, and the lorry rumbled to life. I waited for a second, holding my breath, and then in a rush I released the clutch and stomped on the accelerator. The lorry bucked, then jumped a couple of feet, and my temple hit the half-rolled driver's-door window. I put my finger to my skin, and it came away wet with blood. The engine stammered and died, and everything went back to silence.

Siju wrenched open the door and dragged me out of the cab. He grasped two handfuls of my shirt and shook me.

"What's wrong with you?" he said. "What kind of idiot are you?"

When I didn't answer, he let go of my shirt. His pants were unzipped, and I looked at the V-shaped flap that was hanging open. He saw me looking and said, "What?"

"Nothing."

"Just say it, Guna."

"Nothing," I said.

He zipped his pants.

"Then get inside," he said. "We're going home."

"What about Manju?" I asked.

"She wants to sit in the back."

"It's going to rain," I said. "She'll get wet."

"Just get inside the bloody lorry, Guna," Siju said. "Don't argue."

Inside the cab I hugged my body and tried to stay awake. The cold air was still coming in, and I wanted to roll up my window, but Siju had his open, his elbow resting on it, head leaning on that hand, the other guiding the lorry. He was driving slowly now, taking care to avoid the bumps and dips in the uneven ground. We passed a rock, ghostly white, that I didn't remember from the journey out. From the corner of my eye, I looked at him, my sullen brother. Not a raja but a fourteen-year-old lorry driver in a Bellary mine.

"What's going to happen now?" I asked.

He drew his hand inside. "What's going to happen to what?"

To everything, I wanted to say. But I said, "Manju's mother."

He let a few moments go by before answering. And when he did, what he said was, "Come on, Guna. You're smart. You know."

"We could have given her the money from my school fees," I said.

"For what?" He sounded like an old man. "So she can die in three months instead of two?"

After that we didn't talk. The trees fell away, and the ground became smoother. The camp came into view, almost completely dark, just a few remaining fires that would burn throughout the night. Siju parked in the lorry yard and jumped out. I stayed sitting in the cab. A few drops of rain fell on the windshield and created long glossy streaks as they traveled down. The camp would wake to find itself afloat. The rats would come looking for dry ground. Munna would need to be nursed. Amma would put her hand behind his soft downy head to soothe him. Appa would bail out the water that pooled in the roof of our tent. Amma would tie an old *lungi* of Appa's to two of the bamboo poles to create a hammock for Munna that would keep him above the reach of the rats. Manju's mother would shift to a more comfortable position and wait for the rain to stop. There didn't seem to be a reason for any of it, a logic that I could see. There was repetition and routine and the inevitability of accident. Tomorrow Mr. Subbu would drink a Pepsi, and we would dig for iron.

I heard Siju say my name, and I heard the panic in his voice. It was raining in earnest now, the windshield a silver wash. I pushed open the door and nearly fell out. My feet sank into the soft mud. Siju was standing at the back of the truck, the back panel open. His hair hung draggled around his face, and drops of water clung to the tips. He pointed wordlessly to the lorry bed. I forced my eyes to scan the entire space for Manju, but she wasn't there.

We stood there for what seemed like an hour, though I knew it was less than a minute. I pictured her walking across the plains, her face directed to some anonymous town. She would walk for hours, I knew, and when she got tired, she would sleep exactly where she stopped walking, her arms shielding her face from the rain. I imagined her curled up on the ground. I imagined that her hair would plaster her cheek. I imagined that her uniform would be washed back into white, a beacon for anyone watching, except no one would be.

Over the following months Siju began sucking diesel out of the lorries and selling it back to the drivers at 20 percent below pump prices, and by the time the monsoons ended, he had earned enough money for one year of school fees for me. He gave it to Amma without telling me, and I never thanked him directly. We had spoken very little since the night of the lorry ride. I watched him closely for a while, worried that he would disappear too, but he came back night after night, sometimes after we had all fallen asleep, never smiling, never saying much. I knew he took the lorry out sometimes, but he never took me with him again. He stopped swaggering, and the lorry cleaners seemed disappointed. I went to school in the mornings and returned to the mine afterward.

The next August, after the flooded pits were starting to dry out again, Mr. Subbu arrived at the mine late one afternoon and announced that he was giving everyone the rest of the day off. He smiled at the responding cheer. Then from his Esteem he brought out a small color television and a white satellite dish and hooked them up to the generator, setting them on a rickety table with the help of the one of the laborers. He fiddled with the antenna until a picture flickered on the screen.

We all gathered around to watch the magnificent round stadium in China fill with color and light and music and movement. We watched graceful acrobats and women with feathers and children with brightly painted faces. We watched glittering fireworks and slender athletes in shiny tracksuits and flapping flags with all the shades of the world. We watched as the stadium slowly filled with red light, and thousands of people arranged themselves into gracious, shifting shapes in the center. Thousands more gathered in the seats, their faces reflecting the same awe we felt. We watched, all of us, in silence, stunned by the beauty of what we had created.

CONTRIBUTORS' NOTES

Sherman Alexie is the author of twenty-two books, including *The Absolutely True Diary of a Part-Time Indian*, winner of the 2007 National Book Award for Young People's Literature; *War Dances*, winner of the 2010 PEN/Faulkner Award; and *Face*, a book of poetry. His latest collection of stories is *Blasphemy*.

Ana Arana is a reporter for Fundación MEPI. Prior to that, she was a Knight International Journalism Fellow who trained investigative reporters in Mexico. Her work has appeared in *Foreign Affairs*, *Marie Claire*, *Newsweek*, *Salon*, the *Columbia Journalism Review*, *Business Week*, and the *Village Voice*. Arana is a graduate of the Columbia Graduate School of Journalism and San Francisco State University.

Lynda Barry has worked as a painter, cartoonist, writer, illustrator, playwright, editor, commentator, and teacher, and found they are very much alike. She is the author of *100 Demons*, *The Freddie Stories*, *Blabber Blabber Blabber*, and the creative how-tos *What It Is* and *Picture This*. She lives in Wisconsin.

Sibylla Brodzinsky is a journalist who has spent more than twenty years writing about Latin American politics, human rights, and social issues in publications including the *Economist*, the *Christian Science Monitor*, and the *Guardian*.

Pamela Colloff is an executive editor at *Texas Monthly*, where she writes primarily about criminal justice. Her work has also appeared in *The New Yorker* and has been anthologized in three editions of *Best American Crime Reporting* as well as the e-book collection, *Next Wave: America's New Generation of Great Literary Journalists*. She was raised in New York City and attended Brown University. She now lives in Austin with her husband and their two children.

Jennifer Egan is the author of *A Visit from the Goon Squad, The Keep, Look at Me, The Invisible Circus,* and the story collection *Emerald City*. Her stories have been published in *The New Yorker, Harper's, GQ, Zoetrope,* and *Ploughshares,* and her nonfiction appears frequently in the *New York Times Magazine*. She lives with her husband and sons in Brooklyn.

Isaac Fitzgerald has been a firefighter, worked on a boat, and has been given a sword by a king, thereby accomplishing three out of five of his childhood goals. He has also written for the *Bold Italic, McSweeney's, Mother Jones,* and the *San Francisco Chronicle*. He is a co-owner of the *Rumpus* and co-founder, with Wendy MacNaughton, of the Tumblr Pen & Ink, which will be published as a book in 2014. He can be found at isaacfitzgerald.net.

Jim Gavin's fiction has appeared in *The New Yorker,* the *Paris Review, Esquire,* the *Mississippi Review, ZYZZYVA,* and *Slice*. He lives in Los Angeles.

Josh Gondelman is a writer and comedian who incubated in Boston before moving to New York City. Josh's writing has appeared on McSweeney's Internet Tendency, *New York* magazine's The Cut blog, and in *Esquire*. He is the co-creator of @SeinfeldToday, and his own Twitter feed was named one of 2012's best by *Paste* magazine.

Cynthia Gorney, a contributing writer for *National Geographic,* is also on the faculty of the Graduate School of Journalism at UC Berkeley. A former national features writer and South America bureau chief for the *Washington Post,* she is the author of *Articles of Faith: A Front-*

line History of the Abortion Wars, and has also written for the *New York Times Magazine, The New Yorker, Harper's, Sports Illustrated,* and many other magazines. She and her husband, Bill Sokol, live in Oakland, California.

Peter Hessler is a staff writer at *The New Yorker,* where he served as the Beijing correspondent from 2000 to 2007, and is also a contributing writer for *National Geographic.* He is the author of *River Town,* which won the Kiriyama Prize; *Oracle Bones,* which was a finalist for the National Book Award; *Country Driving;* and *Strange Stones,* a collection of shorter work. He won the 2008 National Magazine Award for excellence in reporting, and he was named a MacArthur Fellow in 2011. He lives in Cairo.

Nick Hornby is the author of the memoir *Fever Pitch* and six novels, the most recent of which is *Juliet, Naked.* He is also the author of *Songbook,* a finalist for a National Book Critics Circle Award for criticism. His screenplay for *An Education* was nominated for an Academy Award. He lives in North London.

Katharyn Howd Machan is the author of thirty published collections, and her poems have appeared in numerous magazines, anthologies, and textbooks, including *The Bedford Introduction to Literature* and *Sound and Sense.* She is a full professor in the Department of Writing at Ithaca College in central New York State. In 2012 she edited *Adrienne Rich: A Tribute Anthology.*

Kiese Laymon is a black southern writer, born and raised in Jackson, Mississippi. He attended Millsaps College, Jackson State University, and Oberlin College before earning an MFA from Indiana University. He is the author of the novel *Long Division* and a collection of essays, *How to Slowly Kill Yourself and Others in America.* He has written essays and stories for numerous publications, including *Esquire,* ESPN.com, NPR, *Truthout, Hip Hop Reader, Mythium,* and *Politics and Culture.* Laymon is currently an associate professor of English and Africana Studies at Vassar College.

EDW Lynch is an American humorist and humanitarian. He lives in the San Francisco Bay Area.

Wendy MacNaughton is an illustrator based in San Francisco. Her work appears in publications such as the *New York Times*, the *Wall Street Journal*, and *Print*. She has illustrated the books *Lost Cat: A True Story of Love, Desperation, and GPS Technology*; *The Essential Scratch & Sniff Guide to Becoming a Wine Expert*; the forthcoming *Meanwhile, San Francisco—the City in Its Own Words*; and *Salt, Fat, Acid, Heat*. Along with Isaac Fitzgerald, she is a co-founder of the Tumblr Pen & Ink, which will be published as a book in 2014. She can be found at wendymacnaughton.com.

Alexander Maksik is the author of the novels *You Deserve Nothing* and *A Marker to Measure Drift*. His fiction has appeared in *Harper's*, *Tin House*, *Harvard Review*, and *Narrative Magazine*, among others, and has been translated into more than a dozen languages. He lives in New York.

Kyle Minor's second collection of short fiction, *Praying Drunk*, will be published in February 2014. His stories and essays have appeared in the *Southern Review*, the *Gettysburg Review*, *Gulf Coast*, and *The Best American Mystery Stories 2008*. He is finishing a first novel, *The Sexual Lives of Missionaries*. He corresponds with readers at kyleminor.com.

Jack Moore is a comedian, playwright, and TV writer. He created @SeinfeldToday with his friend Josh Gondelman and has written about sports all over the Internet. Follow him on Twitter: @JackPMoore.

Walter Mosley is the author of more than forty-three critically acclaimed books, including the major best-selling mystery series featuring Easy Rawlins. His work has been translated into twenty-three languages and includes literary fiction, science fiction, political monographs, and a young adult novel. His short fiction has been widely published, and his nonfiction has appeared in the *New York Times Magazine* and *The Nation*, among other publications. He is the winner of numerous awards, including an O. Henry Award, a Grammy, and PEN America's Lifetime Achievement Award. He lives in New York City.

Alix Ohlin is the author of the novels *Inside,* which was shortlisted for the 2012 Scotiabank Giller Prize, and *The Missing Person.* She has also published two story collections, *Signs and Wonders* and *Babylon and Other Stories.* Her work has appeared in *Best American Short Stories, Best New American Voices,* and on public radio's *Selected Shorts.*

Peter Orner is the author of two novels, *The Second Coming of Mavala Shikongo* and *Love and Shame and Love,* as well as the story collection *Esther Stories.* His latest book, in which "Foley's Pond" appears, is *Last Car over the Sagamore Bridge.* Orner is also the editor of the oral histories, *Underground America* and *Hope Deferred: Narratives of Zimbabwean Lives.* Born in Chicago, Orner now lives in Bolinas, California.

Miroslav Penkov was born and raised in Bulgaria. His debut collection *East of the West* has been published in a dozen countries and his stories have appeared in *A Public Space, Granta, One Story, The Best American Short Stories 2008,* and the *PEN/O. Henry Prize Stories 2012.* Winner of the BBC International Short Story Award 2012, he teaches creative writing at the University of North Texas, where he is a fiction editor for the *American Literary Review.*

Kim Philley was born in Singapore and grew up in Indonesia, Thailand, and Virginia. Her work has appeared in the *New York Times, Indiana Review,* and *Epiphany,* among other publications. Recently, she reported on the Cambodian-Thai border war at Preah Vihear temple for the *Caravan,* and on Burmese spirit possession ceremonies from Mandalay for the BBC's "From Our Own Correspondent." A former Henry Hoyns Fellow in poetry at the University of Virginia, she has taught at both the University of Virginia and Boise State University. She currently lives in a turret of the historic Idanha Hotel in Boise, Idaho.

Sebastian Rotella is an award-winning foreign correspondent and investigative reporter. He worked for almost twenty-three years for the

Los Angeles Times, covering everything from terrorism to the arts to the Mexican border. He served most recently as a national security correspondent in Washington, D.C., and his previous posts include international investigative correspondent and bureau chief in Paris and Buenos Aires. In 2006, he was named a Pulitzer finalist for international reporting for his coverage of terrorism and Muslim communities in Europe. Rotella is the author of two books: *Twilight on the Line: Underworlds and Politics at the U.S.-Mexico Border,* which was named a *New York Times* Notable Book in 1998, and the novel, *Triple Crossing,* published in August 2011. He is a graduate of the University of Michigan and was born in Chicago.

Davy Rothbart is the creator of *Found* magazine, a frequent contributor to *This American Life,* and the author of a collection of stories, *The Lone Surfer of Montana, Kansas,* and a book of personal essays, *My Heart Is An Idiot,* from which "Human Snowball" is excerpted. He writes regularly for *GQ* and *Grantland,* and his work has appeared in *The New Yorker,* the *New York Times,* and the *Believer.* His documentary film *Medora,* about a resilient high school basketball team in a dwindling town in rural Indiana, premiered in March 2013 at the SXSW Film Festival. Rothbart is also the founder of Washington II Washington, an annual hiking adventure for inner-city kids. He splits his time between Los Angeles and his hometown of Ann Arbor.

Karen Russell is the author of the story collection *St. Lucy's Home for Girls Raised by Wolves* and *Swamplandia!,* a Pulitzer Prize finalist and one of the *New York Times*'s Top 5 Fiction Books of 2011. Her latest story collection is *Vampires in the Lemon Grove.*

Alexis Schaitkin's stories and essays have appeared in the *Southern Review, Southwest Review,* and *Ecotone,* among other places. She is a graduate of the University of Virginia's MFA program in fiction. She lives in New York, where she is at work on a novel.

Max Schoening is a researcher in the Americas division of Human Rights Watch. He contributed research to *Violentology: A Manual of the Colombian Conflict,* a forthcoming photography book by Stephen Ferry.

Brendan Todt received his MFA from Vermont College of Fine Arts. His poetry and prose can be found in *Ninth Letter, South Dakota Review, NANO Fiction,* and elsewhere. He lives with his wife and dog in Sioux City, Iowa. You can find him teaching at Western Iowa Tech, riding his bike into stiff headwinds, or refereeing soccer across Siouxland. Visit him at brendantodt.com.

Andrew Tonkovich edits the literary magazine *Santa Monica Review,* blogs about books at the *OC Weekly,* and hosts the literary arts program *Bibliocracy* on Pacifica radio station KPFK in Southern California. His essays and short stories have appeared recently in *Ecotone, Faultline, Portside,* and the *Los Angeles Review of Books.* He teaches writing at UC Irvine and represents librarians and fellow lecturers on behalf of the American Federation of Teachers.

Madhuri Vijay received her MFA from the Iowa Writers' Workshop, where she was an Iowa Arts Fellow. Her short story "Lorry Raja" won *Narrative Magazine*'s 30-Below Contest. She currently lives in India.

Kurt Vonnegut was born in Indianapolis in 1922. He studied at Cornell University and the University of Chicago. Vonnegut published his first novel, *Player Piano,* in 1952. He would go on to write over twenty-five books, among them *Cat's Cradle; God Bless You, Mr. Rosewater; Breakfast of Champions;* and *Galápagos.* During the Second World War he was held prisoner in Germany and was present at the bombing of Dresden, an experience that provided the setting for his most famous work, *Slaughterhouse-Five.*

Shari Wagner is the author of two books of poems, *The Harmonist at Nightfall* and *Evening Chore,* as well as the editor and cowriter of her father's memoir of Somalia, *A Hundred Camels.* Her poems have appeared in *North American Review, Shenandoah, Poetry East,* and *The Writer's Almanac.* She lives with her family in Westfield, Indiana, and teaches for the Indiana Writers Center.

Dan Wakefield is the author of the novel *Going All the Way* and a collection of essays, *Spiritually Incorrect.* His memoirs include *New York* *in the Fifties* and *Returning: A Spiritual Journey.* He edited and wrote the introduction to *Kurt Vonnegut: Letters.*

Teddy Wayne is the author of the novels *The Love Song of Jonny Valentine* and *Kapitoil,* which won a 2011 Whiting Writers' Award, was a runner-up for the PEN/Bingham Prize, and a finalist for the New York Public Library Young Lions Fiction Award and the Dayton Literary Peace Prize. He is the recipient of an NEA creative writing fellowship, and his work regularly appears in *The New Yorker,* the *New York Times, McSweeney's,* and elsewhere. He has taught at Washington University in St. Louis and Marymount Manhattan College, and he lives in New York.

Originally from Henderson County in the North Carolina mountains, **Robert West** now teaches in the Department of English at Mississippi State University. His poems have appeared in the *Christian Science Monitor, Poetry, Southern Poetry Review, The Southern Poetry Anthology,* Ted Kooser's *American Life in Poetry,* and elsewhere. His latest collection is the chapbook *Convalescent.*

Tim Wirkus's fiction has appeared in *Subtropics, Gargoyle,* the *Cream City Review, Sou'wester,* and *Ruminate Magazine.* He is currently finishing work on his first novel, in which two Mormon missionaries investigate the disappearance of a man they baptized. Tim is a student in the University of Southern California's PhD program in creative writing and literature.

Jim Wise is a poet whose work has appeared in *Gay and Lesbian Review Worldwide, RFD,* and a number of online journals and zines. He can usually be found reading Walt Whitman in a cottage just outside Indianapolis, which he shares with his partner and muse, Steven Chen.

THE *BEST AMERICAN* *NONREQUIRED READING* COMMITTEE

The student committee at 826 Valencia in San Francisco was joined by an outfit of brilliant high schoolers at 826 Michigan in Ann Arbor. Together, these two groups scoured the magazines and journals of America in order to find the best work of the year. What you hold in your hands is the product of their tireless research and intense deliberation.

Hanel Baveja is a senior at Huron High School in Ann Arbor. This is her fourth year as part of the *BANR* editing committee. She prefers pancakes to waffles and plain paper to lined. She enjoys reading and writing short stories, poetry, and plays. She is also fond of traveling and eating blue cheese, zucchini bread, and crepes.

 Lianna Bernstein is a senior in high school and lives in Ann Arbor. This is her second year in *BANR* and she also participates in tennis, bowling, and basketball at her school. She is passionate about peppermint tea, bike rides, and her weekly phone calls with her older siblings. She is often quoted as saying "I am done," "so done," and "someone bring me chocolate." This summer she'll be rereading Harry Potter and spending way too much money at Starbucks.

Claire Butz is a senior at Pioneer High School in Ann Arbor. She loves the smell of Crayola crayons, flipping to the cold side of the pillow, and arriving at her destination just as a song ends. Her heart lies in Long Island, and not a day goes by where she doesn't wish she were sailing on Tomahawk Lake. Claire's bucket list includes seeing the Rolling Stones in concert and learning to speak Italian.

 Sophie Chabon was born in October of 1994 in Los Angeles, CA. She migrated north at the age of two and lived in Berkeley for a number of years, until she packed up again and headed to the woods of Central Connecticut to attend Wesleyan University. She loves the works of Whedon and Kerouac and is well aware that winter is coming. She is 5'6½".

After living in Idaho and Utah, **Aimee Echols-Chase** finished high school in San Francisco. She is now traversing the Parisian streets whilst attending NYU Liberal Studies. She is fascinated with economic theory and long fiction. Aimee also possesses an ever-evolving affinity for string instruments. She is currently inclined toward bass, and you'll be happy to know that she is already performing sub-par renditions of Radiohead and Cake songs.

Gladis Figueroa is sixteen years old and a junior at Immaculate Conception Academy in San Francisco. Her hobbies include playing sports and singing. After school, she usually hangs out with her friends or takes care of her younger sisters. Her ethnicity is El Salvadoreña and Guatemalteca. She has been a student at 826 Valencia for seven years.

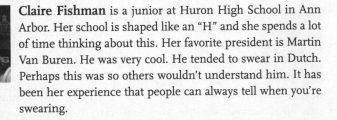 **Claire Fishman** is a junior at Huron High School in Ann Arbor. Her school is shaped like an "H" and she spends a lot of time thinking about this. Her favorite president is Martin Van Buren. He was very cool. He tended to swear in Dutch. Perhaps this was so others wouldn't understand him. It has been her experience that people can always tell when you're swearing.

Sarah Gargaro is a senior at Greenhills High School in Ann Arbor. This is her fourth year spent reading nonrequired, occasionally bizarre pieces in the basement of the Robot Shop. She makes a mean lasagna, her handwriting is fluid (she changed both her "f's" and "g's" just this year), and she enjoys writing in marker.

 Valerie Guevara, eighteen years old, was planted and cultivated in the heart of San Francisco. She now ventures farther than ever, attending the University of California, Berkeley. The way to her heart is through high-quality coffee and expensive cheese. She wishes her mango eating skills had more pizzazz, like her stories.

Quinn Johns is a senior at Huron High School in Ann Arbor. When he is not sleeping or rowing on the nearby river, he is most likely enjoying a good book outside, unless of course it's raining. This fall begins the fourth of a quatrain of fantastic *BANR* experiences. He enjoys an excellent cup of hot chocolate or regular water.

 Roger Krupetsky is a student at Skyline College in San Bruno, CA, and a graduate of Independence High School in San Francisco. He has a 65 percent encounter rate at Dolores Park in the summer, dropping to 10 percent in all other seasons. Other popular encounter locations include various MMORPGs and his local taquería. He can be lured out of his nest with promises of social interaction during colder months.

Shalini Lakshmanan is a sophomore at Huron High School in Ann Arbor. She enjoys reading short stories and long novels as well as baking cookies and muffins of different varieties. Her favorite pastime is encountering new and different authors as well as recipes. She hopes to continue participating in *BANR* next year.

Rebecca Landau is a senior at Berkeley High School. When she is not reading or writing, she is usually busy procrastinating. She enjoys the works of Stephen Sondheim, Tony Kushner, and Ursula K. Le Guin. Her shoelace is probably untied right now but hey, the entropy of the universe is ever increasing so don't blame her.

Elizabeth Malan is a senior at Skyline High School in Ann Arbor. This has been her second year in *BANR* and she is very much looking forward to a third. Generally, Beth enjoys activities such as painting, writing and, naturally, reading. She believes that dragons and tea are both excellent pastimes, and one of her favorite books is *The Thinker's Thesaurus*.

Flavia Mora, seventeen, is a freshman at City College in San Francisco. She is a graduate of San Francisco's Ruth Asawa School of the Arts. This past year was her second year on the *BANR* committee. She is hoping to pursue her interest in integrating social science and art in her future career.

Annabel Ostrow is a senior at Lick Wilmerding High School in San Francisco, where she swims, stage manages, and strives to be politically correct at all times. One summer she took a course exploring the idea of the epic hero through the lens of the Harry Potter books, and she remains unembarrassed by the geekiness this reveals. Meanwhile, she loves working on *BANR* and discovering new and unconventional voices.

Marco Ponce, fourteen, is a sophomore at George Washington High School in San Francisco. Marco has attended the 826 Valencia after-school tutoring program since he was in third grade. He loves soccer and learning new things. He is passionate about fighting for what is right, and he may or may not want to be president.

Milton Pineda, eighteen, graduated from Academy of Arts and Sciences in San Francisco and is now a freshman at San Francisco State University. His hobbies include activities that require minimal movement and physical effort, such as music, video games, Reddit, and hanging out with friends and family. He plans to major in business administration or anything else that grabs his attention.

Hosanna Rubio is a senior at the Ruth Asawa School of the Arts in San Francisco, as well as a proud descendent of African slaves. She wants to learn how to weave baskets, whittle, and freestyle straight off the dome. She is infatuated with the music of Jermaine Cole (J. Cole) and loves life whenever it involves Abigail Schott-Rosenfield. Hosanna is learning "the system" so she can change it. She's almost there.

Anna Sanford is a senior at Piedmont High School in the Bay Area. She has spent much of her seventeen years in the company of books, many of whom she considers best friends. When not reading, Anna enjoys running, cooking, and spending time with friends. This is her first year of *BANR*, an experience that has not only taught her about the unusual longevity of a remote Greek island and the courage of a one-eyed matador, but changed her perspective on life itself.

Frances Saux is a senior at San Francisco's Ruth Asawa School of the Arts, where she studies creative writing. She spends most of her free time reading books by David Foster Wallace. She hopes to someday publish her own stories and essays.

Abigail Schott-Rosenfield, seventeen, is a senior at the Ruth Asawa School of the Arts in San Francisco. At the moment she is enjoying *Tell Me a Riddle* by Tillie Olsen. She is also learning Arabic (Ahlan wasahlan. Ismi samir). She is pleased to have completed her second term on the *BANR* committee. Her muse is Hosanna Rubio.

Hannah Shevrin is a senior at Community High School in Ann Arbor. This is her third year on *BANR*, where she has spent her Tuesday evenings laughing with her fellow readers/editors about the oddities of life. She enjoys walking long distances on overcast days while listening to early 2000s R&B soul. One of the neatest moments of her life was when she was on a piece of land owned by a man whose last name was Land. She frequently receives compliments on her handwriting, and she is thinking of selling it. Watch out, Comic Sans!

Kate Shrayber is seventeen years old and a senior at Gateway High School in San Francisco. In her spare time she enjoys dirty chais and long walks on the beach. She's currently completing a twelve step program with Bookaholics Anonymous due to her addiction to novels.

Sarah Starman is a senior at Pioneer High School in Ann Arbor. Summer is by far her favorite season, and her friends are tired of her saying that. She bakes cakes for people on their birthdays. She has an old-fashioned rotary telephone on her bed, and even when it rings at 2 A.M. she doesn't disconnect it (mostly because she's so tired she falls back asleep). She loves '80s music, raspberries, and of course, *BANR*.

Miranda Wiebe is seventeen and a senior at Piedmont High School in the Bay Area. She enjoys running, gardening, ROFL-ing, and listening to Foxy Brown. Being on the *BANR* committee taught her many important life lessons, such as the theory of Schrodinger's Cat and how to listen.

Emma Pearl Willmer-Shiles has too many names, is sixteen years old, and a senior at Sacred Heart High School in San Francisco. She enjoys reading science fiction in both English and Spanish, and has been obsessed with Greek mythology since her brother gave her *The Golden Fleece* in fifth grade. Drawing is one of her favorite activities and almost everything she owns has doodles on it.

Sabrina Yerena, fifteen years old, is a sophomore at Immaculate Conception Academy in San Francisco. At ICA, she is part of student council. After school, she can be found at 826 Valencia's drop-in tutoring program, which she has attended for seven years now. In her free time she likes to play basketball and draw.

Oscar Zapata graduated from Abraham Lincoln High School in 2013 and has lived in San Francisco for the majority of his life. His hobbies include but are not limited to: taking apart his computer and putting it back together again, engaging strangers in friendly conversation, spending way too much money on his collection of hi-fi headphones, and wasting time on the internet.

Very special thanks to Scott Cohen, Nicole Angeloro, and Mark Robinson. Thanks also to 826 National, 826 Valencia, 826 Michigan, Laura Howard, Dan McKinley, Sunra Thompson, Brian McMullen, Alyson Sinclair, Isaac Fitzgerald, Jordan Bass, Sam Riley, Henry W. Leung, Jia Tolentino, Mimi Lok, Juliana Sloane, McKenna Stayner, Rachel Khong, Soraya Okuda, Jordan Karnes, Clara Sankey, Em-J Staples, Cliff Mayotte, Brian Christian, Chelsea Hogue, Gerald Richards, Ryan Lewis, Yalie Kamara, Raúl J. Alcantar, Emilie Coulson, Lauren Hall, María Inés Montes, Miranda Tsang, Gretchen Schrafft, Dana Riess, Naoki O'Bryan, Allie Washkin, Nolan Boomer, Erica Plumlee, Jessica McHugh, Paolo Yumol, Alex Ryan Bauer, and Nate Rogers.

NOTABLE
NONREQUIRED READING
OF 2012

CHRIS ADRIAN
  Grand Rounds, *Granta*
DANIEL ALARCÓN
  The Provincials, *Granta*
KATYA APEKINA
  Maureen and Marjorie, *The Iowa Review*

MATTHEW BAKER
  A Cruel Gap-Toothed Boy, *The Missouri Review*
SHANE BAUER
  Solitary in Iran Nearly Broke Me. Then I Went Inside America's
  Prisons, *Mother Jones*
JOSH BEGLEY
  A Gated Community, *Tomorrow Magazine*
BRIAN BOIES
  A House Well Furnished, *Zyzzyva*
GINA LUJAN BOUBION
  The American Dream is a Combination Lock, *The Antioch Review*
CHARLES BOWDEN
  Return to the Arkansas Delta, *National Geographic*

DAVID GESSNER
    Brant's Requiem, *Orion Magazine*
ELIZABETH GILBERT
    The Finest Wife, *The Rumpus*
JENNIFER GONNERMAN
    The Man Who Charged Himself With Murder, *New York Magazine*
RIGOBERTO GONZÁLEZ
    The Great Poetry Caper, *The Poetry Foundation*
AMELIA GRAY
    These Are the Fables, *Hobart*

L.K. HANSON
    Some Pages from the Story of My Hand, *Ploughshares*
JOSHUA HARMON
    The Annotated Mix-Tape #8, *Make Magazine*
JOEANN HART
    Piece of History, *Fifth Wednesday Journal*
JUSTIN HECKERT
    The Hazards of Growing Up Painlessly, *The New York Times Magazine*
ALEKSANDAR HEMON
    War Dogs, *Granta*
A.M. HOMES
    Hello Everybody, *Electric Literature*
RENÉ HOUTRIDES
    Griffonia, *The Georgia Review*

GEETHA IYER
    The Glass World-Builder, *Gulf Coast*

TANIA JAMES
    The Scriptological Review, *A Public Space*
LACY M. JOHNSON
    The Addict, *Creative Nonfiction*
HEIDI JULAVITS
    This Feels So Real, *Harper's*

ELI SANDERS
 The Shooter, *River Teeth*
ELI SASLOW
 A Trip to the Threshing Floor, *ESPN the Magazine*
GEORGE SAUNDERS
 The Semplica-Girl Diaries, *The New Yorker*
ELIZABETH SCHULTE
 Borders, *Ninth Letter*
MOLLY SENTELL HAILE
 Wild Man Blues, *Oxford American*
MAGGIE SHIPSTEAD
 The Great Central Pacific Guano Company, *American Short Fiction*
JOHANNA SKIBSRUD
 The Electric Man, *Ecotone*
ANNA DELLA SUBIN
 A Very Still Life, *Bidoun*

LAURA VAN DEN BERG
 Lessons, *American Short Fiction*

MARK WARREN
 Daddy: My Father's Last Words, *Esquire*
DANIEL WESSLER RIORDAN
 The Earth Will Swallow You, *Indiana Review*
TOM WILLIAMS
 The Hotel Joseph Conrad, *Jelly Bucket*
JANE WONG
 Unsent Correspondence, *Memoir Journal*

JENNY ZHANG
 Outsider/Insider, *Rookie*

ABOUT 826 NATIONAL

Proceeds from this book benefit youth literacy

A LARGE PERCENTAGE OF the cover price of this book goes to 826 National, a network of eight youth tutoring, writing, and publishing centers in eight cities around the country.

Since the birth of 826 National in 2002, our goal has been to assist students ages 6–18 with their writing skills while helping teachers get their classes passionate about writing. We do this with a vast army of volunteers who donate their time so we can give as much one-on-one attention as possible to the students whose writing needs it. Our mission is based on the understanding that great leaps in learning can happen with one-on-one attention, and that strong writing skills are fundamental to future success.

Through volunteer support, each of the eight 826 chapters—in San Francisco, New York, Los Angeles, Ann Arbor, Chicago, Seattle, Boston, and Washington, DC—provides drop-in tutoring, class field trips, writing workshops, and in-schools programs, all free of charge, for students, classes, and schools. 826 centers are especially committed to supporting teachers, offering services and resources for English Language Learners, and publishing student work. Each of the 826 chapters works to produce professional-quality publications written entirely by young people, to forge relationships with teachers in order to create innovative workshops and lesson plans, to inspire students to write and appreciate the written word, and to rally thousands of enthusiastic volunteers to make it all happen. By offering all of our programming for free, we aim to serve families who cannot afford to pay for the level of personalized instruction their children receive through 826 chapters.

The demand for 826 National's services is tremendous. We work with more than 6,000 volunteers and over 30,000 students nationally. We host hundreds of field trips and workshops, and we welcome over 200 students per day for after-school tutoring. At many of our centers, our field trips are fully booked almost a year in advance, teacher requests for in-school tutor support continue to rise, and the majority of our evening and weekend workshops have waitlists.

826 National volunteers are local community residents, professional writers, teachers, artists, college students, parents, bankers, lawyers, and retirees from a wide range of professions. These passionate individuals can be found at all of our centers after school, sitting side-by-side with our students, providing one-on-one attention. They can be found running our field trips, or helping an entire classroom of local students learn how to write a story, or assisting student writers during one of our Young Authors' Book Programs.

All day and in a variety of ways, our volunteers are actively connecting with youth from the communities we serve.

To learn more or get involved, please visit:

826 National: www.826national.org
826 San Francisco: www.826valencia.org
826 New York: www.826nyc.org
826 Los Angeles: www.826la.org
826 Chicago: www.826chi.org
826 Ann Arbor: www.826mi.org
826 Seattle: www.826seattle.org
826 Boston: www.826boston.org
826 Washington, DC: www.826dc.org

826 VALENCIA

Named for the street address of the building it occupies in the heart of San Francisco's Mission District, 826 Valencia opened on April 8, 2002 and consists of a writing lab; a street-front, student-friendly retail pirate store that partially funds its programs; and satellite classrooms in two local middle schools. 826 Valencia has developed programs that reach students at every possible opportunity—in school, after school, in the evenings, or on the weekends. Since its doors opened, over fifteen hundred volunteers—including published authors, magazine founders, SAT course instructors, documentary filmmakers, and other professionals—have donated their time to work with thousands of students. These volunteers allow the center to offer all of its services for free.

826 NYC

826NYC's writing center opened its doors in September 2004. Since then its programs have offered over one thousand students opportunities to improve their writing and to work side by side with hundreds of community volunteers. 826NYC has also built a satellite tutoring center, created in partnership with the Brooklyn Public Library, which has introduced library programs to an entirely new community of students. The center publishes a handful of books of student writing each year.

826 LA

826LA benefits greatly from the wealth of cultural and artistic resources in the Los Angeles area. The center regularly presents a free workshop at the Armand Hammer Museum in which esteemed artists, writers, and performers teach their craft. 826LA has collaborated with the J. Paul Getty Museum to create Community Photoworks, a months-long program that taught seventh-graders the basics of photographic composition and analysis, sent them into Los Angeles with cameras, and then helped them polish artist statements. Since opening in March 2005, 826LA has provided thousands of hours of free one-on-one writing instruction, held summer camps for English language learners, given students sportswriting training in the Lakers' press room, and published love poems written from the perspectives of leopards.

826 CHICAGO

826 Chicago opened its writing lab and after-school tutoring center in the West Town community of Chicago, in the Wicker Park neighborhood. The setting is both culturally lively and teeming with schools: within one mile, there are fifteen public schools serving more than sixteen thousand students. The center opened in October 2005 and now has over five hundred volunteers. Its programs, like at all the 826 chapters, are designed to be both challenging and enjoyable. Ultimately, the goal is to strengthen each student's power to express ideas effectively, creatively, confidently, and in his or her individual voice.

826 MICHIGAN

826 Michigan opened its doors on
June 1, 2005, on South State Street
in Ann Arbor. In October of 2007
the operation moved downtown,
to a new and improved location on
Liberty Street. This move enabled
the opening of Liberty Street Robot

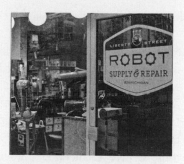

Supply & Repair in May 2008. The shop carries everything the robot
owner might need, from positronic brains to grasping appendages to
solar cells. 826 Michigan is the only 826 not named after a city because it serves students all over southeastern Michigan, hosting in-
school residencies in Ypsilanti schools, and providing workshops for
students in Detroit, Lincoln, and Willow Run school districts. The
center also has a packed workshop schedule on site every semester,
with offerings on making pop-up books, writing sonnets, creating
screenplays, producing infomercials, and more.

826 SEATTLE

826 Seattle began offering after-
school tutoring in October 2005,
followed shortly by evening and
weekend writing workshops and, in
December 2005, the first field trip
to 826 Seattle by a public school
class (Ms. Dunker's fifth graders

from Greenwood Elementary). The center is in Greenwood, one of
the most diverse neighborhoods in the city. And, thankfully, enough
space travelers stop by the Greenwood Space Travel Supply Company at 826 Seattle on their way back from the Space Needle. Rev-
enue from the store, like from all 826 storefronts, helps to support
the writing programs, along with the generous outpouring from
community members.

826 BOSTON

826 Boston kicked off its programming in the spring of 2007 by inviting authors Junot Díaz, Steve Almond, Holly Black, and Kelly Link to lead writing workshops at the English High School. The visiting writers challenged students to modernize fairy tales, invent their ideal school, and tell their own stories. Afterward, a handful of dedicated volunteers followed up with weekly visits to help students develop their writing craft. These days, the center has thrown open its doors in Roxbury's Egleston Square—a culturally diverse community south of downtown that stretches into Jamaica Plain, Roxbury, and Dorchester. 826 Boston neighbors more than twenty Boston schools, a dance studio, and the Boston Neighborhood Network (a public-access television station).

826 DC

826 National's newest chapter, 826DC, opened its doors to the city's Columbia Heights neighborhood in September 2010. Like all the 826s, 826DC provides after-school tutoring, field trips, after-school workshops, in-school tutoring, help for English language learners, and assistance with the publication of student work. It also offers free admission to the Museum of Unnatural History, the center's unique storefront. 826DC volunteers helped publish a student-authored poetry book project called *Dear Brain*. 826DC's students have also already read poetry for the President and First Lady Obama, participating in the 2011 White House Poetry Student Workshop.

ScholarMatch

ScholarMatch is a nonprofit organization that aims to make college possible by connecting under-resourced students with donors. Launched in 2010 as a project of 826 National, ScholarMatch uses crowd-funding to help high-achieving, San Francisco Bay Area students who have significant financial need. But it takes more than money to ensure that students successfully complete college. That's why ScholarMatch also offers student support services and partners with college access organizations, nonprofits, and high schools to ensure that students have the network and resources they need to succeed.

More than 80 percent of ScholarMatch students are the first in their families to go to college, and over 50 percent of them have annual family incomes of less than $25,000. ScholarMatch students are resilient young people who have overcome harrowing challenges and maintain their determination to seek a better future through college.

With commitments from donors, we ensure that young people in our community receive the education they need to succeed in a challenging economic landscape. To support our students' college journey or to learn more about our organization, visit scholarmatch.org.